3/02

# NEW DIRECTIONS IN CRIMINOLOGICAL THEORY

## Advances in Criminological Theory
### Volume 4

# NEW DIRECTIONS IN CRIMINOLOGICAL THEORY

*Edited by*

**Freda Adler**

**William S. Laufer**

**Advances in Criminological Theory**

**Volume 4**

Transaction Publishers

New Brunswick (U.S.A.) and London (U.K.)

ISSN: 0894-2366
ISBN: 1-56000-046-5
Printed in the United States of America

# Contents

# Editors' Note

The contributions to the first three volumes of *Advances in Criminological Theory* have generated lively discussion and comment. These comments themselves are contributing to the advance of criminological theory. In this issue we shall present the first of these comments. The editors invite others to contribute their reflections on issues raised by the contributions to this series. Comments need not be in article form. Brief notes are equally welcome.

# 1

# The Future of Labeling Theory: Foundations and Promises

*Charles F. Wellford*
*Ruth A. Triplett*

In the twentieth century the history of criminological theory has been one of competing theoretical perspectives. Throughout this period numerous explanations for crime and deviance have emerged that have been offered as better explanations than other theories or perspectives.[1] Research is done on one of the perspectives. The research demonstrates the limited value of that theory or perspective and the community of criminological scholars moves on to develop a new theory, test a new theory, or lament the stagnation in criminological theory.

In recent years, renewed and increased attention has been given to the need to organize a variety of theories into an interdisciplinary or integrated theory that captures the contributions that can be made from the many explanatory approaches that have emerged over the last one hundred years (Messner et al. 1989). This move towards integrated or interdisciplinary theory represents a new stage of development in the field and requires a careful reassessment of the perspectives that have formed the core of criminological thought.

Labeling theory represents for criminological thought a major school of social thought—symbolic interactionism. Labeling has as

1

its foundation symbolic interactionist theory and, therefore, represents for criminologists one way in which a prominent school of
social thought could be included into a comprehensive explanation
of crime and deviance. In earlier analyses of labeling theory authors
have, in the tradition noted above, attempted to assess its value as
an explanation of crime or deviance (e.g., see Wellford 1975, 1987;
Mahoney 1974; Thomas and Bishop 1984). Our goal in this paper is
not to establish that labeling theory on its own cannot explain in
any meaningful way significant amounts of criminal behavior (given
our interest in integrated theory we take that to be axiomatic) but
to assess the essential elements of labeling theory, to review its
likely contributions, and to describe the developments that we think
are necessary to capture the advantages that labeling theory would
bring to a comprehensive explanation of crime or deviance.

In this paper we will first briefly sketch the foundations of
labeling theory. Then we will discuss the problems of labeling
theory that have been faced in the criminological literature. This
will be followed by a review of empirical research indicating the
elements of labeling theory that may be most critical to include in a
comprehensive explanation of crime, and a discussion of the emerging trends in labeling theory research. Finally, we will conclude
with an assessment of what we think should be done to advance
labeling theory as part of a more comprehensive explanation of
crime.

## The Foundations of Labeling Theory

In one of the most thoughtful discussions of the origins of human
behavior, Leslie White observed, "In the word was the beginning,
the beginning of man and of culture" (White 1969, 22). White's
analysis of the role of "the word" or as he preferred to refer to it,
"the symbol," represents a clear statement of an important tradition in social thought. This tradition emphasizes that the unique
characteristics of humans and of their behavior is in the use of
symbols. Again to quote White,

It was the symbol which transformed our anthropoid ancestors into men and
made them human. All civilizations have been generated and perpetuated only

by the use of symbols. It is the symbol which transforms an infant of homo sapiens into a human being. All human behavior consists of or is dependent upon the use of symbols. Human behavior is symbolic behavior. Symbolic behavior is human behavior. The symbol is the universe of humanity. (White 1969, 22)

The symbol then represents that summation of the characteristics of human beings that set them apart from their animal ancestors and contemporaries. The symbol represents an important element within social thought.

As defined by White the symbol is, "as a thing, the value or meaning of which is bestowed upon it by those who use it" (White 1969, 25). Thus, the symbol represents that which the individual attaches to something in the environment or to oneself. The symbol can represent a physical thing, a social thing, a biological thing, or any element of the environment, internal or external, in which the individual operates. The critical element, then, of being human is the ability to interpret one's environment, to attach symbols to it.

This approach, made most explicit by Leslie White, was captured for American sociology much earlier by the concept of the looking-glass self as enunciated by Charles Horton Cooley. That concept emphasized for social theorists the role of an individual's perceptions (or in White's terms, symboling) of other people's behavior in the formation of that individual's behavior. To quote from Cooley (Cooley 1964, 189), "the looking-glass self consists of three parts: the imagination of our appearance to the other person, the imagination of his judgment of that appearance, and some sort of self feeling, such as pride or mortification." For Cooley, the symbolic process involves the manner in which the individual interprets the social environment. The individual's characteristics and the social environment are neither in tension nor time ordered. They are related to each other in an interactive way, such that the self and its social environment emerge coterminously. For Cooley there is no distinction between the individual and the environment, they are inextricably related.

While Cooley's work is often cited in American sociology as a foundation for those theories that emphasize symboling, perhaps the more influential theorists in this tradition is George Herbert Mead. Mead's analysis was more complex because of his understanding of the relationship between the social environment and the individual. Mead's concepts of I and me represent attempts to describe the way in which the individual both effects and is effected by the social environment through the process of interpretation. The concept of the generalized other, which represents an entity comparable to Freud's superego, provides another important theoretical component to Mead's work. For our purposes, there are two essential components of Mead's social thought. The first is the recognition that roles and rules play a critical part in the formation of the self. The second is how, after a self begins to interpret the environment, react to and understand these rules, the self then begins to act back on the environment. The potential of tension or conflict between these two aspects of self, present clearly in Mead and Freud but not in Cooley, represent an important advance in social thinking in this tradition—one of critical importance to labeling theory.[2]

For those who emphasize symboling, however, the critical element is the interpretation of others' activities. This subjective process of interpretation represents the critical element in this tradition in understanding the formation of an individual's understanding of oneself, the determination of the link between self-assessments and behavior, and the role that the individual plays within a society. This tradition, while always having been recognized within American sociology, has not been a dominant one.

In American sociology, given the emphasis during the last fifty years on the scientific aspect of the discipline, those traditions that emphasized internal, unobservable, and individualized concepts tended to be given less status and less attention. As sociology began to emerge to develop its own unique identity, its emphasis on structural, cultural, external elements in the Durkheimian tradition placed symbolic interactionism at a much lower level of importance than other theoretical traditions. As noted earlier, our position is that such attempts to limit theoretical models is at best problematic. For a discipline such as criminology that is trying to explain a particular behavior rather than a discipline-created behavior, the theoretical approach to explanation needs to be as comprehensive as possible.[3] Therefore, even though it represents great difficulties for scientific analysis, our contention is that symbolic interactionism and its representation within the criminological field (labeling theory) should be given strong consideration as a component in a comprehensive understanding of crime and deviance.

## Labeling Theory

It is not necessary to once again describe the essential elements of labeling theory. This has been done many times by many authors (e.g., Schrag 1971; Siegel 1986). Our interest is in understanding how labeling theory has emerged within criminology and why its contributions have been so minimal. Neither do we wish to review the extensive research that has been done on labeling, most of which has noted its empirical shortcomings (for a recent summary see Adler et al. 1991). Rather we wish to discuss three reasons that we believe explain why labeling theory has not achieved the level of importance that it can have in a comprehensive theory of crime and deviance. These are first, the previously noted tendency in much of criminological theory to offer relatively narrow theoretical models to explain all of deviance; second, the tendency in the 1970s and 1980s for labeling to be connected with conflict theory; and third, the failure of labeling theorists and advocates to pay attention to the symbolic nature of labeling.

When Clarence Schrag (1971) summarized the propositions of labeling theory, the first element he identified was that no act was intrinsically criminal. He further stated that a component of labeling theory was the proposition that laws are made for and enforced in favor of more powerful interests. Nowhere in the symbolic interactionist literature or in the writings of those who have been most careful in delineating the labeling perspective, does one find these propositions. Still, Schrag's analysis was correct for that time. As labeling theory emerged, it emerged as a critic of government institutions established to control crime. Its central notion was that these institutions may, through their actions, in fact be perpetuating and exacerbating the problem they are established to control. This theme is consistent with the writings of conflict theorists on the formation of law and its operation. The similarity of these themes led many who were initially drawn to labeling theory to expand their thinking to include other aspects of critical criminology.

To the extent that labeling theory began to be a part of or merged with conflict theory (Davis 1972; Quinney 1973), it opened itself up to the obvious criticisms that have been made of that perspective. Both analytically and empirically these propositions turned out to be of questionable value in democratic societies and, therefore, labeling theory suffered from its affiliation with this approach. It is important, however, to emphasize that the labeling perspective is no more linked to critical or conflict theoretical models than it is to structural, historical, or any other explanation of behavior.

In his analysis of the importance of symbolic interactionism for understanding crime and deviance, Edward Lemert laid out clearly the ways in which labeling theory could be linked to other theoretical models (Lemert 1972). This linkage tends to be associated with the distinction between primary and secondary deviance, that is, primary deviance could be explained by other theoretical models, whereas secondary deviance would be explained by labeling. The need identified by Lemert to link labeling to other theoretical models was not developed by later theorists. On the contrary, the works of Schur (1971) and others (e.g., Scheff 1974) took a very narrow view of labeling, understanding it as the primary if not sole explanation of secondary deviation. The concept of primary deviation was generally left without explanation except by Lemert, who carefully considered its sources and relationship to secondary deviance (e.g., Lemert 1972, 48). Thus, while some labeling theorists recognized at least an understanding of the distinction between primary and secondary deviance and the need to link labeling to other theoretical models, the primary thrust was to focus on labeling as (the) cause of crime and deviant behavior. As criminology has progressed we have, as noted above, come to understand the difficulties of such single-dimension theoretical models and have opted for interdisciplinary and integrated theories. The future of criminology clearly rests on this approach to theory building and the value of labeling will only increase as we begin to understand other theoretical perspectives and complete the decoupling of labeling and conflict theories.

Another problem that has limited the contributions labeling has made to theories of crime and deviance is the failure of labeling theorists and researchers to understand or to remember the central elements of labeling theory. As a symbolic interactionist perspective, the primary concern in labeling should be on the individual's interpretation of the response of others. Yet, labeling theorists focused primarily on the simple application of the label. There was no attention to the changes that were actually occurring in the self, how these might be effected by other characteristics of the individual, or how the strength of the label might also be a part of understanding its impact.

This tendency to deal only with the manifestation of the label and not its interpretation is similar to what has occurred in deterrence theory. As many have pointed out (e.g., Paternoster 1987), deterrence theory emphasizes primarily the role of informal and experiential deterrence rather than formal deterrence. And yet, much of the thinking and early work in criminology focused upon external, formal deterrents. Only recently have we moved to understanding the importance of informal deterrence and more importantly, the individual's perception of deterrence and its impact. Thus, in both deterrence and labeling theory we have seen a tendency to emphasize the external aspect without attention to the internal. This is particularly troubling for labeling because the central value of labeling theory is its emphasis on the interpretation that occurs when an individual responds to the social environment.

Therefore, labeling theory has suffered from the inattention to its central element, the symbolic process, by its tendency to drift into an association with critical and conflict criminology, and the tendency to treat labeling as a single explanation of secondary deviance. These are not necessary elements of labeling theory. In fact, in Lemert's analysis one finds none of these components and yet in the interpretation and use of labeling theory by criminologists in the 1970s and 1980s these have been essential ingredients. As we move into the 1990s labeling theory has the potential to become of much more value to theories of crime and deviance as it moves away from these misleading and misguiding approaches and we seek new ways to gain the full value of a symbolic interactionist perspective for understanding crime and deviance.

## Recent Advances

The recent advances made in the development and testing of labeling or as it is increasingly referred to today the deviance amplification hypothesis may be divided into three different approaches. The first approach deals with specifying those factors on which the effects of formal labels are contingent. The second approach attempts an integration of aspects of labeling theory with other criminological theories. One such attempt integrates labeling with social learning theory. Another (Farrell 1989) focuses on a "psychological elaboration" of an integrated theory drawing on strain, interaction, and social cultural theories. Finally, the third development centers around changing the focus of the type of label under consideration. As noted above, past research has focused almost exclusively on formal labels such as arrest, conviction, or sentencing (see Thomas and Bishop 1984 for an exception). Two new attempts at revitalizing labeling theory focus on the effects of informal, subjective labels. This section of the paper discusses each of these developments.

In a recent review of labeling, Paternoster and Iovanni (1989) suggest that one reason empirical research is not supportive of labeling is that researchers have not specified the conditions under which labeling is effective. This approach to labeling involves two areas of research and theoretical development. The first deals with specifying the variables with which labels may interact such as group membership. The second area attempts to clearly define the process through which labeling works.

The group membership of an actor may interact with the label to define the label's effect. Harris (1976) posits that labeling someone who by their "cast" does not already have full social membership in the society is redundant (433). Thus labeling such an individual will have little effect on self-identity or behavior. Labeling someone who is accepted as a full member of society, however, may have dramatic effects. For this individual labeling devalues the individual's status and group membership.

Past research provides some support for these predictions, demonstrating that labeling effects are weakest among blacks and the lower class (Ageton and Elliott 1974; Harris 1975, 1976; Jensen

1972; and Thornberry 1971). However, further development and testing of this hypothesis is needed. Besides the need for verification of past findings it is important to continue theoretical development in this area. Future research might focus on further specifying the types of group membership which make labels redundant or ineffective. For example, Paternoster and Iovanni (1989) suggest that the group membership of both the actor and the labeler is important in determining effects.

There is more to this approach, however, than simply specifying different groups for which labels' effects vary. The task also includes defining the process through which labels enhance the probability of delinquent behavior. One criticism of labeling is that official labels are neither necessary nor sufficient conditions for movement to a sustained pattern of criminal activity (Mankoff 1971). However, labeling theorists do not argue that deviance amplification is simply a matter of labels directly causing delinquent behavior. Ever since Lemert (1951, 1972), they hypothesize that the movement to secondary deviance is a *process* actors go through.

In describing the process, labeling theorists insist on a variety of conditions that must accompany or follow the label for it to work as a deviance amplifier. For example, Becker (1963) emphasizes the importance of membership in an organized group which promotes the learning of deviant motives and interests. Lofland (1969) describes a variety of conditions which may "facilitate" the movement to secondary deviance. Some of the conditions which he specifies include self-orientation of the actor, and degree of attachment of actor to normal or deviant others. A change in self-concept and role engulfment are other factors long associated with the movement to secondary deviance.

After an extensive review of the literature, Paternoster and Iovanni (1989) outline the most recent attempt in defining the process through which labels increase the probability of delinquent behavior. The process begins with the labeling event that may or may not become publicly known. The label, if publicly known, can then lead to either exclusive or inclusive societal reactions. Exclusion from conventional activities and others can then cause an alteration in the identity of the actor to one of deviant or criminal.

An alteration in identity leads the actor to seek the support of deviant others. Being rewarded for deviant behavior leads to a greater probability of secondary deviance. Paternoster and Iovanni allow for the possibility that in this process an actor may actively seek the label.

While there has been some recent theoretical development in this area, little attempt has been made to test these hypotheses. Thus, the greatest need for this approach is empirical testing. This presents a challenge to criminologists because of the difficulty in testing such a model as the one outlined by Paternoster and Iovanni (1989). However, labeling cannot be verified or dismissed without such a test.

Related to specifying the process by which labeling works is the attempt to integrate labeling with another criminological theory. Two such attempts at the integration of aspects of labeling with other theories are by Triplett (1990) and Farrell (1989).

Triplett (1990) argues that both Becker (1963) and Lemert (1967) saw labels as indirectly effecting deviant behavior through changes in the actor's reward and motivation systems. As previously discussed Becker (1963) saw labeling as only the first part in a process leading to secondary deviance. Membership in a group that supports deviant activity is another necessary step in the process. Lemert (1967) expands on this idea when he proposes that the movement from primary to secondary deviance involves learning. Actors moving to secondary deviance learn how to exploit their new, degraded status by changing what they view as rewarding. Again, membership in a group that rewards deviant behavior promotes this learning.

Beginning then with the notion that labeling alone does not cause delinquent behavior, Triplett (1990) tests the hypothesis that labels will only be effective if they cause a change in the actor's reward system, beliefs, motivations, and friends. She argues with Matsueda (1982) that variables such as attachments and involvement measure who we learn from and who rewards us. Triplett then tests for the direct effects of labels on beliefs, attachment to family, proportion of delinquent friends, involvement with those friends and their effects on delinquent behavior. Using four waves of the Elliott National Youth Survey she finds that labels do have a significant impact on the proportion of delinquent friends one has. The proportion of delinquent friends then has a consistently, significant effect on delinquent behavior. The effects of labels on the other variables was nonsignificant though in the expected direction. She concludes that while labels effect motivations to delinquent behavior by increasing social supports for delinquent behavior they do not effect beliefs or attitudes towards conventional behavior.

In 1989 Farrell presented what he termed a "psychological elaboration of an integrated systems model." In this work Farrell centers on integrated theory which draws upon interaction, strain and social and cultural support theories around the personality characteristic of ambiguity tolerance. He predicts that individuals come under a certain amount of conflict in terms of the way they are defined by others. This creates a tension or strain for individuals that can be reduced by redefining and reorganizing their self image. The less individuals can tolerate ambiguity the more susceptible they are to the strain and also to the stereotypical imputations of others. Their reaction may be to accept this stereotypical identity, associate with those similarly labeled and thus to increase their deviant activities.

The question surrounding these two approaches is under what conditions does formal action by the society (a label) deter delinquent behavior, increase delinquent behavior or have no effect. This question was raised by Thorsell and Klemke in 1972, repeated by Tittle in 1975 and yet has received little attention. Past research either ignores the question or suggests we make a theoretical choice between labeling and deterrence. The answer, however, does not lie in such a choice but in determining the conditions under which the effects of formal criminal justice agency contact vary.

While the first two approaches deal with specifying the process in which labeling causes deviant behavior, the third approach takes a different turn. In response to several damaging criticisms of labeling (see Tittle 1980 and Wellford 1987) and the writings of labeling theorists, researchers have begun to focus on the effects that informal, subjective labels have on self-identity and behavior. Such efforts have led us to one of the more promising developments in labeling—the rediscovery (see discussion above) of the importance of informal labels.

Informal labels are defined as

an attempt to characterized a person as a given "type" (such as "good student" or "troublemaker") by persons who are not acting as official agents of formal social control agencies, and in social situations that are not formal social control "ceremonies." (Paternoster and Triplett 1989, 6)

Informal labels then are, for example, those which parents give when they perceive their children as "dumb" or "bad" and transmit these feelings to their children.

The emphasis on informal labels answers several damaging criticisms of labeling. Informal labels may be applied long before actors have contact with formal agencies of control and before self-concept has completely developed. It is important to note that labeling theorists themselves did not ignore the possible effects of informal labels (see for example Lemert 1951; Schur 1971; and Tannenbaum 1938). However, their effect may have been downplayed because of the historical context in which labeling theory developed (see Paternoster and Triplett 1989 for a more detailed discussion).

Another long ignored aspect of labeling is the subjective interpretation of that label (see Mead 1974 for an early statement on the importance of subjective interpretations). The importance of focusing on subjective labels, the actor's perception of how others perceive them, derives from the fact that the actor's perception may differ from the objective label, which is the perception of the one assigning the label. Thus, while it is important to know that parents label their child "criminal" it is equally important to know how the child interprets this label. If a child is labeled "good" but perceives a different label, "criminal," which one will have the effect? Testing for the effects of subjective labels takes into consideration the possibility of misinterpretation between actors.

Another development in this area is the distinction between types of labels. Orcutt (1973) notes that informal social reactions to deviant behavior may be exclusive or inclusive in form. Inclusive reactions are attempts by the social group to bring the deviant "into conformity with the rules of the group without excluding him from it.[11] Exclusive reactions are those attempts at social control which operate to reject the rule-breaker from the group and revoke his privileges and status as an ordinary member'' (260). While Orcutt was concerned mostly with the determinants of inclusive versus exclusive reactions this distinction also has importance for deviance amplification. It might be predicted that exclusive reactions and inclusive reactions will have opposite effects on the probability of future delinquent behavior.

One early test of the effects of informal labels is that of Thomas and Bishop (1984). They test the effects of self-reported suspension or being thrown out of a classroom on delinquent involvement, self-identity, and perceptions of risk. Thomas and Bishop find no significant effect of informal labels and conclude that there is little support for labeling's predictions. However, there is a difference between informal sanctions and informal labels. Sanctions given by an informal authority, like a parent or teacher, do not necessarily imply a label. A teacher, punishing a child for inappropriate classroom behavior, may not generalize that punishment to describe the child's general behavior or the child.

Two recent attempts at testing labeling have tested the impact of informal, subjective labels. One is Triplett's (1990) attempt at integration discussed previously. Another attempt is Paternoster and Triplett (1989).

Paternoster and Triplett (1989) develop a theory of informal labeling that focuses on the subjective interpretation of informal labels, both inclusive and exclusive. They propose that informal labels that actors interpret as signifying that they are delinquent result in a weakening of conventional ties while simultaneously strengthening unconventional ties. Informal labels which are interpreted as inclusive, signifying the actor is "sick" instead of "bad," however, work to reestablish the offender's ties with the conventional community.

They use the child's perception of the parental label "delinquent" as a measure of exclusive labels and "sick" as inclusive. They then hypothesize that exclusive labels will decrease family and school involvement, school grades, conventional aspirations and beliefs while increasing the proportion of delinquent friends and the commitment to those friends thus increasing delinquent behavior. Inclusive reactions are predicted to have the opposite effect. Paternoster and Triplett (1989) find that indeed exclusive reactions work in the predicted manner. However, their measure of inclusive reactions did not consistently work as predicted. While they increased school involvement and conventional beliefs and decreased commitment to delinquent friends as predicted, they also negatively effected conventional aspirations and school perform-ance (grades): "Perceptions that others think of one's self as 'messed up' and 'having personal problems' may constitute a more temperate form of a negative label than a perception that others view one as a 'trouble maker,' but it appears to be a derisive label nonetheless" (27).

The focus on informal, subjective labels is perhaps the most promising area of development in labeling research. However, this preliminary work requires further careful testing and development. One particular difficulty of this approach is the measurement of informal labels. As mentioned in connection with Thomas and Bishop's (1984) study it is difficult to specify when an informal response is a label. The possible distinction between label and sanction that does not pose a problem for formal labels poses considerable difficulty when discussing informal labels.

Another difficulty that needs to be addressed is the meaning that these labels have for both the giver and the one being labeled. As measured by Paternoster and Triplett (1989) and Triplett (1990) we know when a child perceives a negative label by their parents but not what this label means to the child. The work of Link and his associates (Link 1982, 1987; Link and Cullen 1983; Link et al. 1987, 1989) addresses the area of the expectations of the labeled person and the effects these expectations have on behavior. Their work, though focusing on mental illness, has implications for criminology. Any discussion of advances in labeling would not be complete without a discussion of their work.

Link and his associates developed a modified labeling perspective towards mental illness based on the work of Scheff (1966). They propose that our society has formed conceptions of what it means to be a mental patient that involve the ideas of devaluation and discrimination. These conceptions are known by all the members of the society but become personally relevant when they are applied to oneself. Those labeled respond depending on their expectations of societal reactions. Their responses include secrecy, withdrawal, or education. The labeled person's response may have negative consequences for self-esteem, earning power, or ties with society. Lack of self-esteem, lower earning power and a change in one's social network can then lead to increased vulnerability to a new disorder (Link et al. 1989).

In testing this model Link et al. (1989) examine the expectations of patients and untreated community residents, their strategies to cope with labeling or the possibility of labeling, and the effects of these strategies. They find that both samples believe mental patients face devaluation and discrimination. In terms of coping strategies, Link et al. discovered that the people in their sample endorse secrecy, withdrawal and education. Testing the effects of these responses on social support networks they find they create a greater reliance on household members for support and lessening of reliance on nonhousehold members. This effect remains even when controlling for behavior. They conclude, "Our study strongly challenges the notion that labeling and stigma are inconsequential in the lives of psychiatric patients" (1989, 421).

One point that Link (1982) makes is that labels have debilitating effects that go beyond the creation of deviant behavior. Awareness and exploration of these effects as well as a movement away from exploring only those factors considered to be *the* primary cause of criminal or delinquent behavior may be one of the many contributions of labeling to criminological theory.

### The Future of Labeling Research and Theory

One of the most thoughtful contributors to and analysts of labeling theory, Edwin Lemert (especially 1972), described the emergence and future of labeling theory in ways that if they had been followed would have prevented many of the problems that we have noted in this paper. Lemert observed that there was no necessary link between labeling and theories that saw social control as arbitrary, discriminatory, and as the sole source of deviance. He also recognized the importance of other theoretical perspectives in the development of comprehensive theories of crime and deviance. He understood how these could complement and be integrated with labeling. Most importantly, from our perspective, Lemert recognized the significance of symbolic interactionism and the work of George Herbert Mead for labeling theory. Unfortunately many labeling theorists, researchers, and critics have not paid careful enough attention to the richness of Lemert's analysis. The future of labeling theory as we have outlined it and as we see it developing depends very much on its ability to in a sense "get back on track." The period of the 1970s and early 1980s has seen little development in labeling theory as critics noted its obvious shortcomings and other perspectives became more prominent.

The future of research on labeling theory seems quite clear. Such research must be longitudinal; it should focus on the labeling process in the family, school and community as well as by more formal labelers; it should emphasize early labeling; it must necessarily have a developmental component to provide for the ways in which a developing self may in fact react to labels and interpret them; and it must avoid the problem of treating labels as objects rather than symbols of objects. In recent years criminologists have come to understand the importance of longitudinal research (Tonry et al. 1991) and comprehensive longitudinal studies are underway in the field of delinquency (see the 1991 Symposium issue of the *Journal of Criminal Law and Criminology*) and, more generally, for delinquency and crime (Earls and Reiss 1990). These studies demonstrate the importance of longitudinal designs in sorting out complex casual models. We believe such efforts should be incorporated into the models organizing the research measures of the components of labeling theory.

We have argued throughout this paper that official labels are less important than informal labels in part because formal labels occur late in the period when one's self-conception is forming. Therefore, it is critical that future research on labeling better understand the process of labeling as it occurs in preschool and elementary school years as the child's conception and understanding of self begins to take form. This requires a truly developmental perspective to allow for an understanding of the interaction between emerging self and the social environment and requires that the researcher understand that the important measure of a label is the individual's perception of labels, whether formal or informal, and not the actual behavioral manifestation of the label by an external source. Finally, this research, as it develops, will begin to allow us to focus on the interaction between informal and formal labels as these change through the development of an individual. Clearly, this type of research has begun. The work noted earlier by Triplett (1990) represents an attempt to address the longitudinal component and to focus on informal labels. Our hope is that as we begin to understand the contribution labeling theory can make to the understanding of crime that other longitudinal studies focusing on early development and its relationship to crime and deviance will pay greater attention to the labeling perspective.

While the agenda for research development is clear, the future of labeling theory and its development raises a much more complex set of concerns. First, as we noted at the very beginning of this paper, criminological theories have often been presented as comprehensive explanations of crime and deviance with little recognition of the limits the theories carry with them. This certainly applies to labeling theory. Self-perceptions, self-interpretations of self and environment, the actions of those who provide reactions and labels are all in some sense limited by the characteristics of individuals and their environment. As a simple example, no matter how intense one is, no matter how one peceives oneself, no matter how the environment reacts, it is generally impossible for someone under four feet to dunk a basketball. This simple example is offered to note that even biological characteristics may have an impact on the influence that labels and labeling can have. This is certainly the case also with other characteristics of individuals and environments. This, of course, is not to say labeling has no effect; simply, that it will have, as any single theory or theoretical perspective must have, limits on its ability to explain behavior. This brings us to our earlier point that for labeling theory to fully develop, it must be seen as part of a larger theoretical model.

It has recently been argued that a distinctive characteristic of criminology is its commitment to an interdisciplinary of integrated theory of criminal behavior (Wellford 1989). While many have debated the value or possiblity of such theories, there is no debate about their potential value. The approach that seems to offer the best foundation for a model for interdisciplinary theory is one that provides for sources of explanation interacting together from cultural, social, psychological and biological spheres of knowledge. Labeling theory clearly represents an important element in the interaction between social and psychological levels of explanation. Still, it needs to be integrated into not only other social and psychological theories (as has been suggested by, for example, Farrell, 1989), but also with theories that include biophysical characteristics and components representing cultural and subcultural aspects.

This approach should not lead us into a distinction that marrs the contributions of Lemert—that is that labeling theory explains secondary deviance and all other theories explain primary deviance. Such an approach has proven to be inadequate. Certainly the impact on secondary deviance can come from theories that also explain primary deviance and the basic factors of symbolic interactionism and labeling may well be important in understanding some forms of primary crime or deviance. It is the integrated model that would explain through the operation of the same conceptual elements, perhaps differently weighted, perhaps operating at different times, the sources of primary and secondary deviance.

Finally, advances in labeling theory must provide more information on the process by which informal and/or formal labels actually effect delinquent or criminal behavior. Most of the research that we have reviewed and most of the theoretical development has focused on whether a label, either real or perceived, has some relationship to subsequent behavior. The theoretical question that needs further development is how a label has an effect. Is its effect primarily on the individual or the environment; is the effect primarily in terms of its subsequent change in the behavior of the individual; is its effect primarily on the way in which the individual is responded to by certain segments of the environment; and so on. The models that have been developed so far leave the connection between the label and the behavior relatively undeveloped.

We consider the future of labeling theory to be quite promising. We believe that as a representation within the criminological field of a major source of social thought (symbolic interactionism) it will be an important part of our understanding of crime and delinquency. Its value is significantly enhanced by the degree to which we are able to remove it from any direct association with critical or conflict criminology. Its value is becoming more apparent as research addresses its essential symbolic elements. Its ability to provide explanations will be enhanced as it is integrated with other theories in a comprehensive model of crime and delinquency. While it is easy to criticize much of the past theory and research on labeling, it is also easy to understand its importance. It is the importance that we wish to encourage other criminologists to consider and, in so doing, to begin to develop a better understanding of crime, delinquency and their prevention and control.

## Notes

1. Particularly in discussions of labeling, but also for other approaches, there is the discussion of whether it is a theory (Schur 1971) or a perspective (e.g., Gibbs 1966; Tittle 1975). We do not find this discussion very illuminating or important. Certainly almost any current explanation of crime could be more fully and formally developed. Labeling and other approaches are offered as explanations of crime and deviance. Whether they meet some definition of a theory or not is separate from the potential value of the explanation and the steps necessary to further develop and/or test the explanation.
2. For those who want to more fully understand Cooley and Mead we suggest the following original works—for Cooley, *Human Nature and Social Order* (1964); *Social Organization* (1962) and for Mead, *Mind, Self and Society* (1934). Excellent summaries and analyses of their contributions can be found in Rieff's (1962, 1964) introductions to the above noted books by Cooley and Coser's (1971) analyses of Cooley and Mead.
3. Many social science disciplines have been able to define a fundamental dependent variable that is appropriate to a discipline specific theory. For example, the concept of rational economic behavior created by economists has allowed the development of simple economic theories that utilize few concepts, models, etc. from other disciplines. Criminology, however, attempts to explain criminal behavior — a set of behaviors whose definition is not controlled by the discipline (see Gottfredson and Hirschi, 1990 for a discussion of this point).

## References

Adler, Freda, G. Mueller and W. Laufer
    1991    *Criminology*. New York: McGraw-Hill.
Ageton, Suzanne and Delbert Elliott
    1974    The effect of legal processing on delinquent orientations. *Social Problems* 22: 87–100.
Becker, Howard
    1963    *Outsiders*. New York: Free Press.

Cooley, Charles Horton
    1962    *Social Organization*. New York: Schocken.
    1964    *Human Nature and Social Order*. New York: Schocken.
Coser, Lewis A.
    1971    *Masters of Sociological Thought*. New York: Harcourt Brace Jovanovich.
Davis, Nanette
    1972    Labeling theory in deviance research. *Sociological Quarterly* 13: 447–474.
Farrell, Ronald
    1989    Cognitive consistency in deviance causation: A psychological elaboration of an integrated systems model. Pp. 77–92 in Steven Messner, Marvin Krohn and Allen Liska (eds.) *Theoretical Integration in the Study of Deviance and Crime: Problems and Prospects*. Albany: State University of New York Press.
Felton, Earls and A. Reiss
    1990    *Program on Human Development and Criminal Behavior*. Cambridge, Mass: Harvard School of Public Health.
Gibbs, Jack P.
    1966    Conceptions of deviant behavior: The old and the new. *Pacific Sociological Review* 9: 9–23.
Gottfredson, Michael R. and T. Hirschi
    1990    *A General Theory of Crime*. Stanford, Cal.: Stanford University Press.
Harris, Anthony
    1975    Imprisonnment and the expected value of a criminal choice: A specification and test of aspects of the labeling perspective. *American Sociological Review* 40: 71–87.
    1976    Race, commitment to deviance and spoiled identity. *American Sociological Review* 41: 432–42.
Jensen, Gary
    1972    Delinquency and adolescent self-conceptions: A study of the personal relevance of infraction. *Social Problems* 20: 84–103.
Lemert, Edwin
    1951    *Social Pathology*. New York: McGraw Hill.
    1967    *Human Deviance, Social Problems and Social Control*. Englewood Cliffs, N.J.: Prentice Hall, Inc.
Link, Bruce
    1982    Mental patient status, work and income: An examination of the effects of a psychiatric label. *American Sociological Review* 47: 202–15.
    1987    Understanding labeling effects in the area of mental disorders: An assessment of the effects of expectations of rejection. *American Sociological Review* 52: 96–112.
Link, Bruce and Francis Cullen
    1983    Reconsidering the social rejection of ex-mental patience: Levels of attitudinal response. *American Journal of Sociology* 11: 261–73.

Link, Bruce, Francis Cullen, James Frank and John Wozniak
    1987    The social rejection of former mental patients: Understanding
            why labels matter. *American Sociological Review* 92: 1461–1500.
Link, Bruce, Francis Cullen, Elmer Struelning, Patrick Shrout, and Bruce
Donrenwend
    1989    A modified labeling theory approach to mental disorders: An
            empirical assessment. *American Sociological Review* 54: 400–
            23.
Lofland, John
    1969    *Deviance and Identity.* Englewood Cliffs, N.J.: Prentice-Hall,
            Inc.
Mahoney, Ann R.
    1974    The effect of labeling upon youths in the juvenile justice system:
            A review of the evidence. *Law and Society Review* 8: 583–614.
Mankoff, Milton
    1971    Societal reaction and career deviance: A critical analysis. *The
            Sociological Quarterly* 12: 204–18.
Matsueda, Ross
    1982    Testing control theory and differential association: A causal
            modeling approach. *American Sociological Review* 47: 489–504.
Mead, George H.
    1934    *Mind, Self and Society.* C. Morris (ed). Chicago: University of
            Chicago Press.
Messner, Steven F., M. D. Krohn, and A. E. Liska
    1989    *Theoretical Integration in the Study of Crime: Problems and
            Prospects.* New York: SUNY Albany Press.
Orcutt, James
    1973    "Societal Reaction and the Response to Deviance in Small
            Groups." *Social Forces* 52: 259–67.
Paternoster, Raymond
    1987    The deterrent effect of the perceived certainty and severity of
            punishment: A review of the evidence and issues," *Justice
            Quarterly* 4: 173–218.
Paternoster, Raymond and LeeAnn Iovanni
    1989    The labeling perspective and delinquency: An elaboration of the
            theory and assessment of the evidence. *Justice Quarterly* 6: 359–
            394.
Paternoster, Raymond and Ruth Triplett
    1989    The Effect of Subjective Labels on Delinquency. Paper pre-
            sented at American Society of Criminology.
Rieff, Philip
    1962    Introduction. C. H. Cooley. *Social Organization.* New York:
            Schocken.
    1964    Introduction. C. H. Cooley. *Human Nature and Social Order.*
            New York: Schocken.
Scheff, Thomas
    1966    *Being Mentally Ill.* Chicago: Aldine.
    1974    Labeling theory of mental illness. *American Sociological Review*
            39: 444–52.

Schrag, Clarence
    1971    *Crime and Justice: American Style.* Washington, D.C.: Government Printing Office.
Schur, Edwin
    1971    *Labeling Deviant Behavior.* Englewood-Cliffs, N.J.: Prentice Hall.
Siegel, Larry J.
    1986    *Criminology.* St. Paul: West Publishing
Tannenbaum, Frank
    1938    *Crime and the Community.* New York: McGraw Hill.
Thomas, Charles and Donna Bishop
    1984    The effect of formal and informal sanctions on delinquency: A longitudinal comparison of labelling and deterrence theories. *Journal of Criminal Law and Criminology* 75: 1222–46.
Thornberry, Terrence
    1971    Punishment and crime: The effect of legal dispositions on subsequent criminal behavior. Unpublished Ph.D. Dissertation, University of Pennsylvania.
Thorsell, Bernard and Lloyd Klensky
    "The labeling process: Reinforcement vs. deterrence." *Law and Society Review* 6: 393–403.
Tittle, Charles
    1975    Deterrents or labeling. *Social Problems* 22 :332–45.
    1980    Labeling and crime: An empirical evaluation, Pp. 241–68 in Walter Gove (ed.) *The Labeling of Deviance: Exploring a Perspective, Second Edition.* Beverly Hills, Cal.: Sage Publications.
Tonry, Michael, L. E. Ohlin and D. P. Farrington
    1991    *Human Development and Criminal Behavior.* New York: Springer-Verlag.
Triplett, Ruth
    1990    Labeling and Differential Association: The Effects on Delinquent Behavior. Unpublished Ph. D. Dissertation, University of Maryland.
Wellford, Charles F.
    1975    Labeling theory and criminology: An assessment. *Social Problems* 22: 226–41.
    1987    Delinquency prevention and labeling. Pp. 257–267 *From Children to Citizens,* Volume 3 (J. Q. Wilson and G. C. Loury, eds.). New York: Springer-Verlag.
    1989    Toward an integrated theory of criminal behavior in S. F. Messner et al. *Theoretical Integration in the Study of Crime* New York: SUNY Albany Press.
White, Leslie A.
    1969    The symbol. *Science and Culture* (L. White) New York: Farrar, Strauss, Giroux.

# 2

# A Proposed Resolution of Key Issues in the Political Sociology of Law

*Austin T. Turk*

Criminologists working from conflict or radical perspectives have emphasized the point that definitions of criminality are meaningful only in reference to the sociolegal contexts in which they are created, interpreted, negotiated, and imposed. It follows that to explain the forms and patterns of criminality, one must learn how the identification of events and persons as criminal depends upon the processes of lawmaking and enforcement. These processes are found to be intrinsically political, reflecting class and other conflicts, and generally biased more toward perpetuating than reducing social inequalities. Explaining crime thus requires explaining its context—that is, a political sociology of law.

Since its revival in the 1960s, the sociology of law has been a storm center of intellectual and political controversy. The comfortably limiting assumptions of moral functionalism and technocratic empiricism have been exposed, and shown to be quite inadequate for either justifying or guiding research. Though persistent as ideologies, reverential and servile conceptions of law are no longer worth challenging except for political or pedagogical reasons. The question now is not whether but how a political sociology of law is to be developed. Understanding of what that means, the issues encountered, and strategic options for their resolution is to be sought in the dialogues among analysts inspired mostly by the legacies of Marx and/or Weber.

## From Programs to Research

Misleadingly dubbed "conflict sociology," the efforts of Marxians and Weberians until recently were devoted mainly to the critique of functionalism and empiricism, secondarily to formulating alternative conceptions and research programs. The initial objective has been achieved: Marxians and Weberians have jointly succeeded in establishing the fundamental importance of their concerns (cf. Hunt 1982). Law is now widely understood to be (1) not merely a social phenomenon but a political creation; (2) a complex form of power, and thus a means and object of conflict; (3) understandable only in contextually specified terms; and (4) entirely problematic in its relationship to justice, however either law or justice is defined.

Natural law as secularized in moral functionalism and the ideologies of populist informalism has been left behind. We now know better than to look for the sources of law in mysterious evolutionary, systemic, psychological, or spiritual forces. Law does not just happen, somehow emerging out of a natural sociality or wondrous enlightenment. It is not mandated by structural necessities or molded by a universal process of rationalization. Rather, however complex may be the causal linkage, legal cultural and organizational particulars, as well as the concept of law itself, are demonstrably political creations. That is, law is deliberately produced by the individual and joint efforts of people to stabilize their relations with others on the best possible terms for themselves. It follows that the instrumentalists have not been wrong after all, just theoretically shortsighted and methodologically naive.

Having won a beachhead for the conception of law as power, neither Marxians nor Weberians have yet really capitalized on that victory. We are still groping for a way to theorize the connections between hegemony and violence, consensus and coercion, liberalism and socialism, law and state. Recognizing that law is a complex and variable mixture of military, political, economic, ideological, and diversionary power resources is a start (Turk 1976; see also

Schermerhorn 1961, 17–18), but merely sets up the problem. The problem is to describe and explain particular mixtures of legal power, and their variations, without imposing our respective predilections for a primarily economic, political, or other explanatory mode. Still, to understand that law is a multidimensional and, unless proven otherwise, multidirectional form of power is a significant achievement. Given that legal power is real power, of course people struggle over it in the hope of using it to coerce, constrain, and convince others to end or lessen their resistance or interference. *How*, no longer *whether*, people struggle over and with the power of law is at last unavoidably on the research agenda.

To have established the need for contextual specification is a major accomplishment. Observed legal relationships and behavior patterns are not assumed to be invariant, but linked to the social-cultural and historical settings in which they occur and with which they interact and change. Bits and pieces of "the" law or "the" legal process can no longer excusably be portrayed and analyzed as if they existed in a timeless undifferentiated social space. There remains, however, the question of how far specification can go without degenerating into uniquism. While it is essential to be clear on where and when observations were made, it is unhelpful to insist on specificity to the point of abandoning the effort to construct a general—which is to say predictive—theory of law. Particular constellations of legal power and other social phenomena are ultimately meaningless unless interpreted so as to inform causal understanding and, it follows, political calculation. The need for not just specification but *purposive* specification—that is, theoretically informative as well as politically useful—has yet to be unambiguously shown and fully accepted.

That law and justice are not necessarily joined or even compatible has been amply demonstrated. But unease persists over losing the ideal of justice with, under, through, or despite law. Philosophical projects abound in the quest for a theory of justice; invariably they fail but continue to attract some of the toughest and most sophisticated minds around. Why? Nonlogical and empirically unfounded assumptions about the value, sanctity, capacity, and significance of individual humans continue to be set against equally untenable assumptions about the importance of collectivities, social movements, and humanity in toto. In demystifying law, Marxians and Weberians alike have left in ruins not only the absolutes of particular legal constructions but also their own nonlogical assumptions. Establishing that law is a political creation, a complex form of power, and a contextually specific production implies what many find a disturbing relativism. For the committed and concerned, there is a need to show that it is intellectually possible to discredit the ideological pretensions of capitalist, state socialist, or other political-legal formations without abandoning their own faiths. Whether or not it is necessary, we have yet to justify our critical achievements in a political sociology transcending the nonlogics of absolutism and relativism.

Having won the intellectual case for a political sociology of law, the victors are under greater pressure to "get on with it." Arguably, our fundamental problems are now methodological: how to study law as a political creation and form of power; how to do purposive contextual specification; how to deal with the relativism implicit in the political conception of law.

Marxians and Weberians have generated a considerable literature arguing among themselves over how to approach the research task. Happily, programmatic debates over the relative merits of different Marxisms, and of Marxian and Weberian perspectives, have gradually subsided as the limits of presupposition have been reached. The need for doing research instead of debating approaches has come to be generally accepted. As they move from philosophizing about science to the design and execution of empirical studies, even the most theoretically sensitive researchers have to settle upon precise working resolutions of several thorny issues.

## Research Issues and Strategies

Of the many issues that have been debated, there are five of particular methodological import: (1) the meaning of "value-free"; (2) the significance of the quantitative-qualitative distinction; (3) how to do comparative research; (4) the proper uses of history; and (5) the nature of dialectical analysis.

*The research meaning of "value-free"*

One of the most unfortunate modifiers ever invented, "value-free" has precipitated often fierce exchanges over such nonsensical questions as whether scientists have or should have values and whether research without value implications is possible or desirable. Regardless of Weber's (1949) good intentions, his mighty effort to clarify the difference between scholarship and propaganda abetted the thorough confusion of science with its philosophy. Instead of wrestling continuously with substantive questions, many social scientists have been diverted by an excessive—frequently paralyzing and ultimately fruitless—concern with finding unassailable epistemological grounds for their inquiries. Attempts to do so have led some to the evasions of Wright Mills' (1959, 25–75) "abstracted empiricism" and "grand theory" (i.e., procedural and conceptual formalism), claiming to exclude values from the research process. Rightly rejecting such claims, others have been led into the opposite error of inadvertently or polemically confusing the methods of casuistry with those of science (e.g., Ayre 1982, in an exchange with Turk 1979, 1982).

The research of the casuist is demonstrative and conclusive, that of the scientist (dis)confirmatory and tentative. Casuistic research is designed to build a case for premises whose validity is assumed. Scientific research is designed to test the implications of premises whose validity is never beyond question. In each kind of research, success is a matter of degree and is intersubjectively defined. This means that only the judgments of competent others are accepted by the researcher as measures of success or failure in conceptualization, observation, or interpretation. Competence among scientists is defined by recognized understanding and use of experimental reasoning and observational techniques. Among casuists, competence is defined by recognized skill in articulating, applying, and defending the premises. In both scientific and casuistic research, analytical logic and empirical observation are employed, but with fundamentally different objectives and priorities. The prime objective and value in science is theoretical knowledge: predictively useful causal generalizations. Given unquestionable premises, the priority value in casuistic research is practical knowledge: polemically useful evidence and arguments.

Being a dangerous and political place, this world needs both science and casuistry. Prediction and causal explanation are essential if humanity is to have a chance of surviving the testing constantly imposed by nature and social struggles. For scientific knowledge to be effectively disseminated and applied, necessarily on behalf of some values rather than others, casuistry provides the tools. The "value-free" issue becomes one only when casuistic standards are used to evaluate scientific research, and vice versa, or when casuistic methods are used in what are ostensibly scientific studies.

Casuists stir up opposition and weaken their case by attacking or misrepresenting unsupportive works deemed competent among scientists. It is better tactics to ignore competent but unsupportive studies, or better still to elaborate one's arguments so as to make such studies appear to be supportive or at least irrelevant. Good casuists (e.g., skilled lawyers, theologians, publicists) are adept at enlisting science in their cause, and understand the advantages of enlisting good science as against the dangers of linking their cause to poor science.

Scientists, on the other hand, waste their time and undermine their own claims to competence (knowing what is science) in attacking or misrepresenting casuistic studies as if they were scientific. The language and data may be similar, but the universes of discourse are vastly different. Scientific criticism is only pertinent when casuistic methods are used in what is misrepresented to be scientific research. Because of the likelihood of attack by scientists, such misrepresentation may well be counterproductive. Even if scientists are too busy, uninformed, or parochial to attack on behalf of the values of science itself, ideological opponents are very likely to make the most of the opportunity to discredit the cause by exposing its pseudoscientific supports.

All this suggests that the values of both casuistic and scientific research are best served when individual researchers themselves take care to maintain in their own work the distinction between casuistry and science. Obviously an individual may work sometimes as a scientist and other times as a casuist, with neither role being intrinsically superior to the other. No one can "do the scientific handstand" (Becker 1950, 34) all the time, and to be entirely uncaring about values other than those of science would be pathological if it were possible. Conversely, to be uncaring about the values of science is to be ignorant or pathologically indifferent to the need for science if one values humanity in whatever terms. As a casuist, the person with scientific research skills would seem obliged to use them on behalf of the cause, and perhaps may be able to make a stronger case than an associate without such skills. Even so, the casuistic uses of the methods and products of science must not be confused with scientific research if the values of science as well as nonscientific values are to be most effectively promoted.

How does all this help resolve the "value-free" issue? First, the impossibility of excluding values from research is taken for granted. Second, an operational tactic is proposed, not a philosophical solution. Third, the investigator is asked to decide what the priority is in a particular study, not to make a total commitment to be either a casuist or a scientist. Fourth, casuistic and scientific research are recognized to be equally necessary, complementary instead of conflicting. And fifth, the argument for maintaining the distinction between science and casuistry is not absolutist or abstract but pragmatic: that the goals of both are more likely to be attained.

If the "value-free" issue is so resolved, the other four issues become more amendable to resolution along similarly pragmatic lines.

## Quantitative-Qualitative

Here again, regrettable numbers of social scientists and casuists alike have been led astray by abstractions. Mesmerized by the wondrous subtleties and occasional insights of such luminaries as Blumer, Habermas, Levi-Strauss, Merleau-Ponty, Schroyer, and Schutz, some have imagined with St. Augustine that numbers are not merely useless but diabolical:

> The good Christian should beware of mathematicians and all those who make empty prophecies. The danger already exists that the mathematicians have

made a covenant with the devil to darken the spirit and to confine man in the bonds of Hell. (Quoted in Martindale 1963, 98–99)

Others have been conversely bemused by the ingenious mathematizing of such virtuosi as Blalock, Davis, Duncan, Goodman, Rapoport, Simon, and White. Armed with faith in numbers, they have disdained as not "empirical" the verbal descriptions and analyses of ethnographers and historians. Between them, the verbalists and the numerologists have infected generations of students with an intellectual pathology identified by Karl Schuessler (1965) as "the number complex."

The number complex is a disorder threatening to both science and casuistry. In its antinumbers form, there is an extreme aversion to numerical or other symbolic notation, statistics, surveys, experiments, computers, and even people associated with such things. In its pronumbers form, the complex is manifested in fascination with "all of the above," along with the identification of numbers with reality, loss of ability to distinguish substantive from methodological issues and priorities, and total indifference to ideas or information communicated through words.

Scientists afflicted with the antinumbers complex become unable to communicate with other scientists, and perhaps even with themselves, as experimental reasoning and observational techniques are abandoned. Those afflicted with the pronumbers complex are in great danger of premature recognition, making the fall harder when the fruits of their labors are critically examined by healthy scientists or skilled casuists interested in discrediting those fruits. A common symptom is failing to understand that scientific knowledge is established by repetition of results, not by passing a one-shot test of statistical significance (Tukey 1969).

As Lynn McDonald (1976, 17–18) and David Greenberg (1979, xiii–xvi) have indicated, antinumber casuists not only throw out a very useful and powerful set of tools, but incapacitate themselves for defending their cause against opponents who do use such tools. Pronumber casuists risk mistaking numerical displays for convincing arguments—for example, body counting implies military victory, declining arrest rates mean success in crime control, rising unemployment rates signal the revolutionary "moment," international loan defaults mark the "final crisis" of capitalism. Sooner or later, events and hostile critics discredit such number games, and therefore the causes for which they are played.

The therapeutic solution to the quantitative-qualitative issue is obvious: Get help! Neither fear nor love mathematical tools, for they are merely tools—clearly usable for some research tasks, clearly not for others. If one needs to count and can get adequate numbers, why not? If ones does not need to count, mathematization is pointless formalism. If one cannot get adequate numbers, mathematization is pseudoresearch. Which numbers are adequate? Technical measurement theory suggests all sorts of rules for manipulating numbers of varying adequacy, but the bottom-line tests for determining when numbers are eligible for manipulation are not a priori but pragmatic: Can one get (devise) the numbers? Can one persuade competent others that the numbers are meaningful? Does manipulating the numbers add demonstrably to anyone's ability to predict, explain, or persuade?

Regardless of when one needs or is able to count, both scientists and casuists are interested in maximizing their capacity to identify and analyze complex structures and processes. There is no more efficient and powerful tool than mathematics for ordering and analyzing observations, and mathematical or other symbolic logics are often useful for articulating and understanding complicated ideas and arguments. But more importantly, there is no tool designer and user more creative and skilled than the human investigator. Sometimes the limitless universe of observations can be mathematically coded, sampled, ordered, and analyzed in what are found to be predictively useful and causally meaningful ways. When this occurs, the economies of intellectual effort are tremendous—which makes it always worthwhile to consider how adequate numbers might be generated. Given that genuine mathematization is not possible most of the time (and most unlikely ever to be), competent scientists and casuists are adept at devising verbal approximations. Whether the research is scientific or casuistic, is focused upon general or specific questions, the researcher will explicitly or implicitly code (conceptualize), sample (select), order (arrange), and analyze (describe and explain) some universe of observations.

One universe is the political sociology of law as I earlier defined it: a conception of law as politically created, a form of power, having no necessary connection with justice, and understandable only in purposively specified contexts. Contextual specification presupposes that the methodological issues of how to do comparative research and to use history have been operationally resolved.

## Comparative Research

All research is comparative. One compares observations with either other observations or with some conceptual universe of empirically or hypothetically possible observations. Though epistemological relativists deny the possibility of meaningfully comparing anything with anything else, their arguments dissipate in the conundrum of having to define the unique case in terms of what is unique about it—which presupposes some way of distinguishing it from others (cf. Beirne, 1983). The issue, then, is not whether but how to compare so as to accomplish either casuistic or scientific research objectives.

Marxians and Weberians have clashed at times because the two kinds of objectives may seem to require different solutions. Some Marxians, especially the "philosophical Marxists," have claimed "a privileged insight into the truth about history that could be opposed to any merely empirical, sociological account of historical events in all their disturbing nastiness" (Bottomore 1975, 47–48). No scientist could accept such cavalier dismissal of scientific values and methods. Neither can skilled casuists, who understand that effective arguments cannot be built upon mere assertions, anecdotes, associations, or analogies. These are the tactics of sloganeering and exhortation, not of research, and are eventually counterproductive because they produce not only misrepresentations and distortions but also valid propositions whose validity cannot be defended (Turk 1979).

The question of whether Marxian research should be comparative has been debated primarily among Marxists. Weberians have helped fuel the controversy by stressing the many deficiencies of vulgar and/or philosophical Marxist writings: dogmatism, parochialism, determinism, semanticism, scholasticism, and other sins. Much of the Weberian critique has been irrelevant: nonscientific works have been treated as if they could be expected to meet scientific standards, nonscience as if it were science (e.g., the philosophizing of sundry "critical theorists"; the opportunistic propagandizing of Vyshinsky and his ilk; the fulminations of myriad self-defined "Marxist" radicals and revolutionaries). Among Marxists themselves, the issue has not been one of science but of casuistry: whether the cause is served by detailed speculations on the features of postcapitalist society, or by comparisons of present-stage capitalist and socialist societies. Futuristic speculation has been overwhelmingly rejected; the need for research to counter invidious comparisons by anti-Marxist casuists has been increasingly accepted.

Marxian comparative researchers face the same basic problem as everyone else: finding the optimal balance between appropriateness and equivalence (Armer 1973). The utility in one setting of concepts and techniques developed in another has to be demonstrated. Otherwise, modifications or new ones have to be devised that are usable within the cultural and/or structural constraints of the research setting. But tailoring concepts and techniques to fit the case at hand makes it more difficult to demonstrate their utility elsewhere. The problem is especially tough for Marxian researchers because the code, the conceptual universe, with which they begin has been developed almost entirely in the critique of European and American capitalism. It is still unclear how far they can use Marxian concepts and explanations, or modify them without losing what has been distinctively Marxist. Regardless, the Marxian research effort so far has been particularly helpful in demonstrating the need not only to balance appropriateness and equivalence but also to consider the possibility and nature of cross-societal linkages (e.g., the impact of colonialism in its various guises upon political-legal institutions and developments in Third World areas, Snyder 1980; Sumner 1982).

Granted the need for comparative research, how is it to be done? Because the problems of comparing are encountered in any research, there is in one sense nothing to be done beyond learning how to do research. The trade-offs involved in balancing appropriateness and equivalence (detailed vs. generalizing studies) and the problem of independent observation (multicollinearity, interviewer bias, feedback effects, etc.) are well known. However, these problems are highlighted in cross-societal and trans-historical comparisons. At least one methodological necessity has been made plain: a conceptual universe encompassing the societies or eras to be compared, and therefore not reducible to descriptions and explanations of just one of them. In some degree, appropriateness has to be sacrificed; culture-specific description and explanation have to be subordinated within a nonspecific conceptual universe.

Researchers have three options: *imposition*, *promotion*, or *abstraction*. First, they can pretend that site A is identical to site B, and see how well such "imposed" descriptions and explanations enable them to achieve their research aims: predictive causal generalizations or defensible casuistic arguments. Second, they can promote their conceptual universe to a higher level—for example, an analysis of nineteenth century capitalist law and politics is reformulated as a general theory of legal power, or a Euro-American universe is redefined as a "world system." Third, researchers can redefine the conceptual universe at a higher level of abstraction—for example, the study of class struggle and class structure becomes social conflict and authority structure analysis.

Each option has advantages and disadvantages, and no one option is intrinsically superior. *Imposition* is parsimonious and draws attention to similarities and parallels, but its track record is not too good in the political sociology of law. *Promotion* sensitizes researchers to continuities and interpenetration, but tends to slide into a "higher form" of imposition in which all history or the entire world is amalgamated into a conceptualization unable to recognize or explain diversity and change. *Abstraction* makes it easier to treat diversity and change (e.g., in terms of variables), but there is a risk of minimizing significant qualitative shifts and differences. In addition, applicability is harder to demonstrate and validity to test. If we agree that the limits of imposition have been reached in our field, then we should concentrate on seeing how far promotion and abstraction can take us.

Marxians have led in trying promotion and Weberians in trying abstraction; but Marxian promotion has clearly involved "neo-Marxian" abstractions, while Weberian abstraction has as clearly involved the promotion of some Euro-American (including some

Marxian) conceptions. Both approaches are worth trying, with some promise of complementarity if not convergence. The debate over how to do comparative research is resolved by showing that the purposes of science or casuistry are advanced by trying to do comparative studies, either way. Whether through promotion or abstraction, contextual specification is achieved insofar as we establish the conditions under which our concepts and techniques serve our purposes.

## The Proper Uses of History

For casuists and scientists, the issue is not how to do historical research but how to use it for their respective purposes. Historiography is not in question; to do historical research is to meet the expectations of competent historians. There have been social scientists who imagined studying persistence and change without regard for history, but they have thereby doomed themselves to the dustbin of intellectual history. The methodological issue is whether history is properly used as explanation or as description.

The "materialist conception of history" has been widely misinterpreted to exclude the role of human consciousness in social causation; to warrant deterministic explanations of later events as simply the results of earlier ones; to make the causal primacy of economic over all other factors an invariant uniformity, a constant instead of a variable; to misconstrue research as illustration instead of verification; and to reject scientific explanation in favor of a concept of "historical explanation" incorporating all the preceding fallacies. Insofar as philosophical cum polemical Marxism has encouraged such misinterpretation, it has been demonstrably counterproductive, helping to justify the stereotyping of research by Marxians as only and irredeemably antiscientific casuistry (cf. Parkin 1979).

Despite the stereotyping and the antic productions sustaining it, competent British Marxist and other historians have been at work. E. P. Thompson (1968, 1975), Douglas Hay (1975), and their colleagues have revealed how English law permeated society, not always to the detriment of the working class, and how class dominance was largely achieved through violence legalized by the ideology of law. A diverse array of "revisionist" and "postrevisionist" historians have shown how law, psychiatry, reformism, and penology jointly contributed to social control (a slippery concept they find) in various European and American settings (Cohen and Scull, 1983). Such historical studies have been crucial in establishing that law-and-society relationships are extremely complex in capitalist societies, as indeed in any society:

> Law, society, economy, state and ideology . . . constitute heterogeneous entities, whose external and internal relations are characterized by continuity *and* discontinuity, function *and* disfunction, mediation, refraction and reinforcement. This renders problematic the relation between law, state, economy and society. (Sugarman 1983, 2)

Whether contributors or consumers, scientists and casuists have to find ways to use such scholarly contributions in their own research.

To make use of history, researchers have to be sure of their objectives—which are not to be confused with those of the historian. Historical research is intended to produce a detailed and defensible account of what happened over some time period. The aim is to connect observations at "Time 1" with observations at "Time 2" and so on to "Time N." It may also be intended to contribute to casuistic or scientific goals, but these do not define the historian's research task. Because such goals are extraneous to historical research, the casuist or scientist cannot achieve their objectives just by doing historical research. The historian cannot do competent research (acceptable to other historians), anymore than can the scientist or casuist, if constrained by requirements and goals other than those intrinsic to the enterprise. Consequently, the casuist or scientist may be able to use the fruits of historical research but not historical research per se to advance their respective causes.

The proper use of history is not the same for casuistry and science. Casuistry requires competent history, but must encourage the dissemination of favorable rather than unfavorable accounts. "Equal time" for both is a nonsensical idea in casuistry; the cause is not served by facilitating the spread of heresies. Even if a "free marketplace of ideas" is the casuist's ideal, freedom of speech and belief do not extend to even reasoned attacks upon that freedom—

as has been amply demonstrated in historical, casuistic, and scientific studies. Casuistry implies discrimination in every sense: using only competent history that favors the cause, while ignoring, belittling, or suppressing even competent history judged to be unfavorable.

Science, in contrast, requires the use of all competent history as a source of data and potentially of ideas (Turk 1973). The goal of predictive causal generalizations implies that historical observations must be treated like any others—that is, as indicators of similarity and difference, continuity and change. It follows that the scientist cannot accord unique details the same respect as that properly given by the historian. The relevance of historical details for scientific purposes is determined by whether they can be fitted into the scientist's conceptual universe so as to help articulate and test general propositions.

What then of historical explanation? Strictly speaking, historical explanation is showing connections through time among observations made within an explicitly delimited field. Such "actuarial" explanation is difficult but essential, logically equivalent to the mathematizing of descriptive statistics. When anyone begins asking *why* the connections are as the historian shows, the line is crossed between history and either casuistry or science. If one's purposes are casuistic, the "meaning of history" will be the revelation and vindication of one's cause. If one aims at scientific knowledge, the connections are to be explained as particular outcomes of casual processes understood in general but contextually specified terms. The purpose determines the adequacy of explanation.

## Dialectical Analysis

Marx's rejection of Hegel is usually seen as a clean break with his idealist philosophizing, but may rather be viewed as a logical or methodological extension of it. Instead of a mysterious endless unfolding of thought, counterthought, and internally contradictory synthesis, Marx's conceptual universe was the successive transformations of social life resulting from the working out of the structural contradictions intrinsic to each new "social organization of production." The analytical object was no longer defined in terms of philosophical abstractions but of concrete realities: the humanly created material conditions of existence. The Hegelian dialectic model itself was not questioned, but was to be applied to the "external world" as well as the world of ideas. In Marx's conception, and as emphasized by Engels (1972), the dialectical process was to be understood in terms of "the general laws of motion" through which both human consciousness and social structure progressively changed. Research would proceed by tracing in detail the historical unfolding of the dialectic, the irremediable contradictions in the present synthesis (capitalism), and the path of change as the current structure inevitably disintegrated and a new resolution was created (Marx and Engels 1962, 387–88).

Whatever its merits as a philosopher's device, the dialectical model has been a problem for scientists and casuists ever since Marx brought it to earth. It has been often misconstrued to be the final analysis instead of an analytical tool, or to be an alternative to science instead of a contribution to it. Scientists have, of course, rejected both misconstructions; but their inutility for casuistry has been less evident.

If one is building an argument against capitalism, one will find enormously attractive the idea that scientifically established "laws of motion" ensure its collapse. However, as every informed Marxist knows, it has become increasingly hard to sustain that idea. There are several difficulties. First, the concept of "laws" is an anachronism; early mechanical and deterministic conceptions of science as "exact" have been displaced by processual and probabilistic conceptions of the kind Marxism's own genitors seem to have dimly envisioned. Second, structural contradictions are not as readily demonstrated as are logical ones. Third, assuming that one succeeds in demonstrating structural contradictions, it is not easy to demonstrate the primacy of contradictions in the social organization of production. And fourth, it is exceedingly hard to demonstrate the necessity or inevitablity of structural collapse because of whatever contradictions are found. Given such difficulties, how does or can one reconcile dialecticism with science?

One option is to leave dialectics to philosophers and logicians. Marx's extension of Hegelian dialectics to the "external world" might simply be considered a pioneering effort in the history of social science. Thus, dialectical analysis would be dismissed as a primitive method long since superseded by a more powerful, objective, and fruitful research technology. However, this resolution is unworkable because it ignores the central importance of dialectics for a distinctively Marxian casuistry. Moreover, it is unacceptable because empirically grounded dialectical analysis can be a powerful addition and corrective to the descriptive empiricism dominant in contemporary social science methodology (cf. Freiberg 1980).

More promising options emphasize dialectical *analysis* without necessarily imposing the dialectic *model*. Frank (1973), for instance, has ably defended a holistic and flexible conception of dialectical analysis against van den Berghe's (1963) proposed "theoretical synthesis" of dialecticism and functionalism. By implication (and as demonstrated in Frank's own works), holistic dialectical analysis can be scientifically useful for interpreting observations—for example, of profit-taking from Third World "development" investments—in terms of the *promoted* model of capitalism. The procedure and results are decidedly substantive: descriptive analyses of capitalist exploitation without any logical necessity of asserting the inevitablism of the dialectic model (or of the functionalist one).

Another approach is to redefine or "loosen" the concept of dialectical analysis so that it is not limited to descriptive studies of capitalism. "Power structure research" (Domhoff, 1980) exemplifies this option. Even though such studies have focused mainly upon the class structures of the United States and other advanced capitalist societies, there is in principle no reason why the power structures of state socialist and other kinds of societies cannot be similarly examined—as of course they long have been by both casuists and scientists. The methodological limitation of power structure analysis, as of holistic dialectical analysis, is that the strong descriptive emphasis tends to lose the essential idea of dialectic as *process*. A kind of dialectic without a dynamic (or "law" without "motion") is the consequence, leading the theorist to look *outside* relationships for explanations of their "movement" instead of looking *within* them. This outcome meets neither casuistic nor scientific needs: the key insights of dialectical analysis have resulted since Marx from seeing how power structures "contain within themselves the seeds of their own destruction''—or at least causal forces generating both stabilizing and destabilizing tendencies.

A more satisfactory option in this respect is to demystify ''the dialectic'' by stressing dialectical *processes*—minimally defined as social conflicts generated by exploitation and oppression, and tending to destabilize and perhaps destroy their structural bases. The scientist's cautious ''perhaps'' is hardly inspiring, so casuists will necessarily be less restrained in interpreting social conflicts both as the products of structural inequalities and as moving toward their elimination. Nonetheless, good casuists will avoid determinism in favor of probabilism, and leave room for human creativity and effort. William Chambliss and Erik Ohlin Wright have provided notable examples of such casuistry, advancing Marxist interpretations within carefully developed illustrative analyses of social conflicts and the structural sources of material inequalities.

Chambliss has been particularly alert to the dangers of an excessively abstract and deterministic ''dialectical paradigm.'' In an important article, ''On Lawmaking,'' he stipulated that law creation is ''a process aimed at the resolution of contradictions, conflicts and dilemmas which are inherent in the structure of a particular historical period'' (Chambliss 1979, 152). He went on to offer an ''admittedly abstract depiction'' of a contradiction as being

established in a particular historical period when the working out of the logic of the social structure and ideology must necessarily destroy some fundamental aspects of existing social relations. (Chambliss 1979, 152)

Subsequently, Chambliss moved from abstraction to reality, averring that ''the logic of the dialectic'' leads not to determinism but instead to an emphasis upon the point ''that people, not 'systems,' 'societies,' or 'the legal order,' but people make laws, people acting in the face of extant resources and constraints'' (Chambliss and Seidman 1982, 144).

In similar fashion, Wright has stressed that the dialectical processes arising from the contradictions of capitalism may lead to several possible ''futures''—as opposed to the traditional Marxist view ''that capitalism is part of a single historical trajectory which inevitably leads to socialism and then communism'' (Wright 1979a, 40). He has also contributed significant theoretical and methodological insights on how to conceptualize in empirically defensible, nondeterministic terms the class relationships and struggles, historical transformations, and bureaucratic structures of capitalism (Wright 1979b).

Summing up, the problem of dialecticism is resolved for research purposes insofar as four conditions are met in dialectical analysis:

1. The dialectic model is treated heuristically instead of being imposed upon the complexities of particular social realities.
2. Dialectical analysis is not assumed to be applicable only to capitalism.
3. Dialectical analysis is not equated with describing patterns of exploitation and oppression, or structures of power, but instead is focused upon dialectical processes—that is, conflicts arising from and potentially threatening such patterns and structures.
4. The presence and causal significance of dialectical processes are treated as objects of investigation, not as assumptions about the precise nature and direction of social conflicts and changes.

## Conclusion

Marxians and Weberians have shown that a political sociology of law is needed, and have agreed that it must be empirically as well as theoretically defensible. The commitment to research means that a number of contentious methodological issues will have to be resolved in practice even if not necessarily in philosophical principle. Those issues have been examined, and working strategies for dealing with them have been proposed. Despite ideological and theoretical differences between and among Marxian and Weberian researchers, the possibility of a methodological convergence exists. If the distinction between casuistry and science is accepted, and the need for both understood, everyone's research aims are more likely to be advanced—as we learn to use both words and numbers, comparisons and histories, in analyzing the fundamental and potentially transforming social processes which some call "dialectical" and others simply call "conflict."

The traditional preoccupation of criminologists with explaining ill-defined individual offenses has so far been largely unaffected by the argument that a viable criminology requires a political sociology of law. Indeed, there has been a resurgence of theorizing that simply ignores or misconstrues the issues (e.g., Wilson and Hernstein 1985; Gottfredson and Hirschi 1990), while politically conservative funding policies continue to favor narrowly conceived technocratic exercises in eclectic data collection and analysis. Nonetheless, the untenable assumptions of traditional criminology are increasingly evident in failures of explanation and policy, and must eventually give way to the new criminology—the contextually specified analysis of linkages between (a) perceptions and measures of criminality, and (b) "the direct exercise of legal power to articulate and impose normative demands" (Turk 1984, 329).

## References

Armer, Michael
   1973    "Methodological problems and possibilities in comparative research." Pp. 49–79 in Michael Armer and Allen D. Grimshaw (eds.), *Comparative Social Research: Methodological Problems and Strategies*. New York: Wiley.
Ayre, Richard
   1982    "Objectivity versus political and moral commitment? For science and partisanship in criminology." *Contemporary Crises* 6: 133–54.
Beirne, Piers
   1983    "Cultural relativism and comparative criminology." *Contemporary Crises* 7: 371–391.
Becker, Howard P.
   1950    *Through Values to Social Interpretation*. Durham, N.C: Duke University Press.
Bottomore, Tom
   1975    *Marxist Sociology*. New York: Holmes and Meier.
Chambliss, William J.
   1979    "On lawmaking." *British Journal of Law and Society* 6: 149–71.
Chambliss, William J. and Robert Seidman
   1982    *Law, Order, and Power*. Reading, Mass.: Addison-Wesley. Second edition.
Cohen, Stanley and Andrew Scull (eds.)
   1983    *Social Control and the State*. Oxford: Martin Robertson.
Domhoff, G. William (ed.)
   1980    *Power Structure Research*. Beverly Hills, Cal.: Sage Publications.
Engels, Frederick
   1972    *Dialectics of Nature*. Moscow: Progress Publishers.

Frank, Andre Gunder
  1973   "Functionalism and dialectics." Pp. 62–73 in William J. Chambliss (ed.), *Sociological Readings in the Conflict Perspective.* Reading, Mass.: Addison-Wesley.
Freiberg, J. W.
  1980.   "Dialectical method." Boulder, Co.: The Red Feather Institute for Advanced Studies in Sociology, No. 57.
Gottfredson, Michael R. and Travis Hirschi
  1990   *A General Theory of Crime.* Stanford, Cal.: Stanford University Press.
Greenberg, David
  1979   *Mathematical Criminology.* New Brunswick, N.J.: Rutgers University Press.
Hay, Douglas, Peter Linebaugh, John G. Rule, E. P. Thompson, and Cal Winslow.
  1975   *Albion's Fatal Tree: Crime and Society in Eighteenth-Century England.* New York: Pantheon.
Hunt, Alan
  1982   "Dichotomy and contradiction in the sociology of law." Pp. 74–97 in Piers Beirne and Richard Quinney (eds.), *Marxism and Law.* New York: Wiley.
Martindale, Don
  1963   "Limits to the uses of mathematics in the study of sociology." Pp. 95–121 in James C. Charlesworth (ed.), *Mathematics and the Social Sciences: The Utility and Inutility of Mathematics in the Study of Economics, Political Science, and Sociology.* Philadelphia: American Academy of Political and Social Science.
Marx, Karl and Frederick Engels
  1962   *Marx-Engels Selected Works.* Moscow: Foreign Languages Publishing House. Volume 2.
McDonald, Lynn
  1976   *The Sociology of Law and Order.* London: Faber and Faber.
Mills, C. Wright
  1959   *The Sociological Imagination.* New York: Oxford University Press.
Parkin, Frank
  1979   *Marxism and Class Theory: A Bourgeois Critique.* New York: Columbia University Press.
Schermerhorn, Richard A.
  1961   *Society and Power.* New York: Random House.
Schuessler, Karl
  1965   "The number complex in sociology." *The Ohio Valley Sociologist* 31: 3–11.
Snyder, Francis G.
  1980   "Law and development in the light of dependency theory." *Law and Society Review* 14: 723–804.
Sugarman, David (ed.)
  1983   *Legality, Ideology and the State.* New York: Academic.

Sumner, Colin (ed.)
  1982   *Crime, Justice and Underdevelopment*. London: Heinemann.
Thompson, E. P.
  1975   *Whigs and Hunters: The Origin of the Black Art*. New York: Pantheon.
  1968   *The Making of the English Working Class*. New York: Penguin.
Turkey, J. W.
  1969   "Analyzing data." *American Psychologist* 24: 83–91.
Turk, Austin T.
  1973   "The sociological relevance of history: a footnote to research on legal control in South Africa." Pp. 285–300 in Michael Armer and Allen D. Grimshaw (eds.), *Comparative Social Research: Methodological Problems and Strategies*. New York: Wiley.
  1976   "Law as a weapon in social conflict." *Social Problems* 23: 276–291.
  1979   "Analyzing official deviance: for nonpartisan conflict analyses in criminology." *Criminology* 16: 459–476.
  1982   "Values and objectivity in criminological inquiry: Ayre's dilemma." *Contemporary Crises* 6: 155–59.
  1984   "Criminology and sociolegal studies." Pp. 309–34 in Anthony N. Doob and Edward L. Greenspan (eds.), *Perspectives in Criminal Law*. Aurora, Ontario: Canada Law Book, Inc.
van den Berghe, Pierre
  1963   "Dialectic and functionalism: toward a theoretical synthesis." *American Sociological Review* 28: 695–705.
Weber, Max
  1949   *The Methodology of the Social Sciences*. New York: The Free Press. Translated and edited by Edward A. Shils and Henry A. Finch.
Wilson, James Q. and Richard J. Hernstein
  1985   *Crime and Human Nature*. New York: Simon and Schuster.
Wright, Erik Ohlin
  1979a   "Capitalism's futures: A provisional reconceptualization of alternatives to capitalist society." Toronto: University of Toronto, Department of Sociology, Structural Analysis Programme, Working Paper No. 7.
  1979b   *Class, Crisis and the State*. London: NLB.

# 3

# Contrasting Crime General and Crime Specific Theory: The Case of Hot spots of Crime

*David Weisburd, Lisa Maher, and*
*Lawrence Sherman with Michael Buerger, Ellen Cohn,*
*and Anthony Petrosino*

Criminological theory has been dominated by the search for underlying root causes common to all deviant behavior. Some scholars have found these antecedents of criminality in the social disorganization that characterizes communities where crime rates are high (Thrasher 1927; Shaw and McKay 1931, 1942). Others have looked to the differential associations that provide both the normative and educational foundations of deviance (Sutherland and Cressey 1970), or the normlessness that follows from contradictions in culture and aspirations of offenders (Merton 1938). Still others have been primarily concerned with the failures of social control (Hirschi 1969), or at times its excesses (Erikson 1962). Common to all of these approaches is the assumption that most crime will fall within a single explanation for criminality. Indeed, even white collar crime, which has often been seen to contradict conventional theorizing, was developed as a concept in order to illustrate the advantages of one general theory (see Sutherland 1973), and has recently been used to provide support for another (Hirschi and Gottfredson 1987a).

Search for a general theory for explaining crime continues (see Hirschi and Gottfredson 1987b; Gottfredson and Hirschi 1990; Wilson and Hernstein 1985) but a number of criminologists have shifted their focus to crime specific rather than general analysis. Here the concern has most often been with crime prevention rather than criminological theory (see Hope 1986; Poyner 1983, 1988; Webb 1988; for an important exception see Cohen and Felson 1979). Nonetheless these finding have led some to challenge the focus of traditional explanations for the etiology of crime and deviance. As Cornish and Clarke argue, crime specific analysis leads us away from a unitary explanation of "divergent criminal behaviors" to one that identifies the vast differences between them as "crucial to the tasks of explanation and control" (Cornish and Clarke 1986, 6; see also Clarke and Cornish 1985).

The debate between crime general and crime specific theories has generally been raised in the context of the behavior of persons. For example, studies have examined the degree to which individual offenders evidence degrees of crime specialization (e.g., see Wolfgang et al. 1972; Blumstein et al. 1986; Bursik 1980; Kempf 1986; Albrecht and Moitra 1988), or the extent to which there are similarities or differences in the nature of those who commit very different types of crimes (e.g., see Hirschi and Gottfredson 1987a; Wheeler et al. 1988; Steffensmeier 1989). In this paper we examine the salience of crime specific and crime general approaches in the context of the distribution of crime across places. Applying computer mapping techniques to police call for service data, we identify and analyze the distribution of specific offenses in what are defined as "hot spots" of crime.

## Crime Causation Theory and Crime at Places

Focus upon the environments in which crime occurs has a long history in criminological study. In the first half of the nineteenth century, for example, French scholars sought to identify relationships between crime and social characteristics of geographic areas or regions (e.g., see Guerry 1833; Quetelet 1842). These "cartographic criminologist" as Smith calls them matched "spatial (usually regional) patterns of crime and offender rates with variations in 'moral' statistics (including literacy, population density, wealth, occupation, nationality and the home environment) and with physical phenomena (such as climate)'' (Smith 1986, 3). Following upon the work of the French, scholars in England began to examine what was to become a major American concern, the link between urbanization and crime (Rawson 1839; Mayhew 1862, Booth 1902–3). Despite groundbreaking work in providing explanations for the distribution of crime, these ecological perspectives were quickly overtaken by scholars who looked for the causes of crime in the biological and physiological framework of individuals (Morris 1958).

The emergence of the Chicago school of American sociology in the first quarter of this century brought about a resurgence of interest in the role of ecological factors in crime causation as well as a clearly developed theoretical perspective for understanding variations in crime rates across physical space. These urban sociologists, led by Robert Park, looked to characteristics of the urban environment to explain the crime problem in American cities. They identified "interstitial areas" in Chicago where social control was weak and social disorganization pervasive (Thrasher 1927), and theorized that such factors were responsible for variations in urban crime rates (Burgess 1925). While these scholars centered their interests upon juvenile delinquency, their work sought to demonstrate the more general roles of economic deprivation, ethnic heterogeneity, and high rates of social mobility in the production of crime rates (Shaw 1929; Shaw and McKay 1931, 1942).

Perhaps because the ideas of the Chicago school were so well accepted and became so obvious a part of our understanding of city life, interest in the ecological correlates of crime faded. Shaw's confident assertion that the "study of such a problem as juvenile delinquency necessarily begins with a study of its geographical location" (Shaw 1929, 10) was not heeded by those who followed him. Rather, the next generation of researchers sought to explain why certain individuals within these high crime areas (or outside them) chose to commit crimes while others did not (Merton 1938; Sutherland 1939). These sociologists shifted focus from the ecology of crime to the predisposition of persons to criminality, though they continued to search for a unitary explanation for criminal behavior.

Recent interest in the ecology of crime, much like that of the

Chicago school,[1] developed primarily from a desire to further public policies for crime control. This "environmental criminology" as it is called by Brantingham and Brantingham (1981) is generally more concerned with applied crime prevention than crime causation theory (for critiques see Cohen 1985; South 1987). It is thus not surprising that scholars who have made important contributions to recent research in this area have been drawn from a diverse set of scholarly disciplines. Represented among them are geographers (see Harries 1974, 1976, 1980; Herbert 1980; Herbert and Harries 1986) architectural designers and planners (see Angel 1968; Gardiner 1978; Jacobs 1961; Newman 1972, 1980) as well as traditional criminologists (see Clarke 1980; Clarke 1983; Clarke and Mayhew, eds. 1980; Heal and Laycock, eds. 1986).

Environmental strategies of crime control began with efforts to alter specific aspects of urban design (Jeffrey 1977) or urban architecture (Newman 1972), but broadened to take into account a much larger set of characteristics of physical space and criminal opportunity (e.g., Brantingham and Brantingham 1975, 1977, 1981a; Mayhew et al. 1976; Duffala 1976; Rengert 1980, 1981, Stoks 1981; Scott, Crow, and Erikson 1985; Jeffrey, Hunter, and Griswold 1987; Le Beau 1987; Hunter 1988; Cromwell 1991). Advocates of the environmental perspective argued that the physical space where criminal events occur should be the focus of criminological inquiry (Brantingham and Brantingham 1975, 1981; see also Herbert 1982; Herbert and Hyde 1985; Herbert and Harries 1986), but they did not stake out a clear position on whether this switch of concern would also demand rejection of the traditional assumptions of crime causation theory. Environmental criminology's basic contribution lay in its call for a change in the unit of analysis from persons (or criminality) to places (or crimes), and the identification of new variables to add to ecological models (e.g., see Taylor et al. 1981, 1984; Taylor and Gottfredson 1986; Byrne 1986; Sampson 1986a, 1986b, 1987).

Two perspectives that have benefited from these recent contributions to environmental and ecological study are particularly pertinent to the questions raised in our paper. One provides a definitional framework for examining the distribution of crime across places. The other questions to what extent ecological or opportunity analyses alter the parameters of conventional criminological theory.

In a recent article in *Criminology*, Sherman, Gartin, and Buerger (1989) define what they describe as the "criminology of place." Place, as they understand it, is "a fixed physical environment which can be seen completely and simultaneously, at least on its surface, by one person's naked eyes" (Sherman et al. 1989, 31; see also Sherman and Weisburd 1987), a definition that allows them to examine the concentration of police call data across addresses (the smallest unit of visual space) in the city of Minneapolis. Their analysis "reveals substantial concentrations of all police calls, and especially calls for predatory crime, in a relatively few 'hot spots.'" (1989, 37; see also Beavon 1984; Brantingham and Brantingham 1981b). On the surface, such findings appear to support the salience of a common set of antecedents for much criminal conduct, at least that portion labelled as "predatory." Yet, Sherman et al. did not examine the relationship among specific crimes at the addresses they examined. Nor were they able to aggregate their data beyond individual addresses. Their work thus left open the possibility that crime concentration at places reflects the clustering of particular and specialized forms of criminality in discrete environments.

It is this latter concern which forms the basis for Clarke and Cornish's critique of conventional crime causation theory (Clarke and Cornish 1985; Cornish and Clarke 1986). Following upon a series of situational crime prevention studies for specific offenses (e.g., in regard to burglary, theft, and vandalism), they argue that there is a substantial body of evidence challenging attempts to develop a unitary theory for explaining crime. Cornish and Clarke suggest that a more crime specific focus is called for, which would develop models of criminal decision making "in relation to particular types of crime" (Cornish and Clarke 1989, 104). While they provide a general framework for developing such models they argue that the "desire to construct general statements about crime, deviancy and rule breaking has consistently diverted attention from the important differences between types of crime—the people committing them, the nature of the motivations involved and the behaviors required" (Clarke and Cornish 1985, 165).

## Identifying Hot Spots of Crime

Our data for examining the distribution of crime at places are drawn from the Minneapolis police dispatch system between June 6th of 1987 and June 5th of 1988. While police calls have not generally been used as an indicator of crime events, as Sherman et al. note they "provide the widest ongoing data collection net for criminal events in the city" (1989, 35). Call data often include criminal activities that get filtered out by police discretion or victim fear in official crime reporting.

Sources of error in call data in Minneapolis, however, as elsewhere, are not insubstantial (for a review of this problem, see Sherman et al. 1989). Crimes identified by the dispatch system may represent intentional lies or a misinterpretation of events by victims, bystanders, or call takers. In poorer areas, where private telephones are not as prevalent, address information may be indicative of places where victims are able to find a phone rather than where crime events occur. While our observations of call-generated crime reporting suggest that call operators are sophisticated in their identification and classification of crime (see also Manning 1988), we recognize that there may be a substantial degree of reporting error in our data. Whether the count of crime as measured by dispatched calls is a less reliable indicator than other traditional reporting methods such as analysis of complaint reports we cannot say. Other data suggest that there is a very high correlation between reported crime and police calls (see Taylor et al. 1981). Moreover, as Biderman and Reiss (1967) note there is no "true" count for crime events, only socially organized counting methods each with its own sources of bias and error.

Because police call data include a substantial amount of information that is not reflective of criminal activity, we chose to extract from the Minneapolis file a series of fifty-two crime call categories (see appendix 3-1). These ranged from serious criminal events such as stabbings, shootings, rapes, or robberies to relatively minor violations such as disorderly conduct or even noise on the street. Using these criteria for extraction of call data we identified a sample of 194,668 events.

Our identification of places of high call activity from these data was facilitated by site selection work in the Minneapolis Hot Spots Patrol Experiment (Sherman and Weisburd 1989).[2] We began by selecting only addresses that included three or more "hard" crime calls (see appendix 3-1). The distinction between "hard" and "soft" crime is one suggested by Albert Reiss, Jr. (1985) in order to contrast more serious predatory offenses and what some have identified as incivilities or crimes of public disorder.[3] This distinction was used in our analysis primarily because we sought to identify places amenable to police intervention which, relative to other locations, included a large number of serious property or person offenses. Some 5538 addresses fit our criteria for initial inclusion in the analysis out of an estimated 115,000 addresses in the city of Minneapolis.

But we did not want to stop with identification of what might be called high rate addresses, since we believed it likely that the addresses would cluster together into what we defined as crime hot spots. Accordingly, we utilized computer mapping techniques to identify the spatial relationships among the 5538 high rate addresses.[4] As we expected, we found a substantial degree of clustering of those addresses, which allowed us to define discrete areas, usually less than a block long as "hot spots of crime."[5]

As we did not want to examine every cluster of crime activity as identified by calls for service, but rather only high activity clusters, we set a threshold of twenty separate hard crime call events for initial inclusion in our sample. This left us with 420 preliminary hot spots that were then examined in Minneapolis by two observers. The observers were able to distinguish addresses that were visually close on the maps, but in reality distant one from another or separated by natural or man-made boundaries. Conversely they linked addresses that were proximate, but appeared distant on our computer maps. Following these observations we were left with 365 valid crime hot spots.[6]

These 365 hot spots of crime account for more than a quarter of the total number of crime call events in the city of Minneapolis in the year we examined (see table 3.1), though we estimate that the hot spots comprised no more than 2.5 percent of the city's street segments or blocks.[7] While our initial criteria for selection of hot spots was based only on hard crime calls, we also find that the

TABLE 3.1
Comparison of Crime Calls within Hot Spots to Minneapolis City Totals

|  | Soft Crime Calls | Hard Crime Calls | Total Crime Calls |
|---|---|---|---|
| Hot spots | 36,248 (27.82%)* | 17,594 (27.33%)* | 53,842 (27.66%)* |
| City total | 130,296 | 64,372 | 194,668 |

*% of city total calls located in hot spot boundaries.

relative proportion of hard and soft crime events is very close to the overall city-wide distributions. Nonetheless, there is considerable variation in the proportion of the total number of specific crime calls found in the hot spots. In the case of "thefts" and "morals" (mostly street prostitution), for example, more than half of all calls city wide are found in our sample. In contrast, fewer than ten percent of "prowler" and "hot rod" calls are found in the hot spots. For the majority of call categories, somewhere between twenty and forty five percent of total calls were linked to addresses in the 365 hot spots.

## Analysis

The debate between advocates of specific and general theories of crime causation can be directly related to the distribution of crime across places. If there is a common set of underlying causal factors that influence all crimes, we would expect to find relatively little specialization in the types of crimes that are committed at hot spots. Rather we would expect a heterogenous group of crimes where crime events are clustered. As James Q. Wilson and George Kelling (1982) argue in their influential article "Broken Windows" in regard to neighborhoods of developing social and physical decline:

Such an area is vulnerable to criminal invasion. Though it is not inevitable, it is more likely that here, rather than in places where people are confident they can regulate public behavior by informal controls, drugs will change hands, prostitutes will solicit, and cars will be stripped. That the drunks will be robbed by boys who do it as a lark, and the prostitutes purposefully and perhaps violently. That muggings will occur. (1982, 3)

In some sense, our finding of a very high concentration of crime calls at hot spots in Minneapolis provides initial support for a general theory of crime causation at places. This is because we find that crime is indeed disproportionately concentrated at certain hot spots, places that presumedly have common characteristics that make them "criminogenic." Yet, the concentration of crime in particular hot spots does not tell us whether there is something specific to certain environments that leads to the occurrence of particular forms of criminality. If the premise of crime specific theory is correct, then we would predict that specific types of crimes would occur in specific hot spots. By implication we would expect there to be little relationship or a negative among crimes at hot spots (since such places are assumed to evidence specialization in crime occurances).

In order to contrast these two general models for crime causation at places—one that predicts little specialization at hot spots and another that suggests a high degree of specialization—we analyze the correlation of crime calls across hot spots. Our analysis is based on the hot spots described above, though we do not examine all crime call categories. Our decision to exclude certain crime types was due both to the relative infrequency of some of the crimes and the lack of clear definition of a number of others. The fourteen crime call types we examine include damage to property, domestic disputes, morals offenses, drunks, rape, burglary of a business, burglary of a dwelling, robbery of a business, robbery of a person, thefts, shootings, stabbings, auto theft, and assault.[8] Overall these categories accounted for 56.4 percent of the crime calls that are found in our hot spots sample.

Examination of the correlations among crime call occurrences across places raises a strong challenge to the hypothesis that all crimes are linked (see table 3.2). In some cases such a finding seems obvious when we turn from places to persons in explaining criminality. For example, it is not surprising that burglaries of dwellings and burglaries of businesses are negatively related. It is often impossible to commit both of these offences in a hot spot—since many hot spots are made up wholly of either business or residential addresses. But such obvious constraints on what crimes may be committed in a particular place, do not apply to the small or negative correlations found between such crimes as burglaries of businesses and auto theft, or shootings and robberies. Indeed, it is common today for scholars to identify a link between serious crimes such as stabbings or shootings, and minor offenses such as thefts, moral offences, and auto theft. But our data do not.

The relationship of morals (primarily prostitution) calls and other offenses is particularly interesting in the light of theoretical links that have been made between public disorder and serious crimes (e.g., see Wilson and Kelling 1982; Reiss 1986). Contrary to these perspectives, we find weak links at hot spots, between morals calls and other calls with the exception of "drunks," burglaries of businesses, robberies of persons, and assaults. In turn, though these correlations are significant, with the exception of robbery of persons they are relatively small.

While there is substantial evidence in table 3.2 that crimes often assume to be linked are not in fact correlated (and often negatively correlated) at hot spots, our data also indicate that certain crime categories are strongly related. Domestic calls and burglaries of dwellings for example, are correlated at over .70. Robberies of persons and drunk calls, as well assaults and robberies of person, and domestic and assault calls, and stabbing and assault calls, are all correlated at hot spots at greater than .50. While we do not have the kind of supplemental quantitative or qualitative detail necessary to define the specific reasons why these particular types of crime calls are so strongly linked, such relationships may be understood to some extent with reference to the crime categories themselves. Domestic violence and burglaries of dwellings for example demand residential locations, and we might speculate that nondomestic assaults and stabbings are often the product of street disputes.

Similar explanations may be used for call categories that reflect somewhat weaker though still significant relationsihps. For example, rapes are unrelated to such crime calls as morals, drunks, thefts or auto theft, but related to crime calls of violence such as shootings, stabbings, and assaults. In turn, it is not surprising that morals offenses are moderately related to robberies of persons, or that domestics are moderately related to shootings and stabbings. Prostitutes are often assumed to victimize their "johns," and police

TABLE 3.2

Correlation Matrix for Frequency of Crime Calls at Hot Spots (N = 365)

| Correlations: | 1 | 2 | 3 | 4 | 5 | 6 | 7 | 8 | 9 | 10 | 11 | 12 | 13 | 14 |
|---|---|---|---|---|---|---|---|---|---|---|---|---|---|---|
| Damage Property (1) | 1.0 | | | | | | | | | | | | | |
| Drunk[1] (2) | .21* | 1.0 | | | | | | | | | | | | |
| Morals[2] (3) | .04 | .18* | 1.0 | | | | | | | | | | | |
| Thefts[1] (4) | .37* | .49* | .13 | 1.0 | | | | | | | | | | |
| Autotheft (5) | .39* | .11 | .13 | .33* | 1.0 | | | | | | | | | |
| Burglary Business (6) | .20* | .22* | .18* | .23* | -.04 | 1.0 | | | | | | | | |
| Burglary Dwelling (7) | .19* | -.18* | -.07 | -.12 | .01 | -.09 | 1.0 | | | | | | | |
| Robbery Business[1] (8) | .01 | .18* | .07 | .27* | .02 | .21* | -.05 | 1.0 | | | | | | |
| Robbery Person (9) | .26* | .52* | .39* | .46* | .26* | .07 | .04 | .20* | 1.0 | | | | | |
| Assault (10) | .36* | .46* | .16* | .28* | .13* | .04 | .36* | .13 | .58* | 1.0 | | | | |
| Domestics (11) | .21* | -.05 | -.05 | -.05 | .01 | -.13 | .73* | -.11 | .13 | .54* | 1.0 | | | |
| Shootings (12) | .09 | .02 | .01 | .02 | .02 | -.02 | .27* | -.07 | .19* | .27* | 38* | 1.0 | | |
| Stabbings (13) | .17* | .28* | .02 | .06 | -.01 | -.01 | .27* | -.02 | .27* | .55* | .41* | .16* | 1.0 | |
| Rape (14) | .14* | .12 | .04 | .02 | .05 | -.08 | .27* | .02 | .20* | .35* | .35* | .28* | .27* | 1.0 |

[1]Variable was logged to correct for non-linearities

officers often speak of the potential violence that surrounds domestic disputes.

One way of gaining an overall view of the strength of association among the call categories examined is to standardize the correlation coefficients according to their magnitude. In a widely used measure of "effect size" Cohen (1988) suggests that a correlation of less than .30 represents a "small effect," one of between .30 and .50 a "medium effect" and one of over .50 a "large effect." Using these criteria it is clear that the relationships among crime occurrences at places are generally very small (see table 3.3). Of the ninety-one potential correlations in the matrix, a total of seventy-three evidence small relationships (of which some forty-two are not statistically significant at the .01 level). Only thirteen (or 14 percent) show medium "effects" and only five reach what Cohen describes as a large "effect size." Accordingly, while we noted earlier that there are some strong relationships found between call categories at places, overall there is relatively little association among the crime call categories examined.

Can we conclude then that our data are consistent with the assumptions of crime specific as contrasted with crime general theorizing? If we examine more closely the nature of crime specialization at hot spots, such an assumption appears unwarranted. In table 3.4 we look at the number of hot spots with selected proportions of specific crime call categories included in our analyses. The crime specific perspective would predict that there would be a concentration of particular crimes at particular hot spots: for example hot spots for burglary or auto theft distinct one from another. Yet, our data indicate relatively little crime concentration at hot

TABLE 3.3
Examination of "Effect Sizes" in Correlation Matix

|  | # | % |
|---|---|---|
| Non-significant "Effects[x]": | 42 | 46.15 |
| "Small Effects" (r < .30): | 31 | 34.07 |
| "Medium Effects" (.30 < r < .50): | 13 | 14.29 |
| "Large Effects" (r > .50): | 5 | 5.49 |
| Total | 91 | 100% |

[x]$p < .01$

spots. Only in the case of thefts is there any hot spot in which more than 60 percent of the total crime calls are generated by one crime category, and with the exception of thefts and domestic disturbances there are very few hot spots where even 30 percent of the crime calls can be attributed to a particular crime type.

## Discussion

Our findings are not consistent with either crime general or crime specific theorizing, but rather provide a position somewhere between the polar extremes that are often associated with this debate. Before we turn to a discussion of the implications of this finding for our understanding of crime at places, we want to address some specific limitations that derive from our particular approach to these problems.

A simple explanation for the divergence of our findings from those suggested by crime general theory could be found in the fact that we have chosen places for examination rather than individuals. It could very well be that general causes motivate offenders but particular environments provide opportunities for specific types of crime. In some ways this approach is very much consistent with traditional understandings of crime causation. For example Sutherland and Cressey note that the "objective situation" of criminal acts provides the specific opportunities for crime, but address themselves in detail only to the factors that lead certain individuals to take advantage of crime prone situations (see 1970, 74–75, see also Hirschi and Gottfredson 1990). Though such an explanation would not challenge our finding that general causes do not predict the distribution of crime across places, we recognize that general propositions relating to the causes of individual offending are not necessarily inconsistent with our data.

Our choice of hot spots may have also accentuated characteristics unique to particular forms of offending, precisely because we examine crimes in relatively small discrete places that have very specific environmental qualities. When applied to places criminological theory has been developed with reference to the large worlds of neighborhoods and communities, not the small worlds represented by clusters of addresses. We believe that such precision is

**TABLE 3.4**

**Number of Hot Spots with a Specific Proportion of Selected Crime Call Categories**

| Crime Types | None | .01–10% | 10.01–20% | 20.01–30% | 30.01–60% | 60.01–100% | N |
|---|---|---|---|---|---|---|---|
| Damage property (N = 1915) | 3 | 331 | 31 | 2 | 0 | 0 | 365 |
| Drunk (N = 2280) | 81 | 252 | 29 | 3 | 0 | 0 | 365 |
| Moral (N = 610) | 288 | 70 | 3 | 1 | 3 | 0 | 365 |
| Thefts (N = 9376) | 0 | 155 | 107 | 49 | 48 | 6 | 365 |
| Autotheft (N = 1086) | 56 | 295 | 14 | 0 | 0 | 0 | 365 |

| | | | | | | |
|---|---|---|---|---|---|---|
| Burglary of a business (N=851) | 108 | 243 | 13 | 0 | 1 | 0 | 365 |
| Burglary of a dwelling (N=1911) | 69 | 254 | 37 | 4 | 1 | 0 | 365 |
| Robbery of a business (N=278) | 254 | 107 | 4 | 0 | 0 | 0 | 365 |
| Robbery of person (N=1563) | 62 | 296 | 7 | 0 | 0 | 0 | 365 |
| Assault (N=3816) | 13 | 274 | 73 | 5 | 0 | 0 | 365 |
| Domestic disturbance (N=6209) | 30 | 169 | 79 | 57 | 30 | 0 | 365 |
| Shootings (N=120) | 292 | 73 | 0 | 0 | 0 | 0 | 365 |
| Stabbings (N=361) | 207 | 158 | 0 | 0 | 0 | 0 | 365 |
| Rape (N=265) | 228 | 137 | 0 | 0 | 0 | 0 | 365 |

essential to gaining a clearer understanding of the causes of crime. Yet, this strategy of analysis could serve to mask features common to all types of crime. In some sense the fact that we find concentrations of hot spots in certain parts of the city supports a more general view of crime causation, and we have no doubt that there are structural conditions like social disorganization, which are in some way related to offending. At the same time, there are hot spots even in the better neighborhoods in Minneapolis, and even in the worst ones there are discrete areas free of crime hot spots. What is clear from our findings, is that crime call categories are not strongly related across hot spots, a fact that challenges those who would link all crime at places into some broad category for explanation.

The choice of hot spots as a unit of analysis may also be seen as masking substantial clustering of individual offense types at individual places, and thus underestimating the degree to which places evidence crime specialization. Crime specific advocates usually begin their analyses by searching for areas where specific crimes are known to be concentrated. We have already shown that few hot spots in our study are dominated by a particular crime category. Nevertheless, it might be argued that our strategy for identifying hot spots of crime has underestimated the number of places with relatively few but nonetheless specialized crime events.

A final issue relating to our method develops from our use of cross-sectional rather than longitudinal data. Theories that define general causes to crime in neighborhoods often identify a causal chain that begins in time with minor crime events and culminates in the most serious crimes. Indeed, from the time of the Chicago school, a number of those who have studied crime have looked to the histories of communities and the ways in which these histories impact the nature and types of crime in urban areas (e.g., see Burgess 1925; Shaw and McKay 1942; Reiss 1986). In this regard Wilson and Kelling (1982), who we cited earlier, expect a growing disorganization in neighborhoods that begins with broken windows and other incivilities and leads to serious property and person crimes over time. Clearly, a longitudinal study of hot spots of crime would provide a more powerful test of such propositions. Nevertheless, the fact that there are generally weak correlations in our study even among crime call categories of similar seriousness provides a direct challenge to the notion that general causes lead to particular stages in the development of what has been defined as the crime problem.

## Conclusions

Most crime causation theories are consistent with the premise that crime is a unified phenomenon with a common set of general "causes" (Steffensmeier 1989). Our examination of the distribution of crime calls across places, within the limitations described above, provides a challenge to this proposition. But our data also depart from what we might expect if we posit a specific "cause" to each crime type (e.g., Clarke and Cornish 1985). Indeed, we find that a number of specific crimes are related one to another across hot spots of crime, a result that would suggest that attention to common causes of particular clusters of crimes at places is warranted.

While our results are at first glance contradictory, they are consistent with the observations of a number of other scholars (e.g., see Wheeler et al. 1988; Steffensmeier 1989), and with a broader criminological tradition that recognizes the social nature of definitions of criminal conduct (see Durkheim 1933, 1982; Becker 1963). Clearly, the labels assigned to crime calls are socially determined and accordingly they may obscure much that is common to the underlying behaviors that they are meant to define. Thus, we are not surprised that certain crime calls are strongly related in our study. But beyond this, we think it more a matter of criminological polemic than of the reality of the distribution of crime across both places and persons that some have assumed the preeminence of either a general or specific approach to explaining crime. We find no inconsistency in recognizing that both specific and general causes play an important part in the development and distribution of crime and criminality.

## Appendix 3.1
### Definitions of Call Categories Identified as Hard or Soft Crimes

*Hard Crime*

ASLT    Assault, with or without a weapon (or display of weapon)

ALSTP    Assault in progress

AUTOTH   Auto theft

BURGB    Burglary of a business

BURGBP   Burglary of a business, in progress at the time of call

ABURGB   Attempted burglary of a business (unsuccessful)

BURGD    Burglary of a dwelling (residential burglary, includes both private homes and apartments)

BURGDP   Burglary of dwelling, in progress

ABURGD   Attempted burglary of a dwelling (unsuccessful)

CSCM     Criminal sexual conduct (molester)

CSCR     Criminal sexual conduct (rape)

KIDNAP   Kidnapping abduction

AROBBZ   Attempted robbery of a business (involves a face-to-face confrontation between a would-be robber and an intended victim), without a successful conclusion; taking of property by force or threat of force

ROBBIZ   A (successful) robbery of a business

ROBBZP   Robbery of a business, in progress (telephone report from a source other than a hold-up alarm)

AROBPR   Attempted robbery of a person (can be either armed or strong-arm robbery; includes purse-snatching)

ROBPER   Robbery of a person (armed or strong-arm), usually in a public place

ROBDWL   Robbery of a dwelling (house or apartment)

SHOOT    Someone hit by bullets; various causes

STAB     Stabbing (nonaccidental)

THEFT    Taking of property, without force or threat of force

THEFTP   Theft, in progress

THEFTA   Theft from auto (frequently involves damage to the auto, broken windows, etc.)

## Soft Crime

AOA      Assist other agency; frequently but not exclusively law-enforcement related, this category also includes assisting city building inspectors and child protection agency officers conduct their business in potentially explosive situations

ASTOFF  Assist police officer, nonemergency situations

BOOK  Booking; a self-initiated arrest (on warrants, on probable cause for felonies, or for misdemeanors occurring in the officer's presence; these are usually not distinguished in the call data)

CUSTRB  Customer trouble at a local business

DABUSE  Domestic abuse, involving assaults and/or threats within a family or intimate relationship; also includes reports of violations of restraining orders

DAMPRP  Damage to property, vandalism

DIST  Disturbance, with no further specification; often overlaps with "domestics" and "fights," as well as non-classified calls like "party" and "music" complaints

DK  A drunk, usually standing or mobile

DOMES  A domestic quarrel (between/among relatives or house-hold members), *without* physical assaults, threats, or violations of restraining orders

DOMESW  A domestic fight in which weapons are used, or displayed (a subset of DABUSE which has been retained as a separate category: it allows dispatchers to recognize it as a higher priority call in the "calls pending" queue, and provides a warning to assigned officers that they are going into a situation of heightened danger)

HDOMES  Heavy domestic, used to signify a domestic fight which was in progress at the time of the call (call-taker could hear sounds of a fight or assault over the phone)

DOWN  Person down on the ground or sidewalk; unknown details, could be either drunk or ill, or an accident or assault victim

FC  Firecrackers; FC calls are given out to squads as an "in-service" call (i.e., check the area, but do not contact the complainant)

FIGHT  Usually distinguished from ASLT by the number of people involved; fights take place among larger groups, and there is no immediately identifiable "victim"; the vicarious victimization to passersby is more attenuated

FIGHTW  Fight, with weapons

HOTROD  Noise or other disturbance created by mobile motor vehicles

KIDTRB  Kid trouble; a catch-all identification of juveniles acting
up in a variety of ways

MORALS  A police-initiated category, usually indicating the arrest
of a prostitute or hustler; occasionally denotes other
offenses

NBRTRB  Neighbor trouble; another catch-all, this time involving
people who live near and are known to each other

PERGUN  Person with a gun; unlike ASLT, vicarious victimization
is still only potential

PERWEA  Person with a weapon, nonfirearm

PROWL  Prowler; also includes peeping toms

SHOTS  Sounds of shots fired, no data to indicate any injuries or
even potential victims

SUSPP  Suspicious person; sometimes related to prostitution activity

SUSPV  Suspicious vehicles

THEFTH  Theft, holding one; shoplifting calls, usually confined to
the interior of business locations, with extremely attenuated "public" victimization

THREAT  Verbal, phone, or mails threats against a person's life,
safety, or property; usually, no immediate danger is indicated.

UNKTRB  Unknown trouble; call-taker is unable to elicit information
from the caller; approximately half turn out to be Domestic calls, while another 10–20 percent are kids playing
with the telephone

UNWANT  Unwanted person; a catch-all that includes some domestic
situations, some guests who have worn out their welcome,
and a lot of drunks and derelicts either sleeping it off
where they don't belong, or trying to get into places they
don't belong to sleep it off (ringing doorbells, panhan-
dling, and "harassment" also fall into this category)

This research was supported by Grant Number 88-IJ-CX0009 from the National
Institute of Justice and a Research Council Award from Rutgers University. Points
of view or opinions expressed do not necessarily represent the official positions or

policies of the U.S. Department of Justice or Rutgers University. An earlier version of this paper was presented at the American Sociological Association Meeting, San Francisco, 1989. Helpful comments on earlier drafts were provided by Marcus Felson, Patricia Brantingham, Ronald Clarke, and David Greenberg.

## Notes

1. As Matza (1969) notes, the Chicago school had a "correctional" approach to crime that emphasized the control and amelioration of such common urban problems as delinquency and vagrancy.
2. The task there was to identify a specialized group of hot spots of multiple addresses in the city of Minneapolis that would evidence a high degree of crime stability year to year, a high likelihood of activity that was amenable to deterrence through police presence, and enough distance one to another to prevent treatment contamination of control groups. In order to develop such a sample it was necessary to examine the distribution of crime events as represented by call data throughout the city of Minneapolis, a process that allowed us as well to identify and analyze the entire "universe" of hot spots as we define them.
3. We depart from Reiss's classification in one important way. He describes vandalism or damage to property as a "hard" crime, primarily because there is significant monetary loss. Our observations suggest that most of the calls in this category involve only very minor losses to victims. Accordingly damage to property is included as a soft crime in our site selection process.
4. To facilitate this process we sought as a first step to merge our 5538 addresses with a computer map provided by Mapinfo Corporation (1988). While we experienced some difficulty in this process because of different definitions of places used by the City of Minneapolis and Mapinfo, we were able to overcome most of these. In cases of very high activity addresses that were not defined by Mapinfo we hand plotted addresses. However, our final computer map did not include some 5 percent of the hot addresses we identified. Almost all of these excluded addresses included fewer than ten hard crime calls.
5. Where blocks were very small and "hot addresses" relatively contiguous (and where visual sighting could easily go beyond a block) the "one-block rule" was violated.
6. Disagreements on hot spot boundaries between the observers were most often encountered in fringe addresses in places where crime concentration generally was high. For the final 110 sites in the Minneapolis Hot Spots Experiment, observers reported 75 percent agreement on hot spot boundaries. However, agreement was much lower earlier in the selection process where resolutions of disagreements were made by a project principal investigator. Observers also identified and deleted known magnet phone addresses which drew calls primarily from other places outside the hot spot boundaries.
7. Mapinfo identifies some 15411 street segments in the city. Hot spots were almost always less than one street segment in length.
8. For a general description of call categories see appendix 3.1. We combine related crime categories as follows:

| theft | = THEFT + THEFTP + THEFTH |
|---|---|
| autotheft | = AUTOTH + THEFTA |
| burglary business | = BURGB + BURGBP + ABURGB |
| burglary dwelling | = BURGD + BURGDP + ABURGD |
| robbery business | = ROBBIZ + AROBBZ + ROBBZP + ALARMH |
| robbery person | = ROBPER + AROBPR |
| assault | = ASLT + ASLTP |
| domestic | = DABUSE + DOMES + HDOMES + DOMESW |

# References

Albrecht, H. J. and Moitra, S. (1988). Escalation and specialization: A comparative analysis of patterns in criminal careers. In G. Kaiser and I. Geissler *Crime and criminal justice: Criminological research in the 2nd decade at the Max Planck Institute in Frieburg* (115–36). Frieburg, Eigenverlay Max-Plack-Institut.

Angel, S. (1968). *Discouraging crime through city planning.* Working Paper No. 75. Berkeley, University of California, Institute of Urban and Regional Development.

Beavon, D. J. K. (1984). *The use of micro-spatial data and its implications for crime prevention.* Paper presented at the annual meeting, American Society of Criminology, Cincinnati.

Becker, H. (1963). *Outsiders: Studies in the Sociology of Deviance.* New York, Free Press.

Biderman, A. D., and Reiss A. J. (1967). On exploring the "darkfigure" of crime. *Annals of the American Academy of Political and Social Sciences* 374: 1–15.

Blumstein, A., Cohen, J., Roth J. A., and Visher C. A. (1986). *Criminal Careers and Career Criminals.* Washington, D. C., National Academy Press.

Booth, C. (1902–3). *Life and Labor of the People in London*, 17 volumes (3rd Edition), London, Macmillan.

Brantingham, P. J., and Brantingham, P. L. (1975). *Residential burglary and urban form.* Urban Studies 12: 273–84.

Brantingham, P. L., Brantingham, P. J., eds. (1977). Housing patterns and burglary in a medium-sized American city. In J. F. Scott and S. Dinitz (eds.), *Criminal Justice Planning* (63–74). New York, Praeger.

Brantingham, P. J. and Brantingham, P. L. (1981a). *Environmental Criminology.* Beverly Hills and London, Sage.

Brantingham, P. L. and Brantingham, P. J. (1981b). "Mobility, notoriety, and crime: a study in the crime patterns of urban nodal points." *Journal of Envirnomental Systems* 11, 89–99.

Burgess, E. W. (1925). The growth of the city. In R. E. Park, E. W. Burgess, and R. D. McKenzie, *The City* (47–62). Chicago, University of Chicago Press.

Bursik, R. J. (1980). The Dynamics of specialization in juvenile offenses. *Social Forces* 58: 851–64.

Byrne, J. M. (1986). Cities, citizens and crime: the ecological/nonecological debate reconsidered. In J. M. Byrne and R. J. Sampson (eds.), *The Social Ecology of Crime* (77–101). New York, Springer-Verlag.

Clarke, R. V. G. (1983). Situational crime prevention: Its theoretical basis and practical scope. In N. Morris and M. Tonry, *Crime and Justice: An Annual Review of Research*, volume 4. Chicago, University of Chicago Press.

Clarke, R. V., and Cornish D. B., (1985). Modelling offenders' decisions: A framework for research and policy. In M. Tonry and N. Morris (eds.), *Crime and Justice: An Annual Review of Research*, volume 6 (147–85). Chicago, University of Chicago Press.

Clarke, R. V. G., and Mayhew P., eds. (1980). *Designing out crime*. London. HMSO.

Cohen, Jacob. (1988). *Statistical Power Analysis for the Behavioral Sciences*, second edition. Hillsdale, N. J. Lawrence Erlbaum Associates.

Cohen, L. E., and Felson, M. (1979). Social change and crime rate trends: A routine activity approach. *American Sociological Review* 46: 558–608.

Cohen, S. (1985). *Visions of Social Control: Crime, Punishment and Classification*. Cambridge, Polity Press.

Cornish, D. B., and Clarke, R. V. (1989). Crime specialization, crime displacement and rational choice theory. In H. Wegener, F. Losel and J. Haisch (eds.). *Criminal Behavior and the Justice System: Psychological Perspectives* (103–17). New York, Springer-Verlag.

Cornish, D. B., and Clarke, R. V., eds. (1986). *The Reasoning Criminal*. New York, Springer-Verlag.

Duffala, D. C. (1976). Convenience stores, armed robbery and physical environmental features. *American Behavioral Scientist* 20: 227–46.

Durkheim, E. (1933). *The Division of Labor in Society*. Glencoe, Ill., The Free Press.

Durkheim, E. (1982). *The Rules of Sociological Method*. New York, The Free Press.

Erikson, K. T. (1962). Notes on the sociology of deviance. *Social Problems* 9: 307–14.

Gardiner, R. A. (1978). *Design for Safe Neighborhoods*. Washington, D. C., Government Printing Office.

Gottfredson, M. R., Hirschi, T. (1990). *A General Theory of Crime*. Stanford, Cal., Stanford University Press.

Guerry, A. M. 1833). *Essai sur la statistique moral de la France avec cartes*. Paris, Crochard.

Harries, K. D., (1974). *The Geography of Crime and Justice*. New York, McGraw-Hill.

Harries, K. D. (1976). Cities and crime. A geographical model. *Criminology* 14: 369-86.

Harries, K. D. (1980). *Crime and the Environment*. Springfield, Ill. C. C. Thomas.

Heal, K., and Laycock, F., eds. (1986). *Situational Crime Prevention: From Theory into Practice*. London, HMSO.

Herbert, D. T. (1980). Urban crime and spatial perspective: The British experience. In D. E. Georges-Abeyies and K. D. Harries (eds.), *Crime: A Spatial Perspective* (26–46). New York, Columbia University Press.

Herbert, D. T. (1982). *The Geography of Urban Crime*. London, Longman.

Herbert, D. T. and Harries, K. D. (1986). Area based policies for crime prevention. *Applied Geography* 6: 281–95.

Herbert, D. T., and Hyde, S. W. (1985). Environmental criminology: Testing some area hypotheses. *Transactions, Institute of British Geographers* 10 (3): 259–74.

Hirschi, T. (1969). *Causes of Delinquency*. Berkeley, University of California Press.

Hirschi, T. and Gottfredson, M. (1987a). Causes of white collar crime. *Criminology* 25: 949–74.

Hirschi, T. and Gottfredson, M. (1987b). Toward a general theory of crime. In W. Buikhuisen and S. Mednick (eds.) *Explaining crime: Interdisciplinary approaches* (8–26). Leiden, Brill.

Hope, T. (1986). School design and burglary. In K. Heal and G. Haycock (eds.), *Situational Crime Prevention: From Theory into Practice* (73–79), London, HMSO.

Hunter, R. D. (1988). *Environmental characteristics of convenience stores robberies in the state of Florida*. Paper presented at the annual meeting, American Society of Criminology, Chicago.

Jacobs, J. (1961). *The Death and Life of Great American Cities*. New York, Random House.

Jeffrey C. R. (1977). *Crime Prevention Through Environmental Design*. Beverly Hills and London, Sage.

Jeffrey, C. R., Hunter, R. D., and Griswold, J. (1987). Crime prevention and computer analysis of convenience store robberi in Tallahassee, Florida. *Security Systems*, August, 1987.

Kempf, K. (1986). Offense specialization: Does it exist?. In D. B. Cornish and R. V. Clarke (eds.), *The Reasoning Criminal* (186–99). New York, Springer-Verlag.

LeBeau, J. L., (1987). The method and measures of centrography and the spatial dynamics of rape. *Journal of Quantitative Criminology* 3: 125–141.

Manning, P. K. (1988). *Symbolic Communication: Signifying Calls and the Police Response*. Cambridge, MIT Press.

Matza, D. (1969). *Becoming Deviant*. Englewood Cliffs, N. J., Prentice Hall.

Mayhew, H. (1862). *London Labour and the London Poor*. London, Griffin, Bohn.

Mayhew, P. M., Clarke, R. V. G., Sturman, A. and Hough, J. M. (1976). Steering column locks and car theft. Home Office Research Study. No. 34, London, HMSO. (Reprinted 1983). Crime as opportunity. In R. V. G. Clarke and B. Cornish (eds.), *Crime Control in Britain: A Review of Policy Research* (235–47). Albany, State University of New York Press.

Merton, R. (1938). Social structure and anomie. *American Sociological Review* 3: 672–82.

Morris, T. M. (1958). *The Criminal Area*. London, Routledge and Kegan Paul.

Newman, O. (1972). *Defensible Space: Crime Prevention Through Urban Design*. New York, Macmillan.

Newman, O. (1980). *Community of Interest*. New York, Doubleday.

Poyner, B. (1983). *Design Against Crime*. London, Butterworths.

Poyner, B. (1988). *Design modifications to prevent crime in mass housing—Fallacies and realities*. Paper presented at the 40th annual meeting, American Society of Criminology, Chicago.

Quetelet, A. J. (1842). *A Treatise of Man*. Gainsville, Fla.: Scholars' Facsimiles and Reprints (1969).

Rawson, R. W. (1839). An injury into the statistics of crime in England and Wales. *Journal of the Statistics Society of London* 2: 316–44.

Reiss, A. J., Jr. (1985). *Policing a City's Central District: The Oakland Story*. National Institute of Justice, U. S. Department of Justice, Washington, D. C., March 1985.

Reiss, A. J., Jr. (1986). Why are communities important in understanding crime? In A. J. Reiss Jr. and Mr. Tonry (eds.), *Communities and Crime* (1–33). Chicago, University of Chicago Press.

Rengert, G. F. (1980). Theory and Practice in urban police responses. In D. E. Georges-Abeyies and K. D. Harries (eds.), *Crime: A spatial perspective* (47–57). New York, Columbia University Press.

Rengert, G. F. (1981). Burglary in Philadelphia: An opportunity structure model. In P. J. Brantingham and P. L. Brantingham (eds.), *Environmental Criminology* (189–201). Beverly Hills and London, Sage.

Sampson, R. J. (1986a). Crime in cities: The effects of formal and informal social control. In A. J. Reiss Jr. and M. Tonry (eds.) *Communities and Crime* (271–311). Chicago, University of Chicago Press.

Sampson, R. J. (1986b). The effects of urbanization and neighborhood characteristics of criminal victimization. In R. M. Figlio, S. Hakim and G. F. Rengert (eds.) *Metropolitan crime patterns* (3–25). New York, Willow Tree.

Sampson, R. J. (1987). Personal violence by strangers: An extension and test of the opportunity model of predatory victimization. *Journal of Criminal Law and Criminology* 78: 327–56.

Scott, L., Crow, W. J., and Erikson, R. (1985). *Robbery as Robbers See It*. Dallas, Southland Corporation.

Shaw, C. R. (1929). *Delinquency Areas*. Chicago, University of Chicago Press.

Shaw, C. R., and McKay, H. D., (1931). *Social factors in juvenile delinquency*, volume 2 of *Report on the Causes of Crime*, National Commission on Law Observance and Enforcement, report no. 13, Washington, D. C., U.S. Government Printing Office.

Shaw, C. R., and McKay, H. D., (1942). *Juvenile delinquency and urban areas* (revised edition 1969). Chicago, University of Chicago Press.

Sherman, L. W., Gartin, P. R., and Buerger, M. E. (1989). Hot spots of predatory crime: Routine activities and the criminology of place. *Criminology* 27 (1): 27–56.

70    New Directions in Criminological Theory

Sherman, L. W., and Weisburd, D. (1987). *Policing the hotspots of crime.* Funded proposal, National Institute of Justice.
Sherman, L. W., and Weisburd, D. (1989). *Policing the hotspots of crime: A redesign of the Kansas city preventive patrol experiment.* Washington, D. C., Crime Control Institute.
Smith, S. J. (1986). *Crime, Space and Society.* Cambridge, Cambridge University Press.
South, N. (1987). The security and surveillance of the environment. In J. Lowman, R. J. Menzies, and T. S. Palys (eds.), *Transcarceration: Essays in the Sociology of Social Control* (p. 139–52), Cambridge Studies in Criminology, London, Gower.
Steffensmeier, D. (1989). On the causes of "white-collar" crime: An assessment of Hirschi and Gottfredson's claims. *Criminology* 27 (2): 345–58.
Stoks, F. G. (1981). Assessing urban public space environments for danger of violent crime—Especially rape. Ph.D. Dissertation, University of Washington, Seattle, Wash.
Sutherland, E. H. (1939). *Principles of Criminology.* Philadelphia, Lippincott.
Sutherland, E. H. (1973). *On Analyzing Crime.* Chicago, University of Chicago Press.
Sutherland, E. H., and Cressey, D. R. (1970). *Criminology*, 8th edition. Philadelphia, Lipincott.
Taylor, R. B., and Gottfredson, S. D. (1986). Environmental design, crime and prevention: An examination of community dynamics. In A. J. Reiss and M. Tonry (eds.), *Communities and Crime* (387–417). Crime and Justice: An Annual Review of Research, volume 8. Chicago, University of Chicago Press.
Taylor, R. B., Gottfredson, S. D. and S. Brower. (1981). *Informal social control in the residential urban environment.* Baltimore, Md., Center for Metropolitan Planning and Research.
Taylor, R. B., and Gottfredson, S. D., and S. Brower (1984). Block crime and fear: Defensible space, local social ties and territorial functioning. *Journal of Research in Crime and Delinquency* 21: 303–31.
Thrasher, F. M. (1927). *The Gang.* Chicago, University of Chicago Press.
Webb, B. (1988). *Reducing shoplifting in a large central London store.* Paper presented at the 40th annual meeting, American Society of Criminology, Chicago.
Wheeler, S., Weisburd, D., Waring, E. and Bode N. (1988). White Collar Crimes and Criminals. *American Criminal Law Review* 25 (3): 331–57.
Wilson, J. Q., and Kelling, G. (1982). Broken windows: The police and neighborhood safety. *Atlantic* (March): 29–38.
Wilson, J. Q., and Hernstein, R. J. (1985). *Crime and Human Nature.* New York. Simon and Schuster.
Wolfgang, M. E., Figlio, R. M. and Sellin, Thorsten, (1972). *Delinquency in a Birth Cohort.* Chicago, University of Chicago.

# 4

# Strategy, Structure, and Corporate Crime: The Historical Context of Anticompetitive Behavior

*Sally S. Simpson*

In the past two decades criminologists have seriously turned to the study of corporate illegality and other forms of white-collar crime.[1] Though scholars like Sutherland (1939), Clinard (1946), Cressey (1953), and Geis (1962) set a research agenda earlier, most criminological research has focused on more traditional types of crimes and criminals. Consequently, the corpus of knowledge about "the crime problem" has been heavily influenced by street crime paradigms and the causes of illegality within an organization often reduced to individual motivations, pathologies, and/or "human nature" (e.g., Hirschi and Gottfredson 1988).[2] Given the complexity of much corporate illegality (Harris and Simpson 1987; Shapiro 1984; Wheeler Weisburd, and Bode 1982), this reductionism is ill-conceived and shortsighted. The goal of this paper is to embed corporate criminality within the organization, specifically changes in strategy and structure. To do so, however, requires a brief review of the corporate crime literature.[3]

## Review of the Literature

### *The Corporate Environment*

The call for closer examination of intraorganizational processes and their relationship to corporate illegality emerges in part from dissatisfaction with earlier research that examines the impact of extraorganizational pressures on various types of corporate offending. The argument that a firm is apt to resort to criminal means in order to remain competitive when its profitability is threatened has mixed empirical support (Barnett 1986; Clinard and Yeager 1980; Lane 1953; Simpson 1986, 1987).

Some types of corporate offending appear to be unrelated to industry profit pressures (such as environmental violations, see Clinard and Yeager 1980, 129). Indeed, large-scale economic downturns and industry declines may differentially affect criminality within broad crime categories. Using Simpson's (1986) research on antitrust violations as illustrative, her data support the external profit squeeze-crime relationship only for serious types of anticompetitive behavior (Simpson 1987). And, though significant, none of her economic measures of "poverty" account for much variation in anti-competitive behavior between 1927 and 1981.[4]

Besides industry profitability or economic munificence, other factors believed to influence firm criminality include industry concentration, number of competitors, style and strength of product distribution networks, trade association members, and product differentiation (Asch and Seneca 1975; Clabault and Burton 1970; Hay and Kelley 1974; Posner 1970; Sonnenfeld and Lawrence 1978; Staw and Szwajowski 1975). There is little agreement, however, as to the consistency and reliability of observed relationships. For instance, Clabault and Burton (1970) find low industry concentration associated with various kinds of trade violations. Conversely, Asch and Seneca (1975) and Hay and Kelley (1974) find companies convicted of Sherman Act criminal violations to be located in highly concentrated industries. In Sonnenfeld and Lawrence's (1978) study of the forest products industry, price fixing was associated with greater buyer power vis-à-vis suppliers. Yet, industries characterized by atomistic buyers produced more antitrust conspiracy cases in Asch and Seneca's study (1975).

These somewhat contradictory and/or weak findings may be due to different samples, measures, and kinds of analysis. However, another explanation is that important causal factors are ignored. Intraorganizational factors, in conjunction with environmental pressures, may affect not only the occurrence of crime, but its historical patterns (i.e., which types of illegality are apt to occur). As Clinard and Yeager (1980) remind us, causality is multidimensional and theory must account for such etiological and historical complexity.

*Intra-Organizational Factors*

*Corporate culture.* There are many studies that highlight the importance of both corporate culture[5] and structure on crime. Beginning with Sutherland (1949) but taken up later by Geis (1967) and Vaughan (1983), deviant cultures and subcultures (Zey-Ferrell et al. 1979, 1982) are implicated as agents of criminal socialization. New personnel learn the techniques of crime as well as the language of neutralization (e.g., "everybody does it"; "no one is really hurt"; "it isn't really *criminal.*") from significant others within the corporation and/or task unit (Benson 1985; Sykes and Matza 1957).

Vaughan (1983) suggests that deviant cultures arise in firms when personnel experience pressures to achieve culturally defined success goals but cannot because the legitimate means to compete are limited, restricted, and/or are unsuccessful. As illegitimate means are increasingly substituted for legitimate ones, they become institutionalized. Illegality becomes normative.

Victor and Cullen (1988), in their studies of work environments, find that "ethical" climates are multidetermined by societal norms, organizational form, and firm-specific factors. In one company, the ethical climate varied between the home office and its branches. In another, there were significant differences between the main facility and less central departments that were located elsewhere. They also found that perceptions of an ethical work environment were related to how people felt about their work. Employees reported more satisfaction when they observed higher levels of caring and lower levels of instrumentalism in their environments. This research suggests that even within the same organization, actors may perceive multiple cultures.

*Corporate structure.* Firm structure is also correlated with the incidence of corporate crime. Illegality varies by corporate size (Clinard and Yeager 1980; Simpson 1986), business type (Sonnenfeld and Lawrence 1978), division strength (Ross 1980), and the degree of firm delegation (Braithwaite 1978) and diversification (Asch and Seneca 1975; Clinard and Yeager 1980). However, none of these variables (with the possible exception of firm size) is particularly robust in its relationship with corporate illegality. This is certainly the belief of Clinard and Yeager (1980, 132) who, after examining the impact of firm characteristics on manufacturing, financial, labor, and other types of violations, conclude that "information on firm financial performance and structural characteristics is, by itself, insufficient for explaining corporate crime."

The culture-structure-crime literature, while informative, is conceptually imprecise. Yeager (1986) points out that few studies of corporate culture and crime are systematic; most are impressionistic. Consequently, it is unclear how norm erosion occurs and at what point illegal means are substituted for legal ones. The quantitative studies of corporate structure and crime are less vulnerable to these criticisms, but they have other problems. For instance, some interpret large corporations as more criminogenic than smaller firms because they are more impersonal and alienating. However, size probably reflects different rates of business transactions across firms, not necessarily the criminal propensities of corporate actors. Diversification is apt to enhance the corporate criminal's ability to disguise illegal acts from colleagues and supervisors, thereby providing greater opportunities for misconduct (Coleman 1987). Thus, structural correlates may not be etiological. And, if structure is not per se criminogenic,[6] it is necessary to identify the conditions under which particular corporate structures produce organizational illegality.

The failures of intraorganizational studies to specify the conditions and relationships of corporate illegality are, to a large degree, theoretical failings. Therefore, it is important to link corporate crime to a well-developed theoretical framework. Because much corporate crime occurs within particular task groups or organizational subunits (Zey-Ferrell and Ferrell 1982; Vaughan 1989), our theory takes subunit analysis as its conceptual starting point. Of particular concern is how criminality is affected by changes in organizational strategy and structure as reflected in subunit domination of organizational goals and resources.

Others (most notable Finney and Lesieur 1982) opt for a more inclusive theory that embraces micro, intermediate, and macro levels of analysis. But, this theoretical approach may be too ambitious considering the paucity of systematic research on corporate illegality and the lack of conceptual sophistication surrounding extant corporate crime typologies (see Simpson 1986). Thus, we begin with a discussion of the relationship between subunit domination and organizational strategy and structure.

*Subunit power.* In all organizations there is an unequal balance of power between organization members and subunits (Rex 1961). Power within organizations is determined by the relative importance of what organizational actors do and their skill in doing it (Pfeffer 1981, 98). Hickson, Hinings, Lee, and Schneck (1971, 218) specify the conditions under which subunit power will vary within organizations. They argue that intraorganizational power is a function of (1) uncertainty; (2) substitutability; and (3) centrality.

If a subunit is critical to an organization's activities and those activities are not easily substitutable, "the critical factor affecting subunit power . . . is its ability to cope with uncertainty in the organization" (Pfeffer 1981, 110). The degree to which different subunits can cope with and manage uncertainty affects the power balance within a firm. But, if what that subunit does is not central to organizational outputs, "successful coping brings little power" (Hinings, Hickson, Pennings, and Schneck 1974, 22). Power also can be gained through pervasive organizational linkages. Subunits that forge the greatest number of connections to other subunits are potentially more influential within the organizational power game.

One way to determine which subunit has the most power at any given time is to examine managerial succession. The selection of a CEO from a sales and marketing background suggests that sales and marketing is more "essentially" situated in the firm; it represents a new or, if the past CEO was also from sales and marketing, proven strategic direction for coping with environmental uncertainties (Fligstein 1987).

*Strategies and structure.* The internal organization of the firm is composed of two main features: strategy and structure. Strategy is defined by Chandler (1962, 13) as "the determination of the long term goals and objectives of an enterprise, and the adoption of courses of action and the allocation of resources necessary for carrying out these goals." He defines structure as "the design of the company through which the enterprise is administered" (14). Structure is composed of authority and communication lines, including information and data shared between administrative offices. Changes in corporate strategies and structures follow logical historical patterns and appear to have industry coherence (Fligstein 1987). For the most part, changes in strategy precede and affect changes in organizational form (Chandler 1962; Rumult 1974).

The relationship between subunit competition for organizational dominance and changes in strategy and structure form the core of our theorizing about crime. As subunits compete for scarce resources and power over organizational direction and decision making, illegality may result from internal pressures to achieve organizational goals without the necessary means to do so successfully (Vaughan 1983). The source of these pressures may rest with top management (Gross 1978).

Recent studies confirm the importance of top managers in setting both the moral tone and strategic direction for the firm (Simpson 1992). Yet, when certain types or styles of top managers pursue unobtainable directives, the criminal consequences may be dire. In his interviews with middle managers, Clinard (1983) cites the role of top management and the various pressures placed on middle management as the chief causes of illegality in organizations.

Clinard's managers emphasize how different types of CEOs can influence the internal structure of the corporation. So-called "entrepreneurial and/or financially-oriented" CEOs are more concerned with personal prestige and quick profits from the company than "fiduciary or technical" types who are more cautious and ethically committed to promoting the company as a whole (Clinard 1983, 136). Unfortunately, middle managers are often left out of strategy and resource allocation decisions, but are expected to deliver when "the dictum goes out to meet company directives." Because their future is closely tied to their ability to "serve up whatever the boss demands," ethical dilemmas are more likely to appear among middle managers (*Wall Street Journal*, 8 November 1979).

The types of illegality in which a company engages may reflect particular subunit "courses of action" (Chandler 1962, 13). This is not to say that the strategies themselves are criminal (though some may be); rather dominant strategies will produce organizational subgoals and directives that may be criminogenic. For instance, finance subunits will pursue different corporate strategies with different corporate pressures and tensions than, say, manufacturing subunits. Given these relations, it is plausible that corporate illegality will pattern according to which strategies and structures are dominant. And, as new subunits rise to power, bringing with them new goals and innovative strategies, we can expect different types of illegal acts to emerge.

The form an organizations takes is strategically *and* environmentally driven. As subunits pursue innovative strategies for firm success, a change in the organizational structure may be required. For instance, if sales and marketing subunit strategies call for increased product diversification requiring advanced technologies and highly specialized employees, a multidivisional structure may be the best organizational form to successfully implement this strategic direction. A company might also change form in response to its economic, political, or cultural environment. For example, legal changes in a firm's environment might limit or encourage mergers or promote vertical over horizontal integration. If the industry leader changes from a functionally oriented company to a multidivisional structure (like General Motors did in 1920), competitors may mimic the structure.

In sum, organizational strategies produce tensions and strains on particular managers or subunits to achieve strategic goals. They provide motivation for crime. Firm structure shape criminal opportunities. Thus, we expect that the amount and type of corporate crime will vary as different subunits strategies prevail and new organizational structures emerge.

There is no reason to believe that this theoretical perspective cannot explain all kinds of corporate illegality. However, given the complexity and diversity of corporate crime, it makes little sense to examine all crime types in this limited space. Instead, historical changes in subunit strategies and organizational forms will be linked to changes in the patterns of anticompetitive behavior. Trade violations are selected, in part, because we know the most about them. Anti-competitive corporate illegality, especially price fixing and other collusion, has been the subject of numerous quantitative

(Asch and Seneca, 1975; Clabault and Burton, 1966; Hay and Kelley; 1874; Lean et al., 1982; Simpson, 1986; 1987; Sutherland, 1949) and qualitative studies (Geis, 1967; Sonnenfeld and Lawrence, 1978).

## Types of Anticompetitive Behavior

There are several broad categories of anticompetitive behaviors that are relevant for our theory (Gellhorn 1981; Posner 1976). *Horizontal restraints* of trade are those where there exists an agreement of competitors that restrains competition among sellers (or buyers) at the same level of distribution. So, for example, competitor cartels, conspiracies to fix prices, allocate territories, boycott mavericks, and so on are restricted by law. Under the Sherman Act (1890), some of these behaviors are defined as not only illegal, but as criminal. The Sherman Act is broadened by the Federal Trade Commission Act of 1914, the goal of which is to stem more generally defined unfair and deceptive trade practices.

*Vertical restraints* of trade are those imposed by the seller on the buyer or vice-versa. These include such behaviors as distribution restraints (resale price maintenance, consignments and distribution in agents, territory and customer restrictions) and supplier power (e.g., refusal to deal, tying arrangements, exclusive dealing). The relevant body of law for these offenses includes the Clayton Act (1914) and the Robinson-Patman Act (1936). Some market restraints, especially those "downstream" are seen to produce criminogenic tiers (Farberman 1975; and Denzin 1977). As producers pass constraints downward to franchise dealers (often through illegal means), the pressures to commit violations are also passed.

Other types of anticompetitive acts can fall under one or both of these categories. Unlawful *mergers* can be horizontal (buying one's product line competitor) or vertical (buying one's supplier or buyer). *Patents* are protected as a type of legal monopoly and violations of patent protection often occur in conjunction with price discrimination. *Interlocking directorates* are illegal under the Clayton Act and tied to the cartel idea of sharing important information about pricing, territories, aggressive targeting, and so on. *Unfair advertising* is regulated under the FTC Act. (For more detail, see appendix 4.1.)

In figure 4.1, changes in corporate strategy and structure are placed in historical context using the empirical research of Chandler (1962), Rumult (1974), and Fligstein (1987). Anticipated patterns of anticompetitive behavior are linked to these changes.

## Subunit Power, Strategy, and Structure: 1900–1979[7]

In the early years of monopoly capital, corporations sought to control their environments through mergers. This strategy was problematic because monopolization as a strategy required efficiency, but the dominant structure at the time—a holding company often lead by different organizational subunits representing entrepreneurial capitalist-owners or lawyers—was inefficient. The holding company, most famously represented by U.S. Steel, operated similarly to the conglomerates of today, that is, as a set of companies operating autonomously. But internal coordination, especially in the areas of investment and planning, was difficult. To pursue this new strategic direction, a new organizational form was necessary. The holding company gave way to a new type of structure— the functional form. Functionally structured companies (like American Car Foundry and American Can) were hierarchial and divided into separate departments for sales, finance, production, engineering, and other critical task units. This centralized structure "appeared to be the only one that could assure effective administrative control over a large industrial consolidation" (Chandler 1962, 41). Not surprisingly, this organizational form (which caught on rapidly in the metal-making industries) reproduced a manufacturing strategy.

By 1919, a struggle ensued between entrepreneurs, lawyers, and manufacturing strategists, but because manufacturing personnel had specialized knowledge of the firm product, they won the power struggle over how to manage a large firm (Fligstein 1987, 48). Monopolization and control of competition as a strategy began to falter as companies looked to new product development as a growth strategy (Chandler 1962). To handle diversification, a new organizational form developed. Two firms, Du Pont and General Motors,

# FIGURE 4.1
## Anticipated Patterning of Antitrust Criminality

| DEPENDENT VARIABLE SET | | INDEPENDENT VARIABLE SET | | | | | |
| --- | --- | --- | --- | --- | --- | --- | --- |
| | | ORGANIZATIONAL RESOURCES | | | | | |
| Period | Antitrust Crime Types | Dominant Strategy | Innovative Strategy | Dominant Structure | Innovative Structure | Dominant Subunit | Subunit on Rise |
| 1919–39 | 1. Horizontal restraints; advertising  2. Vertical restraints; upstream pressure on *suppliers*; advertising; some downstream pressure on buyers | Manufacturing Integration | Product-Related | Functional | Multi-divisional | Manufacturing | Sales & Marketing |
| 1939–59 | 1. Vertical restraints with Robinson-Patman. Advertising  2. Conglomerate mergers, illegal tying of *diverse* products | Product-Related | Product-Related | Multi-divisional | | Manufacture/Sales & Marketing | Finance |
| 1959 to present | 1. Conglomerate mergers, illegal tying of diverse products.  2. Finance capital related, international combinations | Product—Related/ Unrelated | | Multi-divisional | | Finance/ Manufacturing | |

*Adopted from Fligstein (1987:48)

[1]Anticompetitive acts predicted by dominant strategies, structures, and subunits, by period.

[2]Anticompetitive acts predicted by newly emerging strategies, structures, and subunits, by period.

improved on the functional structure, offering instead a multidivisional one.

Product diversification was a sales and marketing strategy that had three primary goals: (1) product differentiation; (2) ending price competition; and (3) new product development to gain market share across related products (Fligstein 1987, 48). As the multidivisional form gained adherents, sales and marketing subunits gained power.

Sales and marketing subunits within multidivisional corporations dominated through the 1950s. Their emphasis on new product development as a survival strategy (tested during the Great Depression) outperformed the old manufacturing/functional structure corporation. But, a threat to their power was on the horizon. The product cycle concept challenged the hegemony of sales and marketing strategies and portended the rise of the finance subunit.

The product cycle concept required a shift of capital away from mature product markets toward either new markets for the old product (e.g., international) or new product development. The underlying logic of product unrelated diversification was an attempt to "escape the cyclical nature" of some businesses (e.g., the auto business) or to "reduce the evident risk of remaining totally committed to a declining or stagnant product-market area" (Rumult 1974, 81).

After the Celler-Kefauver Act closed the asset loophole in Clayton in 1951, the number of vertical and horizontal mergers (reflective of a sales and marketing strategy) decreased. The new political environment required new responses—a conglomerate strategy that emphasized growth in new product lines and deemphasized market share. Environmental shifts gave rise to finance subunits. "Since the firm was no longer involved in a few product lines, manufacturing expertise proved too narrow and sales and marketing strategy applied only to growth in market share of related products" (Fligstein 1987, 50).

*The Historical Context of Antitrust Offending: Patterns of Crime*

These historical shifts in organizational strategy and structure (reflecting environmental changes and subunit power struggles) are likely to produce (1) different types of anticompetitive behavior over time and (2) variations in the incidence of illegality over time. The following hpyotheses are represented in figure 4.1.

*Hypothesis 1:* Functionally oriented firms pursuing manufacturing integration and single product strategies, will produce a greater incidence of horizontal restraints of trade, especially mergers, conspiracies to price fix, monopolize, and/or allocate territories than firms dominated by other subunits.

These acts may be either noncoercive (cooperative competitors who voluntarily eliminate competition among themselves, e.g., the steel industry) or coercive (firm or firms attempt to eliminate or coerce competitors). Some advertising violations are also expected as firms try to influence buyer choice, but not in excessive amounts since manufacturing strategies emphasize market dominance through cost efficient production.

These expectations are based in the kinds of organizational goals and subgoals that emerge from manufacturing strategies and the strains inherent in achieving them. In the early 1900s, most companies were producing a single product group. Corporate growth was highly dependent on *control* of the market. Yet, there were few barriers to entry in most industries and lots of competition (Chandler 1962). Because the functional form was highly centralized administratively, with a few top managers entrusted with decision-making responsibility (Chandler 1962, 41), targeting competitors through monopolization practices made sense and, given management style, was relatively easy to pursue and cover up.

*Hypothesis 2:* With the rise of sales and marketing subunits, there will be a greater incidence of upstream pressure on suppliers (tied to the manufacturing influence) and later downstream restraints of trade (with the focus on the customer and distributor).

Sales and marketing strategies emphasize related product development and market share growth. Thus, there will be more pressure internally to focus on the customer. A likely consequence is more unlawful vertical mergers (as firms try to control the distribution network), tying arrangements, reciprocal buying and exclusive dealing, and price discrimination.

The passage of Robinson-Patman in 1936 will increase the number of price discrimination violations as firms attempt to cope with new legislative proscriptions that protect small competitors from volume sellers and buyers (Finney and Lesieur, 1982:273).[8] Also, sales and marketing strategies are apt to produce a large number of advertising violations as firms attempt to distinguish their products from their competitors.

*Hypothesis 3:* Firms controlled by finance subunits are apt to pursue strategies that increase the likelihood of illegal international combinations, unlawful conglomerate mergers, some illegal tying of diverse products, and patent violations (tied to pressures for new product development).

The product cycle concept, with its attendant concern for capital mobility and flexibility, has spawned a new decade of merger activity. Depending on the political environment, these mergers have either been discouraged (Carter) or encouraged (Reagan).[9] Thus, while financial subunits and strategies are expected to produce more illegal conglomerate mergers, these numbers will vary by political administration.

The primary strategic goals of finance subunits are maximum growth and profitability (Fligstein 1987). Finance goals, perhaps more than any others, are apt to permeate the entire corporation. Intense intraorganizational pressure on all departments and personnel is likely if goals are not met. Consequently, we might hypothesize that firms dominated by finance subunits will produce the greatest amount of corporate crime. And, if all kinds of corporate illegality are included (e.g., foreign bribery and corruption, environmental violations, worker health and safety violations, financial fraud, stock manipulations, and so on), we would hypothesize this relationship. However, it is not expected to be true in the case of anticompetitive behavior.

*Hypothesis 4:* The sheer volume of anticompetitive illegality will be greatest in firms that have powerful sales and marketing subunits and multidivisional forms.

There are several reasons to expect multidivisional firms dominated by sales and marketing subunits to have higher rates of anticompetitive behavior than other firms, *ceteris paribus.* First, subunits with the greatest exposure to the external environment are more vulnerable to its vicissitudes and have greater opportunities to violate the law (Gross 1980). Sales and marketing, much more than production and finance, depend on such external relationships. Moreover, it is through their contacts with customers and relaying these desires and concerns that sales and marketing subunits maintain power and influence corporate strategies. Second, sales and marketing subunits are more regulated by relevant antitrust law than other subunits, that is, their organizational activities are more relevant to the concerns of antitrust law. For example, the strategies favored by manufacturing subunits may lead to some horizontal combination violations, but the emphasis on cost efficiency is equally likely to produce illegal squeezes on labor and/or manufacturing violations through the production of "cost efficient" but unsafe/substandard products. Similarly, as finance strategies seek more profitable ways to shift capital, securities fraud and/or other financial violations such as tax evasion or accounting fraud are probable outcomes.

Finally, Vaughan (1983) asserts that subunits with skills and resources most relevant to the profit-seeking goals of the corporation are most affected by structural "tensions" (i.e., pressures to violate the law) when organizational goals are not met. Under dominant sales and marketing subunits, strategies of market growth and product diversification are reinforced by marketing ideologies that justify and rationalize producer interests by embedding them in notions of consumer sovereignty (Smith 1987). The coupling of ideology and strategy creates powerful definitions of what is expected from sales and marketing personnel. The ideology of profit maximization is translated into sales and marketing product "subgoals" (Perrow, 1970).

The diffuse layers of personnel and bureaucracy are more likely to produce evaluations of employee performance that rely on quantitative rather than qualitative criteria. Top managers will typically evaluate divisions based on financial performance, paying less attention to day to day operations. As employees come to realize that only numbers count, the substitution of illicit means to achieve organizational goals is more easily rationalized.[10]

The multidivisional form isolates subunits, decreasing internal communication while increasing autonomy and task group cohesion. If deviant subcultures emerge because of difficulties in achieving organizational goals, they will be less amenable to direct corporate detection and control (Finney and Lesieur, 1982). Drexel Burnham Lambert's split into east and west coast operations dramatically highlight these problems (Zey 1989) as do findings that organizational cultures differ across Standard Business Units and parent corporations (Victor and Cullen 1988).

Given the greater law, opportunities, and pressures to achieve organizational goals placed on sales and marketing subunits during market growth and product diversification strategies, the multidivisional structure will serve to facilitate anticompetitive acts.

> *Hypothesis 5:* As firms within the same product market become more isomorphic (similar subunits in power and competitive strategies), criminality within that industry will tend toward homogeneity.

A firm's cultural environment is composed of other companies to whom it looks for successful strategies and organizational forms. Firms will take on these strategies and structures if it appears that they give others a competitive edge. DiMaggio and Powell (1983) refer to this process as organizational mimicry.

Through the exchange of personnel and mimicry, firms tend to homogenize their actions and forms to such a degree that they begin to closely resemble one another (DiMaggio and Powell 1983; Hannon and Freeman 1977). This is particularly true within industries where competitors are apt to duplicate successful strategies. And, if illegal conduct is perceived to benefit some competitors to the detriment of other, more honest, corporate actors, we can expect that the latter "may then adopt what they define as an industry standard of honesty, rationalizing their action by the need to remain competitive" (Barnett 1986, 565). A good example of mimicry occurred in 1936 when Packard, Nash, Reo, Hudson, Chrysler, American, and General Motors (just to name a few) all advertised a 6 percent interest rate for a new car loan that "misrepresented the cost of the credit charge for purchasing motor vehicles on the installment or deferred payment plan" (FTC Case Decisions 8 December 1939).

## Conclusion

Very little is actually known about how and why corporate crime varies within and across firms and industries over time. Some theoretical perspectives explain etiology by emphasizing the flawed personality characteristics of corporate managers. Others, more informed by small group theory, assert social learning or subcultural processes. Anomie theory postulates extraorganizational and internal sources of strain that motivate corporate representatives to substitute illegal for legal means.

Each of these diverse perspectives may help explain a piece of the theoretical puzzle, but if the goal is to gain a more comprehensive understanding of corporate crime, we need explanations that are informed by organizational theory. Specifically, any theory of corporate illegality must be embedded in existing corporate structure.

In this paper, the anticompetitive behavior of companies over time is tied to historical changes in organizational strategies and form. As strategic goals for the organization shift, the motivations for corporate crime reflect these adjustments. Likewise, changes in organizational structure adjust crime opportunities. Such an approach allows us to understand the occurrence and configuration of corporate illegality within firms, across industries, and over time.

Clearly, this is not a formal theory of corporate crime and it is perhaps more speculative than is ideal. But, the examination of corporate strategy and structure leads us toward new theory and away from the insularity of criminological paradigms. As a next logical step, it makes sense to examine the predictive capacity of the perspective and, if it proves insightful, to extend it to other types of corporate offending.

**Appendix 4.1**

*Relevant Antitrust Legislation, by year.*

| Year | Legislation and Intent. |
| --- | --- |

1890   Sherman Act:    Section 1. Every contract, combination in the form of trust or otherwise, or conspiracy, in restraint of trade or commerce among the several states, or with foreign nations is declared illegal.
Section 2. Every person who shall monopolize, or attempt to monopolize, or combine or conspire with any other person or persons to monopolize any part of the trade or commerce among the several states, or with foreign nations shall be deemed guilty of a felony.

1914   Clayton Act:    Declared four restrictive practices illegal but not criminal:
Section 2, price-discrimination (sales of a product at different prices to similarly situated buyers);
Section 3, tying and exclusive dealing contracts (sales on condition that the buyer stop dealing with sellers competition);
Section 7, corporate mergers (acquisitions of competing companies via *stock* acquisitions);
Section 8, interlocking directorates (common board members among competing companies).

1914   Federal Trade Commission Act:    Unfair methods of competition in or affecting commerce, and unfair or deceptive acts or practices in or affecting commerce are hereby declared unlawful.

*Amendments*

| 1936 | Robinson-Patman Act: | Sought to limit the purchasing power of large buyers, enforceable against buyers seeking and sellers offering unjustified price discounts. |
|------|----------------------|-----------------------------------------------|
| 1950 | Celler-Kefauver Act: | Section 7 of the Clayton Act is rewritten to close the asset acquisitions loophole. Applies to vertical and conglomerate as well as horizontal mergers. |
| 1970 | Magnuson-Moss Act: | Increased the FTC jurisdiction to matters affecting commerce, especially consumer protection actions. |

## Notes

This research was funded as part of a post-doctoral research fellowship at the Harvard Graduate School of Business Administration. The author is grateful to Dean John McArthur and the Division of Research for their support. Thanks also to Harold Barnett, Alfred Chandler, Jr., Amitai Etzioni, Jurg Gerber, Rosabeth Moss Kanter, N. Craig Smith, and members of the marketing faculty at HBS for their helpful comments on earlier drafts. I am indebted to an anonymous reviewer whose detailed suggestions provided a direction for final revision.

1. For the purposes of this discussion, corporate crime/illegality is defined as acts committed by corporate personnel on behalf of the corporation that are in violation of civil, administrative, and/or criminal law (Clinard and Yeager 1980; Kramer 1982). These include securities, antitrust, financial, environmental, manufacturing, labor, and other violations. Victims of corporate crime may range from competitors, the government, employees, the general public, suppliers, customers, and society as a whole.
2. Notable exceptions to this rule include Clinard and Yeager (1980), Conklin (1977), Ermann and Lundman (1978), Finney and Lesieur (1982), and Kramer (1982). See Coleman (1987) and Gross (1978) for a mixture of individual and organizational theorizing. Noting the problems with individual-level analysis of organizational phenomena, Schrager and Short (1978, 41) argue, "preoccupation with individuals can lead us to underestimate the pressures within society and organizational structure which impel those individuals to commit illegal acts." But, see Cressey (1989) and Braithwaite and Fisse (1990) for arguments supporting and opposing a return to reductionist approaches.

3. For an in-depth review of the corporate crime literature, especially as it relates to causation, see Yeager (1986).
4. Barnett's (1986) research on corporate tax compliance in Sweden finds no significant differences in industry profitability between an industries in which compliance is high versus those where it is low. He does find, however, that extreme cases of industry decline (as measured by minor and total bankruptcy per enterprise) are significantly related to higher tax noncompliance.
5. Barnett (1986) also examines the relationship between *industry* culture and tax noncompliance, concluding "that industry culture is an important factor in explaining relative noncompliance across industries." The theoretical relevance of industry culture will be noted later in this paper.
6. Gross (1978) does not share this point of view. He argues that corporations, by virtue of their goals and structures, are inherently criminogenic.
7. This historical section essentially restates the findings of Chandler (1962) and, more typically, Fligstein (1987).
8. Fligstein (1987) argues that changes in the legal environment are affected by corporate conduct, that is, anticompetitive acts precede antitrust legislation, resulting in new forms of organizational behavior not yet defined as illegal but apt to be anticompetitive. Corporations act on and are acted upon by the external environment. The nonrecursive nature of law and illegal corporate conduct presents a thorny theoretical knot that I acknowledge, but one not formally confronted in this research.
9. On 15 January 1981 in FTC testimony, a lawyer for a corporate defendant noted that "there is perhaps, if not a change in attitude, a different view in Washington" regarding the resolution of friction "between business, regulatory agencies, and consumers." This impression is supported by FTC Chairman Daniel Oliver in a recent letter to former President Reagan. Oliver wrote, "I am sometimes asked, 'why would a deregulator be put in charge of a regulatory agency?' I answer, 'only people who know how dangerous guns are should be allowed to play with guns.' " Oliver goes on to add, "During much of the history of antitrust the harm the government has done has exceeded the good it has done. But not for the last eight years" (FTC News, 16 May 1989).
10. I am indebted to Professor Ray Corey of the Harvard School of Business Administration for this observation.

## References

Asch, Peter and Joseph J. Seneca. 1975. "Characteristics of Collusive Firms." *Journal of Industrial Economics* 23: 223–47.

Bacharach, Samuel B. 1982. *Research in the Sociology of Organizations*, volume 1. Greenwich, Conn.: JAI Press.

Barnett, Harold C. 1986. "Industry Culture and Industry Economy: Correlates of Tax Noncompliance in Sweden." *Criminology* 24: 553–75.

Benson, Michael. 1986. "Denying the Guilty Mind: Accounting for Involvement in a White-Collar Crime." *Criminology* 23: 583–607.

Braithwaite, John. 1978. "Corporate Crime and the Internationalization of Capital." Unpublished manuscript, Australian Institute of Criminology, Canberra.

Braithwaite, John and Brent Fisse. 1990. "On the Plausibility of Corporate Crime Theory." In William S. Laufer and Freda Adler (eds.), *Advances in Criminological Theory*, volume 2. New Brunswick, N.J.: Transaction Publishers.

Chandler, Alfred D., Jr. 1962. *Strategy and Structure: Chapters in the History of the American Industrial Enterprise*. Boston: MIT Press.

Clabault, M. J. and J. F. Burton Jr. 1966. *Sherman Act Indictments, 1955–1965: A Legal and Economic Analysis*. New York: Federal Legal Publications.

Clinard, Marshall B. 1946. "Criminological Theories of Violations of Wartime Regulations." *American Sociological Review* 11: 258–70.

Clinard, Marshall B. 1983. *Corporate Ethics and Crime: The Role of Middle Management*. Beverly Hills, Cal.: Sage.

Clinard, Marshall B. and Richard Quinney, eds. (1967). *Criminal Behavior Systems: A Typology*. New York: Holt, Rinehart and Winston.

Clinard, Marshall B. and Peter C. Yeager. 1980. *Corporate Crime*. New York: The Free Press.

Coleman, James. 1987. "Toward an Integrated Theory of White-Collar Crime." *American Journal of Sociology* 93: 406–39.

Conklin, John. 1977. *Illegal but not Criminal*. Englewood Cliffs, N.J.: Prentice-Hall.

Cressey, Donald. 1953. *Other People's Money*. New York: The Free Press.

Cressey, Donald. 1989. "The Poverty of Theory in Corporate Crime Research." In William S. Laufer and Freda Adler (eds.). *Advances in Criminological Theory*, volume 1. New Brunswick, N.J.: Transaction.

Denzin, Norman. 1977. "Notes on a Criminogenic Hypothesis: A Case Study of the American Liquor Industry." *American Sociological Review* 42: 905–20.

Denzin, Norman, ed. 1978. *Studies in Symbolic Interaction,* volume 1. Greenwich, Conn.: JAI Press.

DiMaggio, Paul J. and Walter W. Powell. 1983. "Institutional Isomorphism." *American Sociological Review* 48: 147–60.

Ermann, M. David and Richard J. Lundman. 1978. "Deviant Acts by Complex Organizations." *Sociological Quarterly* (Winter): 64.

Farberman, Harvey A. 1975. "A Criminogenic Market Structure: The Automobile Industry." *Social Science Quarterly* 16: 438–57.

Finney, Henry C. and Henry R. Lesieur. 1982. "A Contingency Theory of Organizational Crime." In Samuel B. Bacharach (ed). *Research in the Sociology of Organizations*, volume 1. Greenwich, Conn.: JAI Press.

Fligstein, Nail. 1987. "The Intraorganizational Power Struggle: Rise of Finance Personnel to Top Leadership in Large Corporations, 1919–1979." *American Sociological Review* 52: 44–56.

Geis, Gilbert. 1962. "Toward a Delineation of White-Collar Offenses." *Sociological Inquiry* 32: 160–71.

Geis, Gilbert. 1967. "White Collar Crime: The Heavy Electrical Equipment Antitrust Cases of 1961." In Marshall B. Clinard and Richard Quinney (eds.), *Criminal Behavior Systems: A Typology*. New York: Holt, Rinehart and Winston.

Geis, Gilbert and Ezra Stotland. 1980. *White-Collar Crime: Theory and Research*. Beverly Hills, Cal.: Sage.

Gellhorn, Ernest. 1981. *Antitrust Law and Economics in a Nutshell*. St. Paul, Minn.: West.

Gross, Edward. 1978. "Organizational Crime: A Theoretical Perspective." In Norman Denzin (ed.), *Studies in Symbolic Interaction*, volume 1. Greenwich, Conn.: JAI Press.

Gross, Edward. 1980. "Organization Structure and Organizational Crime." In Gilbert Geis and Ezra Stotland (eds.), *White-Collar Crime: Theory and Research*. Beverly Hills, Cal.: Sage.

Hannan, Michael T. and John H. Freeman. 1977. "The Population Ecology of Organizations." *American Journal of Sociology* 82: 929–64.

Harris, Anthony R. and Sally S. Simpson. 1987. "The Serial Production of Corporate Crime." Presented at the Annual Meeting of the Society for the Study of Social Problems, Chicago.

Hay, George A. and Daniel Kelly. 1974. "An Empirical Survey of Price-Fixing Conspiracies." *The Journal of Law and Economics* 13: 13–38.

Hickson, D., C. R. Hinings, C. A. Lee, R. E. Schneck, and J. M. Pennings. (1971). "A Strategic Contingencies Theory of Intraorganizational Power." *Administrative Science Quarterly* 16: 216–29.

Hirschi, Travis and Michael Gottfredson. 1987. "Causes of White-Collar Crime." *Criminology* 25: 949–74.

Kramer, Ronald C. 1982. "Corporate Crime: An Organizational Approach." In Peter Wickman and Timothy Daily (eds.), White Collar and Economic Crime. Lexington, Mass.: D. C. Heath.

Lane, Robert E. 1953. "Why Businessmen Violate the Law." *Journal of Criminal Law, Criminology and Police Science* 44: 151–65.

Laufer, William S. and Freda Adler. 1989/1990. *Advances in Criminological Theory*, volumes 1 and 2. New Brunswick, N.J.: Transaction.

Lawrence, Paul R. and Jay W. Lorsch. 1967. *Organizations and Environment*. Boston: Harvard Business School Press.

Lean, David F., Jonathan D. Ogru, and Robert P. Rogers. 1982. *Competition and Collusion in Electrical Equipment Markets: An Economic Assessment*. Bureau of the Economics Staff Report to the FTC.

Perrow, Charles. 1970. *Organizational Analysis: A Sociological View*. Belmont, Cal.: Brooks/Cole.

Pfeffer, Jeffrey. 1981. *Power in Organizations*. Marshfield, MA.: Pitman.

Posner, Richard A. 1976. *Antitrust Law: An Economic Perspective*. Chicago: The University of Chicago Press.

Posner, Richard A. 1970. "A Statistical Study of Antitrust Enforcement." *Journal of Law and Economics* 13: 365–419.

Post, James E. 1986. *Research in Corporate Social Performance and Policy*, volume 8. Greenwich, Conn.: JAI Press.

Rex, John. 1961. *Key Problems in Sociological Theory*. London: Routledge & Kegan Paul.

Ross, Irwin. 1980. "Illegal Corporate Behavior: Big Companies?" *Fortune* (December): 57–61.

Rumult, Richard P. 1974. *Strategy, Structure, and Economic Performance*. Boston: Harvard Business School Press.

Schrager, Laura S. and James F. Short, Jr. 1978. "Toward a Sociology of Organizational Crime." *Social Problems* 25: 407–19.

Shapiro, Susan. 1984. *Wayward Capitalists*. New Haven, Conn.: Yale University Press.

Simpson, Sally S. 1986. "The Decompositon of Antitrust: Testing a Multi-level, Longitudinal Model of Profit-Squeeze." *American Sociological Review* 51: 859–75.

Simpson, Sally S. 1987. "Cycles of Illegality: Antitrust Violations in Corporate America." *Social Forces* 64: 943–63.

Simpson, Sally S. 1992. "Corporate Crime and Corporate Crime Deterrence: Views from the Inside." Forthcoming in Kip Schlegel and David Weisburd (eds.), *Essays in White Collar Crime*. Boston: Northeastern University Press.

Smith, N. Craig. 1987. "The Ideology of Marketing." Paper presented to the MEG Conference, University of Warwick.

Sonnenfeld, Jeffrey and Paul R. Lawrence. 1978. "Why do Companies Succumb to Price Fixing?" *Harvard Business Review* 56: 145–57.

Staw, Barry N. and Eugene Szwajkowski. 1975. "The Scarcity-Munificence Component of Organizational Acts." *Administrative Science Quarterly* 20: 345–54.

Sutherland, Edwin. 1939. "White-Collar Criminality." Presidential Address to the American Sociological Association.

Sutherland, Edwin. 1949. *White-Collar Crime*. New York: Dryden Press.

Sykes, Gresham M. and David Matza. 1957. "Techniques of Neutralization." *American Sociological Review* 5: 1–12.

Vaughan, Diane. (1983). *Controlling Unlawful Organizational Behavior: Social Structure and Corporate Misconduct*. Chicago: University of Chicago.

Vaughan, Diane. 1989. "Ethical Decision Making in Organizations: The Challenger Launch." Presented at a special workshop on organizational deviance, Harvard School of Business Administration.

Victor, Bart and John B. Cullen. 1988. "The Organizational Bases of Ethical Work Environments." *Administrative Science Quarterly* 33: 101–25.

The Wall Street Journal. 1982. November 8.

Wheeler, Stanton, David Weisburd, and Nancy Bode. 1982. "Sentencing the White-Collar Offender: Rhetoric and Reality." *American Sociological Review*, 47: 641–59.

Wickman, Peter and Timothy Dailey. 1982. *White Collar and Economic Crime*. Lexington, Mass.: D. C. Heath.

Yeager, Peter C. 1986. "Analyzing Corporate Offenses: Progress and Prospects." In James E. Post (ed.) *Research in Corporate Social Performance and Policy*, volume 8. Greenwich, Conn.: JAI Press.

Zey, Mary K. 1989. "The Consequences of Insider Trading and Securities Fraud: The Case of Drexel Burnham Lambert." Presented at a special workshop on organizational deviance, Harvard School of Business Administration.

Zey-Ferrell, Mary K., Mark Weaver, and O. C. Ferrell. 1979. "Predicting

Unethical Behavior among Marketing Practicioners.'' *Human Relations* 32: 557–69.

Zey-Ferrell, Mary K. and O. C. Ferrell. 1982. ''Role Set Configuration and Opportunity as Predictors of Unethical Behavior in Organizations.'' *Human Relations* 35: 587–604.

# 5

# Employee Theft: An Examination of Gerald Mars and an Explanation Based on Equity Theory

*Edward W. Sieh*

"Employee theft, is defined as the unlawful and unauthorized intentional taking of an employer's property, with the purpose of benefiting the worker or someone who is not entitled to the property" (Sieh 1987, 174). This behavior differs from white-collar crimes or grand larceny in that it is not intended to include the theft of large quantities of inexpensive material or of small quantities of very expensive materials. These actions would likely call for an investigation by the authorities if only to comply with insurance company formalities. The behavior under consideration here, for the most part, is considered petty theft, pilfering or fiddling. Nonetheless, over time the consequences can be considerable. Theft by employees can lead to business failures, particularly during a recession, lost employee benefits, defaulted loans, diminished trust and cooperation among workers, and a lack of faith in the business sector.

Any discussion of the etiology of human behavior can be frustrating because there are so many varied explanations. Whenever an explanation is offered it seems that someone else offers an alternative account of the event. This paper will discuss just one of the many possible explanations of employee theft by attending to

95

one set of concepts with full recognition that there are other accounts that may prove valid as well. In order to focus on an explanation of behavior one must consider the dynamic nature of the event and the rules of behavior that apply to everyone.

Some of the many different explanations for employee theft range from the rotten apple theory (U.S. Chamber of Commerce 1974) to the "gin, girls and gambling" hypothesis offered by Peterson (1947). Ross (1961) believes that some employee theft is due to the cynical worker's desire to supplement the worker's wages. Carson (1977) argues that employees steal in order to enhance their social status. These explanations focus on blaming the perpetrator for the crime while leaving the employer free of fault. The problem is seen as intrinsic to the worker while nothing is said about the pressures that are inherent to the work environment.

While there are other important contributors to the discussion of employee theft, including Hollinger's work (1978, 1982a, 1982b, and 1986), this article will consider a work that has received a great deal of attention both in the United States and in Great Britain. This paper will analyze an explanation offered by Gerald Mars (1983), by indicating various points of deficiency, and offering an alternative account which emphasizes fairness at work.

Mars (1973, 1974, and 1983), Henry (1978), and Ditton (1977a and 1977b) utilized the ethnographic approach when presenting their understandings of theft. "These show the informal economy activities are not just restricted to extra or part-time work, outside formal employment, but that they are comprised of the activities of ordinary people in full-time jobs who take part in fiddles, pilfering, and amateur trading in ways that are integral to, "subsidized" by and, some would say, parasitic on their formal jobs" (Henry 1982, 467).

Mars (1983) wrote a valuable and thorough account of employee fiddling. Fiddling is defined as the

movement of resources to individual private use that do not appear in official accounts—or that appear in official accounts under different headings and which are acquired by individuals through their relationships to a job. These resources may derive directly from the job itself or be allocated from an outside source that relates to the job. (Mars 1983, 10)

He prefers to use the term "fiddling" not to condone theft, but to allow for the possibility of alternative methods of transaction that "theft" does not adequately describe. Using the term theft effectively prejudges the action because it recategorizes the acts that are being discussed (Mars 1983, 166).

Mars analyzed the worker's social environment by using Douglas's (1970, 1978) concepts of a grid (autonomy) and strength of group (constraints). Mars presented a taxonomy of four job categories. The hawks (entrepreneurs, small businessmen, and innovative professionals) are isolated individualists who bend organizational rules to their own advantage. The donkeys (cashiers, machine operators, and transport workers) are also isolated but they are constrained. Their response is to engage in sabotage or fiddling. The wolves (dockworkers) work in well-organized and highly regulated groups engaged in theft. The vultures (writers and travelling salesmen) fiddle in ways which reflect the individualistic and competitive nature of their work.

Fiddling too, can be understood as a multistranded transaction. It is just one of several ways that people deal with each other, albeit outside conventional market exchanges (Mars 1983, 168). Fiddling becomes not necessarily the "wrong" way of doing something but rather another way of doing something (Mars 1983, 166). This has important implications for the morality of "part-time" fiddling.

> When he fiddles he divides his life, as Ditton (1970a) skillfully shows, into a working life, public and impersonal, and a fiddling life, private and personal. However, he lacks both the psychic equipment and the split-level moral framework needed to cope with this division. . . . The individual has to square his fiddling self with his working self. (Mars 1983, 169–70)

Reconciling the straight with the sinful self is accomplished through the absorption of the work group's world view. The work group clarifies social relationships and the accompanying transactions (Mars 1983, 170). Furthermore, the work group establishes the system of morality. It establishes both quantitative and qualitative limits on what and how much can be taken. The work group helps to establish an equilibrium between the sinful self and the everyday self (Mars 1983, 170–71).

Mars explains the worker's fiddling by linking the social environment of the job with the worker's world view.

A lack to fit between job and cosmology can have a number of effects: first, if a person cannot adapt his values, beliefs and attitudes to suit the job's demands, he can resign or withdraw mentally from the conflict; secondly, he can suffer breakdown; or thirdly, he may survive incompatibility in that state of tension sometimes called alienation. In such a state he may respond through a higher than usual sickness rate; a greater than usual turnover in the number of jobs; through sabotage, through absenteeism, and through fiddling. (Mars 1983, 35)

Compatibility between world views and work, according to Mars, produces job satisfaction. The worker may be paid appropriately, but if the worker also fiddles, the worker can add excitement to the work, beat the system, gain control of his/her fate, develop a measure of self-expression, and acquire prestige in the community. It is an empowering mechanism. "Fiddling" should be seen as something more than an index of worker dissatisfaction, it should also be seen as pointing to ways in which the status quo could be changed so as to bring workers from the periphery into the center of work place control (Carlen 1983, 806).

Ditton (1982, 356) suggests that Mars reports "no new data, and that he concentrates on providing a novel and artful rearrangement of existing anecdotal evidence." The value of his presentation, however, lies in its simple, clearly expressed and unmoralistic way of dragging all the usually concealed crooks and nannies of the real shady world into broad daylight (Ditton 1982, 356).

Pahl (1983) criticizes Mars for using sexist terms (e.g., donkeys to describe female cashiers) but also for showing signs of ethnocentricism particularly as it relates to Mars's apparent preference for the entrepreneurial activities of the hawk, who acts with a degree of flair. "It is surely naive to imagine that setting up a paradise for hawks would reduce fiddles. . . . One fears that Mars is a natural hawk who can only perceive hawk-like solutions" (Pahl 1983, 295).

Levi (1983) argues that Mars comes close to suggesting that fiddles would occur far less often if the work atmosphere, in particular, interpersonal relationships, were better. Levi believes this hypothesis needs better testing than is offered by what is considered ad hoc references to girls who cease fiddling when they get more interesting work. This might be considered another example of endorsing the Hawthorne effect. He also believes that Mars may exaggerate the lack of interest some may have in their fiddles. For many it becomes an integral part of their income. There are also doubts about the union mitigating the need for the fiddle (Levi 1983, 584). Levi believes that the workers would continue to act as they have whether unionized or not.

Based on his selection of examples, Mars's work seems to be about working-class crimes. It draws attention to various work-related activities that we take for granted or seek consumer protection from but rarely consider to be examples of systematic theft. Fiddling takes place within the various transactions conducted at work between the worker, the work group, the employer, and sometimes an outside customer. Fiddling is presented not as a real crime but as another way of doing business. His style of reporting on fiddling appears to give the impression that it is a victimless crime with few serious consequences (Levi 1983, 583). Levi (1983) believes he may hae been colonized by the subject matter. In part this may be the outcome of Mars's attempt at maintaining a sense of methodological disinterest in the activities of the fiddler. From the perspective of the victim these actions cannot be understood so dispassionately.

It is apparent that Mars's workers, in part, are violating the work group's limits identified by Horning (1970), Sieh (1987) and others. His concept of theft would include theft from employers and customers alike, particularly customers who are exploited by thieves who engage in what is labeled as passing trade—individuals who have a temporary relationship with the employee. It seems that he makes no distinction between picking a customer's pocket, watering down the customer's drinks, selling day-old bread, or shortchanging a customer. Moreover, these are not necessarily the same phenomenon. Some of these employees could be honest employees who feel pressured to steal or they could be crooks, who just happen to have jobs, and have found an opportunity to steal. The victim is undifferentiated and, in many cases is undeserving.

This does not mean that we ought to prosecute all offenders, but why should the fact of being in employment confer a "master status" of "respectable", while being out of lawful work puts us beyond the pale, as a member of the dangerous class? The author provides no guide as to where the line between "fiddling" and "crime" ought to be drawn, and in the instances I have mentioned, worker control offers no protection. (Levi 1983, 584)

Mars offers some valuable insights into the world of work and fiddling but while his explanation seems to provide a breadth of description it lacks depth of content. His account lacks a mechanism for explaining what occurs at work to specifically instigate employee theft. It appears that the transactions he mentions are another form of innovation brought on by the frustration generated by the lack of success with conventional approaches to the job which was conceptualized by Merton (1968).

Mars mentions that theft may be attributable to the worker's sense of alienation and desire for control. Moreover, he places a great deal of importance on the squaring of the fiddling self with the working self particularly through the acceptance and absorbing the work group's assumptions (Mars 1983, 170). It seems problematical that Mars does not spell out what specifically are these assumptions. This writer believes that one of the work group's assumptions is that when the worker is treated unfairly at work, the worker has a right to seek redress which under the proper conditions may take the form of employee theft.

### Acceptable Rationalizations

It is assumed that most workers are both law abiding and committed to a legitimate life-style, therefore, it is necessary to ask: How does a worker come to take the step to steal something from the employer?

> There are those, however, whose commitment to conventional morality and law would normally prevent them from taking part in illegal activity in the first place. But if an acceptable account can be found in advance to rationalise such action, then the person could feel free to engage in it. (Henry 1978, 46)

C. W. Mills (1963) provides a useful discussion of motives. He argues that people develop a "vocabulary of motives" for justifying behavior when explaining it to others. People vocalize and impute motives to themselves and to others. Motives then are accepted justifications for present, future, or past programs or acts. "Justifications are explanations through which the responsibility for the act is accepted but any 'wrongfulness' is denied" (Henry 1978, 46).

These processes "indicate mechanisms for the linkage of vocabularies of motives to systems of action" (Mills 1963, 440). This process originates not from within the individual but from the situation in which the person finds themselves (Mills 1963, 442). Different social groups, including work groups, have different vocabularies of motives. When workers appeal to others involved in their work milieu, motives become strategies for action. The worker is looking for acceptance from co-workers. In many social actions, the person seeks agreement from co-workers, tacitly or explicitly, otherwise the acts will be forsaken.

In the work environment two reference groups, managers and workers, both strongly influence the actions of the worker, and in turn, each provides support for employee theft. Henry (1978), Mars (1983) and Sieh (1987) have reported that managers were actively involved with fiddling. Employer-directed deviance, in turn, instigates reciprocal employee deviance (Kemper 1965). Supervisors have been known to exacerbate the taking of company property through their meta communicative, nonverbal clues (winks) which let employees know that taking something is not wrong because it is "given away," "cheap," "spare," or "extra" (Ditton 1977b). The work group helps to interpret these signals.

Despite the actions of the supervisors, the most important social mechanism for rationalizing theft is provided by the work group that assists the worker in identifying acceptable motives or justifications. It can provide the worker with a collective sense of job dissatisfaction and with the appropriate motives needed to rationalize theft. In this normative system, employee theft is approved through the development of a particular perspective toward the company. In one particular case the employees felt it was their company, it was compensation, the company expected it, and the managers did it (Horning 1970). Dockworkers shared common attitudes that justified employee theft as an entitlement due them for being exploited (Mars 1974). Hotel employees evolved a justification of the fiddle as a necessity to compensate for low wages and high turnover (Mars 1973).

The work group tends to mitigate technical, safety, and security limitations that act against access to the desired items and thus expands the number of opportunities for theft at work (Mars 1974).

Moreover, it can provide important knowledge of what use a stolen item has and how to dispose of it. Limits are established on the taking of property, particularly by identifying appropriate targets. Paradoxically, through the efforts of the work group, the total volume of property stolen increases (Robin 1967; Stoddard 1968; Horning 1970; Snizek 1974; Bradford 1976; Ditton 1977a; Altheide et al. 1978; Mars 1973, 1974, and 1983; and Sieh 1987).

Hollinger and Clark (1982b, 339) found the strength of the work group's norms were much stronger than the formal control mechanism present at work. Mars (1974) found that supporters of these norms avoided prosecution because the other workers refused to testify against them. The employee is encouraged to take only what is perceived to be owed to that individual because to take more jeopardizes the group's activities and violates the group's norms regulating the amount of theft.

As part of the work group's socialization process, and through the acquisition of a "vocabulary of motives" the new worker assimilates a particular world view of the work experience. In developing this particular view the employee, borrowing from Sutherland (1978), learns certain attitudes, motives, and appropriate techniques which both rationalize and facilitate the taking of company property. "The normative system of the work subculture may provide the means of neutralizing acts of pilfering" (Horning 1970, 60–61). One particularly useful technique is the denial of the victim (Sykes and Matza 1957).

[T]he moral indignation of self and others may be neutralized by an insistence that the injury is not wrong in light of the circumstances. The injury, it may be claimed, is not really an injury; rather, it is a form of rightful retaliation or punishment. By a subtle alchemy the delinquent [employee] moves himself into the position of an avenger and the victim is transformed into a wrong-doer. (Sykes and Matza 1957, 68–69)

Other factors also contribute to this view. To some degree, the internal social conditions found at work reflect the existing conflict between blue-collar and white-collar workers. Conflict arises when managers flaunt their privileges or when obligations are not met. As a function of the employee adopting the world view of the work group, a different perspective toward the company is acquired that enables the worker to rationalize his or her actions by perceiving themselves as a victim. What might at first appear as unprovoked theft, proves to be an aggressive response to misconduct; a manifestation of the self-help theory identified by Black (1983, 34). Much of this employee-initiated conduct also resembles a form of conflict management. Property is confiscated as a form of social control. Paradoxically, this means the workers who take things, are actually reaffirming the necessity that order be maintained in the distribution of benefits, and that limits be placed on the benefits granted those in power.

## Equity as a Motivational Theory

Moore (1978) proposes a concept of human nature that incorporates the existence of a natural morality. "Rather than playing a dependent, derivative role in human affairs, the concern with justice seems to provide the central and guiding theme in our lives" (Lerner 1977b, 4). Lerner (1975, 1977a, and 1977b) and Lerner and Whitehead (1980) support the notion that behavior is motivated by a positive concern for fairness. In both the earlier formulations of Adams (1965) and the later discussions of Walster et al. (1973), inequity (unfairness) produces stress which motivates people to reestablish equity. When the inequity continues and the stress builds, the worker feels frustrated and seeks relief by engaging in employee theft. The strength of the motivation is proportional to the magnitude of the perceived inequity (Adams 1965). "Specifically, the theory postulates that a perceived inequity creates tension in the perceiver that is proportional to the magnitude of the inequity, and that the perceiver is motivated by his tension to reduce the inequity" (Greenberg 1982, 381). Consequently, we are led to the general assertion of the reactive position that inequity motivates behavior (Greenberg 1982, 391). Equity may explain some behavior but how does it specifically relate to the workplace?

## Fairness at Work

Dalton (1959) argued that employee theft derives its meaning from the social context in which it takes place. As one worker said in reference to another's actions, "You could say he's robbin' them, but he don't see it as robbery because them bastards have robbed us in the beginning" (Henry 1978, 49). In another example, when a worker does well, his expense account will expand as a form of reward but if the worker has worked hard and finds that the rewards stay the same and that any efforts go unrequited the worker will punish the organization by stepping up his expense account too (Mars 1983, 35–36).

Recent discussions of employee theft based on research in a variety of settings view it as an attempt to resolve various workplace inequities that are generally expressed in terms of job dissatisfaction (Sieh 1987; Altheide et al. 1978; Ditton 1977; Hollinger and Clark 1982a; Mangione and Quinn 1975; Quinney 1977; and Zeitlin 1971). A theme "that runs through much work place deviance (theft, sabotage, sleeping at work, using drugs, etc.), suggests that it is motivated by strains or inequities internal to the work environment (Hollinger 1986, 56). By coming to work late, leaving early, taking long lunch and coffee breaks, or falsifying sick leave, these discontented but trapped employees can perhaps achieve a personal "equity" within the work milieu (Hollinger 1986, 71). The norms and practices through which workers are disciplined, laid off, assigned wage rates, awarded promotions, and so on are crucial in that they affect the worker's sense of equity (Blauner 1964). The purpose here is to provide an explanation of employee theft by presenting a detailed account of how a sense of inequity experienced at work can provide a motivation to engage in employee theft.

One of the principal maxims found at work calls for a fair day's wage for a fair day's labor. Fairness is central to the work environment. If one wishes to "reduce economically disadvantageous industrial unrest an understanding of inequity is important" (Adams 1963, 422). Equity and justice, when properly dispensed at work, promote efficiency and reduce conflict (Jaques 1970, 144). The employee is socialized in the community and by the work group to seek wealth and status. Borrowing from strain theory, stress and frustration result when the employee feels unfairly treated and blocked from achieving these values. The stronger the blocked drive, the more intense the aggressive reactions, and consequently, the greater the likelihood that some hostility will be revealed openly (Berkowitz 1962, 38).

This theory of equity is comprised of what Dubin (1978) calls relational units. Relational units are complex units that have two or more properties. In the present model, equity is constituted of three relational units: obligation, balance, and unjust deprivation. These properties provide the means for describing and analyzing the interrelated features of the concept and are played out in the interactions between the worker and the boss. These three elements comprise the concept of equity in that they provide an indication that equity has not been achieved.

According to Moore (1978) there exists a (conscious) psychological contract between the employer and the employee whereby an employer assumes an obligation to provide a certain reward for a given amount of effort. This arrangement is considered fair when the contract is fulfilled. This employer-employee contract can be viewed as a formalization of the personal contract. "The personal contract represents a person's resolution to orient himself to the world on the basis of what he earns or deserves via his prior investments" (Lerner, Miller, and Holmes 1976, 135).

The concept of balance provides the basis for determining the fairness of the exchange between the employer and the employee. The contract between the employer and the employee obligates the balancing of the reward (outcome) with the effort (input). The state of equity is considered fair when proportions are neither too much nor too little. If the amount is more or less than what is subjectively perceived as fair, then an imbalance exists. It is this perception of a disequilibrium that is experienced as a grievance (Jaques 1970, 183).

One of the canons of the proactive approach to equity is the recognition that various forms of justice emerge from the person's perception of where he stands in relation to others. There is a comparative process inherent in the development of expectations and perceptions of injustice (Adams 1965). One measures what one has by what one expects to have. The experiencing of unjust deprivation is understood as a matter involving the perception of an imbalance in the weighing of one's contributions and rewards versus the contributions and rewards given to others. "When the normative expectations of the person making social comparisons are violated, when he finds that his outcomes and inputs are not in balance in relation to those of others, feelings of inequity result" (Adams 1965, 280). Adams (1965, 281) provides this formula:

**Figure 5.1**

$$\frac{\text{Outcomes of Person A}}{\text{Inputs of Person A}} = \frac{\text{Outcomes of Person B}}{\text{Inputs of Person B}}$$

Inequity or injustice exists when the ratios are unequal, with the person for whom the ratio is smaller experiencing unjust deprivation (Crosby and Gonzalez-Intal 1984, 144).

There are a variety of sources of stress at work, ranging from obnoxious fellow workers to the ordinary dangers of the job. One particular source of stress is wage-inequity. Wage-inequity is defined as the employee not receiving his or her fair share of wages due to being treated unfairly at work. A sense of disequilibrium sets in when, for example, the employee's benefits are diminished because he or she has been unfairly suspended without pay. When the employee feels his or her wages and benefits are not in balance with what is expected of the employee, one way to reestablish this equilibrium is to engage in theft from the employer. These concerns are not experienced in isolation. The work group reinforces the employee's perception of being treated unfairly and provides the means for viewing criminal counteractions as appropriate responses.

A sequential ordering of events reflecting an escalation in stress brought on by repeated experiences with unfairness at work further explains the occurrence of theft. Responses to inequity will be influenced by a lack of opportunities for legitimate problem resolution. Legitimate actions intended to reduce the stress are undertaken first, but degenerates into illegitimate and eventually criminal responses as each response proves inadequate in meeting the problem. Frustration sets in when the worker realizes that he or she cannot reduce the stress through legitimate channels such as filing a union grievance. In turn the worker chooses the illegitimate response, employee theft.

"[A]ggressive responses aroused by a frustration tend to be directed toward the perceived frustrater" (Berkowitz 1962, 308). The company is considered the appropriate target for aggression since the company, through the actions of its representatives, is the source of inequity. This person, in the "representative role," epitomizes the organization from the point of view of those below him (Kemper 1965, 291). "When the organization either as an entity, or in the person of a superior [in a representative role], has defaulted on the obligations of the organization to its members, 'reciprocal deviance' can result" (Kemper 1965, 293). Reciprocal deviance refers to compensated employee behavior which is intended to reconcile organizational failures to "recognize merit" or "any attempt to abrogate the pay-productivity ratio in a downward direction" (Kemper 1965, 294).

It is apparent that the worker has some basic concerns about wage-inequity relative to meeting obligations, providing some measure of balance with respect to effort and reward, and in terms of meeting concerns for unjustified deprivation. When problems are not addressed through conventional means, the worker will respond aggressively. This leads to the formulation of a number of hypotheses.

## Hypotheses

The three dimensions of equity: obligation, balance, and unjustified deprivation, when considered in light of employee theft, suggest this proposition. Employees who "perceive" they are treated unfairly "in comparison with what others have received," will respond by "taking only what is owed to them."

This theory leads to the development of a number of hypotheses. First, the more frequently employees perceive the employer to have failed to fulfill the employer's obligation to the employee by not meeting the conditions of the contract, the more likely the employee is to steal company property. Second, the more frequently the employee finds his/her income adversely affected by what the employee perceives to be unfair treatment, the more likely the employee is to engage in theft in order to reestablish a balance between inputs and outcomes. It is also hypothesized that the more frequently the employee feels he or she has been unfairly treated in comparison to the treatment given others, the more likely the employee is to engage in theft in order to achieve a sense of equity. Lastly, it is hypothesized that the more frustrated the worker becomes in attempting to respond to inequity generated stress at work, the more likely it is that the worker will act aggressively toward the company and thus engage in theft.

The individaul member of the work group will engage in theft relative to the constraints of the work group, the available opportunities, the perception of risk, and the understanding that satisfaction can be achieved this way. The sense of satisfaction is measured in terms of the amount of stress reduced through the various applied techniques.

## Discussion

Employees can make a variety of responses to inequity that can be viewed from a mild reaction to a very dramatic response. Some employees will do nothing but others will get drunk, "get stoned," get mad and holler at the boss, call on the union for help, or talk over their problems with their spouses. As the problems continue or seem to get worse, the employees move into the intermediate response level where one finds employee theft along with responses such as minor cases of industrial sabotage, the filing of formal union grievances or law suits, and limited job actions. With respect to theft, an intermediate response, it will be strongly influenced by the social context. If things get worse there may be major incidences of sabotage, union organized strikes, wildcat strikes, and even violence. On a grander scale, these conditions can lead to political unrest and revolution.

It should be recognized that for a worker, employer-employee obligations can be met but the employee may still feel unfairly treated when comparisons are made with the treatment given other workers employed in other sectors of the industry. We should also be mindful that the use of technology will change the worker's concerns. It is possible for an employer to view the addition of technology as a labor saving device while the employees view it as an additional burden that will reduce their wages and pose a potential threat to their jobs. The problems at the Hormel plant in Austin, Minnesota clearly indicate as much. (See Hage and Klauda 1989.) Lastly, we should be aware of the constant changes that take place in the expectations of the worker. With increased productivity, rising salaries, and growing education levels in the work force, it is possible that matters involving equity will be a continual concern in management-labor relations.

What has been presented thus far should be viewed as a dynamic example of an environment which is subject to change. The work group and the environment are not static entitles. Moreover, as one problem involving unfairness is dealt with, the employee may be faced with another. Through the presence of inequity, an imbalance exists in the social system, but by reestablishing equity, a social equilibrium is maintained and an integrated, adjusted and relatively stable system can emerge.

## References

Adams, J. S. 1963. Toward an understanding of inequity. *Journal of Abnormal and Social Psychology* 67, 422–36.

Adams, J. S. 1965. Inequity in social exchange. In L. Berkowitz (ed.), *Advances in Experimental Psychology*. New York: Academic Press.

Altheide, D. L., Adler, P. A., Adler, P., and Altheide, D. A. 1978. The social meaning of employee theft. In J. M. Johnson and J. D. Douglas (eds.), *Deviance in Business and the Professions*. New York: J. B. Lippincott.

Berkowitz, L. 1962. *Aggression: A Social Psychological Analysis*. New York: McGraw-Hill.

Black, D. 1983. Crime as social control. *American Sociological Review* 48, 34–45.

Blauner, R. 1964. *Alienation and Freedom*. Chicago: University of Chicago.

Bradford, J. A. 1976. "A general perspective on job satisfaction: The relationship between job satisfaction, and sociological, psychological and cultural variables" (Doctoral dissertation, University of California, San Diego, 1976). Ann Arbor: Dissertation Abstracts International.

Carlen, P. 1983. Review of *Cheats at work*. *Sociological Review* 31, 805–07.

Carson, C. R. 1977. *Managing Employee Honesty*. Los Angeles: Security World.

Crosby, F. and A. M. Gonzalez-Intal 1984. Relative deprivation and equity theories: Felt injustice and the undeserved benefits of others. In R. Folger (ed.), *The Sense of Injustice: Social Psychological Perspectives*. New York: Plenum.

Dalton, M. 1959. *Men who Manage*. New York: John Wiley, 1959.

Ditton, J. 1977a. *Part-Time Crime*. London: Macmillan

Ditton, J. 1977b. Perks, pilferage and the fiddle: The historical structure of invisible wages. *Theory and Society* 4, 39–69.

Ditton, J. 1982. Honest dishonesty (review of *Cheats at Work*). *New Society* 62, 355–56.

Douglas, M. 1970. *Natural Symbols*. London: Crescent Press.

Douglas, M. 1978. *Cultural Bias*. London: Royal Anthropological Institute.

Dubin, R. 1978. *Theory Building*. New York: Free Press.

Greenberg, J. 1982. Approaching equity and avoiding inequity in groups and organizations. In J. Greenberg and R. Cohen (eds.), *Equity and Justice in Social Behavior*. New York: Academic Press.

Hage, D. and P. Klauda. 1989. *No Retreat, No Surrender*. New York: Morrow.

Henry, S. 1978. *The Hidden Economy: The Context and Control of Borderline Crime*. Oxford: Martin Robertson.

Henry, S. 1982. The Working Unemployed. *Sociological Review, 30,* 460–477.

Hollinger, R. C. 1978. "Employee deviance against the formal work organization." Unpublished doctoral dissertation, University of Minnesota, Minneapolis.

Hollinger, R. C. and J. P. Clark. 1982a. Employee deviance: A response to the perceived quality of the work experience. *Work and Occupation* 9, 97–114.

Hollinger, R. C. and J. P. Clark. 1982b. Formal and informal social controls of employee deviance. *The Sociological Quarterly* 23, 333–43.

Hollinger, R. C. 1986. Acts against the workplace: Social bonding and employee deviance. *Deviant Behavior* 7, 53–75.

Horning, D. M. 1970. Blue-collar theft: Conceptions of property attitudes toward pilfering and work group norms in a modern industrial plant. In E. O. Smigel and H. L. Ross (eds.), *Crime Against Bureaucracy*. New York: Van Nostrand Reingold.

Kemper, T. D. 1966. Representative roles and the legitimization of deviance. *Social Problems* 13, 288–98.

Lerner, M. J. 1975. The justice motive in social behavior: An introduction. *Journal of Social Issues* 31, 1–20.

Lerner, M. J. 1977a. The justice motive: Some hypotheses as to its origins and forms. *Journal of Personality* 45, 1–52.

Lerner, M. J. 1977b. The justice motive in social behavior: Hypotheses as to its origin and forms, II. Research Grant Proposal to the Canada Council.

Lerner, M. J. and L. A. Whitehead. 1980. Procedural justice viewed in the context of justice motive theory. In G. Mikula (ed.), *Justice and Social Interaction*. New York: Springer-Verlag.

Lerner, M. J., D. T. Miller, and J. G. Holmes. 1976 Deserving and the emergence of forms of justice. In L. Berkowitz and E. Walster (eds.), *Advances in Experimental Social Psychology*, vol. 9. New York: Academic.

Levi, M. 1983. Review of Cheats at Work. *Journal of Social Policy* 12, 583–84.

Mangione, Thomas W. and Robert P. Quinn. 1975. Job satisfaction, counter-productive behavior and drug use at work. *Journal of Applied Psychology* 60, 114–16.

Mars, G. 1973. Hotel pilferage: A case study in occupational theft. In M. Warner (ed.), *The Sociology of the Work Place*. New York: Halstead.

Mars, G. 1974. Dock Pilferage. In P. Rock and M. McIntosh (eds.) *Deviance and Social Control*. London: Tavistock.

Mars, G. 1983. *Cheats at Work: An Anthropology of Workplace Crime*. London: Unwin.

Martin, J. 1986. When expectations and justice do not coincide: blue-collar visions of a just world. In H. Bierhoff, R. L. Cohen and J. Greenberg (eds.), *Justice in Social Relations*. New York: Plenum.

Merton, R. K. 1968. *Social Theory and Social Structure*. New York: Free Press.

Mills, C. W. 1940. Situated actions and vocabularies of motive. In I. Horowitz (ed.), *People, Power, and Politics*. New York: Oxford University Press.

Moore, B. 1978. *Injustice: The Social Basis of Obedience and Revolt*. White Plains, N.Y.: M. E. Sharpe.

Pahl, R. E. 1983. Review of Cheats at Work. *British Journal of Criminology* 23, 294–95.

Peterson, V. W. 1947. Why honest people steal. *Journal of Criminal Law and Criminology* 38, 94–103.

Quinney, R. 1977. *Class, State and Crime*. New York: McKay.

Robin, G. D. 1967. *Employees as Offenders*. Report for National Analysis, 1967.

Ross, I. 1961. Thievery in the plant. *Fortune* 64, 139–43.

Sieh, E. W. 1987. Garment workers: Perception of inequity and employee theft. *British Journal of Criminology* 27, 174–90.

Snizek, W. E. 1974. Deviant behavior among blue-collar worker-employees: Work-norm violations in the factory. In C. D. Bryant (ed.), *Deviant Behavior*. Chicago: Rand McNally.

Stoddard, E. 1968. The informal code of police deviance: A group approach to blue-coat crime. *Journal of Criminal Law, Criminology and Police Science* 59, 201–13.

Sutherland, E. and D. R. Cressey. 1978. *Criminology*. New York: Lippincott.

Sykes, G. and D. Matza. 1957. Techniques of neutralization: A theory of delinquency. *American Sociological Review* 22, 664–70.

U.S. Chamber of Commerce. 1974. *White-Collar Crime*. Washington: Chamber of Commerce.

Walster, E., E. Berscheid, and G. W. Walster. 1973. New directions in equity research. *Journal of Personality and Social Psychology* 25, 151–56.

# 6

# Alcohol and Theories of Homicide

*Robert Nash Parker*

In his landmark study of the social and behavioral aspects of homicide, Marvin Wolfgang reports that 64 percent of homicide offenders and victims he studied had been drinking alcohol (1958). With the reporting of this fact, long known to those with direct law enforcement experience with homicide and other forms of violence, the important role of alcohol in violent behavior was acknowledged in the research literature. However, nearly twenty-five years later, one researcher wrote that "The results of Wolfgang's (1958) research on 588 cases of homicide in Philadelphia . . . are typical" (Collins 1981, 290). Wolfgang's Philadelphia study was landmark in part because it stimulated a great deal of research into the causes of homicide, as represented in a number of empirical studies (Hackney 1968; Gastil 1971; Loftin and Hill 1974; Luckenbill 1977; Parker and Smith 1979; Blau and Blau 1982; Messner 1982; Doerner 1983; Bailey 1984; Williams 1984; Huff-Corzine et al. 1986; Sampson 1987; Williams and Flewelling 1988; Parker 1989) and the development of at least four major theories:[1] subculture of violence (Wolfgang and Ferricuti 1967), economic deprivation (Loftin and Hill 1974; Braithwaite 1979), deterrence theory, especially involving capital punishment (Sellin 1967; Erlich 1975; Phillips 1980; Blumstein et al., 1978), and routine activity or life-style theory (Hindelang et al. 1978; Cohen and Felson, 1979; Cohen et al. 1981). However, none of the empirical studies cited nor any of the four

**113**

theories deal with the role which alcohol might play in the genesis or explanation of homicide.

This paper addresses this disjunction between this observed relationship and theoretical/empirical research on homicide by specifying the manner in which alcohol as a concept might fit into these four theories, and to propose some hypotheses based on this theoretical integration. The kinds of data necessary to test some of these hypotheses will also be described. In pursuing this effort, some aspects of the typology for theory construction outlined by Pernanen (1981) are utilized, particularly with regard to the discussion below concerning the possible relationships (or lack of relationships) that exist between alcohol and other major concepts in these four theories of homicide.

What possible roles could alcohol play in the genesis of homicide? Although alcohol could be directly related to homicide, most reviews of alcohol research and crime reject this type of direct effects model as unlikely because of the simplistic model of causation it implies (Collins 1981, xiii; Pernanen 1981). As these authors note, however, there is very little direct evidence from research in which alcohol consumption is measured and included in the analysis along with measures representing the concepts found in most theories of crime causation. The possibility exists alcohol may have a direct effect on homicide even when other important variables are controlled for in a statistical sense. Although the likelihood of such a finding may be small, and the effects found would be small, their import for social theory and public policy would be substantial because alcohol is a state-regulated commodity. Substantial impetus for control of alcohol and, explicitly, for the reduction of alcohol consumption, already exists in the context of attempts to reduce drunk driving (see Jacobs 1989). If alcohol consumption were found to have important direct effects on homicide independent of other major predictors, the politically potent efforts directed towards the reduction of drunk driving could result in a reduction in homicide rates. Thus, alcohol may present a unique situation for attempts to utilize public policy to control interpersonal violence, as it is a politically viable, socially acceptable, and practically achievable means of reducing homicide by reducing alcohol consumption. This contrasts markedly with the policy situation of previously identified important causes of homicide like poverty, regional subcultures, or social disorganization (see Land et al., 1990).

A second and more likely role for alcohol in the causation of homicide is that alcohol could mediate or intervene between homicide and its other major causes. In an example to be discussed below in greater detail, it could be that alcohol helps to explain the often cited relationshipship between geographic region and homicide rates. Living in the South may lead to a distinct pattern of alcohol consumption, which in turn could help to explain that region's traditionally high homicide rates. This sort of model implies that once alcohol consumption has been controlled for, the direct relationship between regional location and homicide disappears.[2] Although such an argument suggest a direct relationship between alcohol and homicide, this type of effect can only be understood in terms of a fully specified theoretical model. This suggests an important conceptual distinction between the simple direct effects discussed above and the role of alcohol as an intervening variable in a causal process. This distinction has little or no impact on the interpretation of the effect of alcohol on homicide, but it may have a great deal to do with understanding of the effects of regional subculture, poverty, deterrence, or life-style on homicide, as the impact of the former on the latter may change from direct to indirect in the context of a fully specified model in which alcohol is an intervening variable.

A third possible role for alcohol is an interactive one, in which alcohol is related to other important causal factors. In this type of relationship, alcohol changes the way in which other variables effect homicide. An example of this type of relationship involves the possibility that alcohol changes the way poverty is related to homicide. This relationship, the subject of considerable controversy in criminology (see Messner 1982, 1983b; Parker 1989; Land, et al., 1990), is often found to be an important one in statistical analyses. It may be that alcohol consumption and poverty rates interact, such that the positive association between poverty and homicide often reported in the literature would decrease in magnitude if a location also had lower rates of alcohol consumption. On the other hand, if a similar location had very high rates of alcohol consumption, the presence of a relatively large poor population might be even more strongly associated with high homicide rates. Notice that if alcohol is excluded from the model, the high poverty, high consumption and high homicide rate places, and the high poverty, low consumption, and low homicide rate places are averaged, producing the reasonably strong association often observed. The association between homicide and poverty would be much higher in the high consumption places and much lower in the low consumption places. Although these sorts of relationships are often difficult to find empirical evidence for, they can provide the most interesting and substantively important findings; consider the impact on targeting of intervention programs designed to reduce alcohol related problems if empirical support could be found for the hypothesized interaction described here.

A final possibility considered here is that alcohol and homicide are in fact *not* related, that the evidence amassed thus far in support of this relationship is spurious in nature. The sort of model that this notion implies, referred to as a common cause model by Pernanen (1981), specifies that alcohol and homicide appear to be related because of the influence of some third variable that has been excluded unintentionally from consideration. This approach emphasizes the difference between association and causality, a distinction that is next to impossible to make without fully specified theories. One example could involve economic deprivation, a concept found to be important in a number of prior studies of homicide. Perhaps the frustration which results from severe deprivation leads both to increased alcohol consumption and to increased rates of violence. In this example, economic deprivation acts in the role of the common cause or third variable, and when the impact of this variable is accounted for in an empirically estimated model, the relationship between alcohol and homicide vanishes.

Additional evidence from criminological ethnographies and biographies suggests some support for the general notion that alcohol use and criminal activity are not related (see Collins, 1981, for a review). Offenders often report that use of alcohol and criminal activity are incidental to one another, such that both occur in socially defined situations in which conventional expectations for behavior have been removed or modified. In this case it could be argued that the excluded variable is the existence of a "time out" from the usual normative conventions, which produces both criminal behavior and alcohol consumption. It might be difficult to measure an excluded variable of this type, but this model again implies that if one could do so, evidence for a relationship between alcohol and crime would disappear.

Despite the logical case that could be made for this latter alternative, I will not consider the notion that the alcohol/homicide relationship is spurious in this essay. First, the theoretical analyses presented below lead to a very different conclusions for all four of the theories of homicide causation considered here. Second, if a well-specified theory can be presented that purports to account for the relationships among alcohol, homicide, and other important concepts, the best way to find support for the notion that the theory is false and that the relationship of interest is indeed spurious is to empirically test the theory. Since this latter effort is the next step in the larger project in which I am engaged, I shall defer consideration of the spuriousness explanation until empirical analyses based on the theoretical arguments presented here can be undertaken.

The remainder of this essay will be devoted to the presentation of summaries of each of the four theories. As each theory is presented, arguments as to how and where alcohol might relate to important concepts in the theory, are presented, leading to a conceptual model that will be specified and discussed. Finally, the kinds of data required to test the models derived from each theory will be described. However, before this discussion can proceed, a metatheoretical assumption which underlies this discussion must be made explicit.

## The Disinhibition Approach and Violence

What is the general impact that alcohol has on human behavior? One answer to this question, which has been thoroughly discussed in the alcohol research literature, is the disinhibition approach (Room and Collins 1983). The disinhibition approach suggests that in general the impact of alcohol on behavior is to remove the effect of social inhibitions which might otherwise restrict or prohibit behaviors that run contrary to important social norms. Although it could certainly be argued that violence falls into this proscribed category, the underlying assumption made here is somewhat different. Despite the existence of moral, religious, and legal arguments and statutes to the contrary, there is plenty of evidence that violence has widespread normative support in Western culture. The popularity of violent professional sports, violent television programs and movies, books that portray extreme forms of violence, and evidence from research on topics such as family violence (Straus 1980) all contribute to the notion that violence is normatively supported in American society. Norms vary in the degree to which institutional support exists for their enforcement and for the application of sanctions to violators. In situations of normative conflict, alcohol can be seen as a disinhibitor of those norms with the *weakest* institutional support. In the case of conflicting norms of interpersonal violence, the institutional structures that support norms of violence are much stronger and more established than that which supports norms against such violence; compare the popularity and economic importance of violent professional and nonprofessional sports like football with the difficulties women have had in establishing the legal right to defend thatselves against physically abusive male partners (for a discussion of the latter, see Browne and Williams 1989). The disinhibiting effect of alcohol on norms that proscribe violence is an important assumption on which this discussion is based and, as such, is exogenous to the theories to be developed here. This assumption means that the general role of alcohol in violent behavior is to *enhance* the rate of violence (Stets 1990; Fagan 1990).

## Economic Deprivation, Homicide, and Alcohol

Socioeconomic approaches focus on the economic structure of society and the disadvantaged position that many individuals find themselves in. The theoretical link between homicide and poverty is based on two distinct but related conceptions of poverty and its impact. Relative deprivation is seen by many (Merton 1957; Box 1971; Gordon 1973; Braithwaite 1979; Blau and Blau 1982) as the mechanism whereby poverty leads to crime. This approach suggests that some individuals evaluate their socioeconomic position in relative terms and are bothered by the perception that others have more desired social and economic resources. Frustration develops as a result of this evaluation process because individuals come to believe there is little they can do to improve their relative standing. It is out of this frustration that violence can arise. Violence is not directed at those at the source of the frustration, such as employers or those who are perceived as being better off, but rather at those who happen to be within range of the frustrated and relatively deprived individual, such as friends, spouses, and co-workers. The latter become targets because the real causes of frustration are inaccessible to the offender, and/or too powerful to be attacked with impunity.

The second variant of the poverty-violence link suggests that absolute deprivation in and of itself can lead to violence. Perhaps violence is one of the few options available to those without the economic means to deal with problems and crises of everyday life. Absolute deprivation may also produce emotional situations that escalate into violence, again directed at those close at hand, spouses, children, friends, and so on. Simply put, the absolute deprivation approach suggests that violence can occur among such individuals because everyday life is difficult to deal with. Early conflict approaches identified such a link (Engels 1969; Bonger 1916), and more recent discussions have also suggested the importance of absolute deprivation (e.g., Rainwater 1974). Recent studies of nonlethal family violence have also suggested the importance of absolute deprivation: unemployment of the male spouse and marital instability, factors which are related to absolute deprivation, have been found to be related to assaults within the family (Straus 1980; Coleman and Straus 1986).

What role does alcohol consumption play in the deprivation/homicide relationship? One possibility is that alcohol consumption interacts with deprivation in the causation of homicide. Considering the absolute variant first, research on the relationship between income and consumption (see Gruenewald 1988, for a review) shows that alcohol consumption is elastic with income, that is, as income declines, consumption declines.[3] However, prices also play an important role, so that consumption increases with declining price. Despite the seeming contradiction, consumption could be relatively high despite widespread poverty if relative prices are low or declining. If alcohol serves to enhance violence, the effect of poverty on homicide would be greatest where alcohol consumption is also highest, that is, where prices are low. If alcohol consumption were low because of high prices or some other factor, the poverty/homicide relationship might disappear or turn negative, since poverty rates might remain constant while homicide could decline to zero, forcing a negative relationship between poverty and homicide. In this case the pattern of alcohol consumption and its relationship to prices conditions the way in which poverty and homicide are related.

Considering the relative deprivation variant, alcohol might play an intervening role. Inequality is seen as leading to frustration, a factor which could increase alcohol consumption. The income/consumption relationship is not relevant here because inequality can occur regardless of the absolute level of income. If inequality leads to higher consumption, increased homicide rates could have been found to be associated with inequality in prior research (Blau and Blau 1982) because alcohol consumption increased, leading to increased homicide rates. The direct relationship between inequality and homicide would disappear in this case. Figures 6.1 and 6.2 summarize these predictions.

### Subcultures of Violence: Southerners and Blacks

Subculture-of-violence approaches focus on the diversity of cultural and normative behavior and expectations existing at any one time in a large, diverse society. This diversity suggests that certain groups may exist in which members may commit homicide as a legitimate alternative dispute resolution method. The notion that there exists a subculture in American society in which the use of violence is a legitimate means of interaction and problem-solving was most fully developed by Wolfgang and Feracuti (1967). Their argument is that among a certain segment of the population, values are held that legitimate the use of violence in some social situations. The origin of such values may be situational, that is, individuals may develop and adhere to such values because their lives involve situations in which violence is seen as a survival strategy or as a more viable option for attaining desired goals than nonviolence.

**FIGURE 6.1**
**Absolute Deprivation and Alcohol**

**6.1A**
**Poverty and Homicide**

**6.1B**
**Poverty, Alcohol, High Prices, and Homicide**

**6.1C**
**Poverty, Alcohol, High Prices, and Homicide**

**FIGURE 6.2**
**Relative Deprivation and Alcohol**

**6.2A**
**Inequality and Homicide**

**6.2B**
**Inequality, Alcohol, and Homicide**

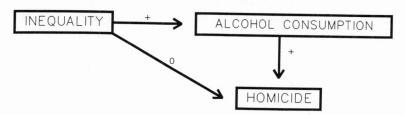

Alternatively, such values may be transmitted intergenerationally through socialization. In addition, an interaction may take place between the situation and prior socialization, so that a person whose socialization might predispose him/her towards the selection of violence in a situation may only do so in certain kinds of situations—situations in which violence is perceived as necessary for survival, thus reinforcing values learned during socialization.

In the United States the focus of empirical investigations of the existence of violent subcultures has focused on two elements of the population: southerners and blacks. Historical evidence links the development of a subculture of violence for both these subgroups with the institution of slavery, and post-Civil War accommodations to the de jure elimination of the slave-based economic system of this region. Two influential studies that make this argument with particular regard to homicide are those of Gastil (1971) and Hackney (1968), which present evidence of a link between state homicide rates and measures of regional location or the degree to which a state's population had southern origins. Despite a number of studies which have failed to find empirical support for this notion (see Sampson 1987; Parker 1989 for reviews), researchers continued to be struck by the plausibility of the Gastill-Hackney thesis applied to both the south and to black urban populations. In addition, researchers continue to find empirical evidence in support of the Gastill-Hackney argument, using variations in the time period analyzed (1960, 1970, or 1980 data have been used) and the exact specifications of independent variables included in the model. Messner (1982) suggests that poverty has a negative impact on homicide, while in another article this same author suggests (Messner 1983a) that poverty has no impact on homicide; in both cases it is suggested that subculture is the dominant predictor of homicide rates. In a third article, Messner (1983b) also find that poverty has a positive impact on homicide, but that so do subcultural indicators, a finding contrary to that presented by Loftin and Hill (1974). Huff-Corzine et al. (1986) also find that both theories are supported.

Evidence from research into regional differences in drinking patterns suggests that southern region/homicide relationship may be explained in terms of the nature and pattern of southern drinking. This evidence suggests that although overall southern rates of alcohol consumption are lower than other regions in the U.S., southerners who do drink alcohol have significantly higher rates of consumption than those from other parts of the country (Room 1983; National Institute on Alcohol Abuse and Alcoholism 1985, 1987). These data suggest that southern drinking patterns differ from those in other regions, even though the South contains a greater number of abstainers, and therefore a lower overall rate of consumption. If this pattern of southern drinking involves relatively high consumption per setting, in social situations, as the data suggest, this would not only be consistent with the situation of one relatively important category of homicide, acquaintance killing acquaintance in a public or semipublic setting, but it would also represent direct evidence of a cultural difference between the south and other regions. It is this kind of direct cultural indicator that is almost universally missing from empirical research on the impact of subculture on violence. In this case, not only does alcohol as a concept lead to gains in the understanding of the causes of homicide, but it also helps to provide a more appropriate test of subculture of violence theory on its own terms. Alcohol plays the role of an intervening variable in this argument, and as such the direct association between region and homicide would disappear if alcohol consumption per drinker is interposed between these two indicators; this hypothesis is summarized in figure 6.3.

Arguments concerning the role alcohol may play vis-à-vis a black subculture of violence are necessarily complicated by evidence concerning drinking patterns by race and by theoretical and empirical evidence on the racial composition/homicide relationship. Research on racial differences in drinking patterns has typically shown that whites drink more than blacks, although there is evidence of an interaction by socioeconomic characteristics. Lower-class black drinking patterns, as reported in ethnographies (see Roizen 1981 for a review), may be more problematic than the sort of drinking behavior engaged in by more affluent blacks, with the former involving heavy weekend binge drinking (Cahalan and Room 1974; Samuels 1976). In addition, recent evidence from a national survey which contained an oversampling of black respondents suggests an inverse relationship between income and drinking, such that for respondents whose incomes were less than 15,000 per year, 17.9

**FIGURE 6.3**
**Regional Subculture and Alcohol**

**6.3A**
**Region and Homicide**

**6.3B**
**Region, Drinking Patterns, and Homicide**

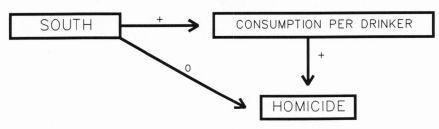

percent of black respondents and 15.8 percent of white respondents reported being heavy drinkers, while in this same income group 21.9 percent of the blacks and 15.5 percent of the whites reported frequent consumption of large amounts of alcohol. Among those with greater than 15,000 incomes, the same percentages were, heavy drinkers, 12.4 percent for blacks and 20.8 percent for whites, and 13.3 percent blacks in the frequent high category, as compared with 19.8 percent of whites (Herd 1989, 31). The race-income-drinking problem patterns showed similar variation: self reported drinking related problems increased among whites as income went up, while the opposite pattern was found among blacks (Herd 1989, 38).[4]

These results suggest the possibility that alcohol consumption intervenes between a racial composition/social class interaction and homicide. If a place has a larger population of lower class or poor blacks, consumption should be elevated, resulting in higher rates of homicide. If a substantial affluent black population resides in a particular place, however, consumption rates should be lower, thus producing lower homicide rates. Once again, alcohol intervenes between other variables of interest in this theory and homicide, explicating the way these variables lead to homicide. These hypotheses are displayed in figure 6.4.

## Capital Punishment and Deterrence

A third approach, made more popular by the conservative political and social shift that has occurred in recent years, has links to the economic philosophers of the Enlightenment such as Jeremy Bentham (Geis 1973) as well as to more modern theories such as Skinner's behaviorism (Braukmann 1975). This approach focuses on the relationship between rates of crime and rates of punishment, arguing in particular that the death penalty is a real deterrent to murder in those places were it is carried out with appropriate frequency and speed. As with the previously discussed theories, research has led to increased rather than decreased controversy about the impact of the death penalty on rates of homicide, with a number of contradictory studies appearing in the past thirty years (Sellin 1967; Ehrlich 1975; Bowers and Pierce 1975; Archer and Gartner 1984). During this period, the U.S. has moved from a relatively high level of executions during the 1950s to a decline in the 1960s ending in the virutal halt of executions into the early

**FIGURE 6.4**
**Racial Subculture and Alcohol**

**6.4A**
**Racial Composition and Homicide**

**6.4B**
**Race, Social Class, Alcohol, and Homicide**

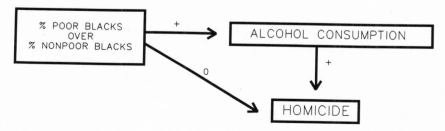

1970s, to a revival of executions during the late 1970s and into the 1980s.

The deterrence approach specifically links the observed rates of any offense such as homicide to the actions taken by authorities to punish those who have committed the offense. Discussions of deterrence theory often involve distinctions among at least four aspects of capital punishment: (1) certainty, or the likelihood that an offender will be executed (indicated by the number of executions divided by the number of murders); (2) severity, or the relationship between those executed and those who receive alternative punishments for murder (indicated by executions per prisoner in the penal system serving time for this offense); (3) celerity, or the length of time between conviction and execution; (4) public knowledge of the execution (see Archer and Gartner 1984, 121). If certainty, severity (more executions per prisoner) and public knowledge are high (or higher if one jurisdiction is compared to another), and if the application of the punishment is swift (celerity), homicide rates should reflect these facts by exhibiting low rates or lower rates over time as deterrence is increased (Ehrlich 1975; Phillips 1980). Most studies have failed to find such an effect, and in some cases homicides were seen to increase following executions (Bowers and Pierce 1980; Sellin 1967; Schuessler 1952; Bailey 1975).

There are at least two distinct approaches to integrating alcohol conceptually with deterrence theory. First, from a sociolegal control point of view, the willingness to have a capital punishment statute in a particular locality, and the further willingness to actually implement such a law via executions, reflects a tendency in favor of strong social control by government of individual behavior. Strict control of alcohol sales and distribution can also be seen in this same light. If both capital punishment and alcohol control are related to an underlying dimension of social control, their joint presence in a community could lead to an enhanced effect of social control such that the presence of one type of control enhances the impact of the other. Therefore, if a locality has both types of laws, we would expect the lowest rates of homicide; in those places where neither law exists, the highest homicide rates could be expected. Places in between, with one form of social control and not the other, should have intermediate levels of homicide. These predictions also represent interactions of alcohol control with capital punishment, as displayed in figure 6.5.

A second approach to the relationship between deterrence and alcohol looks to the internal logic of deterrence theory. Deterrence theory is based on a "rational choice" perspective (Piliavin et al. 1986; Hector 1987) and, as such, depends on the ability of individuals to reliably calculate the relative values of rewards and punishments (as well as the likelihood of each) for any contemplated action. Alcohol consumption can be seen as interacting with the deterrent effect of capital punishment, as it would affect the ability of actors to calculate rationally. This leads to the prediction that in places with capital punishment and high levels of consumption, deterrence theory would be short circuited, resulting in little or no deterrent effect of capital punishment and perhaps higher homicide rates. In places where capital punishment and low levels of con-

**FIGURE 6.5**
**Capital Punishment and Alcohol Regulation**

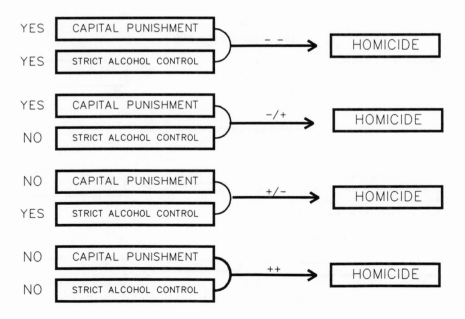

sumption exist, the deterrent effect would be more likely to operate, thus leading to lower homicide rates. Here alcohol changes the causal process by which deterrence is related to homicide, as shown in figure 6.6.

## Life-Style and Routine Activities

Finally, an approach that focuses on the patterns of late twentieth-century life, referred to alternatively as the "routine activity" approach (Cohen and Felson 1979) or the "life-style" approach (Hindelang et al. 1978), has become the focus of many recent efforts to understand violence in general and homicide in particular. This approach suggests that we should expect increasing rates of violence because the pace, tempo, and style in which people live has increased their exposure to potential violence and at the same time reduced the ability of traditional guardians to protect people

**FIGURE 6.6**
**Deterrence Theory and Alcohol Consumption**

**6.6A**
**Deterrence and Homicide**

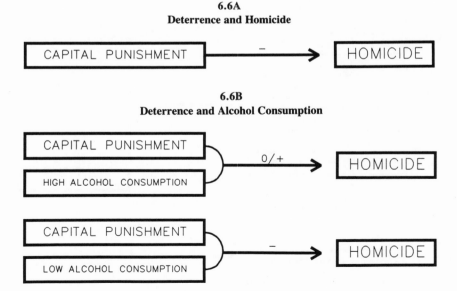

**6.6B**
**Deterrence and Alcohol Consumption**

from such behavior. Cohen and Felson (1979) look at the decreasing size of households, the increasing propensity of people to live alone, the increase in nighttime activities outside of the home such as eating, seeking entertainment, and doing life maintenance activities such as laundry and shopping. In addition, they point to the increased likelihood that families are composed of two wage earners and will thus have increased financial resources to pursue such activities.

This approach suggests that the causes of homicide as well as other offenses may be independent of the social, cultural, economic, and legal contexts of behavior stressed in the three previously discussed approaches. Hindelang et al. (1978) and Cohen and Felson (1979; see also Cohen et al. 1981) have argued that increased in homicide may be explained by social and economic trends that bring together suitable targets, that is, potential victims, motivated offenders, and an absence of effective guardians to protect such targets (Sampson 1987). Cohen and Felson (1979, 600–1) define a household activity ratio, essentially measuring the number of household in the U.S. that are likely to be unoccupied during the day and be composed of members who spend substantial amounts of time away from home. They argue that increases in this indicator reflect life-style changes that have resulted in higher crime rates. They also indicate that this measure is related to such trends as increases in married females being employed outside the home, durable and portable consumer goods distributed in the population, and higher volume of retail and wholesale business. Their findings for the U.S. as a whole show a significant relationship between this ratio and the homicide rate for the period 1947–1974 (1979, 603).

The key to understanding how alcohol is related to routine activities depends on the role alcohol plays in those activities. Routine activities theory directs attention to where an activity like alcohol consumption takes place, and under what circumstances. If most drinking takes place in bars, restaurants, and other public places, this behavior is likely to be part of a set of routine activities that involve going out of the house, often at night, for leisure related pursuits. Nighttime activity is a key indicator in tests of routine activity theory, and it has been found to be an important predictor of victimization (Sampson and Woolridge 1987; Miethe et al. 1987).

Therefore higher rates of consumption in on site facilities like bars and restaurants should lead to higher rates of homicide as more people would be exposing themselves to risk with higher levels of nighttime activity related to alcohol consumption. If, on the other hand, alcohol consumption is done mostly at home, this would imply less exposure to risk of homicide, due to lower levels of nighttime activity related to alcohol consumption.[5] In this case, patterns of alcohol consumption can be seen as indicators of routine activity, the major concept of interest in this approach and, as such, alcohol consumption patterns are predicted to cause homicide rates indirectly, via nighttime activity outside the home.[6] Figure 6.7 displays this hypothesis.

The project of theoretically integrating alcohol into four major theories of homicide has yielded a number of hypotheses suitable for empirical testing. If supported, a number of these hypotheses would lead to increased understanding of the causes of homicide, settle disputes in the existing literature, and/or clarify how and why some of the major concepts of interest in these theories might lead to homicide. However, in order to actually test these hypotheses,

**FIGURE 6.7**
**Routine Activity and Alcohol Consumption**

**6.7A**
**Routine Activity and Homicide**

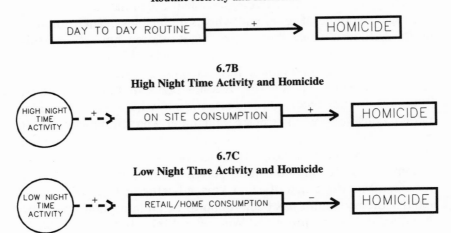

**6.7B**
**High Night Time Activity and Homicide**

**6.7C**
**Low Night Time Activity and Homicide**

certain kinds of data on alcohol consumption, prices, and regulation must be merged with other sources for the independent variables in the four theories as well as with homicide data. The remainder of this essay outlines specifically the kinds of data that are required in order to appropriately test the causal linkages discussed here and given in figures 6.1 through 6.7.

## Data Requirements for Testing Alcohol Integrated Theories of Homicide

Specific data requirements for the empirical evaluation of the hypotheses generated from this theoretical analysis will vary with the nature of the theory and specific hypothesis being tested. However, I believe that some general principles can be described that will provide a context within which the attempt at theoretical integration made in this paper can be more appropriately evaluated. In general, the most fruitful analyses will be those that attempt to contrast hypotheses derived from two or more of the theories analyzed here. Much of the reasoning within each of the four theories involves the construction of an alternative explanation of homicide, alternative to one or more of the other theories in particular (in which case the contrast is made explicit) or to other theories in general. Although it is important to evaluate theories in terms of their own internal logic, the explicit and implicit opposition of these theories suggests that a great deal about homicide may be learned by attempting to contrast these theories empirically. This approach makes the empirical effort contemplated here all the more complex, but the potential theoretical and empirical payoffs of such an approach make the attempt worthy of the effort involved. Within this framework, three general principles can be identified which will guide efforts to secure the necessary data for multiple theory testing.

First, the data bases required for this effort should be dynamic in nature, to the degree that is possible. Dynamic models offer a number of advantages for theory testing over wholly static or cross-sectional designs. All of the concepts of interest in the theories analyzed here have shown wide variation during the last four decades in the U.S., and this is also the case with alcohol consumption. In order to empirically test whether or not two concepts are related, measures of those concepts must vary across the units or cases analyzed. At any one time point, one or more of the measures typically utilized to measure concepts such as alcohol consumption, poverty, or routine activities may show restricted variance, making it difficult at best to understand the manner in which these concepts help to explain variation in homicide rates. By constructing dynamic models, which require data on units analyzed over time, one can guard against the limited variability shown by these concepts at any particular time point.

A second argument in favor of dynamic models is that the theoretical process by which the relationship in question is thought to operate is inherently a dynamic one. For example, in figure 6.1, the hypothesized relationship between prices and consumption is inherently dynamic; adjustments in prices result in differing levels of consumption over time. Similarly, in figure 6.6, the deterrent effect of capital punishment on homicide is thought to operate cumulatively over time, that is, deterrent effects of this sanction occur because of a pattern of sanction application over time which is disseminated to and understood by potential offenders. In either case it does not make sense to analyze these relationships at a particular time point only.

Most statistical approaches designed to analyze dynamic data require relatively long time series or frequent observations in time, or both. Although it may be possible in some of the models specified in figures 6.1 through 6.7 to obtain series with fifty or more observations, this is a severe limitation for measures of most of the concepts discussed here. However, in some cases it is possible and even desirable to combine dynamic data with static data from a number of units cross-sectionally arrayed, thus gaining the advantages of dynamic models without having to meet the usual data requirements. Combining data types in this manner presents special problems for statistical analysis, but solutions to these problems are available (Stimson 1985).

A second guiding criteria in the building of data bases to test theories concerning the relationship between alcohol and homicide is that data from the smallest aggregated units of analysis will be sought. In general it is desirable to analyze data from units that are as homogeneous as possible in all characteristics unmeasured in the model being tested. This helps to minimize the possibility that an unmeasured but important variable exists that varies by unit and that would, if included in the model, have an important impact on the relationships estimated. If the units are largely homogeneous except in those ways that are directly measured in the analysis, it is less likely that such an important excluded variable exists. The aggregated units often analyzed in studies of homicide and alcohol, such as states or entire countries, are often very heterogeneous, suggesting that the possibility of bias from excluded variables and from the aggregation process itself is greater than is desirable. Aggregate units such as metropolitan areas, counties, and cities are smaller and more homogeneous (although by no means perfectly so) and data from such units will be examined where possible.

In addition to minimizing bias from various sources, the use of smaller aggregated units provides additional benefits as well. Multicollinearity has often plagued research on homicide, especially those studies based on the deprivation and/or subcultural perspectives. Measures of concepts such as poverty, inequality, and subcultural membership have often been found to be highly correlated, thus creating statistical problems for the estimation of the independent contribution of such measures to an explanation of homicide. However, this problem is most acute with more highly aggregated units; analyzing data from a larger number of less aggregated units corresponds to the classic "econometric" solution to multicollinearity problems, which is to find additional observations in which the relationship in question is less collinear (Johnston 1972; Parker 1985; Parker and Toth 1990). Analyses based on the deprivation and subculture perspectives as displayed in figures 6.1 through 6.4 would benefit from lower levels of multicollinearity; all of the models discussed here would benefit from less bias due to aggregation or heterogeneity.

In practice, most of the data required to test the proposed theoretical relationships will be available at higher levels of aggregation such as states or SMSAs. Some of the data to be sought for this project will be available at more than one level of aggregation, and in some cases it makes sense to take advantage of this availability and conduct multilevel analyses. For example, the deterrence relationships displayed in figures 6.5 and 6.6 can be conceptualized in multilevel terms. In the U.S. it is the states that determine whether or not capital punishment will be available to local juries, prosecutors, and judges for implementation. Similarly, in many cases states set the limits of alcohol regulation, and localities can either enforce such regulation strictly or loosely; in some cases localities may have "options" within the overall regulatory climate established by state statute. In those cases where multilevel analysis is possible and theoretically interesting, data for such models will be collected.

Finally, multiple measures of the concepts of interest are desirable and will be sought. Multiple measures of concepts are desirable because of the increased reliability gained with their use. All of the measures available for the concepts of interest here are fallible; dependence on only one measure of any concept is a recipe for disaster. The importance of multiple measures of homicide and poverty in the context of theory testing has already been demonstrated (Parker 1985; Parker 1989). A number of regional subcultural indicators have been used, and it may be possible to combine these into a more reliable measure (Gastil 1969; Hackney 1971; Huff-Corzine et al. 1986). Repeated measures of a concept taken over short periods of time can also be utilized to form more reliable measurement of the concept, for example, consumption or homicide rates from three consecutive time points (months, years, etc.) could be used to measure these two concepts more reliably than using any one of the three time points separately (Parker and McDowell 1986).

A second advantage of seeking to account for the multidimentionality of a concept through multiple measures is based on the fact that overall summary measures can often hide important variation. For example, in the state of California, overall consumption of alcohol declined from 3.25 gallons per capita in 1977 to 3.12 in 1986. However, if one examines the trends in beer, wine, and spirits consumption for this same period (these are the components of the overall consumption measure), three different patterns are revealed: wine consumption has gone up gradually (.67 to .79 gallons per capita), spirit consumption has declined sharply (1.28 to .97), and beer consumption has fluctuated around a mean of 1.37 per capita during this same period (Department of Alcohol and Drug Problems 1989). Disaggregated homicide rates by victim/offender relationship, circumstance, and weapon have also demonstrated similar variation (Parker and Colony 1987; Williams and Flewelling 1988; Parker 1989). Multiple measures of concepts used in the theories discussed here will be sought both in terms of measurement reliability and in this latter sense, which may be seen as an attempt to provide increased validity of measurement.

## Summary

Despite common knowledge about the relationship between alcohol and violence, and well-known research findings such as that of Wolfgang's (1958), social scientists have given precious little attention to this relationship. This paper has been an attempt to address this disjunction by examining four prominent theories of homicide and, through both deduction and induction, to bring alcohol as a concept into these theories. A number of testable hypotheses concerning the way alcohol relates to homicide and the major concepts in the four theories have been generated, and a general description of the sorts of data required to empirical evaluate these hypotheses has been provided. Even if every one of the hypotheses advanced about this relationship eventually proves to be empirically untenable, knowledge of how and why violence comes about will have been advanced. Other arguments concerning the way in which alcohol helps to explain violence can be advanced, and it is hoped that this effort will stimulate others to think both theoretically and empirically about this relationship. The analyses presented here also have implications for other important relationships, such as the connection between illegal drugs and violence, and it is also hoped that this effort will stimulate similar efforts focused on that potentially important relationship. Attempts to test these hypotheses, currently in progress, may also yield significant empirical knowledge. By most agreed upon standards of scholarship, then, this effort has been successful; it is hoped that this type of theoretical analysis will be applied to a wide variety of problems and issues in criminology in particular and social science in general.

I would like to thank Judy Gerson, Harold Holder, Robert Saltz, Joel Grube, Paul Gruenewald, Michael Hennessy, Robin Room, Andrew Treno, and Constance Weisner for comments on earlier versions of this paper, and the office staff (especially Jocelyn Wismar) of the Prevention Research Center, Berkeley, California, for their technical support, good humor, and their appreciation of good chocolate. Support for this research was provided by training grant #T32-AA07240 and by center grant, #AA-06282, both from the National Institute on Alcohol Abuse and Alcoholism. NIAAA does not necessarily endorse the analyses and conclusions herein, as these remain the responsibility of the author.

# Notes

1. This enumeration of theories is not meant to be exclusive, but is rather reflective of the bulk of extant research on the causes of homicide.
2. Although this relationship has been the subject of a large number of studies in the homicide literature, recent trends suggest that the South is no longer the region with the highest homicide rates. Since the beginning of the 1980s, the West has had higher overall rates of homicide (10.0 per 100,000 vs. 8.5 in 1985; Parker 1991; Loftin et al. 1990; cf. Land et al. 1990, whose data cover the period 1950 through 1980). More importantly, the hypothesis suggested here, which will be explicated theoretically later in this essay, shows the potential which alcohol has to clarify our understanding of the causes of violence. Empirically, the region/homicide relationship has generated considerable controversy as to its existence; introducing alcohol into theories and empirical models of homicide could provide a resolution to this important problem.
3. There is some evidence that those drinkers in the heaviest consumption categories may engage in substitution effects, such that as income declines a cheaper beverage is substituted, for example, beer is used instead of whiskey as income declines. However, the income/consumption relationship has been well documented in economic research on alcohol consumption (Gruenewald 1988).
4. Herd (1989) suggests that while black alcohol consumption is only somewhat higher than that for whites, blacks report many more drinking related problems than do whites because blacks may be attributing to alcohol problems which are caused by more fundamental structural problems like poverty, discrimination, lack of education and job opportunities, etc. This argument parallels that made by Sampson (1987), in which differences in black and white rates of violence disappear once the economic deprivation/crime relationship is specified completely. Sampson argues persuasively that higher rates of black violence have their roots in economic deprivation, not in a racially based subculture of violence.
5. The theoretical discussion contained here has been kept on the most abstract levels in order to achieve the most general integration of alcohol into the four theories of homicide. However, recent research on homicide has shown the importance of classifying homicide in terms of the prior victim/offender relationship (Parker 1989) and/or in terms of circumstance (Williams and Flewelling 1988). Particularly with regard to the routine activities approach, specific predictions linking routine alcohol-related activities with higher or lower rates of

specific types of homicide are evident. For example, higher rates of on site consumption are most likely to lead to increased rates of robbery homicide and homicides involving disagreements between acquaintances. Increased consumption of alcohol at home relative to other settings might decrease the risk of these types of homicides, but lead to increased risk of homicides involving spouses, lovers, and family members. Similar specifications can be made concerning the other theories as well, but these will be deferred until empirical testing of the hypotheses advanced here is conducted.

6. Nighttime activity, although a central concept in this agrument, cannot be measured at the aggregate level. However, surrogate measures can be entertained, such as the per capita rates of entertainment establishments, or even by using measures of negative outcomes tied to nighttime activity like single vehicle automobile crashes or emergency room admissions. Some care should be taken, however, as these latter measures are often used as surrogates for alcohol related outcomes. Any empirical analysis would need to explore a number of alternatives to measuring nighttime activity at the aggregate level.

# References

Archer, Dane and Rosemary Gartner. 1984. *Violence and Crime in Cross-National Perspective*. New Haven: Yale University Press, Chapter 6, "Homicide and the death penalty: a cross-national test of a deterrence hypothesis," pp. 118–139.

Bailey, William C. 1975. "Murder and the death penalty." *Journal of Criminal Law and Criminology* 65: 416–23.

Bailey, William C. 1984. "Poverty, inequality, and city homicide rates: some not so unexpected results." *Criminology* 22: 531–50.

Blau, Judith R. and Peter M. Blau. 1982. "The cost of inequality: metropolitan structure and violent crime." *American Sociological Review* 47: 114–29.

Blumstein, Alfred, Jacqueline Cohen, and Daniel Nagin, editors. 1978. *Deterrence and Incapacitation: Estimating the Effects of Criminal Sanctions on Crime Rates*. Washington, D.C.: National Academy of Sciences.

Bonger, W. 1916. *Criminality and Economic Conditions*. Boston: Little, Brown.

Bowers, William J. and Glenn L. Pierce. 1975. "The illusion of deterrence in Isaac Ehrlich's research on capital punishment." *Yale Law Journal* 85: 187–208.

Bowers, William J. and Glenn L. Pierce. 1980. "Deterrence or brutalization: what is the effect of executions?" *Crime and Delinquency* 26: 453–84.

Box, Steven. 1971. *Deviance, Reality, and Society*. London: Holt, Rinehart, and Winston.

Braithwaite, John. 1979. *Inequality, Crime, and Public Policy*. London: Routledge and Kegan Paul.

Braukmann, Curtis, 1975. "Behavioral approaches to treatment in the crime and delinquency field." *Criminology* 13: 299–31.

Browne, Angela and Kirk R. Williams. 1989. "Exploring the effect of resource availability and the likelihood of female-perpetrated homicides." *Law and Society Review* 23: 75–94.

Cahalan, D. and Robin Room. 1974. *Problem Drinking Among American Men*. New Brunswick, N.J.: Rutgers Center for Alcohol Studies.

Cohen, Lawrence E., and Marcus Felson. 1979. "Social change and crime rate trends: a routine activities approach." *American Sociological Review* 44: 588–607.

Cohen, Lawrence E., James Kluegal, and Kenneth Land. 1981. "Social inequality and predatory criminal victimization: an exposition and test of a formal theory." *American Sociological Review* 46: 505–524.

Coleman, Diane H. and Murray A. Straus. 1986. Marital power, conflict and violence. *Violence and Victims* 1: 139–53.

Collins, James J., Jr. 1981. "Alcohol use and criminal behavior: An empirical, theoretical, and methodological overview." In James J. Collins, Jr., ed., *Drinking and Crime*, 288–316. New York: The Guilford Press.

Department of Alcohol and Drug Problems. 1989. "Alcohol consumption-california and U.S." Research Activity Memorandum, vol. 8, no. 3, 6.

Doerner, William G. 1983. "Why does johnny reb die when shot? The impact of medical resources upon lethality." *Sociological Inquiry* 53: 1–15.

Ehrlich, Isaac. 1975. "The deterrent effect of capital punishment: a question of life and death." *American Economic Review* 65: 397–417.

Engels, Friedrich. [1845] 1969. *The Condition of the Working Class in England in 1844*. Harmonsworth, England: Penguin Books.

Fagan, Jeffrey. 1990. "Intoxication and aggression." In Michael Torny and James Q. Wilson, eds., *Drugs and Crime*, 241–320, vol. 13, Crime and Justice: A Review of Research. Chicago: University of Chicago Press.

Gastil, Raymond P. 1971. "Homicide and a regional culture of violence." *American Sociological Review* 36: 412–27.

Geis, Gilbert. 1973. "Jeremy Bentham." In Herman Mannheim, ed., *Pioneers in Criminology*, 57. Montclair, N.J.: Patterson Smith.

Gordon, David M. 1973. "Capitalism, class, and crime in America." *Crime and Delinquency* 19: 163–86.

Gruenewald, Paul. 1988. "Analytic Models of Alcohol Consumption: Static Models." Briefing Paper, no. 1. Berkeley, Cal.: Prevention Research Center.

Hackney, Sheldon. 1968. "Southern violence." In Hugh David Graham and Ted Robert Gurr, eds., *Violence in America*, 479–500. New York: Signet.

Herd, Denise. 1989. "The Epidemiology of Drinking Patterns and Alcohol Related Problems Among U.S. Blacks." In Alcohol Use Among U.S. Ethnic Minorities, 3–50. Rockville, Md.: NIAAA.

Hindelang, Michael, Michael Gottfredson, and James Garofalo. 1978. *Victims of Personal Crime: An Empirical Foundation for a Theory of Personal Victimization*. Cambridge, Mass.: Ballinger.

Huff-Corzine, Lin, Jay Corzine, and David Moore. 1986. "Southern exposure: deciphering the south's influence on homicide rates.'' *Social Forces* 64: 906–24.

Johnston, J. 1972. *Econometric Methods*. New York: McGraw-Hill.

Land, Kenneth C., Patricia L. McCall, and Lawrence E. Cohen. 1990. ''Structural covariates of homicide rates: are there invariances across time and social space?'' *American Journal of Sociology* 95: 922–63.

Loftin, Colin and Robert H. Hill. 1974. ''Regional subculture and homicide.'' *American Sociological Review* 39: 714–24.

Loftin, Colin, David McDowall, and Brian Wiersema. 1990. ''Homicide Trends in the United States, 1940–1987.'' Presented at the annual meeting of the American Society of Criminology, Baltimore.

Luckenbill, David F. 1977. ''Criminal homicide as a situated transaction.'' *Social Problems* 25, 176–86.

Miethe, Terance D., Mark S. Stafford, and J. Scott Long. 1987. ''Social differentiation in criminal victimization: a test of routine activities/ lifestyle theories.'' *American Sociological Review* 52: 184–94.

Merton, Robert K. 1957. *Social Theory and Social Structure*. Glencoe, Ill.: The Free Press.

Messner, Steven F. 1982. ''Poverty, inequality, and the urban homicide rate.'' *Criminology* 20: 103–14.

Messner, S. F. 1983a. ''Regional and racial effects on the urban homicide rate: The subculture of violence revisited.'' *American Journal of Sociology* 88, 997–1007.

Messner, S. F. 1983b. ''Regional differences in the economic correlates of the urban homicide rates: Some evidence on the importance of context.'' *Criminology* 21, 477–88.

National Institute on Alcohol Abuse and Alcoholism. 1985. ''U.S. apparent consumption of alcoholic beverages based on state sales, taxation, or receipt data.'' In *U.S. Alcohol Epidemiological Data Reference Manual*. Rockville, Md.: NIAAA.

National Institute on Alcohol Abuse and Alcoholism. 1987. *Alcohol and Health*. Rockville, Md.: NIAAA.

Parker, Robert Nash. 1985. ''Aggregation, ratio variables and measurement problems in criminological research.'' *Journal of Quantitative Criminology* 1: 269–80.

Parker, Robert Nash. 1989. ''Poverty, subculture of violence, and type of homicide.'' *Social Forces* 67: 983–1007.

Parker, Robert Nash. 1991. ''Violent crime.'' In Joseph F. Sheley, ed., *Criminology: A Contemporary Handbook,* 143–60. Belmont, Cal.: Wadsworth.

Parker, Robert Nash and M. Dwayne Smith. 1979. ''Deterrence, poverty, and type of homicide.'' *American Journal of Sociology* 85: 614–24.

Parker, Robert Nash and David McDowall. 1986. ''Constructing an index of officially recorded crime: the use of confirmatory factor analysis.'' *Journal of Quantitative Criminology* 2: 289–308.

Parker, Robert Nash and Catherine J. Colony. 1987. ''Relationships, Homicides, and Weapons: A Detailed Analysis.'' Presented at the Annual Meetings of the American Society of Criminology, November, Montreal.

Parker, Robert Nash and Allison M. Toth. 1990. "Family, intimacy, and homicide: A macro-social approach." *Violence and Victims* 5: 195–210.

Pernanen, Kai. 1981. "Theoretical Aspects of the Relationship between Alcohol use and Crime." In James J. Collins, Jr., ed., *Drinking and Crime*, 1–69. New York: The Guilford Press.

Phillips, David P. 1980. "The deterrent effect of capital punishment: new evidence on an old controversy." *American Journal of Sociology* 86: 139–148.

Piliavin, Irving, Rosemary Gartner, C. Thornton, and Ross Matsueda. 1986. "Crime, Deterrence, and Rational Choice." *American Sociological Review* 51: 101–119.

Rainwater, Lee. 1974. "The slum and its problems." In Lee Rainwater, ed., *Social Problems and Public Policy: Inequality and Justice*, 148–57. Chicago: Aldine.

Roizen, Judy. 1981. "Alcohol and Criminal Behavior Among Blacks: The Case for Research on Special Populations." In James J. Collins, Jr., ed., *Drinking and Crime*, 207–52. New York: Guilford Press.

Room, Robin. 1983. "Region and Urbanization as Factors in Drinking Practices and Problems." In Benjamin Kissin and Henri Begleiter, eds., *The Pathogenesis of Alcoholism: Psychological Factors*, 555–604. Volume 6 in The Biology of Alcoholism series. New York: Plenum Press.

Room, Robin and Gary Collins, eds. 1983. *Alcohol and Disinhibition: Nature and Meaning of the Link*. Washington, D.C.: National Institute on Alcohol Abuse and Alcoholism, Research Monograph, no. 12.

Sampson, Robert J. 1987. "Urban black violence: the effect of male joblessness and family disruption." *American Journal of Sociology* 93: 348–82.

Sampson, Robert J. and John D. Wooldredge, 1987. "Linking the micro- and macro-level dimensions of lifestyle, routine activity and opportunity models of predatory victimization." *Journal of Quantitative Criminology* 3: 371–93.

Samuels, F. G. 1976. *The Negro Tavern: A Microcosm of Slum Life*. San Francisco: R&E Research Associates.

Schuessler, Karl. 1952. "The deterrent influence of the death penalty." *Annals of the American Academy of Political and Social Science* 284: 54–62.

Sellin, Thorsten, ed. 1967. *Capital Punishment*. New York: Harper and Row.

Stets, Jan E. 1990. "Verbal and Physical Aggression in Marriage." *Journal of Marriage and the Family*, forthcoming.

Stimson, James A. 1985. "Regression in Space and Time: A Statistical Essay." *American Journal of Political Science* 29:4, 915–47.

Straus, Murray A. 1980. "A sociological perspective on the cause of family violence." In R. Green, ed., *Violence and the Family*, 7–29. AAAS Selected Symposium, no. 47. Boulder, Col.: Westview Press.

Williams, Kirk R. and Robert L. Flewelling. 1988. "The social production of criminal homicide: a comparative study of disaggregated rates in American cities." *American Sociological Review* 53, 421–31.

Wolfgang, Marvin E. 1958. *Patterns in Criminal Homicide*. Philadelphia: University of Pennsylvania Press.

Wolfgang, Marvin E. and Franco Ferracuti. 1967. *The Subculture of Violence*. London: Tavistock.

# 7

# The Empirical Status of Hirschi's Control Theory

*Kimberly L. Kempf*

Travis Hirschi introduced his theory of social control in 1969 in *Causes of Delinquency* and it has been gaining popularity for nearly twenty-five years. It was argued recently that, "After a number of years of being dominated by strain theories, criminological theory and research has come increasingly under the influence of control theories, particularly as formulated by Hirschi" (Vold and Bernard 1986, 247). There are several indications that social control theory is perhaps the most popular criminological theory, and yet to date there has been no systematic critique of control theory research.

The absence of an evaluation summarizing the research achievements of control theory has not, however, precluded the "wheel of science" from amassing results. As evidence, the theory is a popular subject for dissertations.[1] Scholarly papers either cite the relevance of social control or purport to be formal tests of the theory with perhaps unrivaled frequency. This favored status of control theory has been explained by its testable nature, because the theory lends itself to self-report survey techniques, and because it has achieved support from empirical research (Vold and Bernard 1986, 247; citing Nettler 1984; Arnold and Brungardt 1983; Kornhauser 1978). It also has been argued that "at the beginning of the 1970s, [Hirschi's theory] was the only theoretical formulation that

143

tried to synthesize in a coherent and complex theoretical plan a great deal of information on the causes of delinquent behavior" (LeBlanc 1983, 40; LeBlanc, Ouimet, and Tremblay 1988, 164). The likely acceptance of this theory for future policy development has been noted as well (Williams and McShane 1988, 131).

There are concerns, however, about the scope of social control theory. Just how generalizable are the elements of the social bond? Does the theory explain specific forms of delinquency (e.g., theft, damage, violence), as well as general deviance (LeBlanc et al. 1988, 175)? Is the theory equally applicable across age, race and socio-economic groups? Thio (1978, 49–53), as example, contended that control theory is oversimplified and applicable to unsophisticated delinquent behavior only. Vold and Bernard (1987, 248) argue that neither adult criminality nor truly offensive delinquency actually have been examined (1987, 248). In a similar vein, Albert Cohen commented that Hirschi's theory of social control may be "fertile but not yet fecund" (1985).

"If social bonding theory is to be an 'enduring contribution to criminology' (Gibbons 1979, 121), then the basis for such longevity should be the research results which support, qualify and lead to modification in the perspective" (Krohn and Massey 1980, 539). It is likely that Hirschi would agree to this standard because he has questioned the continued dominance of differential association theory based on its scientific adequacy (Hirschi and Gottfredson 1980, 9). Hirschi also previously acknowledged the need for empirical tests to build on one another to achieve theoretical development. In doing so he stated, "it is easier to construct theories 'twenty years ahead of their time' than theories grounded on and consistent with data currently available" (Hirschi 1969, preface). This paper attempts to determine the extent to which these objectives have been accomplished by the empirical tests of the theory of social control. Has causation been established and, if so, to what degree are the findings generalizable? Hirschi's theory will be outlined briefly and its connections to earlier theories highlighted. An overview of empirical tests of Hirschi's theory will be presented. The current state of the theory research will be identified for scholars interested in testing contol theory today. Not only does the volume of published social control research merit an evaluation of this type, but it is important to determine the knowledge gained in twenty years.

## The Theory of Social Control

"A person is free to commit delinquent acts because his ties to the conventional order have somehow been broken" (Hirschi 1969, 3). This perspective of human behavior offered by Hirschi developed from much earlier ideas, including Hobbes' comments on the contradictions between laws and human nature in *Leviathan*. The influence of Durkheim's anomie, or the weakened collective conscience, and the resulting breakdown of social restraints on behavior also is apparent. Durkheim (1951, 1965ab) discussed the need for rules and the unpredictable behavior of children. Similarly, Piaget (1936) held that behavior is the response to pressures and attempts to influence them.

Control theory seems to accept, at least partially, the Freudian idea that deviant impulses can come forth naturally. For example, Aichhorn (1963) viewed delinquency as the result of unrepressed id freed from restraints by inadequate superego development. Reiss (1951) accepted weak ego and superego development as an explanation for poor personal controls among delinquents. Eysenck's (1964) typology of autonomous nervous system response also included conditions under which punishment fails to inhibit natural tendencies.

Toby (1957) and Briar and Piliavin (1965) introduced the concept "stakes in conformity" to control theory by suggesting that all youths are tempted to violate the law, but some have more to lose in doing so. This contribution clarified that self-interest is an important dimension of the element of commitment in control theory.

Targeting family as the primary source of control, Nye (1958) accepted the Freudian psychology that society must exercise control over our "animal instincts." Internal control occurs when parents socialize children to accept society's values, and thereby develop their conscience. The affection and respect children feel for parents serves as an indirect control. Direct control comes from the presence of parents, friends, police, among others, or from the threat of punishment from these conforming persons. Society also provides legitimate outlets for satisfying the inherent needs of persons in Nye's social control theory.

The theory of delinquency tested by Reckless (1961) included outer containment forces (including poverty, conflict, external restraint, minority group affiliation, and limited access to legitimate opportunities) and inner containment (such as drives, motives, frustrations, rebellion, and hostility).

In *Delinquency and Drift*, Matza (1964) provided a popular explanation for delinquency by integrating earlier ideas of subterranean values, drift, and techniques of neutralization (Matza and Sykes 1961; Sykes and Matza 1957). Drifting to and from delinquency involves freedom from restraint in the social structure. Techniques of neutralization provide delinquents with the opportunity to rationalize their behavior a priori, and thereby neutralize their guilt. Hirschi adapted these techniques of neutralization directly within his element of belief, but he rejected the notion that neutralization motivates delinquents. Instead, control theory contends that the probability of delinquency increases as persons' beliefs in the validity of social norms weakens (Hirschi 1969, 26, 199). The assumption of variation in belief is critical to control theory, and Hirschi incorporates the techniques of neutralization as components of his measures of belief.

The theory of social control offered by Hirschi evolved from many previous contributions. The ability to deviate from normative behavior is considered universal by control theory. Most people do not indulge in deviant behavior because of their bond to society. The social bond was conceptualized by Hirschi through the following four elements:

1. attachment of the individual to others (caring about others, their opinions and expectations),
2. commitment to conventional lines of action (the rational component including risk, energy and self investment in conventional behaviors),
3. involvement (time engrossed in conventional activities), and
4. belief in legitimate order (attribution of moral validity to social norms).

These components of the bond to society were viewed by Hirschi as independent and as having a generally negative association with

the likelihood of engaging in delinquent behavior. Hirschi postulated that as the elements of the social bond become weakened, the
probability of delinquency will increase. Readers not familiar with
Hirschi's theory are encouraged to review the original publication.

Hirschi tested his theory through a survey administered in 1965
to a stratified random sample of 3,605 adolescent males drawn as
part of the Richmond Youth Project in California. Based on a series
of tabular analyses, Hirschi concluded support for his theoretical
model. Hirschi conceded, however, that the theory underestimated
the importance of peers and the Richmond data failed to tap all
domains of this concept. He also accepted that too much importance had been bestowed on the concept of involvement. He deferred revision of the theory until more is learned about the processes that effect the elements of the bond and whether delinquency
itself motivates commitment (Hirschi 1969, 229–31). Hirschi has
not sought these answers through additional empirical investigation.

The intent of this paper is to examine empirical investigations of
the theory of social control since Hirschi's 1969 contribution.
Among subsequent studies, attention will be given to the intent of
the inquiry, the nature of the subjects tested, conceptualization,
technique of investigation, and relevance of findings. This quasi-
meta analysis will provide new information about the status of
control theory and the contribution it has made to our understanding of crime and delinquency.

## Descriptions of the Tests of Hirschi's Theory

Empirical tests of control theory published between 1970 and
1991 were identified through a two-stage process. Studies initially
were located through a search of the *Social Science Citation
Indices, Criminal Justice Abstracts* and *Psychological Literature
Indices* using "control," "social control," "social bond," and
"Hirschi" as key words. The bibliographies of studies identified in
this manner were examined to locate additional investigations with
which to buttress the initial sample. The latter effort was useful for
locating books and articles published in journals perhaps not reviewed in the three indices.

Three criteria were adopted for screening the research. First, there must be an acknowledged test of control theory. Second, Hirschi (1969) must be cited, thereby increasing the likelihood that the test was of Hirschi's version of the theory. And, third, the study must be published, utilizing the assumption that the publication process lends credibility to the scholarly contribution of the article. Although the selection process was rigorous, it was not presumed to be exhaustive and undoubtedly some tests of Hirschi's theory are regrettably omitted. There is, however, no reason to believe the sample studies are not representative of control theory research so they should enable us to ascertain the general level of growth achieved since 1969.

Ultimately, seventy-one empirical tests of control theory were identified (shown in table 7.1). These investigations included a variety of specific research objectives. There were twenty-eight replication efforts, of which many attempted to extend the theory to demographic groups not examined by Hirschi, such as company executives (Lasley 1988), rural youth (Gardner and Shoemaker 1989; Hindelang 1973; Krohn and Massey 1980; Lyerly and Skipper 1981), females (Hindelang 1973) and minority youths (Gardner and Shoemaker 1989; Robbins 1984) and other domains of deviance, including sixteen studies of only drug or alcohol use, four studies of adult crime, two studies of sexual behavior, and one study of mental health disorders. There also were sixteen studies in which social control was compared to another theory. Sixteen additional studies attempted to test theoretical models integrating social control with another theory.[2] The integration efforts with social control most often included social learning or differential association, followed second by deterrence. In a few cases, elements of social control also were combined with strain, social disorganization, culture conflict and conflict of interest theories. Eleven attempts to initiate contributions to theory development were reported. Potential improvements in these eleven studies included the application of new statistical procedures, analyses of unique data, and innovative sample groups.

With the exception of two studies that relied on official adult records (Linquist et al. 1985 and Minor 1977) and one study of aggregated data (Caldas and Pounder 1990), control theory has been

## TABLE 7.1
### Studies on the Relationship between Social Control & Crime

| Author(s) | Data collection year & location | Usable Cases | % Total | Age/grade | % Male | % White | Population | Test Type |
|---|---|---|---|---|---|---|---|---|
| Hirschi (1969) | 1965, Richmond, CA | 3,605 | 65 | 7–12th g. | 100[1] | 59 | student | original |
| Agnew (1985) | 1966, 68, USA | 1,886 | 83 | 10, 11th g. | 100 | 88 | student | replication |
| Agnew (1991) | 1976, 77, USA | 1,655 | 96 | ages 11–17 | — | — | youth | replication |
| Aultman (1979) | 1975, Tallahassee | 1,500 | — | 6–12th g. | — | — | student | comparison |
| Bishop (1984) | —, Virginia | 2,147 | 71 | 6–12th g. | 53 | 75 | student | expansion |
| Buffalo & Rodgers (1971) | 1966, Topeka, KS | 164 | 96 | ages 13–18 | 100 | — | delinquent | replication |
| Burkett & Jensen (197) | —, Seattle | 1,056 | — | 12th g. | 50 | — | student | replication |
| Caldas & Pounder (1990) | 1980, Louisiana | 64[2] | — | — | — | — | — | replication |
| Caplan & LeBlanc (1985) | 1974, Montreal | 1,441 | 98 | — | 100 | — | student | replication |
| Cernkovich (1978) | —, midwest | 412 | — | ages 14–18 | 100 | 100 | student | integration |
| Conger (1976) | 1964, Seattle & midwest | 374 | — | 7th g. | 100 | 28 | student | integration |
| Conger (1976) | 1965, Richmond, CA | 1,493 | 94 | 7–12th g. | 100 | 100 | student | integration |
| Dembo et al. (1985) | 1976, New York City | 258 | 23 | 7–9th g. | 100[1] | 0 | student | replication* |
| Elliott et al. (1988) | 1976–83, USA | 1,501 | 97 | ages 11–22 | 53 | 94 | youth | integration |
| Eve (1978) | 1971, southeast | 300 | — | 11–12th g. | 45 | 79 | student | comparison |
| Finnell & Jones (1975) | 1972, south | 265 | 79 | college seniors | — | 79 | student | replication* |
| Friedman & Rosenbaum (1988) | 1985, midwestern city | 2,926 | 95 | high school | 49 | 56 | student | expansion |
| Gardner & Shoemaker (1989) | 1984, Virginia | 733 | 91 | ages 13–20 | 47 | — | student | replication |
| Ginsberg & Greenley (1978) | 1971, 74, Madison, WI | 274 | 86 | college | — | — | student | comparison |
| Gottfredson et al. (1991) | 1982, 84 4 cities | 3,729 | 93 | junior high | — | 27 | student | integration |
| Hagan & Simpson (1978) | 1971, Toronto | 302 | — | college | — | — | student | replication |
| Hagan et al. (1985) | 1979, Toronto | 458 | 72 | 9–12th g. | 50 | — | student | integration |

*Continued on next page*

**TABLE 7.1—Continued**

| | | | | | | | | |
|---|---|---|---|---|---|---|---|---|
| Hagan et al. (1987) | 1979, Toronto | 463 | — | 9–12th g. | 50 | — | student | integration |
| Hepburn (1977) | 1972, midwest city | 139 | 69 | ages 14–17 | 100 | 100 | stu. & del. | comparison |
| Hindelang (1973) | —, rural NY | 941 | 96 | 6–12th g. | 50 | 98 | student | replication |
| Jensen & Eve (1976) | 1965, Richmond, CA | >4,000 | — | 7–12th g. | — | — | student | comparison |
| Johnson, B. (1973) | 1970, 21 NY colleges | 3,500 | — | college | 48 | 89 | student | comparison |
| Johnson, K. (1984) | —, northwest town | 345 | — | 10–12th g. | 44 | 83 | student | replication |
| Johnson, R. (1987) | —, Seattle | 734 | — | 10th g. | 51 | 71 | student | replication |
| Kaplan et al. (1984) | 1971–73, Houston | 3,052 | 43 | 7–9th g. | — | — | student | integration |
| Kelly & Pink (1973) | 1967, northwest | 284 | 92 | 10th g. | 100 | — | student | replication |
| Krohn & Massey (1980) | —, 3 midwest states | 2,054 | 67 | 7–12th g. | 50 | — | student | replication |
| Krohn et al. (1984) | —, 4 midwest states | 695 | 85 | 7–12th g. | — | 99 | student | comparison |
| LaGrange & White (1985) | —, New Jersey | 341 | — | ages 12, 15, 18 | 100 | — | general | integration |
| Lasley (1988) | —, multinational corp. | 435 | 67 | ages 33–78 | 77 | 77 | executives | replication |
| LeBlanc (1983) | 1974, 76, Montreal | 458 | 51 | ages 12–18 | 100[1] | — | student | expansion |
| LeBlanc et al. (1988) | 1974, 76, Montreal & | 825 | 27 | ages 14–18 | 56 | — | student | expansion |
| | 1985, Montreal | 797 | 72 | ages 14–15 | — | — | student | expansion |
| Levine & Kozak (1979) | 1977, Chicago | 796 | 32 | 5–12th g. | — | — | student | replication* |
| Linden, E. & Hackler (1973) | 1966, Seattle | 200 | — | ages 13–15 | 100 | — | l.c. housing | comparison |
| Linden, R. (1978) | 1965, Richmond, CA | 990 | 62 | 7–12th g. | 100 | 100 | student | replication |
| Linquist et al. (1985) | —, 3 Florida co. | 328 | 63 | adults | 71 | — | offender | replication |
| Liska & Reed (1985) | 1966, 68, USA | 1,886 | 83 | 10, 12th g. | 100 | 88 | student | expansion |
| Lyerly & Skipper (1981) | —, Virginia | 100 | — | teenage | 100 | 100 | delinquent | replication |
| Mak (1990) | —, Canberra, Australia | 793 | — | 8–12th g. | 51 | — | student | expansion |
| Mannle & Lewis (1979) | —, southeast state | 267 | 85 | age 15 | 47 | 53 | delinquent | replication |
| Marcos et al. (1986) | —, southeast | 2,676 | 97 | ages 14–19 | 47 | 83 | student | integration |
| Mathur & Dodder (1985) | —, southwest | 722 | — | youth | 44 | 94 | stu. & del. | expansion |
| Matsueda (1982) | 1965, Richmond, CA | 1,140 | 72 | 7–12th g. | 100 | 100 | student | comparison |
| Matsueda & Heimer (1987) | 1965, Contra Costa co, CA | 2,589 | 75 | high school | 100 | 61 | student | comparison |

*Continued on next page*

**TABLE 7.1—Continued**

| Study | Year, Location | N | | Age/Grade | | | Sample | Type |
|---|---|---|---|---|---|---|---|---|
| Matsueda (1989) | 1966, 68, USA | 1,912 | — | high school | 100 | 100 | students | comparison |
| Meier & Johnson (1977) | 1971, Cook Co, IL | 632w | — | ages 15–18 | — | — | student | integration |
| Menard & Morse (1984) | —, San Diego | 257 | 39 | 9th g. | 40 | — | student | replication |
| Mercer et al. (1978) | 1974, Ontario | 286 | — | — | 43 | — | student | replication |
| Minor (1977) | —, Tallahassee | 260 | 95 | ages 18–50 | 50 | 100 | general | integration |
| Paternoster & Triplett (1988) | 1982, southeast | 1,544 | — | 10–11th g. | — | — | student | comparison |
| Paternoster et al. (1983) | 1975, 76, —— | 300 | — | college | 51 | 90 | student | comparison |
| Poole & Regoli (1979) | 1972, midwest | 72 | 69 | ages 14–17 | 100 | 100 | student | integration |
| Rankin (1977) | 1974, Wayne co, MI | 385 | 79 | 7–11th g. | 50 | 100 | student | expansion |
| Robbins (1984) | 1978–80, 3 reservations | 129 | 70 | ages 10–17 | — | 0 | youth | replication |
| Rosenbaum (1987) | 1977–79, Seattle | 1,612 | — | ages 15–18 | — | 69 | stu. & del. | replication |
| Segrave & Hastad (1985) | —, east coast city | 1,776 | — | ages 14–18 | 51 | — | student | integration |
| Shover et al. (1979) | 1977, southeast | 1,002 | 39 | 8–12th g. | 39 | — | student | comparison |
| Singer & Levine (1988) | 1987, suburban | 560 | 38 | high school | — | — | student | integration |
| Smith (1979) | —, NJ, IA, OR | 1,950 | 98 | ages >= 15 | 42 | — | general | comparison |
| Thompson et al. (1984) | —, southwest | 724 | — | youth | 44 | 94 | stu. & del. | replication |
| Thornton & Voight (1984) | —, Louisiana city | 3,500 | — | ages 11–17 | 50 | 75 | student | expansion |
| Torstensson (1990) | 1953–1983, Stockholm | 791 | 11 | female cohort | — | 0 | delinquent | replication |
| Udry (1988) | 1982, southern city | 201 | 75 | ages 13–16 | 51 | 100 | student | integration |
| Wells & Rankin (1983) | 1966–70, USA | 1,799 | 79 | 10–12th g. | 100 | — | student | expansion |
| Wiatrowski et al. (1981) | 1966, 68, USA | 1,886 | 83 | 10, 12th g. | 100 | 88 | student | expansion |
| Williams & Hawkins (1989) | 1985–87, USA | 483 | 40 | ages >= 18 | 100 | — | married | replication |
| Williams (1985) | —, Texas | 1,342 | 70 | ages >= 16 | — | — | licensed driver | comparison |
| Winfree et al. (1981) | —, rural rocky mtn | 605 | 67 | 6–12th g. | 49 | 83 | student | integration |

1. Complete data were obtained but not analyzed for 1,940 girls (Hirschi 1969, 35–36). Females were omitted from the actual analysis because they were expected to be "less at risk of using various drugs" (Dembo et al. 1985, 273) and to "increase clarity of the interpretation" (La Grange and White 1985, 20).

2. This study used aggregate level data for sixty-four parishes and school districts.

tested with survey data collected primarily through self-administered questionnaires. Although names were recorded in the Richmond data, most surveys assured anonymity. Studies have relied almost exclusively on one-time cross sectional designs. Exceptions include twelve studies based on longitudinal data, however, the majority of these analyzed the data as though they were cross sectional. Data were shared by several studies. For example, six studies used Hirschi's own Richmond data and five studies were based on the Youth in Transition data (Bachman et al. 1975). There also were multiple studies of original data by the same researchers (e.g., Hagan et al. 1985, 1987; Caplan and LeBlanc 1985; LeBlanc et al. 1988). Tests of control theory have included as few as seventy-two subjects and as many as over 4,000. White adolescent students, a majority of whom are male, have been the usual target of the control theory research.[3] In view of the overrepresentation of students, it is not surprising to discover that random selection of any type[4] was not included in most studies.

The apparent lack of variation in design elements precludes this investigation from pursuing an empirically based meta analysis, such as those used by Bridges and Weis (1988) to examine the accumulation of research on criminal violence or the structural covariates of homicide rates by Land et al. (1985). The similarity in research designs may serve as an advantage in this investigation of the empirical status of the theory, however, because differences among the empirical findings may be more readily attributed to operational definitions of the social bond.

*Conceptual and Operational Definitions*

Because these studies were self-acknowledged tests of control theory (rather than subjectively designated as such for our purpose), elements of the social bond were classified according to the original researchers' intent (e.g., if they used the label of attachment, so did I). In the rare event that the study did not mention the social bond specifically, an attempt was made to be inclusive and to categorize variables according to other studies with comparable indicators.

This classification revealed that all four elements of the social bond were included in only seventeen studies. Attachment was the most frequently included element, but there was *no* single element that appeared in every study. The volume and variety of additional measures in these studies also is noteworthy. Many of the variables classified by some researchers as concepts from other theories or spurious factors were defined in other studies as elements of the social bond.[5]

Not only were they omitted from study, but it is equally surprising that justification for the missing elements was rarely provided. One exception, the element of involvement in conventional activities, was subsumed in the measure of commitment (Krohn and Massey 1980; Krohn et al. 1984) and attachment and commitment (Minor 1977) because involvement was viewed as "too conceptually ambiguous to be of theoretical utility" (Minor 1977, 122). Although a significant effect for involvement was shown in Agnew (1985), this investigator chose to ignore the concept in a subsequent test (Agnew 1991). This apriori decision to omit involvement is even more questionable because it is based on findings from Elliott et al. (1985), a study that utilized the same data as Agnew (1991), and which he also criticized. Involvement is the least often measured element in the collection of studies. It is plausible that many investigators dismissed it based on Hirschi's interpretation of its lesser importance or they may have adhered to Minor's argument that involvement is an ambiguous term. The absence of arguments defending the omission of the other three elements of the social bond remains perplexing.

A more parsimonious theoretical model of social control than that presented by Hirschi might have been achieved in the control theory research, and thereby explain the missing elements. In view of this possibility, this inquiry next examines the operational definitions of each element of the social bond adhered to in the sample of studies.

*Attachment to Conventional Others (Parents, Peers, School).*

In Hirschi's own test, the number of measures of attachment exceeded those for the other elements of the social bond. He identified parents, the school, and peers as separate foci for attachment, and multiple dimensions were noted for each target. Based on some of the results, however, Hirschi also commented "that distinctions between the dimensions of attachment to the parent may be artificial" (1969, 93). The law also has been specified as a source of attachment (Jensen and Eve 1976), although Hirschi (1969) had specified this as an element of belief.

*Attachment to Parents*

For attachment to parents, Hirschi was concerned about the direct and psychological holds the parent(s) had on the child, the intimacy of parent-child communication and affection or respect. Virtual supervision was operationalized through a summated index of these questions: *does your mother (father) know where you are when you are away from home? does your mother (father) know whom you are with when you are away from home?* Two intimacy of communication indices were constructed. For the child to parent index, responses to the following items were summed: *do you share your thoughts and feelings with your mother (father)? how often have you talked over your future plans with your mother (father)?* The parent to child index combined these items: *when you don't know why your mother (father) makes a rule, will she explain the reason? when you come across things you don't understand, does your mother (father) help you with them? does your mother (father) ever explain why she feels the way she does?* Affection was noted as the crucial element by Hirschi, although problems were mentioned with available measures (Hirschi 1969, 90–93). Affectional identification was measured by the item: *would you like to be the kind of person your father (mother) is?* Equivalent importance was given to mothers and fathers for all dimensions.

Attachment to parents was the most frequent focus of attachment, as well as the most often examined element in the social bond among the studies reviewed. Fifty studies (70 percent of all studies) included attachment to parents, sometimes specified narrowly as only mother, or broadly as family. Hirschi's four concepts for attachment to parents and the variables used to indicate them are shown in table 7.2. Column one identifies the number of times Hirschi's variable was used to measure attachment; column two

**TABLE 7.2**
**Frequency of measures used across 71 studies of control theory[1]**

| | Same as Hirschi | Same var., other concept | Similar to Hirschi | Other var., same concept | Total |
|---|---|---|---|---|---|
| **Attachment to parents** | | | | 11 | 11 |
| i.   **Virtual supervision** | | | | 11 | 11 |
| Parents know whereabouts | 11 | 2 | 2 | | 15 |
| Parents know w/whom | 8 | 1 | 1 | | 11 |
| | | | | | |
| ii.   **Parent to child intimacy** | | | | 12 | 12 |
| Parent gives reasons for rules | 3 | | 2 | | 5 |
| Parent helps understand | 6 | | 2 | | 8 |
| Parent explains feelings | 2 | | 2 | | 4 |
| | | | | | |
| iii.   **Child to parent intimacy** | | | | 8 | 8 |
| Share thoughts with parent | 8 | | 2 | | 10 |
| Talk about future plans | 4 | | 2 | | 6 |
| | | | | | |
| iv.   **Affection** | | | | 4 | 4 |
| Be like parent | 12 | | 5 | 1 | 18 |
| Total, from 50 studies | | | | | 123 |
| | | | | | |
| **Attachment to peers** | | | | 14 | 14 |
| Be like friends | 8 | | 3 | 1 | 12 |
| Friends' reaction worst | 3 | 1 | | | 4 |
| # delinquent peers | 8 | 5 | 11 | | 24 |
| Respect opinions | 6 | 1 | 4 | 1 | 12 |
| Total, from 39 studies | | | | | 66 |
| | | | | | |
| **Attachment to school** | | | | 8 | 8 |
| like/dislike school | 0 | 12 | 11 | | 23 |
| (respect, care what teachers think) | | | | | 8 |
| (like to be like teachers) | | | | | 2 |
| (grades important) | | | | | 3 |
| (teachers care, are supportive) | | | | | 3 |
| (like schoolwork) | | | | | 2 |
| (gpa, ability, grades) | | | | | 6 |
| Total, from 29 studies | | | | | 55 |

*Continued on next page*

TABLE 7.2—*Continued*

| | | | | | |
|---|---:|---:|---:|---:|---:|
| **Involvement** | | | | 3 | 3 |
| work for $ | 8 | 6 | 1 | | 15 |
| # hrs. homework | 10 | 8 | 2 | | 20 |
| Feel there's nothing to do | 1 | 1 | | | 2 |
| # hrs. w/friends | 4 | 2 | | | 6 |
| # hrs. riding in car | 1 | 1 | | | 2 |
| (Activities, clubs, organizations) | | | | | 8 |
| (Church) | | | | | 4 |
| Total, from 25 studies | | | | | 60 |
| **Commitment** | | | | 20 | 20 |
| i.   **Achievement orientation** | | | | | |
| Good grades important | 4 | 4 | 5 | | 13 |
| Try hard everything | | | 4 | | 4 |
| Try hard school | 2 | 1 | 3 | | 6 |
| ii.  **Adult status** | | | | | |
| Smoking/drinking | 2 | 1 | | | 3 |
| Dating | 3 | 5 | | | 8 |
| iii. **Ed/Emp aspirations** | | | | | |
| Level schooling desire | 3 | 4 | 2 | | 9 |
| Parents want college | 2 | 1 | | | 3 |
| Job is for $ | | | 1 | | 1 |
| Easy life is happy life | | | | | 0 |
| Job desired | 3 | 3 | 1 | | 7 |
| iv.  **Ed/emp expected** | | | | | |
| Job expected | 3 | 2 | 1 | | 6 |
| Shouldn't expect too much | | | | | 0 |
| Competency/race prevent job | | | | | 0 |
| (Educ expect) | | | | | 10 |
| (GPA) | | | | | 6 |
| Total, from 41 studies | | | | | 96 |
| **Belief** | | | | 1 | 1 |
| i.   **Value law/legal system** | | | 1 | 20 | 21 |
| Alright if get away with it | 4 | 1 | 1 | | 6 |
| Respect police | 6 | 3 | | | 9 |
| Concern for teacher's opinions | | 3 | | | 3 |
| (Obey rules) | | | | | 6 |
| ii.  **Techniques of neutralization** | | | | 3 | 3 |
| Criminals shouldn't be blamed | 2 | | | | 2 |

*Continued on next page*

**TABLE 7.2—Continued**

| | | | |
|---|---|---|---|
| Can't seem to stay out of trouble | 3 | 1 | 4 |
| "Delinquency" doesn't really hurt | 7 | | 7 |
| Left keys in car, deserve theft | 5 | 1 | 6 |
| Police should give kids a break | 4 | | 4 |

iii. **Fatalistic statements** 1

Total, from 37 studies 72

1. Variables in parenthesis were not tested by Hirschi, but did appear with such frequency among other studies to merit independent attention.

shows the number of studies for which that item measured a different concept. Comparable but unique measures of Hirschi's concept are shown in column three; alternative variables are shown in column four. As noted, all four concepts of attachment have been measured. Hirschi's items indicating affection for parents, and parental supervision have been replicated the most often. New variables have been most frequently substituted for the parent to child communication index; this occurred in seven studies intended to replicate or improve the theory. Only the virtual supervision measures have been substituted for other concepts.

There were a few unique indicators of attachment to family as well. For example, residing with family was considered attachment by Hagan and Simpson (1978). In their study based on probation files (Linquist et al. 1985), marital status and number of dependents measured attachment to family.

*Attachment to Peers*

Hirschi measured attachment to peers according to the following items: *would you like to be the kind of person your best friends are? a friend's reaction would be the worst thing about getting caught for stealing; do you respect your best friend's opinions about the important things in life? the number of close friends who have been picked up by the police.*

There were thirty-nine studies (55 percent of all reviewed) with indicators of attachment to peers (or friends, associates). Delinquent peer items were by far the most common. Delinquent peer items often differed from Hirschi's use of number of peers and usually specified the type of delinquency involvement or type of feelings for these friends. Interest in being like friends and respect for friend's opinions were equally represented among the studies. Hirschi's item concerning friends' reaction to a theft was rarely studied. Fourteen studies, including nine replication efforts, tested unique peer attachment variables, such as dating, importance of time with family (Agnew 1985), would prefer other friends (Conger 1976), school peers reject me (Johnson 1987), and my friends are among the most popular (Linden 1978).

## Attachment to School

Affection for the school, measured by general like or dislike for school, was Hirschi's variable. There were other school related variables,[6] but they were mentioned in connection with "the causal chain." According to Hirschi, "the casual chain runs from academic incompetence to poor school performance to disliking of school to rejection of the school's authority to the commission of delinquent acts" (Hirschi 1969, 132).

Twenty-nine studies (41 percent of the total) incorporated attachment to school as an element of the social bond, but none of them used Hirschi's measure to do so. Instead, eleven similar variables were substituted. Some of the other school variables Hirschi used, particularly those related to teachers, have since been considered within attachment. Attachment to school was measured by GPA (Jensen and Eve 1976; Wiatrowski et al. 1981) and educational and occupational goals (Aultman 1979). Finally, twelve studies rejected the attachment construct in their tests of the variable like or dislike school; eight of these studies attempted to expand the scope of the theory.

## Involvement in Conventional Activities.

Variables which identify activity type or length of time spent on certain activities account for most of the measures of involvement in conventional activities (shown in table 7.2). Hirschi's items included the following: *currently working for pay; number of hours spent on homework per day; ever feel that 'there's nothing to do'; number of hours spent talking with friends; number of hours spent riding around in a car.* Data also were obtained but results were not reported by Hirschi for involvement in other school activities, clubs, and community organizations.

Involvement was adapted in only twenty-five (35 percent) subsequent investigations of control theory. Among these studies, hours spent on homework, followed by time working most often served to measure the concept. These two indicators also represented other concepts, however, and with nearly the same frequency. Time spent in school organizations, clubs and community activities also were reported as involvement. Church attendance and religiosity were identified as involvement in three studies. Scales or multiple variables were used frequently, although exceptions merit concern, such as a dichotomous measure of church attendance within last year used as the sole criterion of involvement (Hagan and Simpson 1978). Other anomalies among the involvement measures include items more often found as variables for other elements of the bond (e.g., value of good grades, parents know location with whom, like and respect friends, perception of opportunities). Many of the social control measures available in the National Youth Survey data have been equated as indicators of involvement (Jensen 1986, cited in Agnew 1991).

## Commitment to Conventional Lines of Actions.

Hirschi viewed achievement orientation, passage to "adult status," aspirations and expectations as dimensions of commitment. His index of achievement orientation included the following items: *how important is getting good grades to you personally? whatever I do, I try hard; I try hard in school.* A summated index with activities considered adult-like included *smoking, drinking, and dating.* Students were asked which of these they did and at what age they began. The importance of having a car and attitude about school intervention in smoking outside the classroom also were identified. Aspirations and expectations first were measured by Hirschi for education and employment. Individual items included the following: *how much schooling would you like to get eventually? how much schooling do you expect to get? do your parents want you to go to college? the only reason to have a job is*

*for money; you should not expect too much out of life; an easy life
is a happy life; what type of job would you like to get eventually?
what type of job do you expect to get? do you think that either your
competence or racial discrimination will keep you from getting the
kind of job you want to have eventually?*

The items specified as commitment in forty-one studies (58
percent of all reviewed) are summarized in table 7.2. Each of
Hirschi's four concepts is represented, although there was less
consensus among recent studies regarding the measurement of
commitment than was shown for either the elements of attachment
or involvement. Thirteen studies included an item tapping the
importance of grades, with five of them specifying the target of
grade achievement. Aspiration for school level was reported for
nine studies. Expectation for school level also was used, even more
frequently than any of Hirschi's expectation items. Dating, more
often than smoking or drinking, typified "adult status" items. Three
of Hirschi's variables were never utilized. Moreover, many of
Hirschi's variables specified other concepts nearly as often as they
did commitment. There also were twenty commitment variables not
used by Hirschi and the diversity and potential for overlapping with
other elements can be seen through them. For example, commitment to education was identified through amount of time spent on
homework, GPA and liking or disliking of school. Enjoyment of
risk-taking behaviors and value orientations ("conventional," and
those directed at grades, education, the law, and avoiding delinquency) were other criteria for commitment.

*Belief*

Hirschi identified values relative to law and the legal system,
techniques of neutralization, and fatalistic statements as the dimensions of belief. He used items concerning *respect for the local
police and concern for teacher's opinions* as indicative of respect
for impersonal authority. Acceptance of the normative system was
measured by the item: *it is alright to get around the law if you can
get away with it.* The techniques of neutralization were operationalized as follows: *most criminals shouldn't really be blamed for the
things they have done; I can't seem to stay out of trouble no matter*

*how hard I try; most things that people call 'delinquency' don't really hurt anyone; the man who leaves the keys in his car is as much to blame for its theft as the man who steals it; police try to give all kids an even break; suckers deserve to be taken advantage of.* Three fatalistic statements also were tested: *what is going to happen to me will happen, no matter what I do; there is no sense looking ahead since no one knows what the future will be like; a person should live for today and let tomorrow take care of itself.*

In comparison to commitment, the more recent measurement of belief in the legitimate order in thirty-seven studies (52 percent) offers a high level of consistency (shown in table 7.2). The majority of the measures include value orientations toward the law and legal system, although twenty of them differed considerably from Hirschi's variables and six shared the focus of the perceived legitimacy, obedience or likelihood of sanctions. Each of Hirschi's variables for the techniques of neutralization were mentioned, the most frequent item "most things called 'delinquency' don't really hurt anyone." Hirschi's concept of fatalistic statements was never identified.

*Explained Behavior*

Finally, the outcome of the control model should be considered in reviewing the conceptual and operational definitions used in tests of the theory. Hirschi argued, however, that the findings of control theory research should not be dependent on the operational definition of delinquency (Hirschi 1969, 55).

There were several items on the Richmond questionnaire that dealt with delinquency, but Hirschi chose to test only six. Two of the items came from the Nye-Short (1957) scale of delinquency: *have you ever taken little things (worth less than $2) that did not belong to you? have you ever banged up something that did not belong to you on purpose?* The remaining four items were taken from the scale of theft developed by Dentler and Monroe (1961); *have you ever taken things of some value (between $2 and $50) that did not belong to you? have you ever taken things of large value (worth over $50) that did not belong to you? have you ever taken a car for a ride without the owner's permission? not counting fights* *you may have had with a brother or sister, have you ever beaten up on anyone or hurt anyone on purpose?* Hirschi initially created three summated indices from the six items. The standard index measured the total number of acts ever committed. The persistence index took number and recency into account. The recency index tapped only the number of acts committed during the previous year. Despite its skewness and lower predictive capability, only the recency scale was analyzed because it "was considered most appropriate as an operationalization of delinquency in terms of the theory" (Hirschi 1969, 62–3). This argument that better conceptual clarity is obtained from the recent past was the only rationale given for ignoring the other scales.

The theory of social control has been viewed by its researchers as capable of explaining delinquency, crime, adolescent sexual behavior, mental health disorders and conformity. The domain of items cover a full range of deviant behavior, from skipping a school rally or theft of under $2 to armed robbery. Several studies adapted modified versions of the original Nye-Short scale of delinquency;[7] others made a point of including dimensions of crime viewed as serious. A majority of the studies relied on summated scales of the number of infractions reported for each offense category. The recall period was generally limited to activities within the previous one, and sometimes three years. There also were crime-specific criteria, the focus of which was most often alcohol or drug use.

## Discussion of the Findings

The measurement of concepts in the theory of social control has been examined and inconsistencies have been observed. Several studies introduced measurement improvements, yet the research is weakened because little or no attention has been given to the construct validity of the four elements of the social bond. Many studies relied upon factor analyses to identify composite indices, some of which were replicated in several studies. The potential for apparent criterion validity in these efforts is not a substitute for research concern about the integrity of theoretical concepts. This investigation will now turn to the empirical findings and conclusions of the reviewed studies to determine the current state of knowledge on control theory.

Although it achieved most significance in Hirschi's test, attachment was consistently identified as the weakest predictor of delinquency in the research by Krohn and Massey (1980, 538). Johnson (1987) reported no gender differences in attachment. But, perhaps the most consistent finding was the identified need for refinements in the sources of attachment (Conger 1976; Johnson 1987; Linden and Hackler 1973; Mathur and Dodder 1985; Wiatrowski et al. 1981).

Among the attachment foci, the most important indicators were affection for parents (Hindelang 1973, 180), mothers (Krohn and Massey 1980), regulation or pressure from parents and peers (Aultman 1979, 163), and school (Lyerly and Skipper 1981; Mathur and Dodder 1985; Wiatrowski et al. 1981). Johnson (1987, 313) argued that attachment to parents is too broad, misdirected, or nonlinear and "detachment" is more appropriate. Menard and Morse (1984, 1362) argued that school alienation causes family alienation. Finally, although it remains controversial,[8] attachment to delinquent friends contributed to the explanation of crime and delinquency in several studies (Buffalo and Rodgers 1971; Conger 1976; Hepburn 1977; Hindelang 1973; Kaplan et al. 1984; Krohn et al. 1984; Linden and Hackler 1973[9]; Mannle and Lewis 1979; Meier and Johnson 1977; Winfree et al. 1981).

*Involvement in conventional activities* was shown to be fairly unimportant unless it was concerned with commitment (Hindelang 1973, 481–84). Obviously, this sentiment was echoed by those researchers who omitted this element from their models and by Conger, who argued that "involvement can be dispensed with as a crucial element" (1976, 20). On the other hand, involvement in homework and extracurricular school activities was identified as a good predictor in the control models tested by Agnew (1985) and Wiatrowski et al. (1981).

*Commitment*, also considered "stakes in conformity,"[10] was identified as the element with the strongest explanatory value in only the control model examined by Krohn and Massey (1980). Their index and GPA were the most powerful commitment variables; gender differences in commitment also were shown (Krohn and Massey 1980, 538). For Meier and Johnson (1977), age, the proxy they actually used for commitment, was the most influential extralegal variable. Commitment achieved a low explanatory value in Wiatrowski et al. (1981). Lyerly and Skipper (1981) found a significant commitment effect, but not in the direction hypothesized by control theory.

*Belief in the law* had the greatest explanatory value in only one study (Aultman 1979), but the measure was consistently important in each of the five crime specific models she examined. A moderate effect for belief was reported by Paternoster and Triplett (1988). Weak or no effect for belief also was reported (Agnew 1985; Paternoster et al. 1983).

Demographic differences were observed in the findings of several of the control models. Age effects were shown (Agnew 1985; LaGrange and White 1985; Meier and Johnson 1977); peers were more important to older adolescents (LaGrange and White 1985) and the theory fared better for younger subjects (Agnew 1985). Gender differences were identified (Eve 1978; Segrave and Hastad 1985). Race also was important in the study by Eve (1978). Lyerly and Skipper (1981) found no significant variation according to rural or urban residences among their delinquent subjects. During one year, Linden (1978) reported a nonsignificant socioeconomic status effect, while Eve (1978) found socioeconomic status was important.

The noted importance of specifying interactions (Hagan and Simpson 1978; Krohn et al. 1984; Menard and Morse 1984; Poole and Regoli 1979; Thornton and Voight 1984) and establishing causal order among the elements of the social bond (Cernkovich 1978; Hepburn 1977; Johnson 1987; Kelly and Pink 1973; Menard and Morse 1984; Minor 1977; Paternoster et al. 1983; Thompson et al. 1984) is also evident in the multivariate, and especially path analytic models examined. Arguments in favor of longitudinal designs contend that cross sectional data "may have exaggerated the effect [of social control]" (Agnew 1985, 58) and led to erroneous conclusions (Paternoster et al. 1983, 476).

In sum, the empirical models of social control discussed above were tested for a variety of deviant behavior, and different, and sometimes contrary, results were found. When crime specific models were examined, higher levels of explanation were found for the general crime model (Minor 1977), minor delinquency (Aultman 1979; Krohn and Massey 1980) and school infractions (Eve 1978).

## Advice from the Literature

Several recommendations for future control theory research were suggested within these published works. Many proposals were made in favor of theoretical models integrating social control with other theories, including deterrence (Meier and Johnson 1977 and Smith 1979), cultural deviance (Singer and Levine 1988 and Wiatrowski et al. 1981), situational inducements and neutralizations (Minor 1977). Other recommendations included:

1. data need to be collected specifically for the purpose of examining the theory of social control (Mathur and Dodder 1985);
2. control theory needs to be tested on representative samples (LaGrange and White 1985; Lyerly and Skipper 1981; Paternoster et al. 1983; Thornton and Voight 1984);
3. the validity of the theoretical concepts needs to be examined (Wiatrowski et al. 1981);
4. multi-item indicators need to be developed for these constructs (Agnew 1985; Menard and Morse 1984);
5. attention needs to focus on establishing temporal order (Hepburn 1977; Johnson 1987; Paternoster et al. 1983; Thompson et al. 1984);
6. the theory needs to be tested using a complex nonrecursive model with instant and lagged effects (Johnson 1987; Menard and Morse 1984), including measures from more than two time points (Paternoster et al. 1983);
7. serious crime needs to be included (Rankin 1977; Paternoster et al. 1983);
8. crime-specific models developed (Minor 1977; Winfree et al 1981; Wiatrowski et al. 1981).

Many recommendations have been made. Furthermore, many of these recommendations are not new. Hirschi suggested a few modifications for the theoretical concepts and the research procedure following his own test of his theory. Theoretically, mothers and fathers remain equivalent sources of parental attachment (Hirschi 1978, 332). Actually, all conventional attachment foci are equated; "the Simmelian notion that one is cast adrift by one group only to be swallowed up by another is not accurate (Hirschi 1969, 131). Based on the Richmond data, involvement had been accorded too much importance in the theory (Hirschi 1969, 230). And, attachment and belief, at least, are not independent (Hirschi 1969, 200). Hirschi defended his inattention to other plausible interactions as follows: "they do not receive systematic attention here because the task of showing that the bond to conventional order is strongly related to the commission of delinquent acts is considered logically prior (Hirschi 1969, 113).

The Richmond data lack direct operational definitions for affection (Hirschi 1969, 91–92). The skewed distributions of some variables—such as virtual supervision—identified a need for continuous measurement (Hirschi 1969, 89). Hirschi also discussed the roles of academic competence, social class, race, age, grade level, mother's employment, family size, birth order, broken home, and attachments to unconventional others, as potential spurious factors. Without specifying their order or direction in every case, he did acknowledge that "these outside variables may also vary in importance over time" (Hirschi 1969, 113). The importance shown for delinquent peers convinced Hirschi of the need for subsequent research to examine group processes and the sources of these affective ties. He has even encouraged research to defy theoretical assumptions.[11]

Hirschi has since elaborated on his theory of social control, although he has not tested it again. He has made it clear that integrated theoretical models are considered effort without reward (Hirschi 1979). He has explained the distinction between constraints and motives, and the necessity of both in delinquency theories (Hirschi 1978). In doing so, he has criticized most other theories for their absence of constraint and has positioned the plausible conditional variables with secondary importance as motives in his theoretical scheme. Hirschi has debated the relative merits of control theory in comparison to other theories many times (e.g., Hirschi 1979, 1985). Most recently, it has been Hirschi's contention that deterrence and the rational choice perspective already exist in the theory of social control (Hirschi 1985). Should this union be accepted, traditional barriers between the classical and positive schools of criminology may need to be reconsidered.

## The Merits of Control Theory

There are three criteria by which a theory of crime may be judged. First, the degree to which people agree with the theory is a subjective standard. Control theory has succeeded by this gauge and become perhaps the most heralded theory of delinquency. Yet, popularity based on intuitive appeal is not enough to distinguish sound theory from folk wisdom. Second, a theory also may be evaluated according to its relevance for policy and ability to effect program change. From this criteria, the potential importance of the theory of social control is clear. Interventions aimed at enhancing family, school, and peer attachments can easily be envisioned; many are in place now. The rise of curfew ordinances mandate virtual supervision by parents. Activities to occupy after-school and vacation leisure time receive great community support. Many such programs provide role models to help socialize youths to appropriate values and educate them about potential consequences of offending, thereby attempting to affect one or more elements of the bond. However, decisions on policy often reflect feasibility and ease of program administration as much as they consider theoretical merits. The scientific achievements of a theory is the third standard, and the criteria by which criminology must evaluate its theories. To establish causation the scientific method requires a correlation between theoretical elements and the phenomena being explained, clarification of temporal order, and the dismissal of potentially spurious factors. Replication is then required to assure generalizability across time, space, and subjects. By this important measure of scientific merit, social control theory has not fared well. Criminology has not yet determined the capacity of this theory.

### Correlations

Hirschi provided the first test of his theory, and concluded support for it. Subsequently, as Vold and Bernard (1986, 247) surmised, the majority of the reviewed studies also professed at least conditional support for control theory. These failures to refute control theory have been based primarily on associations observed between one or more element of the social bond and delinquency.

Many correlations certainly have been reported among the tests of Hirschi's theory. The qualified conclusions of these studies, however, are misleading. As this review has shown, studies varied in their success with operationalizing elements of the social bond. Many investigations did not incorporate Hirschi's variables. Few attempts to assess the criterion, content or construct validity of new variables were made. Hirschi criticized one study by saying, "Their solution is to use the terms and ignore the claims of control theory" (Hirschi 1979, 34). Unfortunately, his criticism appears to apply more generally to many investigations of control theory.

Attachment has been studied more often than any other element of the bond, but there remains a great deal about this concept to be explored. Aspects of affection and control need to be examined for attachment. The sources and targets of these attachments also need to be disentangled. I support the concern expressed by LeBlanc (1983) to distinguish the relative influences of associations, institutions, and [I add] roles. Schools, for instance, include more than teachers. Not all peer group members are equally important. Families include more than parents. Even parents may not be equally responsible for affection and virtual supervision, plus their effect may vary by gender, age, and family structure (see, for example, Hagan 1989). Other potential sources of attachment surely exist as well. Neighborhood affiliation may hold prominence among some peers. Religion means more than church attendance to many people. Attitudes toward law and the legal system are either attachment or belief, but probably not both. There is nearly consensus among the researchers that theoretical tests of control theory must separate the objects of attachment and identify the mechanisms by which it occurs (Johnson 1979; LaGrange and White 1985; Conger 1976; Linden and Hackler 1973; Mathur and Dodder 1985; Waitrowski et al. 1981).

As an element of the social bond, rational behavior exists within the concept of commitment. In view of the popularity currently bestowed on deterrence, routine activity (Cohen and Felson 1979), and the intuitive appeal of rational choice theory (Cornish and Clark 1986), Hirschi's contention that these theories already are embodied within control theory must be considered. Therefore, in addition to reconciling whether it is the best predictor of delinquency (Krohn and Massey 1980), a sufficiently good correlate (Meier and Johnson 1977), of minimal value (Wiatrowski et al 1981), or in support of the null hypothesis (Lyerly and Skipper 1981), the many dimensions of commitment to conformity need to be better understood. It is important, for example, to disentangle the relationship between aspirations and expectations. Hirschi (1969) includes both as dimensions of commitment, but Elliott et al. (1988) treated three of Hirschi's expectation variables as measures of strain theory.

The time dimension of involvement also must be considered separately from the risk and rationality of commitment. The extent to which the relationship between involvement and delinquency is strong (Agnew 1985; Wiatrowski et al. 1981), conditional (Hindelang 1973), or unimportant (Conger 1976) is far from resolved.

Belief, the moral validity of social norms, is the final element of the social bond. Despite general accord for the importance of the concept, diverse variables have measured belief. It is not surprising, as a consequence, that studies have reported different effects for this element. Tests of control theory must measure values toward the law and legal system, techniques of neutralization and fatalistic orientations.

In addition to research attention directly at establishing the correlations between elements of the social bond and delinquency, control theory may benefit from independent assessments of plausible interactions between elements of the bond. Based on his interpretation of the Richmond data, Hirschi concluded that attachment and belief are not independent (Hirschi 1969, 200). Other studies (Hagan and Simpson 1978; Krohn et al. 1984; Menard and Morse 1984; Poole and Regoli 1979; Thornton and Voight 1984) have argued for the importance of improving our understanding of these interactions, but little progress has been made. The relative effects of individual variables should be better understood with the addition of interaction terms to statistical models. The inclusion of theoretically justifiable interactions should strengthen measurement of the social bond, as well as enhance the explanatory achievements of control theory.

*Temporal Order*

With the focus on observation of associations, the second criteria for establishing causation has received even less attention. It is important to determine, first, whether the elements of the social bond precede delinquency, and, second, the temporal ordering among the elements. Hirschi (1969, 27) acknowledged potential interelement relationships. Bernard (1987, 421) argued that commitment is the only structural element in the social bond, more properly conceived as "an antecedent variable that encompasses attachments, involvements, and beliefs." This reconsideration of the theoretical model is interesting, but remains to be empirically examined. Menard and Morse (1984) argued that school alienation fosters family alienation. Attachment to parents precedes belief, according to Agnew (1985) and Elliott et al. (1988). Liska and Reed (1985) suggest reciprocal effects of attachment and delinquency, but argue that the effects are primarily contemporaneous. The few tests of causal paths have not been replicated successfully. Many studies, however, have conceded the need to determine causal ordering of the elements of the social bond, and their temporal priority to delinquency and crime (Cernkovich 1978; Hepburn 1977; Johnson 1987; Kelly and Pink 1973; Matsueda 1982; Menard and Morse 1984; Minor 1977; Paternoster et al. 1983; Thompson et al. 1984).

The reliance on cross sectional analysis may have precluded this advancement for control theory. Some researchers who retain this view also consider longitudinal data mandatory for establishing temporal order (Agnew 1985; Paternoster et al. 1983). Other researchers refute the necessity of panel data (Hirschi and Selvin 1973; Gottfredson and Hirschi 1987).

Unfortunately, no consensus exists on which statistical techniques are appropriate for analysis of causation based on longitudinal data. Path analysis and LISREL models have been used to compare theories and test integrated theoretical models (Aultman 1979; Dembo et al. 1985; Matsueda 1982; 1989; Matsueda and Heimer 1987; Paternoster et al. 1983). The use of change scores (e.g., $t_2 - t_1$) present another option, but methodological concerns have been noted (Kessler and Greenberg 1981; Markus 1979; Plewis

1985). Some advocates for longitudinal data have argued that these data must include more than two independent observation periods (Kessler and Greenberg 1981; Paternoster et al. 1983), and that analyses must include nonrecursive models with direct and lagged effects examined[12] (Agnew, 1991; Johnson, 1987; Menard & Morse, 1984). However, lagged endogenous variables also have not been used by researchers, even by those researchers who utilized data capable of including them. For instance, as Elliott et al. (1988, 141) explained, "the use of lagged endogenous variables or other change models may mask the effects of variables that are fairly constant over time by including those effects as part of the stability coefficient."

Inclusion of lagged variables in regression models was the option (Markus 1979; Plewis 1985) included in another study of causation with National Youth Survey (Lauritsen et al. 1991). This study of victimization acknowledged the potential specification problem posed by error terms correlated across and within waves for the lagged and predicted terms and used a full-information maximum-likelihood (FIML) simultaneous model to determine whether serial correlation was damaging (Lauritsen et al. 1991, 285–86). This technique also was pursued for testing control theory with the National Youth Survey data by Agnew (1991), who was unable to control for both lagged and contemporaneous effects in one model because the number of lagged variables entailed to specify his theoretical model was too large.[13] Agnew instead used "sensitivity analysis" (following Kessler and Greenberg 1981) to compare a series of more parsimonious models with fixed values for lagged effects. Potential difficulties of serially correlated error terms and multicollinearity were observed, but did not preclude Agnew from concluding "the data suggest that the elements of the bond as described by Hirschi are unimportant in predicting general delinquency among adolescents" (1991, 140).

*Absence of Spurious Factors*

With the other criteria for establishing causation unresolved, it is difficult to interpret the role of potentially spurious factors. Conditional relationships based on extraneous variables have been observed in many studies of control theory, including age (Agnew 1985; LaGrande and White 1985; Meier and Johnson 1977), gender (Eve 1978; Segrave and Hastad 1985), race (Eve 1978), urbanization of area (Gardner and Shoemaker 1989; Lyerly and Skipper 1981), socioeconomic status (Eve 1978) and offense type (Minor 1977; Aultman 1979; Krohn and Massey 1980; Eve 1978; Winfree et al. 1981; Wiatrowski et al. 1981).

With original relationships between elements of the social bond and delinquency not even established, problems occur with the inclusion in some tests of variables that conflict with the tenet of control theory. The role of delinquent friends (Buffalo and Rodgers 1971; Conger 1976; Hepburn 1977; Hindelang 1973; Kaplan et al. 1984; Krohn et al. 1984; Linden and Hackler 1973; Mannle and Lewis 1979; Meier and Johnson 1977; Winfree et al. 1981), whether guided correctly by social control or differential association theory, for example, must be interpreted cautiously. Reducing either of these theories to "number of delinquent peers" does an injustice to the rich conceptual frameworks they provide. Theoretical integration efforts definitely must await resolution of these and other unanswered queries about the effects of the social bond.

*Generalizability Based on Time, Space, and Subjects*

Questions about the extent to which control theory is generalizable to specific crime and across demographic groups remain unanswered as well. Better data, including more representative samples (LaGrange and White 1985; Lyerly and Skipper 1981; Paternoster et al. 1983; Thornton and Voight 1984), are needed. Less than half of the studies included females, and race varied in even fewer. Oversampling of minorities is recommended. Subjects college-age or older were included in only four studies. If control theory is expected to apply to adults as well as youths, the age range must be extended in tests of the theory. Offending must include variation in severity and type. The power of control theory for explaining mental health disorders, sexual behavior, and other forms of norm violation should be considered.

## Conclusion

Many recommendations can be made for future research as criminology attempts to establish the scientific merits of control theory. Data appropriate for the task must be obtained. These data may require primary collection of surveys, but the potential of secondary data resources also has not been exhausted. These data must reflect attention to conceptualization of the social bond and criterion validity for the four elements. Multiple dimensions of each element also should be examined. The benefits accrued from multiple item indices should be determined. Causal order must be determined by all available techniques, until one preferred method is established. All other variables considered potentially spurious to the original relationship must be tested. Replication across time, space, and subjects must continue at least until dissimilar results are no longer common.

Hirschi offered suggestions for modifications and revisions both of the theory and of testing method, most of which subsequent efforts ignored. This review has shown that the control theory research comprises a large number of essentially separate studies which have little relation to each other and fail to build on experience. Thus, the research reveals little about the viability of social control as a scientific theory. Comments about the simplicity (Thio 1978), coherence and robustness of the explanation (LeBlanc 1983; LeBlanc et al. 1988) each are premature. Efforts to expand the theory with additional constructs and calls for the integration of control theory with differential association, deterrence, rational choice, or any other theory will continue to fail until the scientific groundwork for understanding control theory is done. Criminologists need a better understanding of the elements of the social bond as well as the conceptual scheme linking them and the conditions under which they prevail.

Although the large number of studies reviewed should have proved otherwise, it is disheartening to conclude that Cohen was correct in asserting that "Hirschi's theory of social control may be fertile but is not yet fecund" (1985). Criminology has done this theory a disservice. Hopefully, this assessment of control theory research will assist in motivating the growth and development of the theory of social control. Recent criticism about the progression of criminology as a science (Bernard and Ritti 1990; Gottfredson 1988) suggests that the limited growth and development of control theory is not a unique problem. Criminology must attend to the scientific merit of its investigations before any products may be applied successfully to policy reform.

An earlier version of this paper was presented at the Annual Meetings of the American Society of Criminology, Chicago, Illinois, 9–12 November 1988. The author is indebted to Jeffrey Fagan, Janet Lauritsen, Robert Meier, Frank P. Williams, III, and Richard Wright for their helpful comments on earlier versions of this manuscript and to Clint Vestal for his diligent library efforts.

## Notes

1. Dissertations on control theory identified from *Dissertation Abstracts* include Antonio 1972; Bishop 1982; Caplan 1979; Chapman 1986; Creechan 1982; Gardner 1984; Gibbons 1981; Lauritsen 1989; Massey 1983; Matsueda 1984; Meier 1974; Minor 1975; Murcos 1985; Okada, 1987; Rankin, 1978; Riley, 1986; Rosenbaum 1983; Sellers 1987; Slaght 1985; Smith, C. 1983; Smith M. 1980; Smith, W. 1984; Stuck 1985; Taub 1986; Thornton 1977; Tieman 1976; Wiatrowski 1978.
2. Hirschi, however, is critical of integrated theoretical models, particularly the model developed by Elliott et al. (1979) (Hirschi 1979).
3. As with Hirschi (1969), there were a few studies for which data on female and/ or minority subjects were available but not analyzed and notations about their inclusion in future investigations were made, but apparently not yet published.
4. This includes two-stage sampling designs in which schools were typically chosen nonrandomly, then individual classrooms within the schools were randomly selected.
5. For example, Elliott et al. (1988) used GPA, education, and employment expectations as measures of strain theory; whereas, Hirschi defined them as commitment. Parental and peer reinforcement, religiosity, gender role expectations, perceived academic and social success, television viewing, dating, school performance were included in other studies as variables of theories other than social control.
6. Academic competence was measured by grades in English and mathematics (overall GPA was unavailable), Differential Aptitude test score, and self-ratings of school ability. Concern for teacher's opinion of them, another school variable, was identified within the element of belief.
7. Of the twenty-three original items in the Short and Nye questionnaire, eleven were identified as unidimensional (and therefore reliable). Only seven items were included in the final investigation. Use of Guttman scaling to identify unidimensionality among the items was severely criticized by Hindelang et al. (1981, 49–50).

8. Even nine years after his own test of the theory, it was Hirschi's contention that "the ties among delinquents are not equal in quality to those among other peer groups" (1978, 337).
9. They discussed this attachment in terms of "affective ties."
10. This usage follows Toby (1957) and Briar and Piliavin (1965).
11. "Avoid the fallacy fallacy. When a theorist or a methodologist tells you you cannot do something, do it anyway. Breaking rules can be fun." (Hirschi 1973, 171–72).
12. Lagged endogenous variables are included in regression models of change. Lagged variables measure prior behavior as a predictor of current behavior of the same type.
13. Analysis of the effects of change in predictor variables require the inclusion of a lagged predictor variable for each of the variables of interest. Agnew's interest in the effects of change in many social control variables made his model impossible to analyze statistically.

## References

Aichhorn, August
  1963    *Wayward Youth,* New York: Viking.
Agnew, Robert
  1985    "Social control theory and delinquency: a longitudinal test." *Criminology* 23 (1): 47–61.
  1991    "A longitudinal test of social control theory and delinquency." *Journal of Research in Crime and Delinquency* 28 (2): 126–56.
Antonio, Robert J.
  1972    "Accounting for rural-urban crime differentials: a Durkheimian social control model" (unpublished doctoral dissertation, University of Notre Dame). Ann Arbor, Mich.: University Microfilms #ADG72-26800.
Aultman, Madeline G.
  1979    "Delinquency causation: a typological comparison of path models." *Journal of Criminal Law and Criminology* 70: 152–63.
Bachman, Jerald G.
  1975    *Youth in Transition* [MRDF]. Ann Arbor, Mich.: Institute for Social Research for Political and Social Research.
Bernard, Thomas J.
  1987    "Structure and control: reconsidering Hirschi's concept of commitment." *Justice Quarterly* 4 (3): 409–24.
Bernard, Thomas J. and R. Richard Ritti
  1990    "The role of theory in scientific research." In Kimberly L. Kempf (ed.) *Measurement Issues in Criminology.* New York: Springer-Verlag.
Bishop, Donna M.
  1982    "Deterrence and social control: a longitudinal study of the effects of sanctioning and social bonding on the prevention of delinquency" (unpublished doctoral dissertation, State University of New York at Albany). Ann Arbor, Mich.: University Microfilms #ADG82-18700.

Briar, Scott and Irving Piliavin
    1965    "Delinquency, situational inducements and commitment to con-
            formity." *Social Problems* :35–45.
Bridges, George and Joseph G. Weis
    1989    "Measuring violent behavior: effects of study design on corre-
            lates of interpersonal violence." In Neil Weiner and Marvin
            Wolfgang (eds.) *Violent Crime, Violent Criminals,* Newbury
            Park, Cal.: Sage.
Buffalo, M. D. and Joseph W. Rogers
    1971    "Behavioral norms, moral norms and attachment: problems of
            deviance and conformity." *Social Problems* 19 (1): 101–13.
Burkett, Steven R. and Eric L. Jensen
    1975    "Conventional ties, peer influence, and the fear of apprehension:
            a study of adolescent marijuana use." *The Sociological Quar-
            terly* 16 (Autumn): 522–33.
Caldas, Stephen J. and Diana G. Pounder
    1990    "Teenage fertility and its social integration correlates: a control
            theory explanation." *Sociological Spectrum* 10: 541–60.
Caplan, Aaron
    1979    "La theorie de regulation sociale de Hirschi: l'enounce formel
            et ses prolongements," (unpublished doctoral dissertation, Uni-
            versity of Montreal).
Caplan, Aaron and Marc LeBlanc
    1985    "A cross-cultural verification of a social control theory." *Inter-
            national Journal of Comparative and Applied Criminal Justice* 9
            (2): 123–3.
Cernkovich, Stephen A.
    1978    "Evaluating 2 models of delinquency causation." *Criminology*
            16 (3): 335–53.
Chapman, William R.
    1986    "Delinquency theory and attachment to peers," (unpublished
            doctoral dissertation, State University of New York at Albany).
            Ann Arbor, Mich.: University Microfilms #ADG86-14180.
Cohen, Albert
    1985    "Crime and criminal justice in Japan." Presentation at the
            Center for Studies in Criminology and Criminal Law, University
            of Pennsylvania.
Cohen, Lawrence E. and Marcus Felson
    1979    "Social change and crime rate trends: a routine activity ap-
            proach." *American Sociological Review* 44: 588–608.
Conger, Rand
    1976    "Social control and social learning models of delinquency: a
            synthesis." *Criminology* 14 (1): 17–40.
Cornish, Derek B. and Ronald V. Clarke
    1986    *The Reasoning Criminal.* New York: Springer-Verlag.
Creechan, James J. H.
    1982    "Fear of sanctions and social control" (unpublished doctoral
            dissertation, University of Arizona). Ann Arbor, Mich.: Univer-
            sity Microfilms #ADG83-06452.

Dembo, Richard, Gary Grandon, Robert W. Taylor, Lawrence La Voie, William Burgos, and Sames Schmeidler
  1985    "The influence of family relationships on marijuana use among a sample of inner city youth." *Deviant Behavior* 6 (3): 267–68.
Dentler, Robert A. and Lawrence J. Monroe
  1961    "Social correlates of early adolescent theft." *American Sociological Review* 26: 733–43.
Durkheim, Emile
  1951    *Suicide,* New York: Free Press.
  1965    *The Division of Labor in Society,* New York: Free Press.
  1965    *The Rules of the Sociological Method,* New York: Free Press.
Elliott, Delbert S., Suzanne S. Ageton and Rachelle J. Canter
  1979    "An integrated theoretical perspective on delinquent behiavor." *Journal of Research in Crime and Delinquency* 15 (1):
Elliott, Delbert S., David Huzinga, and Scott Menard
  1988    *Multiple Problem Youth: Delinquency, Substance Use, and Mental Health Problems.* N.Y.: Springer-Verlag.
Eve, Raymond A.
  1978    "A study of the efficacy and interactions of several theories for explaining rebelliousness among high school students." *Journal of Criminal Law and Criminology* 69: 115–25.
Eysenck, Hans J.
  1964    *Crime and Personality.* Boston: Houghton Mifflin.
Finnell, William S. and John D. Jones
  1975    "Marijuana, alcohol and academic performance." *Journal of Drug Education* 5 (1): 13–21.
Friedman, Jennifer and Dennis P. Rosenbaum
  1988    "Social control theory: the salience of components by age, gender, and type of crime." *Journal of Quantitative Criminology* 4 (4): 363–81.
Gardner, Robert L., III
  1984    "Social bonding and deliquency: a multivariate analysis" (unpublished doctoral dissertation, Virginia Polytechnic Institute and and State University), Ann Arbor, Mich.: University Microfilms #ADG85-07186.
Gardner, LeGrande and Donald J. Shoemaker
  1989    "Social bonding and delinquency: a comparative analysis." *The Sociological Quarterly* 30 (3): 481–500.
Gibbons, Stephen G.
  1981    "Social control versus social learning: a longitudinal analysis," (unpublished doctoral dissertation, Washington State University), Ann Arbor, Mich.: University Microfilms #ADG81-22414.
Ginsberg, Irving J. and James R. Greenley
  1979    "Competing theories of marijuana use: a longitudinal study." *Journal of Health and Social Behavior* 19 (March): 22–34.
Gottfredson, Don M.
  1988    "Criminological theories: the truth as told by Mark Twain." In William S. Laufer and Freda Adler (eds.) *Advances in Criminological Theory,* vol. 1, New Brunswick, N.J.: Transaction Publishers.

Gottfredson, Denise C., Richard J. McNeil, III., and Gary D. Gottfredson
    1991    "Social area influences on delinquency: a multilevel analysis."
            *Journal of Research in Crime and Delinquency* 28 (2): 197–226.
Gottfredson, Michael and Travis Hirschi
    1987    "The methodological adequacy of longitudinal research on
            crime." *Criminology* 25: 581–614.
Hagan, John
    1989    *Structural Criminology,* New Brunswick, N.J.: Rutgers Univer-
            sity Press.
Hagan, John and John H. Simpson
    1978    "Ties that bind: conformity and the social control of student
            discontent." *Sociology and Social Research* 61 (4): 520–38.
Hagan, John, A. R. Gillis, and John Simpson
    1985    "The class structure of gender and delinquency: toward a power-
            control theory of common delinquent behavior." *American
            Journal of Sociology* 90 (6): 1151–78.
Hagan, John, John Simpson, and A. R. Gillis
    1987    "Class in the household: a power-control theory of gender and
            delinquency." *American Journal of Sociology* 92 (4): 788–816.
Hepburn, John R.
    1977    "Criminology: testing alternative models of delinquency causa-
            tion." *The Journal of Criminal Law and Criminology* 67 (4):
            450–60.
Hindelang, Michael J.
    1973    "Causes of delinquency: a partial replication and extension."
            *Social Problems* 21 (——): 471–87.
Hindelang, Michael J., Travis Hirschi and Joseph G. Weis
    1981    *Measuring Delinquency,* Newbury Park, Cal.: Sage.
Hirschi, Travis
    1969    *Cause of Delinquency.* Berkeley: University of California Press.
    1973    "Procedural rules in the study of deviant behavior." *Social
            Problems* 21 (2): 159–73.
    1978    "Causes and prevention of juvenile delinquency." In Harry M.
            Johnson (ed.), *Social System and Legal Process.* San Francisco,
            Cal.: Jossey-Bass.
    1979    "Separate and unequal is better." *Journal of Crime and Delin-
            quency* 16 (1): 34–37.
    1985    "On the compatibility of rational choice and social control
            theories of crime." In Derek Cornish and Ronald V. Clarke
            (eds.), *The Reasoning Criminal.* New York: Springer Verlag.
Hirschi, Travis and Hanan C. Selvin
    1973    *Principles of Survey Analysis.* New York: Free Press.
Hirschi, Travis and Michael Gottfredson (eds.)
    1980    *Understanding Crime: Current Theory and Research.* Newbury,
            Cal.: Sage.
Hobbes, Thomas
    1957    *Leviathan.* Oxford: Basil Blackwell.
Jensen, Gary F. and Raymond Eve
    1976    "Sex differences in delinquency." *Criminology* 13: 427–48.

Johnson, Bruce D.
  1973   *Marihuana Users and Drug Subcultures*. New York: John Wiley & Sons.
Johnson, Kirk Alan
  1984   "The applicability of social control theory in understanding adolescent alcohol use." *Sociological Spectrum* 4: 275–94.
Johnson, Richard
  1987   "Mother's versus father's role in causing delinquency." *Adolescence* 22 (86): 305–15.
Kaplan, Howard B., Steven S. Martin, and Cynthia Robbins
  1984   "Pathways to adolescent drug use: self-derogation, peer influences, weakening of social controls and early substance use." *Journal of Health and Social Behavior* 25 (September): 270–89.
Kelly Delos H. and William T. Pink
  1973   "School commitment, youth rebellion and delinquency," *Criminology* 10 (4): 473–85.
Kessler, Ronald and David Greenberg
  1981   *Linear Panel Analysis*. New York: Academic Press.
Krohn, Marvin D. and James L. Massey
  1980   "Social control and delinquent behavior: an examination of the elements of the social bond." *The Sociological Quarterly* 21 (4): 529–543.
Krohn, Marvin D., Lonn Lanza-Kaduce and Ronald L. Akers
  1984   "Community context and theories of deviant behavior: an examination of social learning and social bonding theories." *The Sociological Quarterly* 25 (Summer): 353–71.
LaGrange, Randy I. and Helene Raskin White
  1985   "Age differences in delinquency: a test of theory." *Criminology* 23 (1): 19–45.
Land, Kenneth C., Patricia L. McCall and Lawrence E. Cohen
  1985   "Structural covariates of homicide rates: are there any invariances across time and social space?" *American Journal of Sociology* 95 (4): 922–63.
Lauritsen, Janet
  1989   "Adolescent sexual behavior and early childbearing: empirical tests of social control and strain theories" (unpublished doctoral dissertation, University of Illinois), Ann Arbor, Mich.: University Microfilms #8924877.
Lauritsen, Janet L., Robert J. Sampson, John H. Laub
  1990   "The link between offending and victimization among adolescents." *Criminology* 29 (2): 265–92.
LeBlanc, Marc
  1983   "Delinquency as an epiphenomenon of adolescence." in R. Corrado, M. LeBlanc and J. Tre'panier (eds.). *Current Issues in Juvenile Justice*. Butterworths: Toronto.
LeBlanc, Marc, Marc Ouimet and Richard E. Tremblay
  1988   "An integrated control theory of delinquent behavior: a validation 1976–1985." *Psychiatry* 51 (May): 164–76.

Levine, Edward M. and Conrad Kozak
    1979    "Drug and alcohol use, delinquency, and vandalism among upper middle class pre- and post-adolescents." *Journal of Youth and Adolescence* 8 (1): 91–101.
Linden, Eric and James C. Hackler
    1973    "Affective ties and delinquency." *Pacific Sociological Review* 16 (1): 27–47.
Linden, Rick
    1978    "Myths of middle class delinquency: a test of the generalizability of social control theory." *Youth and Society* 9: 407–32.
Lindquist, Charles A., Terry D. Smusz and William Doerner
    1985    "Causes of conformity: an application of control theory to adult misdemeanant probationers." *Journal of Offender Therapy and Comparative Criminology* 29 (1): 1–13.
Liska, Allen E. and Mark D. Reed
    1985    "Ties to conventional institutions and delinquency: estimating reciprocal effects." *American Sociological Review* 50 (4): 547–60.
Lyerly, Robert R. and James K. Skipper
    1981    "Rates of rural-urban delinquency." *Criminology* 19 (3): 385–99.
Mak, Anita S.
    1990    "Testing a psychological control theory of delinquency." *Criminal Justice and Behavior* 17 (2): 215–30.
Mannle, Henry W. and Peter W. Lewis
    1979    "Control theory reexamined: race and the use of neutralizations among institutionalized delinquents." *Criminology* 17: 58–74.
Marcos, Anastasios C.
    1985    "Causal models of adolescent drug use in Arizona and Utah" (unpublished doctoral dissertation, Brigham Young University), Ann Arbor, Mich.: University Microfilms #ADG86-03364.
Marcos, Anastasios C., Stephen J. Bahr, and Richard E. Johnson
    1986    "Test of a bonding/association theory of adolescent drug use." *Social Forces* 65 (1): 135–44.
Markus, Gregory B.
    1979    *Analyzing Panel Data*. Beverly Hills, Cal.: Sage.
Massey, James L.
    1983    "Social bonding and minor adolescent deviance: adolescent tobacco use" (unpublished doctoral dissertation, University of Iowa), Ann Arbor, Mich.: University Microfilms #ADG84-07771.
Mathur, Minu and Richard A. Dodder
    1985    "Delinquency and the attachment bond in Hirschi's control theory." *Free Inquiry Into Creative Sociology* 13 (1): 99–103.
Matsueda, Ross L.
    1982    "Testing control theory and differential association." *American Sociological Review* 47 (4): 489–504.

1984 "Determinants of delinquency: a longitudinal analysis of social control and differential association theories" (unpublished doctoral dissertation, University of California, Santa Barbara), Ann Arbor, Mich.: University Microfilms #ADG84-29892.

1989 "The dynamics of moral beliefs and minor deviance." *Social Forces* 68 (2): 428–57.

Matsueda, Ross L. and Karen Heimer
1987 "Race, family structure, and delinquency: a test of differential association and social control theories." *American Sociological Review* 52 (December): 826–40.

Matza, David
1964 *Delinquency and Drift.* New York: Wiley.

Matza, David and Gresham M. Sykes
1961 "Juvenile delinquency and subterranean values." *American Sociological Review* 26 (October): 712–719.

Meier, Robert F., Jr.
1974 "Marijuana use and social control: a study of the deterrent effects of legal sanctions" (unpublished doctoral dissertation, University of Wisconsin, Madison), Ann Arbor, Mich.: University Microfilms #ADG75-02469.

Meier, Robert F. and Weldon T. Johnson
1977 "Deterrence as social control: the legal and extra-legal production of conformity." *American Sociological Review* 42 (4): 292–304.

Menard, Scott and Barbara J. Morse
1984 "A structural critique of the IQ-delinquency hypothesis: theory and evidence." *American Journal of Sociology* 89 (6): 1347–78.

Mercer, G. William, John D. Hundleby and Richard A. Carpenter
1978 "Adolescent drug use and attitudes toward the family." *Canadian Journal of Behavioral Science* 10 (1): 79–90.

Minor, W. William
1975 "Control theory and deterrence of crime: a theoretical and empirical integration" (unpublished doctoral dissertation, Florida State University), Ann Arbor, Mich.: University Microfilms #ADG76-13820.

1977 "A deterrence control theory of crime in Robert F. Meier (ed.). *Theory in Criminology: Contemporary Views.* Sage Publications: Beverly Hills, Cal.: 117–138.

Nye, F. Ivan
1958 *Family Relationships and Delinquent Behavior.* New York: Wiley.

Nye, F. Ivan and James F. Short, Jr.
1957 "Scaling delinquent behavior." *American Sociological Review* 22, 3 (June), 326–31.

Okada, Daniel W.
1987 "Japanese-American juvenile delinquency: an examination of control theory in a Japanese-American community" (unpublished doctoral dissertation, University of Maryland), Ann Arbor, Mich.: University Microfilms #ADG87-25543.

Paternoster, Raymond, Linda E. Saltzman, Gordon P. Waldo and Theodore G. Chiricos
  1983    "Perceived risk and social control: do sanctions really deter?" *Law & Society* 17 (3): 425–56.
Pasternoster, Raymond and Ruth Triplett
  1988    "Disaggregating self-reported delinquency and its implications for theory." Criminology 26 (4): 591–625.
Plewis, Ian
  1985    *Analyzing Change: Measurement and Explanation Using Longitudinal Data.* New York: John Wiley & Sons.
Poole, Eric D. and Robert M. Regoli
  1979    "Parental support, delinquent friends and delinquency: a test of interaction effects." *Journal of Criminal Law and Criminology* 70 (2): 188–93.
Rankin, Joseph H.
  1977    "Investigating the interrelations among social control variables and conformity." *Journal of Criminal Law and Criminology* 67 (4): 470–80.
  1978    "Investigating the interrelations among social control variables and conformity; changing attitudes toward capital punishment; schools and delinquency" (unpublished doctoral dissertation, University of Arizona), Ann Arbor, Mich.: University Microfilms #ADG78-11515.
Reckless, Walter C.
  1961    *The Crime Problem* (third edition). New York: Appleton-Century Crofts.
Reiss, Albert J. Jr.
  1951    "Delinquency as the failure of personal and social controls." *American Sociological Review* 16: 196–207.
Riley, Judith
  1986    "Empathy and criminal behavior: a look at man's inhumanity to man" (unpublished doctoral dissertation, Florida State University), Ann Arbor, Mich.: University Microfilms #ADG87-.
Robbins, Susan P.
  1984    "Anglo concepts and Indian reality: a study of juvenile delinquency." *Social Casework: The Journal of Contemporary Social Work* 65 (4): 235–41.
Rosenbaum, Jill L.
  1983    "Sex differences in delinquent behavior: a control theory explanation" (unpublished doctoral dissertation, State University of New York at Albany), Ann Arbor, Mich.: University Microfilms #ADG84-04427.
  1987    "Social control, gender, and delinquency: an analysis of drug, property and violent offenders." *Justice Quarterly* 4 (1): 117–32.
Segrave, Jeffery O. and Douglas N. Hastad
  1985    "Evaluating three models of delinquency causation for males and females: strain theory, subculture theory and control theory." *Sociological Focus* 18 (1): 1–17.

Sellers, Christine S.
    1987    "Alcohol, legal experience, and the elderly: a new test of social
            bonding theory" (unpublished doctoral dissertation, University
            of Florida), Ann Arbor, Mich.: University Microfilms #ADG87-
            24964.
Shover, Neal, Stephen Norland, Jennifer James, and William E. Thornton
    1979    "Gender roles and delinquency." *Social Forces* 58: 126–75.
Singer, Simon and Murray Levine
    1988    "Power-control theory, gender, and delinquency: a partial repli-
            cation with additional evidence on the effects of peers." *Crimi-
            nology* 26 (4) 627–48.
Slaght, Evelyn F.
    1985.   "Adolescent deviance as a function of parents, peers, and com-
            munity influence" (unpublished doctoral dissertation, University
            of Maryland). Ann Arbor, Mich.: University Microfilms
            #ADG86-04225.
Smith, Carol F. W.
    1983    "Sanctions and deviant outcomes: the social bond as a qualifier
            of labeling and deterrence effects" (unpublished doctoral disser-
            tation, Washington University). Ann Arbor, Mich.: University
            Microfilms #ADG83-20576.
Smith, Douglas A.
    1979    "Sex and deviance: an assessment of major sociological varia-
            bles." *The Sociological Quarterly* 20 (2): 183–86.
Smith, M. Dwayne
    1980    "A longitudinal analysis of social control theory" (unpublished
            doctoral dissertation, Duke University). Ann Arbor, Mich.: Uni-
            versity Microfilms #ADG81—05683.
Smith, William R.
    1984    "The self-esteem of the incarcerated juvenile: a comparison of
            prisonization, importation and social control theories" (unpub-
            lished doctoral dissertation, Rutgers University, New Bruns-
            wick). Ann Arbor, Mich.: University Microfilms #ADG84-
            24161.
Stuck, Mary F.
    1985    "Adolescents, drugs, and sports involvement: a qualitative
            study" (unpublished doctoral dissertation, Syracuse University),
            Ann Arbor, MI: University Microfilms #ADG86-17336.
Sykes, Gresham M. and David Matza
    1957    "Techniques of neutralization." *American Sociological Review*
            22 (December): 664–70.
Taub, Diane E.
    1986    "Amphetamine usage among high school senior women, 1976–
            1982: an evaluation of social bonding theory" (unpublished
            doctoral dissertation, University of Kentucky). Ann Arbor,
            Mich.: University Microfilms #ADG86-15870.
Thio, Alex
    1978    *Deviant Behavior*. Boston: Houghton Mifflin.

Thompson, William E., Jim Mitchell and Richard A. Dodder
    1984    "An empirical test of Hirschi's control theory of delinquency."
            *Deviant Behavior* 5 (1): 11–22.
Thornton, William E., Jr.
    1977    "Gender roles and delinquency from a social control perspec-
            tive" (unpublished doctoral dissertation, University of Tennes-
            see). Ann Arbor, Mich.: University Microfilms #ADG78-07728.
Thornton, William and Lydia Voight
    1984    "Television and delinquency: a neglected dimension of social
            control." *Youth and Society* 15 (4): 445–68.
Tieman, Cheryl R.
    1976    "Social control and delinquent behavior" (unpublished doctoral
            dissertation, University of Kentucky). Ann Arbor, Mich.: Uni-
            versity Microfilms #ADG77-15979.
Toby, Jackson
    1957    "Social disorganization and stake in conformity: complementary
            factors in the predatory behavior of hoodlums." *Journal of
            Criminal Law, Criminology & Police Science* 48: 12–17.
Torstensson, Marie
    1990    "Female delinquents in a birth cohort: tests of some aspects of
            control theory." *Journal of Quantitative Criminology* 6 (1): 101–
            15.
Udry, J. Richard
    1988    "Biological predispositions and social control in adolescent sex-
            ual behavior." *American Sociological Review* 53 (October): 709–
            22.
Vold, George B. and Thomas J. Bernard
    1986    *Theoretical Criminology*. Oxford: Oxford University Press, third
            edition.
Wells, L. Edward and Joseph H. Rankin
    1983    "Self-concept as a mediating factor in delinquency." *Social
            Psychology Quarterly* 46 (1): 11–22.
Wiatrowski, Michael D.
    1978    "Social control theory and delinquency" (unpublished doctoral
            dissertation, Portland State University). Ann Arbor, Mich.: Uni-
            versity Microfilms #ADG79-05683.
Wiatrowski, Michael D., David B. Griswold and Mary K. Robbins
    1981    "Social control theory and delinquency." *American Sociologi-
            cal Review* 46 (October): 525–41.
Wiatrowski, Michael D. and K. L. Anderson
    1987    "The dimensionality of the social bond." *Journal of Quantita-
            tive Criminology* 3 (1): 65–81.
Williams, Frank P., III
    1985    "Deterrence and social control: rethinking the relationship."
            *Journal of Criminal Justice* 13: 141–51.
Williams Frank P., III and Marilyn D. McShane
    1988    *Criminology Theory*. Englewood Cliffs, N.J.: Prentice Hall.

Williams, Kirk R. and Richard Hawkins
  1989  "Controlling male aggression in intimate relationships." *Law &*
      *Society Review* 23 (4): 591–612.
Winfree, L. Thomas, Harold E. Theis and Kurt T. Griffith
  1981  "Cross cultural examination of complementary social devi-
      ance." *Youth and Society* 12: 465–89.

# 8

# The Social Control of Spouse Assault

*Jeffrey Fagan*

Violence in families re-emerged as a social problem in the United States in the 1960s, launching debates over the social and legal control of spouse assault. These debates took place within a larger context of expansion of governmental regulation of the traditionally private realm of family life (Harvard Law Review 1988). The growth of social services in the 1960s, designed primarily to wrestle with extramarital social problems such as stranger crime or substance abuse, focused public policy not only on the economic behavior of families (Gilbert 1983), but also opened up the family as a social institution amenable to public scrutiny and governmental regulation. Accordingly, family social interactions became increasingly subject to formal social control and legal sanctions (Wexler 1982). In turn, social and legal institutions were mobilized to increase their involvement in marital relations and develop new mechanisms of social control of families.

The expansion of governmental regulation of family relations was aimed in part at concerns about violence among spouses and intimates. Research on the natural history of violence toward spouses led to the framing of specific solutions for marital violence within a legal context (Martin 1976; U.S. Commission on Civil Rights 1978, 1982; Walker 1979; Schecter 1982; Fagan et al. 1984; Langan and Innes 1986; Dutton 1988a). Litigation challenged police practices that discouraged arrest, prompting changes in laws and policies dealing with wife battering (Fields 1978; Lerman 1986), and political activism to strengthen criminal justice responses (Elliott 1989). Law reform focused on statutory changes that permitted or mandated arrests without corroboration in misdemeanor wife assault cases (Browne and Williams 1989), and resulted in the elimination of requirements for abuse victims in divorce proceedings to obtain protection orders. The removal of spousal exemptions in rape laws in many states simplified the prosecution of marital rape (Berger, Searles, and Neuman, 1988).

The problems and limitations in legal responses to women victims of spouse assault also mobilized social institutions to increase the range of formal and informal controls at their disposal. Building on service models developed for rape victims, feminist organizations opened crisis intervention and victim assistance programs for women victims of marital violence, started shelters for victims and their children, trained emergency room workers to diagnose and refer battered women, and formed specialized legal assistance programs for both civil and criminal actions (Schechter 1982).

The social and legal controls that emerged varied according to the explanations and causal theories of spouse assault (Fagan and Browne 1992). Marital violence was alternately explained as a result of family dysfunction or interaction patterns, individual pathology, situational factors that influenced marital dynamics, social pathology, or the behavioral product of ideological supports or cultural beliefs in the partriarchical social and economic organization of society (Fagan and Wexler 1987). Accordingly, reforms and activism gave rise to three approaches to social control that reflected competing theories and assumptions about the etiology of spouse assault.

Feminist approaches to social control focused attention on informal social controls and resources available to the woman victim. Little attention was paid to the family unit as a whole, apart from children who were at risk for injury. In fact, Schecter (1982) suggested that there was a conflict of interest in serving both victim and a "family" unit that included her victimizer. Feminists argued that the control of spouse assault required a restructuring of gender relations (such as sex inequality in the workplace or the home) and the empowerment of women (Ferraro 1989) through social interventions such as shelters.

Social control through therapeutic interventions was promoted by mental health professionals (Fagan and Wexler 1987; Ferraro 1989). These efforts sought to regulate families through interventions that view the family as the "client." The victim was incorporated into this perspective as a cocontributor to the problem and all family members as part of a "system" of violence with roles in maintaining that violence. Social control therefore required "treatment" of all family members where the authority of professionals would exercise control over the "disputants" and coerce or influence family members to stop the violence. These conceptions of social control gravitated to social service agencies, either with formal ties to the courts (e.g., diversion or mediation programs) or under the auspices of protective service or mental health agencies.

Social control through law most often occurred through criminal justice intervention that made salient the risks and costs of spouse assault. Legal controls focused on the victim and the assailant in the context of laws that were being broken with associated costs of punishment, and were rooted in assumptions of specific deterrence (Sherman and Berk 1984b; Berk and Newton 1985; Langan and Innes 1986; Williams and Hawkins 1989). Deterrence approaches emphasized the application of legal sanctions through arrest and prosecution of assailants, or invoking the threat of legal sanction through civil remedies that carried criminal penalties if violated. Legal action was designed to exact a cost, and to the extent that further violence was not evident, its suppression was attributed to the intrinsic consequences of legal sanctions (Dutton et al. 1991). Mandatory arrest policies for incidents in which there is probable cause of wife assault reflect this approach to social control of marital violence (Sherman and Cohn 1989; Fagan and Browne 1992).[1,2]

If legal control is a last resort option after other social controls have failed (Emerson 1981; Miller and Simpson 1991), the mobilization of legal institutions to regulate spouse assault hints at the perceived limitations or ineffectiveness of nonlegal social controls (Williams and Hawkins 1989b). Despite the broader interpretation of spouse assault that informed other approaches to social control of family violence, legal control replaced other formal and informal social controls as the first resort for regulation of family relationships (Fagan 1988; Williams and Hawkins 1989a). The conceptualization of spouse assault in a framework emphasizing legal sanctions made deterrence the favored theory for policy, and arrest the favored policy (Fagan and Browne 1992).[3]

However, research on the effectiveness of law as social control for spouse assault has provided contradictory results: experiments under a range of sampling conditions have yielded no consistent support for specific deterrent effects of arrest (Fagan and Browne 1992).[4] There also is consistent evidence that spousal violence is well controlled by informal (nonlegal) social controls (Bowker 1983, 1984; Berk and Newton 1985; Fagan 1989), while the social costs associated with arrest (job loss, stigma, relationship loss) are more salient in the *perceived* deterrent effects of arrest than are the expected costs of punishment (Williams and Hawkins 1989a).

These new developments provide opportunities for further development of the theoretical basis for the social control of spouse assault. That is the purpose of this chapter. We begin with an examination of the varying conceptualizations of social control as they have been constructed in the discourse on spouse assault: legal controls, both informal and formal social controls, and social psychological controls. Next, we evaluate the empirical and theoretical bases for these concepts. We then integrate these theories and specify the processes that comprise the control dynamics of spouse assault.

## Conceptualizations of Social Control of Spouse Assault

Social control theorists beginning with Durkheim have concurred that social norms were not simply imposed on individuals by societal structures or processes. Rather, they were effective only when internalized through formal and informal processes of socialization (Coser 1975). Yet conceptualizations of the social control of spouse assault often specified control processes that operate at different levels of influence and explanation (compare, for example, Pagelow 1984; Gordon 1988; Williams and Hawkins 1989b). These distinctions complicate comparisons among theories and empirical knowledge.

For example, social control has been examined alternately as: (a) internalized social psychological controls that facilitate conformity or generate greater fear of law violation (Williams and Hawkins 1989b); (b) situational or microinteractional social controls (Eckland-Olsen, Lieb, and Zurcher 1984); (c) social sanctions and perception of sanction risks or costs (Bowker 1983; Berk and Newton 1985; Gelles 1983); or (d) macrolevel cultural or ecological controls (Saunders et al. 1987; Levinson 1989; Yllo and Straus 1984).

Similar diversity marks research on legal controls for spouse assault. Social control through legal sanctions has been examined as a process of legal mobilization and implementation of the law (Black 1980; Sherman and Berk 1984; Elliott 1989; Dunford, Huizinga, and Elliott 1990; Hirschel et al. 1990, 1992; Ford 1991), through the threat of legal punishment in a coercive context to facilitate psychotherapeutic treatment of spouse assailants (Dutton 1986; Saunders and Azar 1989; Hamberger and Hastings 1989; Edelson, Syers, and Brygger 1987), or as the internalization of the perceived costs of law violation (Carmody and William 1987; Williams and Hawkins 1989a; Miller and Simpson 1991). Emphasis on perceived *certainty* vs. *severity* of sanctions also varies in these studies. Only one study (Dutton et al. 1991) has examined the effects of actual legal sanctions on the salience of social controls for spouse assault or perceptions of the costs of law violation.

Distinctions and comparisons among these processes of social control of spouse assault are complicated also by sampling limitations and research design in earlier studies. Most examined effects of social controls on either the behavior or perceptions of *male* assailants, overlooking possible gender differences in evaluations of the salience of various social controls. Few studies have analyzed social controls in the context of the dynamic interactions of spouse assault events or the natural history of violence within relationships. Most examine societal interventions, overlooking the implementation of social control strategies by victims (for exceptions, see Bowker 1983, 1984; Miller and Simpson 1991).

Also, the salience of various forms of social control may be mediated by structural characteristics: gender (Miller and Simpson

1991), age (Fagan 1989), race (Miller and Simpson 1991), and labor force participatin (Sherman et al. 1991). Results vary depending on whether the focus is the assailant or victim. Research with victims has examined the failure of social controls leading to serious forms of intimate violence (e.g., Browne 1987), or the influence of victims' interactions with legal institutions as a mediator of the efficacy of law as social control (e.g., Ford 1991a, 1991b). Few studies have examined the salience of social controls in avoiding spouse assault or promoting its desistance (Fagan 1989).

The reciprocal relationship among legal and social controls also has been neglected in previous research, despite the apparent mutual influence between informal and formal social controls of spouse assault. For example, legal sanctions seem to make social controls more salient by correcting power imbalances within intimate relationships (Dunford et al. 1989; Ford 1991a) or facilitating the influence of extralegal sanctions (Berk and Newton 1985). Thus, legal sanctions carry both direct costs (punishment, deprivation of liberty) and indirect social costs or secondary social sanctions (relationship loss, social disapproval, self-stigma) that contribute to decisions to become or remain violent (Williams and Hawkins 1989a).

Accordingly, if the "quantity of law" or governmental social control is inversely related to nonlegal social control (Black 1976), the salience of legal controls of spouse assault can be understood only as it is influenced by other types of informal social controls that operate in intimate relationships. Research on perceptual deterrence and spouse assault suggests that males view informal social sanctions as more certain than formal legal sanctions, and rate social costs as the most costly consequences of a legal sanction (Williams and Hawkins 1989a). Moreover, males rate these sanctions as significant costs of the act of spouse assault as well as costs of the legal sanction that may be invoked (Williams and Hawkins 1991).

The reciprocity among the different forms of social and legal controls operating at different levels of explanation suggests that their contributions can be integrated in a theoretical framework. This framework also should incorporate social structural and other contextual factors that potentially mediate the salience of social controls. We begin this process first by examining law as social control, and then ecological, situational or societal, and microinteractional or personal processes of social control of spouse assault.

## Social Control through Legal Sanctions

The theoretical basis for social control through legal sanctions rests squarely on deterrence theory. Common sense guides the deterrence doctrine: most individuals would rather avoid prison and accordingly are discouraged from criminal behavior (Miller and Anderson 1986). General deterrent effects depend on the probability that offenders view their behaviors as likely to be detected and punished. Gibbs (1985) refers to this as *vicarious* deterrence. That is, the threat of punishment will regulate perceptions of crime costs and the marginal gains from crime opportunities (Kramer 1990). Specific deterrent effects suggest that offenders, having received some pain or deprivation from punishment, will choose not to pay that penalty or cost again.

The emphasis on arrest and control of offenders in part reflected criticisms of the police and the criminal justice system more generally for failing to more effectively control spouse assault. Until the 1980s, spouse assault rarely invoked any form of governmental social control. For example, Dutton (1987, 1988b) found that arrest occurred in only 21.2 percent of wife assault cases in which prima facie evidence exists for arrest.[5] Elliott (1989) estimated the probability of arrest to vary from 12 to 50 percent. Evidently, the majority of individuals engaged in spouse assault avoids legal sanction and formal social control.

When police did intervene, critics claimed that punitive sanctions for violence against family members were rare or weak, that police and prosecutors did not regard cases of marital violence with the seriousness accorded to stranger violence, that victims of marital violence were not afforded the protection given to victims in stranger violence cases via punishment and control of offenders, and that weak sanction severity actually contributed to or reinforced the underlying causes of marital violence (Elliott 1989). The societal response to these critiques was mobilization of legal institutions to invoke social control of assailants. Efforts were concentrated on the arrest and prosecution of assailants, and also on their compulsory treatment (in lieu of prosecution). However, there was less attention paid to the punitive or retributive dimensions of legal controls, and the ambiguity below reflects that omission.

## Social Control through Specific Deterrence: The Effects of Arrest

Experimental evidence of the specific deterrent effects of arrest compared to nonarrest dispositions (Sherman and Berk 1984a, 1984b; Tauchen, Tauchen, and Witte 1986; Jaffe, Wolfe, Telford, and Austin 1986), and results from nonexperimental studies comparing arrest with other police dispositions of spouse assault cases (Berk and Newton 1985), provided impetus for widespread implementation of proarrest policies for misdemeanor wife assault cases through state law and local policies (Sherman and Cohn 1990). The Minneapolis Domestic Violence experiment (Sherman and Berk 1984a, 1984b) has been the most influential study in the mobilization of law as social control for spouse assault.[6]

However, several reviews (Binder and Meeker 1988; Fagan 1989; Elliott 1989; Lempert 1989) have cited validity problems in the Minneapolis experiment that, together with contradictory results from replications in Omaha (Dunford, Huizinga and Elliott 1989, 1990) and Charlotte, North Carolina (Hirschel et al. 1991, 1992), raise serious questions about the deterrent effects of arrest on repeat spouse assault. In both the Omaha and Charlotte replications, there were no significant differences in recidivism for any type of police response (advise, warning, citation, arrest) for several measures of recidivism. Moreover, the incidence of recidivism in Charlotte was *highest* for the arrest group, directly contradicting the results in Minneapolis.

How could replication results diverge so sharply from the original finding? Is arrest an effective deterrent only in the one location due to its unique circumstances? Or was the experiment flawed and the results simply a Type II error? Several limitations in the design of the Minneapolis experiment suggest that it was a flawed effort.[7] Perhaps the most serious was the exclusion from the Minneapolis experiment of other than "simple (misdemeanor) domestic assaults. . . . Cases of life-threatening or severe injury, usually labelled as a felony . . . were excluded from the design" (263). Thus, the arresting officers' judgment about the severity of violence or the risk to the victim of nonarrest was a source of selection bias in the experiment. Offenders who had left the scene also were excluded from the experiment. These problems were corrected in the replication studies; their contradictory results cast doubt on the validity of the original study.

If incomplete randomization introduced serious sampling biases (Berk 1983) and validity threats (Berk, Smyth, and Sherman, 1988), the effect size of the Minneapolis experiment may be confounded with sample artifacts. Although Sherman and Berk (1984a) report that most of the men in the sample had repeatedly assaulted their partners, prior to the experimental incident, within-group differences are not reported. Berk (1986) states that assailants with lengthier histories of either wife assault or stranger violence had higher recidivism rates than others, regardless of the experimental condition.

The Omaha and Charlotte replications followed experimental designs similar to the Minneapolis study, adding refinements that addressed many of its limitations.[8] Neither study found that arrest was an effective deterrent. In Omaha, for example, "arresting suspects had no more effect in deterring future arrests or complaints than did separating or counseling them" (Dunford et al. 1989, 34). Similarly, victim reports showed "no significant differences between the treatment groups" (34). Moreover, analyses controlling for prior arrests, ethnicity, and other variables showed no significant differences between police responses in terms of reassault and new threats of violence.

The limitations of arrest as social control are evident when the substantive components of arrest are examined. The deterrence experiments focused on the outcomes of arrest and assumed that the content of the intervention, indeed the specific processes of arrest, were invariant. But time in custody following arrest for misdemeanor spouse assault is a relatively unstudied process and a potential source of variability. Thus, if custody is the substantive punishment intrinsic to specific deterrence, then arrest of spouse assailants without incarceration suggests that there is no effective social control in those cases.[9]

Most arrestees in the deterrence experiments spent less than 12 hours in custody. Sherman and Berk (1984a) reported that 43 percent of the arrested group in Minneapolis were released within one day, and an equal number were released within one week.[10] Dunford et al. (1990) reported that less than 20 percent of the arrestees in Omaha were released from custody within two hours of booking; those posting bond (47 percent) were released after about sixteen hours. Hirschel et al. (1990) reported that arrestees in Charlotte were in custody an average of one hour before release.[11] Although average time in custody is likely to vary by community demographics (Lempert 1989) and the "going rate" of punishment for spouse assault (Fagan 1988), these three studies suggest that there is little punitive substance to the arrest process.

As distinguished from other forms of social control, deterrence includes a retributive element, including punishment in the form of deprivation or pain (see Acton 1939, for example, quoted in Zimring and Hawkins 1973). Accordingly, such short times in custody may undermine the deterrent effects of arrest in several ways. First, it may neutralize the intent of the arrest: while arrest may be intended to convey societal rejection of spouse assault, and be a prelude to the delivery of noxious conditions (e.g., deprivation of liberty and physical comforts, placement in unpleasant surroundings, removal from family and friends), a "short arrest" may deliver a quite contrary message: there is little pain attached to an arrest.

This leads to the second effect: this neutralization of the deterrent effects of arrest may create a counterdeterrent effect. That is, arrestees who have learned that arrest is not to be feared and that the deprivation of liberty is almost negligible, may perceive less certainty about the consequences of further violence and will feel even fewer restraints on their behavior. Little is known about the outcomes of previous arrests—whether punishment was imposed, for example. The failure to sanction in earlier arrests may teach an unfortunate lesson to violent spouses about societal indifference (or normative ambiguity) toward intimate violence, as well as the expectation of a low social cost. The oft-arrested assilant may already have learned that he has little to fear from the law, that there is little consequence to his behavior. We return to the relationship between learning and social control later on.

The third effect involves adverse emotional reactions by assailants to an abortive legal intervention. Since violent spouses often are paradoxically dependent on their partners (Dutton 1988a; Dutton and Browning 1988; Walker 1984; Browne 1987), the threat of relationship loss from arrest (one of the social costs of arrest, according to Williams and Hawkins [1989b]) might arouse fear and anger, both toward the spouse and perhaps displaced toward strangers as well. Also, the assailant's anger at the spouse for invoking legal authorities might neutralize whatever sanctions are conveyed by his short involvement with police and brief stay in detention.

Evidently, legal controls are effective only with assailants with less severe histories of spouse assault (Fagan 1989). Less serious assailants also tend to be individuals with little experience in the criminal justice system (Fagan et al. 1984; Fagan and Wexler 1987), and are less likely also to be violent toward strangers (Fagan and Wexler 1987). They are unlikely candidates for felony arrest, and may be more concerned about how employers or neighbors will respond to disclosure of their behaviors. Although the more violent assailants are better prospects for arrest for spouse assault, they also are more likely to have been arrested previously for a violent act (toward a spouse or stranger). Arrest as a sanction has been tried before for this group; apparently, the costs of arrest are not sufficient to convince them to avoid legal sanctions. For this group, achieving social control through legal punishment is unlikely, regardless of whether legal sanction or some other societal intervention is attempted.

It is also possible that legal sanction alone cannot restrain violence for more severe assailants; for this group, the origins of violence may vary from the less severe or infrequent assailant. In families where there are extreme imbalances in marital power, controls may be effective after restoring the balance of power within the couple. Arrest *alone* may not accomplish such a complex task. The processes which lead to a more sustained, injurious violence may neutralize the processes leading to desistance.

Given the lengthy socialization processes that precede the onset of spouse assault (Caesar et al. 1988; Dutton and Strachan 1987), it is unlikely that one arrest or a stint on probation will initiate processes of "unlearning" to desist from a pattern of battering. But for those whose socialization is less strongly linked to normative violence, deterrence may be achieved from social, cultural, or legal sanctions. As we discuss in later sections, these strategies are not necessarily stronger medicine; instead, they rely on different models of social control.

## Expanding Legal Control Through Prosecution

The transfer of social control from legal authorities to women in violent relationships assigns control of legal sources of social control to victims. This process in turn empowers victims to bring about ends that they identify as necessary to change assailants' behaviors, such as participation in treatment or counseling programs (Dunford et al. 1989; Ford 1991a). In other words, the costs of the act can be manipulated by the victim when she is able to invoke legal controls, expanding her salience in an exchange relationship (Gelles 1983; Fagan and Browne 1992). However, in order to manipulate costs, victims need access to resources and, ultimately, sources of power.

Prosecution of assailants is one such power resource that may make salient the costs to the assailant of intimate violence, but only if its control rests with the victim (Ford 1991a). Just as the threat of force is used by violent spouses to maintain their domination (Goode 1971; Yllo and Straus 1990), the threat of prosecution allows victims to raise the specter of a coercive response that will involve punishment or loss. What matters is that the resource is controlled by the victim—if it is controlled by the legal authority, a deterrent threat may be established but *power and resources* remain unbalanced in the relationship. Ford (1983, 1991a) argues that the threat of prosecution, when controlled by the victim, may be more powerful than its reality in managing marital violence because of its relationship to marital power.

But there are problems in the implementation of prosecution and its efficacy as a means of social control. In many jurisdictions, the "criminalization" of marital violence resulted in a rapid increase in the number of wife assault defendants arrested and referred to the lower and superior courts (Goolkasian 1986). In effect, an entire new class of defendants entered the criminal justice system. They differed from drug offenders, burglars, and others who comprise the "daily stream of cases on the offense and offender characteristics that are considered in sentencing."[12] The unique nature of spouse assault cases challenged the established norms within the social organization of the court (Fagan et al. 1984). By introducing a new class of cases into an established "stream," prosecutors may alter the group dynamics, developed over a lengthy period and in response to a shared empirical base, that result in normative decisions across a range of cases.

For example, a felony assault against a spouse may seem quite serious to an arresting officer faced with noninjury domestic incidents, but less serious to a sentencing judge in contrast to stranger cases where defendants have prior criminal records.[13] In sorting cases for prosecution—or prioritizing cases for last resort sanctions including imprisonment—the "working group" in the court (Eisenstein and Jacob 1977) may look to a "going rate" for guidance (Emerson 1983).[14] The relatively brief history of wife assault cases in the criminal courts, and the shifting priorities for prosecution in many urban areas, has not allowed such a rate to develop among the closed social network of court actors involved in prosecution and adjudication policy. This increases risks that, just as arrest often involved no substantive punishment, spouse assault cases in the courts may be assigned a lower priority and seriousness where substantive punishment may be minimized.

The few studies on the specific deterrent effects of prosecution suggest that, like arrest, the effectiveness of prosecution is mediated by the process by which it is launched. Fagan et al. (1984) reported significantly lower recidivism among assailants prosecuted, based on reports from 270 self-selected victims.[15] Nearly all these were victim complaints, and recidivism rates were lower for women seeking prosecution than other legal and extralegal sanctions, including arrest where no prosecution followed.

An experiment in Indianapolis (Ford 1991b) found suppression effects when violence rates were compared for the period preceding and following referral of cases for prosecution. Recidivism rates were lower in cases where women *elected* to continue prosecution (given a choice) compared to *mandatory* prosecution. Effects were evident both in the pretrial period (before sentencing) and for six months afterward. Violence rates also were lower when *victims* initiated prosecution (by victim complaint) compared to prosecutions that were initiated following an arrest (prosecutorial complaint).

Ford argues that social control is most effective when the decision to pursue prosecution is assigned to the victim, making legal institutions a resource for the victim and altering the balance of power in the relationship. He concludes that "actual prosecution . . . probably is less important than . . . the power they gain through bargaining with significant threats of prosecution and punishment" (1991b, 331). That is, legal control is transformed into a form of social control that is wielded by the victim. The costs of the act are set and manipulated by the victim, making the deterrent effect more salient and social control more effective.

*Treatment as Social Control*

The social control of spouse assailants through treatment interventions developed within a framework that combined legal coercion with social control. Court-ordered treatment, under conditions of either diversion or probation, often serves as the social control component of the legal sanction, and usually supplants punitive sanctions (Dutton 1986a, 1987). It was widely embraced and incorporated into legal institutions as part of the criminalization of spouse assault (Ganley 1981; Goolkasian 1986). Treatment dispositions solved a number of organizational and ideological dilemmas that were created by the rapid increase in spouse assault cases in the criminal court (Fagan 1988).

First, treatment provided an "intermediate" sanction and form of social control that is harsher than probation but less drastic than incarceration. Whether or not incarceration is an appropriate sanction in a particular case, judges often are reluctant to invoke such "last resort" sanctions for spouse assault when the victim has not been severly injured (Dutton 1988a; Goolkasian 1986). Judges may fear the consequences to victims of the removal of economic support, and they may still (inappropriately) view spouse assault cases as less serious than stranger violence and thus less deserving of scarce jail or prison space. Treatment meets the need for official sanctions that symbolize disapproval without requiring incarceration (except in the most serious cases). The availability of a dispositional option makes these cases more salient for judges, and in turn prosecutors and police.

Second, treatment offers a means to protect women who chose not to dissolve their relationship, but whose violent partners would not seek treatment voluntarily. Third, treatment placements provide a form of control that strengthens the traditional probation sanction. Monthly, superficial contacts with probation officers for misdemeanor offenses are replaced by weekly or biweekly therapeutic interventions in a structured milieu. Failure to abide by probation conditions mandating treatment participation can result in court action and presumably an escalation in sanction severity. Fourth, treatment interventions often are specifically designed to reinforce the substantive meaning of the arrest sanction (Ganley 1981; Saunders and Azar 1988). The format challenges assailants' belief that their arrest and conviction was unjust, or that their use of violence was justified.

This model has been widely accepted in part because its philosophical basis—individual responsibility and behavioral control—is compatible with explanations of crime causation that stress individual pathology. However, evidence of the social control effects of treatment is inconclusive due to weak evaluation designs and failure to distinguish among diverse treatment models. Recent evaluations (Saunders and Hanusa 1984; Dutton 1986a, 1987; Edelson et al. 1987) reported that 64 to 84 percent of treatment participants were not violent following treatment, although measurement, follow-up times, research designs and definitions of treatment and "success" varied.[16]

Accordingly, whether treatment is an effective form of social control remains unknown. Although legal coercion is intrinsic to court-ordered treatment, and noncompliance carries the threat (but perhaps not the reality) of a punitive response, there is insufficient data to evaluate treatment effectiveness. Moreover, there are competing treatment theories. Important distinctions exist between models using family systems approaches, anger management and assertiveness skills training, and feminist treatment models (Dutton 1988b).

Treatment groups focusing on anger management challenge the assailant's rationalizations that neutralize self-punishment and attribute the cause of their violence to the victim or some other external factor. For these programs, a primary objective is to directly undermine such cognitive, habit-sustaining mechanisms in assaultive males (Browne and Dutton, 1990).[17] Feminist therapy calls for a more basic resocialization of men and, in lieu of anger management, a redirection of their view of women and sex roles and their instrumental use of violence to retain power and domination (Gondolph 1985a). The social and cultural supports that reinforce the maintenance of power are critical to this model (Gondolph 1985b; Bowker 1983; Fagan 1989).

Expanding the social control function of treatment depends on the resolution of critical issues. First, personality characteristics and behavioral problems of participants mediate treatment outcomes (Hamberger and Hastings 1989). Models tailored to specific types of assaultive males are needed. Second, ineffective treatment compromises victim safety and neutralizes the symbolic and substantive components of the legal sanction. The response to treatment noncompliance, dropout or failure needs to be framed in a legal context that reinforces the substantive content of the original punitive sanction. Third, current programs reach only a small fraction of assaultive males. To be salient as social control, and to make credible the court's involvement, increasing the certainty of sanctions will require expansion of treatment options and a more explicit legal control framework for treatment participation.

## Social Control Through General Deterrence

Earlier, the indirect contributions of specific deterrence to social control were examined. Although specific deterrent effects may be weak, there may be secondary, general deterrent effects from the increased incidence of arrest for spouse assault (Williams and Hawkins 1991) and the social disapproval symbolized by changing legal norms. We turn here to the general deterrent effects: to what extent do expectations of social costs attached to an act offer a valid theoretical basis for social control of spouse assault?

General deterrence contributes to social control through the moral-educative function of the law (Zimring and Hawkins 1973), and through creating and disseminating the fear of intrinsic consequences of legal sanctions (Gibbs 1975). Moreover, specific deterrence also complements and enhances general deterrence and social control: the threat and example of punishment educates the public about the expectation of punishment, while punishment also expresses social disapproval for the act. Even where specific deterrent effects of legal mobilization may be weak, the general deterrent effects may become more salient.

Accordingly, the mobilization of law contributes to social control by supplementing and enhancing the moral influence established through education and popularization of the law's functions with respect to social problems. Punishment symbolizes and expresses the level of social disapproval for the act. If the establishment of an expectation of social cost underlies the social control function of deterrence, its effectiveness depends on the success of mobilization of the law and legal institutions. Williams and Hawkins (1989a, 1989b, 1991) expanded the deterrence framework to include both direct costs of legal sanctions (jail time) and social costs attached to legal sanction (job loss, social disapproval, humiliation, relationship loss). They examined the perceived *certainty* of sanctions and both costs resulting from legal intervention. They included both direct and indirect costs as *perceived* ramifications of arrest specific to the assailant's social context, and specified social and legal costs resulting from both the violent act and legal controls that may follow it (1991).

For example, Williams and Hawkins (1989a) analyzed responses from interviews with (N = 494) males in a sample derived from a three-year panel study of the dynamics of intimate violence. Respondents were asked to imagine what would happen if they were arrested for an attack on a spouse or partner, and analyzed the influence of perceived indirect and direct costs of arrest on the decision to participate in spouse assault. All respondents had reported one or more assaults on a spouse or female partner during the year preceding the interview.

Respondents believed that arrest would have deleterious consequences for their personal lives, were it to occur, including disrupted social relationships and humiliation before family and friends. However, responding to hypothetical scenarios, they viewed the loss of job or a jail remand highly unlikely as a consequence for assaults. Even when men perceived arrest for spouse assault as both certain and severe, assailants rated the social costs of arrest as more severe than legal costs (such as jail time). Also, assailants' decision to participate in spouse assault is mediated by the indirect or social costs of arrest (self-stigma, social disapproval, partner loss, and family stigma) more so than the legal costs. Although males did not perceive job loss or jail time as a likely outcome of arrest, job loss coupled with relationship loss, self-stigma and social disapproval were most important in comprising the deterrent effect of arrest.

Carmody and Williams (1987) also analyzed responses about the perceived *certainty* and *severity* of sanctions for wife assault based on telephone interviews with a probability sample of married, cohabitating, or recently separated/divorced couples. Responses from (N = 174) men who reported using physical force against their partners were compared with (N = 1,452) nonassaultive men. Four hypothetical "sanctions" were measured: arrest, social condemnation, separation or divorce from the partner, and retaliatory force by the partner. Men viewed retaliatory force by the partner as the *least* likely consequence of wife assault. The perceived severity of this reaction was quite low as well. The perceived certainty of arrest was also quite low, although the perceived severity score suggested that men viewed this sanction as very serious if it did occur. Male respondents did consider the possibility of a loss of respect from friends and relatives as both likely and severe. However, although the loss of the partner as a result of wife assault was considered a severe outcome, it was perceived as very unlikely.

Assaultive and nonassaultive men did not differ significantly in their perceptions of the certainty (not very likely) and severity (very severe) of arrest or of their partners separating from them or getting a divorce. However, assaultive men did perceive it as more likely that their partners would respond with physical aggression than did nonassaultive men. Conversely, nonassaultive men perceived the certainty and severity of social condemnation as significantly greater than assaultive men. Finally, although the distributions were similar for one-time and repeat offenders, the perceived severity of arrest was significantly lower for men who had assaulted their partners more than once (Carmody and Williams 1987), and presumably where police more often had been called. Evidently, both the perceived and actual deterrent effects of arrest seem to diminish for assailants familiar with the "going rates" of punishment in the criminal justice system for spouse assault.

Perhaps the low expectation of jail time as a component of deterrence reflects their assessment of the "going rate" of punishment for spouse assault. The relatively low base rate of arrest for spouse assault and the relative recency of the societal emphasis on legal sanctions for spouse assault contribute to the normative ambiguity surrounding it and the perception of less serious punishment resulting from arrest. Whether legal mobilization has proceeded sufficiently to establish an expectation of both arrest and a substantive sanction is unknown, and the effects of the moral-educative function of criminalization have not been measured.

## Reciprocity Between Social and Legal Controls

Research on both general and specific deterrence of spouse assault point toward a reciprocal relationship between social and legal sanctions in the social control of spouse assault. Both the direct costs of legal sanctions (the intrinsic punitive consequences of arrest) and the social costs of legal sanctions are salient as controls, although the effects of legal sanctions as social control seem to be indirect and work through their facilitation of social controls. And both the act itself (Williams and Hawkins 1991) and the legal response may levy social costs on the assailant and set in motion the processes that produce informal sanctions.

Arrest of spouse assailants (Berk and Newton 1985; Dunford et al. 1989) results deterrence processes that seem to operate through both threats of formal social controls (legal sanctions) and informal social controls (loss of self-esteem, disrupted social ties, job loss, and shame).[18] These effects were observed in paradigms using both hypothetical scenarios (Williams and Hawkins 1989a, 1989b) and actual arrests (Dutton et al. 1991). Offenders who desist from further violence following arrest may be responding not only to the potential legal costs, but also to the implications of arrest for

relationsips with peers, employers, their spouses, and their neighbors.[19]

Research on perceptual deterrence suggests that although a violent act may not produce such informal controls, they may be set
in motion or facilitated by formal sanctions (Williams and Hawkins
1989a). Results of experiments on arrest (Dunford et al. 1989) and
prosecution (Ford 1991a) show how these processes are set in
motion, and how such informal social controls are invoked by
victims once empowered through an alliance with legal institutions.
Controls that are facilitated by legal sanctions create a coercive
context where social costs are made more salient, and the victim's
security is enhanced.

Dunford et al. (1989) argue that a policy that *encourages* but does
not mandate arrest may be a more effective form of social control
than *mandatory* legal intervention. When victims invoke prosecutorial authority following an arrest or by filing a complaint, they
become active participants in the social controls brought to bear on
their relationship. They argue—similar to Ford's (1983, 1991a)
analysis of prosecution strategies—that victims can then use the
criminal justice process to negotiate their own security with sus-
pects/spouses, set the costs of continued violence or rewards for
desistance, and integrate legal and extralegal social controls (such
as court-ordered treatment).

Thus, according victims the option for arrest is an empowering
process since the decision to invoke legal control is transferred
from legal authorities to the victim. When arrest is mandated, social
control remains with legal authorities, and power differentials between assailant and spouse remain intact. But transferring the
decisions also shifts the locus of social control from institutional
control to a microinteractional process where victims actively manage the process of social control.

The causal linkages that specify how controls mediate assailants'
decision making processes and behavior are still not well understood. The weight of empirical evidence suggests that the social
costs of arrest facilitate extralegal social controls (loss of his
spouse, or the shame that social disclosure might create) that weigh
more heavily in the decision by assailants to avoid violence than
does fear of formal sanctions or legal punishment (arrest or punish-

ment). Conceptualizations of social control through deterrence evidently require a broad framework that includes the cognitive and learning processes through which assailants perceive and weigh the social and legal costs of legal control, the mechanisms by which these perceptions inform behavioral decisions, and other social psychological processes that comprise the decision to avoid spouse assault.

We turn next to the types of social controls invoked by victims apart from legal intervention, and the mechanisms that may make those controls more salient than the threat of punishment.

### Informal Social Control

Social control involves more than the interactions between victims and assailants and the interventions of legal institutions. Social control involves the normative processes and ethics of social interaction that regulate everyday social life (Doyle and Luckenbill 1991), as well as the mobilization that occurs in response to problem behaviors. Thus, informal social controls are effective in several ways: inhibition of problem behaviors, facilitation of conformity, and restraint of social deviance once it appears.

Informal social controls are facilitated and perhaps made more salient by the reciprocity between legal and social controls. These informal, often interpersonal, social controls often involve explicit or remedial actions to raise the social costs of spouse assault. The effects of these informal controls hold important clues for understanding the contexts, motivation, and processes of cessation by assailants.

### Social Disclosure

Bowker's (1984) study of victim-initiated controls involved interviews with over 1,000 victims who had remained in their own homes and minimized abuse based on use of social networks, self-help strategies and available help sources.[20] Three types of strategies were used by victims to control violence: personal strategies, formal help-sources (legal and social agencies), and informal help-sources (social networks).

Social disclosure to neighbors, relatives, friends, and others about the violence in the relationship was an effective control. These informal help-sources also were places where the violence emerged from the private family realm to social knowledge, and social costs attached to spouse assault (stigma to the assailant, social disapproval) were invoked. Second, social interventions, including contracts with the clergy or women's groups, also carried with them the threat of social stigmatization. The third strategy was a group of self-defense strategies, including hiding, taking shelter, or physical self-defense. Accordingly, in addition to self-protection, victims report that social controls from extralegal "authorities" and social sources of support are particularly salient.

Male responses to victim efforts to control violence also show the importance of informal social control. According to victim reports, over half (51 percent) of the males apparently responded to fear: of divorce or legal sanction (Bowker 1983). About one in four also feared loss of their partner, and "wanted to reestablish the relationship." Those who sought help turned mostly to friends, and did so when the victims also initiated social or legal sanctions.

These processes again suggest reciprocity between legal and social sanctions to raise the cost of assaults to the partner. Victims who initiated strategies to control spouse assault in effect threatened or invoked several types of sanctions. Both legal sanctions (contacting the police or prosecutor) or social sanctions (contacting social agencies, disclosure to neighbors and relatives, relationship loss) were cited as enablers for victims to stop assaults. The males also were responsive to sanctions, either the threat of loss of the relationship or the threat of social or legal intervention.[21]

Although the results stop short of identifying specific processes of social control, conditions can be discerned that make social controls salient within the relationship. Certainly, a restoration of the balance of marital power is evident in the strategies used by the women studied by Bowker. This notion fits well with other studies (e.g., Frieze 1979; Walker 1979; Pagelow 1984) which correlate marital violence to imbalances in marital power such as decision making or control of social networks.

Second, raising the costs of battering implicitly suggests that deterrence, social learning and rationale choice perspectives converge as the "costs" of maintaining marital power through force no longer are worthwhile. The actions by victims may represent the introduction of negative reinforcement, or aversive social consequences, for battering. The removal of the gratifying rewards of spouse assault may also result from these strategies, again opening ways to increase the costs of continued assaults. Once these choice dynamics begin, the sociopsychological processes that facilitate self-control of violence can develop.

## Termination

The threat of termination is a form of social control that carries significant costs for males. Bowker (1983, 1984) cites reports from women that males responded quickly and contritely to the threat of losing contact with their wives and children to begin cessation of their violence. Assaultive males also see relationship loss as a social consequence of arrest that would deter them from continued abuse (Williams and Hawkins 1989a, 1991).

But termination also has social, emotional, and economic costs for women victims of spouse assault. Termination of relationships is a "last resort" sanction invoked by women who have exhausted other forms of social control, who no longer can find value in remaining coupled that exceeds the physical (injury) or emotional costs of violence, or who fear for their lives or the lives of their children (Browne 1987). Gender roles provide strong motivations for women to seek alternative social controls to maintain their relationship: dissolution threatens to cut off legitimate avenues of sexual expression, and exposes women to isolation and consignment to some residual pool of "sexual surplus" (Faludi 1991).

Accordingly, the decision by a woman to terminate a relationship is not taken lightly, even in the face of violence, since it raises the prospect of poverty (Sidel 1986) and the loss of valued social capital that derives from remaining coupled (Schecter 1982). These costs, together with the fear of loss of emotional intimacy and financial security, provide strong motivations for women in violent relationships to seek formal and informal sanctions to control violence, sanctions that will help them maintain even unstable, problematic, or violent relationships.

Browne (1987) points to several factors that combine to create difficulties for women in leaving violent relationships: their continuing bond to the male based on a "caretaker" doctrine consistent with their own sex role socialization, the threat of violent reprisals against them or their children if they leave the abuser, shock reactions of victims to abuse, and the practical (emotional, financial, logistic, physical security) problems in actually separating (see Browne 1987, chapters 5 and 7). Long-term and very severe violance may produce a trauma-based bond between victim and assailant (Dutton and Painter 1981).[22] Given threats by males about leaving, as well as threats within the relationship of injury, the constant fear of violence regardless of the action taken leaves no choices that do not carry a high risk of danger.

The cognitive processes leading to a decision to terminate may be age-dependent, with younger women assigning lower costs to termination. Miller and Simpson (1991) surveyed (N = 640) university students. They reported that college-age females who were victims of courtship violence were more likely than males to leave an abusive partner or terminate an abusive relationship. However, termination by females may become more costly and thus less likely as the stakes increase in their relationships: women in more serious relationships, or relationships that were high priorities and more valued, said they were less likely to terminate.

Whether these distinctions and base rates persist at ages beyond college years is unknown. However, the calculus of gains and costs of termination by women victims is likely to change with life circumstances such as the addition of children, entry into career, and other economic considerations enter the decision making process.

If termination is a "last resort" sanction, we would expect it to decrease in response to more effective alternative forms of social control. But the decision to terminate also will vary according to relationship and violence factors: the violence histories of the women preceding the current relationship (Miller and Simpson 1991), the severity of the violence and the trauma of the bond that it produces (Dutton and Painter 1981; Browne 1987), the presence of children and the woman's economic prospects and capital, and access to other sources of informal and formal controls such as friendship networks and social institutions that can both protect victims and express social disapproval.

*Violence as Social Control*

The symbolic meaning of criminal conduct may be interpreted simply as a violation of a legal or moral prohibition, or as a form of self-help and social control (Black 1983). Hobbesian theory would suggest that, in conditions where law and governmental social control are least developed, and where informal social controls are ineffective or unavailable, violence would be evident as a form of social control. In the context of spouse assault, a violent response by a female partner following an assault by a male spouse may be interpreted as self-defense, mutual combat, or a form of social control in response to the weakness of law.

The use of violence by women in intimate relationships is widely acknowledged but little understood (Saunders 1986; Greenblat 1983). Nearly half of all violent relationships involve violence by both partners, while nearly two in three women victims also were violent toward their spouses within one year before or after their victimization (Straus et al. 1980). Although rates of male and female violence are nearly equal (Straus et al. 1980; Straus and Gelles 1986), rates of severe violence are greater among men (Fagan and Browne 1992) and injuries are sustained at a higher rate by women (Stets and Straus 1990). Although the rates of violence by women victims are high, they are engaging in violence in contexts where they are likely to suffer more than their partners.

Women in severely violent relationships who perceive their imminent danger have used homicide as a form of self-defense for themselves or their children (Browne 1987).[23] Although women commit homicides at a rate far lower than males, they more often kill their spouses than do males. In most cases, these women were victims of lengthy periods of severe abuse, and many perceived that the male had lost all control during periods of rage and violence. They also had exhausted or abandoned (as ineffective) other forms of social control. Browne and Williams (1989) showed that the availability of informal social controls (in the form of legislation mandating services) contributed to reductions in state-level homicide rates over a four period following the passage of legislation.

Research on the situational context of women's violence in intimate relationships is rare. Berk, Berk, Loeseke, and Rauma (1983) disputed the depiction of spouse assault as "mutual combat." Despite their participation in retaliatory violence, women more often were injured and turned to the police and other agencies for help. In a small (N = 52) sample of shelter and counseling clients, about 40 percent of the women who used severe violence were responding in self-defense, and another one in three said they were "fighting back" (Saunders 1986). The motives of self-defense and retaliation were indistinguishable among these women, reflecting the mix of anger and fear emotions during a violent episode. Moreover, the labels attached to affix victims' roles in violent episodes often obscure the context and motives (fear, rage, protection, control) that infuse *protective* assaults (Greenblat 1983).

Violence is a risky tactic for women. Bowker (1983) reported that violence by victims was not only ineffective in promoting desistance, but often escalated the man's violence. The few studies that have examined violent interactions between male assailants and their victims are inconclusive on the meaning of violence by women. Apart from self-defense in potentially lethal attacks, there appears to be little gained by women from employing violence as a social control or regulatory strategy in violent relationships. Their disadvantages in strength and size place them at great risk from injury. Without further knowledge on the natural history of intimate violence, there will be little clarity about the effectiveness of victims' violence as social control.

### Social Control, Social Learning, and Social Bonds: Social Psychological Restraints on Spouse Assault

A full specification of social control involves processes by which external social norms are internalized in the personality of social actors. Once internalized, these social psychological structures provide cognitive linkages that mediate the threats of external sanctions and their behavioral outcomes. Thus, compliance with societal rules results from more than just external pressures: it involves the acceptance of social norms and moral obligations to obey them (Coser 1975). The essence of social control involves the shaping of these norms through interaction with external actors that establish the contingencies surrounding the behavior, and the internalization of these norms so that they in turn shape behavioral decisions.

Theories that specify only the role of the external reward-cost choices overlook the importance of rational or subjective cognitive processes that are intrinsic to behavioral decisions (Akers 1989). Rationale choice theorists contend that behavioral outcomes are choices that reflect an assessment of the marginal costs and rewards of the behavior compared to the costs/rewards of conformity (Cornish and Clarke 1985). Deterrence theorists suggest that the intrinsic, direct costs of punishment will result in avoidance of behaviors that lead to pain or deprivation (Gibbs 1975). The empirical evidence from research on perceptual deterrence and victim-initiated controls on spouse assault suggests that these two perspectives are compatible and apparently converge.[24] Yet these perspectives do not address the process of acquisition or learning of the contingencies of reward and punishment that are intrinsic to both theories.

For social control to be effective, the experiential effects of social sanctions, involving self-stigma, fear of job loss, and social disapproval, also must trigger the development or actuation of internal controls that inhibit behavior. Williams and Hawkins (1989b) suggest that these inhibitions or restraints reflect the ties to conventional society that are intrinsic to social bonds of control theory (Hirschi 1969).[25]

Control theory provides mechanisms to explain crime avoidance rather than crime commission. The presence of social bonds suggests that behavioral controls are sufficiently salient to restrain participation in spouse assault. The salience of the direct and indirect costs of social sanctions for spouse assault suggests the fit of the intervening structures of control theory as the mechanism through which spouse assault is restrained. That is, social control inhibits spouse assault by posing painful consequences that threaten the individual's social attachments and beliefs.

An empirical test by Williams and Hawkins (1989b) with a sample of (N = 483) males resulted in validation of attachments and beliefs (but not commitment or involvement) as inhibitors of spouse assault. Assailants also feared the legal consequences of arrest, but in other research expressed those fears in terms of social costs rather than punishment costs. Attachments to significant others was expressed as the importance of social interactions with neighbors, friends and others. Beliefs included normative attitudes about violence, and perceived consequences of arrest.

However, other studies (e.g., Williams and Hawkins 1989a) suggest that the costs attached to arrest also include job loss (conventional behaviors, commitment to conventional goals), social disapproval (beliefs in the law, attachment to conventional others), and relationship loss (attachment to significant others). Evidently, there are attachment, commitment and involvement costs, and pressures to adhere to moral codes, that result from formal and informal social controls, costs also that reflect the social bonds specified by control theory. If deterrence implies a rational behavioral choice based on marginal costs and rewards of conformity, then the strength of social bonds sets the weights attached to the specific costs and rewards.[26]

But social bonds are developmental outcomes, the result of lengthy socialization processes beginning in early childhood and continuing through the transition to early adult years. Akers (1985; 1990, 659) contends that conforming behavior is shaped over time before becoming internalized (self-controlled). Accordingly, the development of social bonds, or the acquisition of the learned component of deterrence, requires a further specification of motivational, reinforcement and acquisition processes by which costs and rewards are learned and evaluated. If socialization is intrinsic to the development of social bonds, then a full specification of the social control of spouse assault also must involve reinforcement or learning principles within the unique context of marital relations and the dynamics of spouse assault.

*Deterrence, Social Control and Social Learning*

This framework for social control of spouse assault expands deterrence beyond legal punishment to include social sanctions that provide costs and rewards for both violence and restraint, and that establish the contingencies associated with these behaviors. Deterrence, control and rational choice theories offer fertile ground for integration, but are incomplete without the inclusion of social learning perspectives to explain the development and natural progressions of behaviors, including its extinction (Akers 1985, 1990; see Fagan and Browne 1992, for a specific application to spouse assault).

The fear of legal punishment and its indirect social costs comprise the deterrent component of social control. Social learning theorists refer to the deterrent component as positive punishment. When these punishment costs are internalized, they are translated into social psychological structures—attachments, commitments, beliefs—that comprise social bonds. The internalization takes place through aversive experiences (painful, noxious stimuli) associated with the behavior. The societal and victim responses to spouse assault—punishment, other legal controls, coerced treatment within a punitive context, social sanctions, relationships costs, retaliatory violence—establishes the contingencies that reinforce the development of social bonds to restrain spouse assault and internalize social controls.

Negative punishment includes the counterdeterrent effects of weak legal sanctions that fail to attach a cost or fear associated with law violation. Also, societal acceptance or acceptance by the victim provide negative punishments, or rewards, for spouse assault. Accordingly, when the police have responded to previous spouse assault incidents without formal reaction, or where arrest results in no substantive punishment (jail time, for example), or where victims do not invoke other controls, negative costs are attached to the behavior. And, at the same time, the behavior is reinforced positively.

These processes suggest that spouse assault, rather than being the calculated behavior of a rational actor, is a contingent behavior where the behavioral outcomes reflect the social experiences of male spouses in legal and social interactions. These interactions occur with both societal institutions of social control and in microinteractions with spouses and others. It is through these interactions that the rewards and costs of punishment are learned and reinforced, as well as the rewards and costs of conformity. And in turn, it is in this context that the bonds of self-control develop, and ultimately are internalized and reinforced.

### Countercontrol: Supports and Motivations for Spouse Assault

The acquisition processes by which behaviors are rewarded and punished is central to this conceptualization of the social control of spouse assault. The difficulty of extinguishing spouse assault attests to its intensive rewards for assailants (Fagan 1989). These rewards also work in opposition to the punishment reinforcement of legal and social sanctions, and apparently win out in many instances.

Accordingly, theories of social control also must address the complex motivations, emotions and contexts of spouse assault that offer their own intrinsic rewards.[27] The learned component of spouse assault and the reinforcement of power-control and domination drives (Fagan and Browne 1992) offer powerful gratification from assaults,[28] and may neutralize or undermine the effects of social controls and social bonds inhibiting spouse assault.[29] These intrinsic rewards of violence and cognitive rearrangements of violent episodes may destabilize or make irrational the learning processes implied in the behavioral decision to assault one's spouse. Three sources of counter-control are briefly reviewed here.

*Patriarchy, Social Networks and Social Embedment*

Social control of spouse assault must counter the cultural norms that facilitate it. Early theories on spouse assault viewed this aggression as an outworking of a culture that engendered and maintained the domination of men over women in every aspect of social life (e.g., Martin 1976; Dobash and Dobash 1979; Walker 1979). Partriarchical influence appears to be culturally normative (Bograd and Yllo 1988): the beliefs that support spouse assault simply express more general cultural norms and values that uphold a hierarchical, patriarchal social organization.[30] Such norms have been linked with wife assault in empirical studies in the United Kingdom (Dobash and Dobash 1979), Canada (Smith 1990) and the United States (Bowker 1983, 1984; Yllo and Straus 1984).

Straus (1976) identified nine specific manifestations of a male-dominant social structure that support wife assault.[31] He concluded that the weakness of legal sanctions for spouse assault (until the 1980s) reflects cultural norms that equate the institution of marriage carrying with a "hitting license": an (implied or explicit) immunity to prosecution for spouse assault by male partners. Economic inequalities, gaps in political representation, and cultural portrayals of women also are cited as manifestations of male orientation and hegemony (Dobash and Dobash 1979; Pagelow 1984).[32] These cultural and economic indicators contribute to male attitudes of superiority and the legitimation of domination.

Less clear, however, are the mechanisms that translate cultural norms into specific social processes that in turn contribute to (or attenuate propensities for) assaultive behavior. For example, subcultural explanations of spouse assault emphasize the translation of broader cultural norms into microsocial interactions within specific networks (Wolfgang and Ferracuti 1967). In Bowker's (1983, 1984) studies, the severity of violence was greater among assaultive spouses who were more deeply embedded in male subcultures.[33] Bowker contends that

the myriad peer-relationships that support the patriarchal dominance of the family and the use of violence to enforce it may constitute a subculture of violence. The more fully a husband is immersed in this subculture, the more likely he is to batter his wife. (135)

The reinforcement of values of male domination and power, or the failure to sanction it negatively, likely occurs through myriad independent social networks that tacitly condone violence toward women. These work in opposition to societal norms that disapprove of spouse assault. Embedment in these networks poses a high risk of severe violence in the home (Fagan and Browne 1992), and also makes it more difficult for males to compromise their cultural identity by discussing their problems with friends or seeking help elsewhere (Miller and Simpson 1991). In addition, engulfment within a network of social relationships often minimizes attachments to people in other social networks (Eckland-Olsen 1982), limiting exposure to other cultural or belief orientations.

With social embedment comes the gratification of social accep-

tance and social identity, often built up over a lifetime of socialization. Alternatively, abandoning the assaultive behavior and losing
control in the home may risk social disapproval. The more deeply
embedded in the social context, the more dependent the assailant
may become on that social world for approval and a positive social
interpretation of his behavior. Conversely, social control of spouse
assault has been shown to be associated with changes in the
micronetworks that comprised the social worlds of assailants (Fagan 1989; Bowker 1983, 1986).

## Motivations for Spouse Assault: Power, Control, and Domination

Although power-motivation theories were first developed by
McClelland and colleagues (McClelland et al. 1972; McClelland and
Davis 1972; McClelland 1975) regarding drinking behaviors, they
follow naturally from patriarchal theories as explanations of assaults by males against their female partners. Although the conceptualization and measurement of power and adherence to traditional
sex role expectations varies extensively,[34] the basic premise unify-
ing the more recent integration of these theories is that assault is
used to assert or maintain power within the relationship (Dutton
and Browning 1987, 1988; Mason and Blankenship 1987). Straus
(1978) and Browne (1987) argue that one episode of violence can
permanently alter the balance of marital power toward a strongly
husband-dominant pattern.

Other studies emphasize the importance of power *balances*
within a partner relationship (Dutton and Strachan 1987). For
example, Coleman and Straus (1986) found that spouse assault was
lowest in "egalitarian" couples that shared domestic chores and
decisions. However, both male and female aggression was highest
in couples in which females were dominant (that is, had the greatest
influence in decision making and control over resources). In couples in which the female partner has greater access to resources
and/or decision-making power, it is unclear whether female aggression is a response to male aggression or an aggressive reaction to
confrontations over power.

Power motives and adherence to patriarchical ideology converge
in research on patriarchy and spouse assault. The translation of

patriarchical ideology into specific attitudes or perceptions of marital power is evident in empirical work by Straus (1976), Yllo and Straus (1984), and Smith (1990). If males are socialized to expect dominance or power within the relationship, aggression may be initiated from frustration over their inability to control their female partners.

Issues of intimacy and the threat of dependency also may trigger violence in partner relationships. Threats to hegemony or control also may result from the male's emotional dependence on, or intimacy with, the victim (Browne 1987).[35] Browning and Dutton (1988) showed that males experience anger most readily in circumstances in which they perceive an impending loss of control over either intimacy or distance.[36] They contend that unsatisfied power needs may produce physiological arousal that is interpreted as anger and expressed through physical aggression. Similarly, increased demands for intimacy may be fear producing, and trigger verbal or physical assaults as a mechanism to produce distance and restore the "balance of power" to the male's control.

In sum, there are powerful rewards from spouse assault that may neutralize or counteract the effects of social controls. The gratification that men experience from marital hegemony and male domination can reinforce aggressive behavior. Gratification from spouse assault may come from achieving/maintaining the instrumental motive of dominance, from the expressive release of anger and aggression in response to perceived power deficits, from the attainment of positive social status in male-dominated networks that domination affords, or even from the restoration of intimacy *on their terms* that flows from the "hearts and flowers" aftermath of many assaults (see Walker 1979, for example).

## Neutralization

Batterers are particularly adept at denial and externalization of blame (Dutton 1986c; Dutton and Strachan 1987; Hamberger and Hastings 1989). Disavowal or accounts help avoid the assignment of an identity to an individual that is consistent with their deviant behavior (e.g., Scott and Lyman 1968). When deviant behaviors occur that violate either self-standards or social norms, a variety of mechanisms may be mobilized to explain the behavior or neutralize self-punishment. Sykes and Matza (1962) suggested that the denial of responsibility was one of several "techniques of neutralization" that individuals use to justify criminal behavior. The perception of being the victim rather than the perpetrator is a common technique used by assailants to neutralize responsibility for their conduct. Such an "excuse function" of spouse assault has cultural determinants.

For example, Shields and Hannecke (1983) found that 68 percent of male spouse assailants externalized the cause of their behavior by attributing it to the wife's behavior or to alcohol. "Excuses" for their spouse assaults were offered by 21 percent of the (N = 75) men studied by Dutton (1985). Although the remainder accepted *responsibility* for their actions, their *justifications* typically blamed the victim for these actions or discounted the behaviors as due to uncontrollable arousal or subgroup norms. Moreover, those who attributed their behavior to their wives were more likely to minimize the *severity* of their actions. Men in treatment for spouse assault (Sonkin et al. 1986) describe both the minimization of spouse assault and victim blaming; or alternatively, they accept responsibility but locate their behavior within cultural norms.

This notion of disavowal of deviance by assaultive males essentially relocates blame for behavior from the individual to an attribute or behavior of their adversary, an imperative in the immediate situational context, or a claim of conformity with cultural norms. This not only serves to excuse aggression, but it also reassures others that the behaviors themselves do not challenge the legitimacy of the violated norms. Thus, spouse assaulters do not challenge the sanctity of marriage nor societal laws against assault.

The cognitive restructuring of events that is necessary to neutralize self-punishment for disapproved behavior involves four types of mechanisms: (1) cognitive restructuring of the behavior itself, through euphemistic labelling of the violence, palliative comparison, or moral justification; (2) cognitive restructuring of the behavior-effect-relationship, through diffusion or displacement of responsibility; (3) cognitive restructuring of the effects of the violence, by minimizing or ignoring them; and (4) cognitive restructuring of the victim, through dehumanizing or victim blame (Bandura 1979). These processes also neutralize perceptions of social controls that proscribe behavior; leading to what Dutton (1982) referred to as "deindividuated violence," in which control over behaviors shifts from external cues to internal stimuli.

Whether assailants can legitimate their behaviors in frameworks that are culturally salient depends on social norms. Collins (1983) suggests that there is a synergistic relationship between cultural acceptance of such accounts and the relocation of blame to external sources that are widely thought to "cause" or at least excuse such behaviors. When cultural evaluations accept that marital conflict can cause aggressive or violent behaviors, then these accounts are more often honored by society, and the use of such excuses also is greater.

## Conclusions

The social control of spouse assault is mediated by the efficacy of the law and legal institutions, the viability of extralegal sources of social control, and the larger context of the natural history of assaults within intimate relationships. Spouse assaults occur in events where the antecedents lead to arousal marked by emotional instability (Browne and Dutton 1990) and irrational behavioral choices.[37] The response to arousal will interact with past external societal responses and internalized social controls to determine the occurrence of spouse assault.

A complex calculus will determine whether a male partner becomes violent under conditions of arousal: earlier lessons about "what works" to quell anxiety or release anger (Sonkin and Durphy 1985),[38] what he perceives as potential costs and consequences (Bowker 1983; Carmody and Williams 1987; Williams and Hawkins 1989a), the salience of internalized social controls (Williams and Hawkins 1989b), what he has seen others do in similar situations (Bandura 1973; Dutton 1988a), and his internalized control over his rage or fear (Browne 1987; Katz 1988).

Social control of spouse assault is likely to change in the future as legal and social controls develop more fully, and as regulative societal norms and customs governing family violence reduce its cultural acceptance. Two trends in particular may increase the effectiveness of legal controls: increasing the expectation of legal sanction through mobilization of legal institutions, and broader access of victims to both social and legal sanctions.

Social control also will reflect victim responses managing legal sanctions to increase the salience of both legal and social controls. Coercion in this case is a complex social phenomenon, not simply a legal one. This includes increasing social stigma and the personal costs of continued violence in the home. Thus, the creation of a shelter not only protects women but offers a social sanction for assailants through increased resources that the women may apply. To the extent that ecological controls at the neighborhood mitigate against violence more generally, social norms will reinforce the moral obligations to refrain from spouse assault.

Unfortunately, changing ecological structures may weaken the development of natural social controls or social norms. Increasing poverty and attendant social disorganization (Elliott and Huizinga 1990; Skogan 1989) and declining labor force participation by non-whites, especially African Americans (Wilson 1987) may erode neighborhood controls against violence generally. These processes also influence the situated social control of families within poor neighborhoods by minimizing the potential effects of job loss as a social cost of spouse assault. Detachment from the labor force preempts the controlling function of job loss and social stigma that result from social control. These dynamics suggest that social control of spouse assault is bound with macrosocial processes of social control, and is likely to vary in efficacy across social areas of varying economic strength and cohesion.

Advances in social control of spouse assault will follow from experimental research to examine the efficacy of social control. Experiments must address the institutional context in which social control is carried out, and the development of internalized social controls following interaction of assailants with legal and social sanctions. Understanding the reciprocity between legal and social controls, and the influences of victim strategies, can advance through research on the natural history of violence in intimate relationships.

# Notes

An earlier version of this paper was presented at the Annual Meeting of the Society for the Study of Social Problems, Washington, D.C., August 1990. The author gratefully acknowledges the contributions of Angela Browne.

1. These three approaches were not exclusive. Feminist approaches converged with the expansion of legal controls through the proliferation of victim-witness programs, creating favorable conditions for shifting the focus of social control to the legal system (Fagan and Browne 1992). Victim-witness programs proliferated in the 1970s, and were magnets within the criminal justice system for female victims of both family and stranger violence. Victimization as a social movement reflected concerns of several constituencies with divergent interests. Groups opposed to what they perceived as lenient sentencing of offenders saw the victims "movement" as a force to balance the rights of the accused with the rights of the victims. Citing tort theory, they viewed crime as a failure of the state to fulfill its part of the social contract, in turn creating an obligation to compensate. The needs of women and children for protection both from offenders and from shabby treatment from criminal justice agencies were seen by victims rights advocates as staking legitimate claims to their share of the "finite rights" in criminal law (Frieze and Browne 1989).

2. Most jurisdictions authorize arrest whenever there is probable cause that a felony assault has occurred. The degree of injury or presence of a weapon generally qualify a felony charge. For misdemeanor cases, there are restrictions on arrest in assault cases including corroboration or "in presence" requirements (Lerman 1986). Thus, victims must initiate a complaint or warrant to effect an arrest. The intent of mandatory arrest statutes is to eliminate these restrictions on misdemeanor wife assault, the most common charge category for domestic assaults, and to allow officers to make misdemeanor arrests on the basis of either the victim's hearsay or their own probable cause determination. In some states, these conditions were established by providing concurrent status as both felony and misdemeanor for domestic assault. Other states (e.g., Washington) have mandated arrest in all domestic assaults based on probable cause or victim complaint.

3. Other forces contributed to the prominence of pro-arrest policies based on deterrence. Civil litigation (Bruno v. Codd, 396 NYS 974, 1977; Scott v. Hart, No. 6-76-2395 [N.D. Cal:1976]; Thurman v. City of Torrington 595 F.Supp. 1521 [D. Conn:1984]) raised the likelihood of damages to police departments for failure to provide equal protection to victims of domestic violence. This combined with activism among feminists and the Reagan administration (Attorney General's Task Force on Family Violence 1984) to increase the political salience of wife assault cases that previously were deemed as "low visibility" behaviors.

4. The evidence from experiments is reviewed later in this chapter. Also, Williams and Hawkins (1991) suggest that the general deterrent effects of these policies have been overlooked in research that examines only the specific deterrent effects. They argue that social costs are risked by both arrest and the violent

acts that may outweigh other costs associated with legal actions (i.e., punishment).

5. Dutton (1987) compares this to the finding of Hood and Sparks (1970) that police made arrests in 20 percent of the cases where they attended and decided that a crime had been committed.

6. Violent family disputes in two Minneapolis police precincts were randomly assigned to one of three police responses: arrest, separation of victim and assailant, and advice/mediation. The study was limited to situations in which the assailant was present when the police arrived. During the six-month follow-up period, biweekly interviews with victims and reviews of official reports of family violence were collected. Sherman and Berk (1984a, 1984b) reported that arrested assailants had significantly lower recidivism rates for both offical records (10 percent) and victim reports (19 percent). There was no evidence of differential effects across conditions based on offender characteristics, though within-group differences were found (Berk 1986). This led to their recommendation that "police adopt arrest as the favored response to domestic assault on the basis (in the original) of its deterrence power" (as cited in Dunford et al., 1). A subsequent reanalysis by Tauchen, Tauchen and Witte (1986) offered more qualified support for the deterrent effects of arrest.

7. First, the follow-up period was relatively short (six months), given the episodic and cyclical patterns of family violence observed by Walker (1979; 1984) and others. Second, self-reports from assailants were not obtained, leaving out the possibility of a "hidden" violence period toward strangers, the original victim, or other victims in the home. Third, distinctions in the level and nature of violence were not made, leaving open questions of the relative harm (e.g., injury, intimidation) that may have accrued from battering incidents. Fourth, the biweekly interview process may have depressed recidivism rates through research effects, response effects, or task-specific biases. Awareness by offenders of victim interviews may have deterred or simply postponed recidivism during the study period. The validity of victim' reports may have been compromised, since assailants often were residing with them during the follow-up period. Fifth, not all precincts in Minneapolis participated in the experiment, and cases were handled from a disproportionately small number of officers. Sixth, other forms of wife abuse, such as persistent denigration or economic reprisal, were not investigated. Seventh, not all shifts were included, nor were the included neighborhoods representative of the social areas of the city of Minneapolis.

8. For example, all police calls for domestic violence during the 4:00 PM to 12:00 PM shift in the city of Omaha were randomly assigned into three treatment groups: (1) those in which the perpetrator would be arrested; (2) those in which the perpetrator would be separated from the victim; and (3) those in which police would "mediate" the dispute. Cases were sampled around the clock in Charlotte, where the use of a police-issued citation also presented a unique intervention option. Randomized treatment was conducted only for cases in which both perpetrator and victim were present at the scene when the police arrived. However, data on those cases in which the perpetrator was not present were collected and analyzed separately in Omaha.

9. Moreover, even when arrested, few defendants for spouse assault serve time (Fagan 1989; Elliott 1989).

10. Sherman and Berk (1984a) reported that their small sample size for the arrest group and the low response rate from victims regarding the time in custody data limit any conclusions on the effects of jail time. The Minneapolis, Charlotte and Omaha studies were unable to obtain official records on time in custody.

11. Hirschel et al. (1990) report that arrestees were routinely transported to the jail pending an appearance before a magistrate to have a warrant issued for the arrest (17). Afterward, most suspects presumably were released on bail.

12. Emerson (1983) defines the "stream of cases" facing officials as influencing legal decisions in several respects. Cases are evaluated for prosecution and sentencing relative to other cases, as well as on their merits. Thus, the relative seriousness of cases changes at different stages of processing, so that a case at arrest may appear to be more serious than at sentencing, when other cases have been winnowed out.

13. This process may be especially sensitive to the different processes of accumulating prior records for intimate violence compared to other crime types.

14. The "going rate" for an offense is *that sanction officials expect an offender to receive for specific offenses*, and is thought to be influenced by organizational factors independent of case specific variables (Casper and Brereton 1984; Hagan and Bumiller 1983).

15. Prosecution rates were low, however. Of the 74 women who sought prosecution, 10 cases were prosecuted and nine were convicted. The others either were dismissed for insufficiency, deferred pending alternative interventions (such as treatment or mediation), or postponed pending a re-evaluation of the assailant's conduct after a probationary period.

16. For example, Dutton (1986a) found that court-ordered mandated treatment resulted in significantly lower recidivism rates compared to nontreated males or treatment dropouts, but sample selection bias in the treatment assignments limits confidence in these findings. Harrell (1991) reported significantly higher rates of physical violence among 157 treated (88 percent) vs. nontreated (57 percent) assailants, based on victim reports over a four-month follow-up period. Treated assailants participated in three programs that varied in their treatment goals and content, and were assigned by judges based on their prior records and violence histories. Victims with nontreated partners also less often called police, and reported no new official charges for spouse assault. Some victims reported increases in the frequency and severity of spouse assault following treatment, although official records did not confirm their reports. Evidently, bad treatment may be iatrogenic, creating greater risks than no treatment at all.

17. For example, to the extent that an assailant believes that his wife's (or partner's) injuries were minimal, or that she was to blame for the conflict, the more likely it is that he will view his subsequent arrest as unjust. Treatment models confront these beliefs, as well as general attitudes about women (sex roles orientation), and beliefs about power in dyadic relationships (Eddy and Myers 1984; Dutton 1988a). Treatment also focuses on anger detection, control, and management to influence cognitive and behavioral abilities.

18. Bowker (1983) included loss of spouse and/or children as an explicit cost of legal intervention.

19. Dutton et al. report that the weight accorded to the threat of jail time is greater

for research on arrestees than was observed in the studies using "hypothetical" arrests.

20. Bowker (1983) interviewed (N = 146) respondents who were recruited through social agencies, religious and cultural groups, and media advertisements in the greater Milwaukee area. The second study (Bowker 1984, 1986) included a larger nationwide sample.

21. Bowker's findings also suggest differential effects by prior violence history. Sanctions were effective primarily in relationships where the history of violence was less severe and power imbalances between partners are minimal (128). For example, the strongest correlates of the assailants' cessation were duration of violence ( − .31) and abuse during pregnancy ( − .15). Again, it appears that more severe and protracted violence may be intractable despite formal, external interventions, legal or otherwise.

22. The bond also may be explained, in part, by the interaction of powerful (negative) reinforcers of extreme maltreatment alternating with positive behaviors (the "hearts and flowers" phase described by Walker [1979, 1984]), and expressions of dependency and remorse by the male abuser. The dependency, and the guilt and gender roles to which it appeals, are created paradoxically by the male's fear of losing the woman whom he has just abused and motivated to leave.

23. Homicides by women to protect themselves were termed victim-precipitated homicides, assigning the causal role to the male based on his instigation of the violence in the couple (Wolfgang 1958, 1967).

24. They also may be "subsumable under the more general differential reinforcement formula in social learning theory. Differential reinforcement refers to the overall balance of rewards and punishments for behavior" (Akers 1990, 655).

25. These bonds include attachments to family and friends, commitment to conventional beliefs and goals, involvement in conventional behaviors, and beliefs in the law.

26. See, Hirschi (1986) and Akers (1990) for discussions of the compatibility of rational choice, deterrence and control perspectives. While the link between deterrence and rational choice has developed a sound empirical footing (Klepper and Nagin 1989; Paternoster 1989), only Williams and Hawkins (1989b) have applied control theory to explain the nature of the utility function applied by decision makers given the opportunity to aggress against spouses.

27. Fagan and Browne (1992) cite three independent variables that increase the probability of violence during microsocial interactions: (1) psychological proclivity toward the exercise of physical violence toward spouses (e.g., personality factors); (2) beliefs that instrumental goals will be achieved through the use of physical force; and (3) arousal that provides the motivation for the (male's) assaultive behavior against the spouse or partner. Each of these factors in turn influences cognitive processes that interpret both the situation and the appropriate behavioral response, and accordingly are likely to mediate either external or internalized social controls.

28. Assailants also often are torn between contradictory ambivalent emotions including dependence, fear, anger, and aggressive impulses (Dutton 1988) that complicate any logical evaluation of alternative behavioral choices. The satisfaction of these emotions (e.g., anxiety reduction, elimination of fear) also

presents an important neutralizer to the perceptions and weighting of the costs of arrest or social sanction.

29. At the extremes of spouse assault, rage states by assailants obviate any calculation, intrinsic or conscious, of the costs or rewards of violence (Dutton 1988; Browne 1987).

30. See: Straus (1976) and Yllo (1983) for specific variables for patriarchy. Gender inequalities (wage differentials, labor market segmentation, political representation) and media portrayals of women are most often cited as indices of patriarchy.

31. Use of force as defense of male authority, normative attitudes supporting violence toward wives, compulsive masculinity, economic constraints and discrimination, burdens of child care (and failure to provide relief to these burdens), myth of the intrinsic weakness of the single parent household, preeminence of the caretaker/wife role for women, women's negative self-image, male orientation of the justice system.

32. Economic inequalities place a lesser value on women's labor and social contributions and reinforce the dominant role played by men in most labor markets. Fewer women occupy elective office than men, and popular culture offers fewer portrayals of women in egalitarian social positions in cinema, television, or print media.

33. The importance of reinforcing societal values, modeled in early childhood and refined in adult years, indicates that both environmental (or normative) supports for domination of women as a group and situational interactions at a social or subcultural level, contribute to male violence toward women.

34. Power is defined alternately in terms of: dominance, decision making, and relative levels of resources (Frieze and Browne 1989) the stronger taking advantage of the weaker; coercion through the threat of physical violence (Straus et al. 1980); or in terms of demographic characteristics that reflect aggregate social status of ethnic or racial groups (Berk et al. 1983).

35. The arousal engendered by emotions of love and desire becomes more anxiety provoking than pleasant. Thus, in addition to proactive desires for dominance and control, the neutralization of dependence and reassertion of emotional distance also may be a powerful reinforcer of spouse assault (Browne 1987; Fagan and Browne 1992).

36. For example, using vignettes, Browning and Dutton found that men reported anger at women's attempts at autonomy in the relationship, as well as attempts by women partners to intensify levels of intimacy and commitment.

37. Arousal also may come from threats of loss of control in the relationship, feelings of rejection or abandonment, threats from intimacy or emotional dependence on his spouse or partner, or threats to social status from outside the relationship (Browne 1987).

38. Especially whether past attacks have been gratifying and reinforcing. That is, whether past violent episodes have resulted in the reduction of arousal, anger or anxiety, or the restoration of control.

# References

Akers, R. L. 1985. *Deviant Behavior: A Social Learning Perspective* (3rd edition). Belmont, Cal.: Wadsworth.

Akers, R. L. 1989. A social behaviorist's perspective on the integration of theories of crime and deviance. In S. Messner, M. Krohn, and A. Liska (eds.), *Theoreteical Integration in the Study of Crime and Deviance: Problems and Prospects*. Albany, N.Y.: SUNY Press, p. 23–31.

Akers, R. L. 1990. Rational choice, deterrence and social learning theory in criminology. *Journal of Criminal Law and Criminology* 81: 653–77.

Bandura, A. 1973. *Aggression: A Social Learning Analysis*. Englewood Cliffs, N.J.: Prentice Hall.

Bandura, A. 1979. The social learning perspective: Mechanisms of aggression. In H. Toch (ed.), *Psychology of Crime and Criminal Justice*. New York: Holt, Rinehart and Winston.

Berger, R. J., Searles, P., and Newman, L. W. 1988. The dimensions of rape reform legislation. *Law and Society Review* 22: 329–58.

Berk, R. A. 1983. An introduction to sample selection bias in sociological data. *American Sociological Review* 48: 386–408.

Berk, R. A. 1986. Personal communication.

Berk, R. A. and Newton, P. J. 1985. Does arrest really deter wife battery? An effort to replicate the findings of the Minneapolis Spouse Abuse Experiment. *American Sociological Review* 50: 253–62.

Berk, R. A., Berk, S. F., Loeske, D., and Rauma, D. 1983. The myth of mutuality in battering. In D. Finkelhor, R. Gelles, G. Hotaling, and M. Straus (eds.), *The Dark Side of Families*. Beverly Hills, Cal.: Sage.

Berk, R. A., Smyth, G. K., and Sherman, L. W. 1988. When random assignment fails: Some lessons from the Minneapolis spouse abuse experiment. *Journal of Quantitative Criminology* 4: 209–23.

Binder, A., and Meeker, J. W. 1988. Experiments as reforms. *Journal of Criminal Justice* 16 (4), 347–58.

Black, D. 1976. *The Behavior of the Law*. New York: Academic Press.

Black, D. 1980. *The Manners and Customs of the Police*. New York: Academic Press.

Black, D. 1983. Crime as social control. *American Sociological Review* 48: 34–45.

Bograd, M. and Yllo, K. 1988. *Feminist Perspectives on Wife Abuse*. Beverly Hills, Cal.: Sage.

Bowker, L. 1983. *Beating Wife-Beating*. Lexington, Mass.: D.C. Heath.

Bowker, L. 1984. Coping with Wife Abuse: Personal and Social Networks. In A. R. Roberts (ed.) *Battered Women and Their Families*. New York: Springer.

Bowker, L. 1986. The meaning of wife beating. *Currents* 2: 39–43.

Browne, A. 1987. *When Battered Women Kill*. New York: Macmillan.

Browne, A. and Dutton, D. G., 1990. Risks and alternatives for abused women: What do we currently know? In R. Roesch, D. G. Dutton, and V. F. Sacco (eds.), *Family Violence: Perspectives in Research and Practice*. Vancouver, B.C.: Simon Fraser University.

Browne, A. and Williams, K. R. 1989. Exploring the effects of resource availability and the likelihood of female-perpetrated homicides. *Law and Society Review* 23: 75–94.

Browning, J. J. and Dutton, D. G. 1986. Assessment of wife assault with the conflict tactics scale: Using couple data to quantify the differential reporting effect. *Journal of Marriage and the Family* 48: 375–79.

Caesar, P. L. 1988. Exposure to violence in families of origin among wife abusers and maritally nonviolent men. *Violence and Victims* 3: 49–64.

Carmody, D. C. and Williams, K. R. 1987. Wife assault and perceptions of sanctions. *Violence and Victims* 2: 25–38.

Casper, J. D. and Brereton, D. 1984. Evaluating criminal justice reforms. *Law and Society Review* 18: 122–44.

Clarke, R. V. and Cornish, D. B. 1985. Modeling offenders decisions: A framework for research and policy. In M. Tonry and N. Morris (eds.), *Crime and Justice: An Annual Review of Research*, vol. 6. Chicago: University of Chicago Press.

Coleman, D. H. and Straus, M. A. 1986. Marital power, conflict, and violence in a nationally representative sample of American couples. *Violence and Victims* 1: 141–57.

Collins, J. J., Jr. 1983. Alcohol use and expressive interpersonal violence: A proposed explanatory model. In E. Gottheil, K. A. Druley, T. E. Skoloda, and H. M. Waxman (eds.), *Alcohol, Drug Abuse and Aggression*. Springfield, Ill.: Charles C. Thomas, 5–25.

Coser, L. A. 1985. The notion of control in sociology. In J. P. Gibbs (ed.), *Social Control: Views from the Social Sciences*. Beverly Hills, Cal.: Sage, 13–22.

Dobash, R. E. and Dobash, R. P. 1979. *Violence against Wives: A Case Against the Patriarchy*. New York: Free Press.

Doyle, D. and Luckenbill, D. 1991. Mobilizing law in response to collective problems: A test of Black's theory of law. *Law and Society Review* 25: 103–16.

Dunford, F. W., Huizinga, D. and Elliott, D. S. 1989. The *Omaha Domestic Violence Police Experiment*, final report, grant 85-IJ-CX-K435, National Institute of Justice. Washington, D.C.: U.S. Department of Justice.

Dunford, F. W., Huizinga, D., and Elliot, D. S. 1990. The role of arrest in domestic assault. *Criminology* 28: 183–206.

Dutton, D. G. 1981. *The Criminal Justice System Response to Wife Assault*. Ottawa: Solicitor General of Canada, Research Division.

Dutton, D. G. 1985. An ecologically nested theory of male violence toward intimates. *International Journal of Womens Studies* 8: 404–13.

Dutton, D. G. 1986a. The outcome of court-mandated treatment for wife assault: A quasi-experimental evaluation. *Violence and Victims* 1: 163–75.

Dutton, D. G. 1986b. Social psychological contributions to criminal justice policy for wife assault. *Applied Social Psychology Annual* 7: 238–61.

Dutton, D. G. 1986c. Wife assaulter's explanations for assault: The neutralization of self-punishment. *Candian Journal of Behavioural Science* 18: 381–90.

Dutton, D. G. 1987. The criminal justice response to wife assault. *Law and Human Behavior* 11: 189–206.

Dutton, D. G. 1988a. Profiling of wife assaulters: Preliminary evidence for a trimodal analysis. *Violence and Victims* 3: 5–30.

Dutton, D. G. 1988b. *The Domestic Assault of Women: Psychological and Criminal Justice Perspectives*. Boston: Allyn and Bacon.

Dutton, D. G. and Browning, J. J. 1987. Power struggles and intimacy anxieties as causative factors of violence in intimate relationships. In G. Russell (eds.), *Violence in Intimate Relationships*. New York: Spectrum.

Dutton, D. G. and Browning, J. J. 1988. Concern for power, fear of intimacy and aversive stimuli for wife abuse. In G. T. Hotaling, D. Finkelhor, J. T. Kirkpatrick, and M. Straus (eds.), *Family Abuse and Its Consequences: New Directions for Research*. Beverly Hills, Cal.: Sage, p. 163–75.

Dutton, D. G. and Painter, S. L. 1981. Traumatic bonding: The development of emotional attachments in battered women and other relationships of intermittent abuse. *Victimology: An International Journal* 6: 139–55.

Dutton, D. G. and Strachan, C. E. 1987. Motivational needs for power and dominance as differentiating variables of assaultive and non-assaultive male populations. *Violence and Victims* 2: 145–56.

Dutton, D. G., Fehr, B., and McEwen, H. 1982. Severe wife battering as deindividuated violence. *Victimology: An International Journal* 7: 13–23.

Dutton, D., Hart, S. G., Kennedy, L. W., and Williams, K. R. 1991. Arrest and the reduction of repeat wife assault. In E. Buzawa and C. Buzawa (eds.), *Domestic Violence: The Changing Criminal Justice Response*. Westport, Conn.: Greenwood.

Eckland-Olson, S. 1982. Social control and relational disturbance: A microstructural paradigm. In D. Black (ed.), *Toward a General Theory of Social Control: Selected Problems*, vol. 2. Orlando, Fla.: Academic Press.

Eckland-Olson, S., Lieb, J., and Zurcher, L. 1984. Some paradoxical impact of criminal sanctions: Some microstructural findings. *Law and Society Review* 18: 159–78.

Edelson, J. L., Syers, M., and Brygger, M. P. 1987. Comparative effectiveness of group treatment for men who batter. Paper presented at the Third National Conference on Family Violence Research. Durham, N.H.: University of New Hampshire.

Eisenstein, J. and Jacob, H. 1977. *Felony Justice: An Organizational Analysis of Criminal Courts*. Boston: Little, Brown and Company.

Elliott, D. S. 1989. Criminal justice procedures in family violence crimes. In L. Ohlin and M. Tonry (eds.), *Family Violence*, volume 11, *Crime and Justice, An Annual Review of Research*. Chicago: University of Chicago Press.

Elliott, D. S. and Huizinga, D. 1990. The mediating effects of the social structure in high risk neighborhoods. Paper presented at the Annual Meeting of the American Sociological Association, Washington, D.C. August.

Emerson, R. 1981. On last resorts. *American Journal of Sociology* 87: 1–22.

Fagan, J. A. 1988. Contributions of family violence research to criminal justice policy on wife assault: Paradigms of science and social control. *Violence and Victims* 3: 159–86.

Fagan, J. 1989. Cessation of family violence: Deterrence and dissuasion. In L. Ohlin and M. Tonry (eds.), *Family violence*, volume 11, *Crime and Justice: An Annual Review of Research*. Chicago: University of Chicago Press.

Fagan, J. and Browne, A. 1992. Violence between spouses and intimates: Physical aggression between women and men in relationships. In A. J. Reiss, Jr. and J. A. Roth (eds.), *The Understanding and Control of Violent Behavior*. Washington, D.C.: National Academy Press (in press).

Fagan, J. and Wexler, S. 1987. Crime in the home and crime in the streets: The relation between family violence and stranger crime. *Violence and Victims* 2: 5–21.

Fagan, J., Friedman, E., Wexler, S., and Lewis, V. 1984. *The National Family Violence Evaluation: Final Report*, Volume 1—Analytic Findings. San Francisco: URSA Institute.

Faludi, S. 1991. *Backlash: The Undeclared War Against American Women*. New York: Crown.

Ferraro, K. M. 1989. Policing woman battering. *Social Problems* 36: 61–74.

Fields, M. D. 1978. Wife beating: Government intervention policies and practices. In U.S. Commission on Civil Rights, *Battered Women and Public Policy*. Washington, D.C.: U.S. Commission on Civil Rights.

Ford, D. A. 1983. Wife battery and criminal justice: A study of victim decision making. *Family Relations* 32, 463–75.

Ford, D. A. 1991a. The preventive impact of policies for prosecuting wife batterers. In E. Buzawa and C. Buzawa (eds.), *Domestic Violence: The Changing Criminal Justice Response*. Westport, Conn.: Greenwood.

Ford, D. A. 1991b. Prosecution as a victim power resource: A note on empowering women in violent conjugal relationships. *Law and Society Review* 25: 313–34.

Frieze, I. H. and Browne, A. 1989. Violence in marriage. In L. Ohlin and M. Tonry (eds.), *Family Violence*, volume 11, *Crime and Justice: An Annual Review of Research*. Chicago: University of Chicago Press.

Ganley, A. L. 1981. *Participants Manual: Court-Mandated Therapy for Men Who Batter: A Three Day Workshop for Professionals*. Washington, D.C.: Center for Womens Policy Studies.

Gelles, R. J. 1983. An exchange/social control theory, In D. Finkelhor, R. J. Gelles, G. T. Hotaling, and M. A. Straus (eds.), *The Dark Side of Families*. Beverly Hills, Cal.: Sage.

Gibbs, J. P. 1975. *Crime, Punishment, and Deterrence*. New York: Elsevier-North Holland.

Gibbs, J. P. 1985. Law and social control. In J. P. Gibbs (ed.), *Social Control: Views From the Social Sciences*. Beverly Hills, Cal.: Sage, p. 83–114.

Gibbs, J. P. 1989. *Control: Sociology's central notion*. Urbana: University of Illinois Press.

Gilbert, N. 1983. *Capitalism and the Welfare State: Dilemmas of Social Benevolence*. New Haven: Yale University Press.

Gondolf, E. W. 1985a. Anger and oppression in men who batter: Empiricist and feminist perspectives and their implications for research. *Victimology: An International Journal* 10: 311–24.

Gondolf, E. W. 1985b. Fight for control: A clinical assessment of men who batter. *Social Casework: The Journal of Contemporary Social Work* 66: 48–54.

Goolkasian, G. A. 1986. Confronting domestic violence: The role of criminal court judges. *Research in Brief*. Washington, D.C.: National Institute of Justice.

Gordon, L. 1988. *Family Violence and Social Control*. New York: Viking Press.

Greenblat, C. S. 1983. A hit is a hit is a hit . . . or is it? Approval and tolerance of the use of physical force by spouses. In D. Finkelhor, R. J. Gelles, G. T. Hotaling, and M. A. Straus (eds.), *The Dark Side of Families*. Beverly Hills, Cal.: Sage, p. 235–60.

Hagan, J. and Bumiller, K. 1983. Making sense of sentencing: A review and critique of sentencing research. In A. Blumstein, J. Cohen, S. E. Martin, and M. H. Tonry (eds.), *Research on Sentencing: The Search for Reform*, vol 2. Washington, D.C.: National Academy Press.

Hamberger, K. L. and Hastings, J. E. 1989. Counseling male spouse abusers: Characteristics of treatment completers and dropouts. *Violence and Victims* 4: 275–86.

Harrell, A. 1991. Evaluation of court-ordered treatment for domestic violence offenders. Final report, grant 90-12L-E-089, State Justice Institute, Washington, D.C.: The Urban Institute.

Hirschel, J. D., Hutchison, I. W. III, Dean, C. W., Kelley, J. J., and Pesackis, C. 1990. Charlotte Spouse Assault Replication Project: Final Report. Grant 87-IJ-CX-K004, National Institute of Justice. Washington, D.C.: U.S. Department of Justice.

Hirschel, J. D., Hutchison, I. W., and Dean, C. 1992. The failure to arrest to deter spouse abuse. *Journal of Research in Crime and Delinquency* 29:6–30.

Hirschi, T. 1969. *Causes of Delinquency*. Berkeley: University of California Press.

Hirschi, T. 1986. On the compatibility of rational choice and social control theories of crime. In R. V. Clarke and D. B. Cornish (eds.), *The Reasoning Criminal*. New York: Springer-Verlag, 106–28.

Jaffe, P., Wolfe, D. A., Telford, A., and Austin, G. 1986. The impact of police charges in incidents of wife abuse. *Journal of Family Violence* 1: 37–49.

Katz, J. 1988. *Seductions of Crime: Moral and Sensual Attractions in Doing Evil*. New York: Basic Books.

Klepper, S. and Nagin, D. 1989. The deterrent effect of perceived certainty and severity of punishment revisited. *Criminology* 27: 721–46.

Kramer, S. 1990. An economic analysis of criminal attempt: Marginal deterrence and the optimal structure of sanctions. *Journal of Criminal Law and Criminology* 81: 398–417.

Langan, P. A. and Innes, C. A. 1986. Preventing domestic violence against women. BJS Special Report NCJ-102937. Washington, D.C.: U.S. Department of Justice, Bureau of Justice Statistics.

Lempert, R. 1989. Humility is a virtue: On the publication of policy relevant research. *Law and Society Review* 23: 145–61.

Lerman, L. G. 1986. Prosecution of wife beaters: Institutional obstacles and innovations. In M. Lystad (ed.), *Violence in the Home: Interdisciplinary Perspectives*. New York: Brunner-Mazel.

Levinson, D. 1989. *Family Violence in Cross-Cultural Perspective*. Newbury Park, Cal.: Sage.

Maiuro, R. D., and Cahn, T. S., and Vitaliano, P. P. 1986. Assertiveness deficits and hostility in domestically violent men. *Violence and Victims* 1: 279–90.

Martin, D. 1976. *Battered Wives*. New York: Kangaroo Paperbacks.

Mason, A. and Blankenship, V. 1987. Power and affiliation, motivation, stess and abuse in intimate relationships. *Journal of Personality and Social Psychology* 52: 203–10.

McClelland, D. C. 1975. Power: *The Inner Experience*. New York: Irvington Publishers.

McClelland, D. C. and Davis, W. N. 1972. The influence of unrestrained power concerns on drinking in working class men. In D. C. McClelland, W. N. Davis, R. Kalin, and E. Wanner (eds.), *The Drinking Man*. New York: The Free Press.

McClelland, D. C., Davis, W. N., Kalin, R., and Wanner, E. 1972. *The Drinking Man*. New York: The Free Press.

Miller, S. and Anderson, A. B. 1986. Updating the deterrence doctine. *Journal of Criminal Law and Criminology* 77: 418–38.

Miller, S. and Simpson, S. 1991. Courtship violence and social control: Does gender matter? *Law and Society Review* 25: 335–67.

Pagelow, M. D. 1984. *Family Violence*. New York: Praeger.

Paternoster, R. 1989. Decisions to participate in and desist from four types of common delinquency: Deterrence and the rational choice perspective. *Law and Society Review* 23: 7–40.

Saunders, D. G. 1986. When battered women use violence: Husband abuse of self-defense? *Violence and Victims* 1: 47–60.

Saunders, D. G. and Azar, S. T. 1989. Treatment programs for family violence. In L. Ohlin and M. Tonry (eds.), *Family Violence*, volume 11, *Crime and Justice: An Annual Review of Research*. Chicago: University of Chicago Press.

Saunders, D. G. and Hanusa, D. R. 1984. Cognitive-behavioral treatment of abusive husbands: The short-term effects of group therapy. Paper presented at the Second National Conference on Family Violence Research. Durham, N.H.: University of New Hampshire, August.

Schecter, S. 1982. *Women and Male Violence*. Boston: South End Press.

Scott, M. B. and Lyman, S. M. 1968. Accounts. *American Sociological Review* 33: 46–62.

Sherman, L. W. and Berk, R. A. 1984a. The Minneapolis domestic violence experiment. *Police Foundation Reports*, 1. Washington, D.C.: The Police Foundation.

Sherman, L. W. and Berk, R. A. 1984b. The specific deterrent effects of arrest for domestic assault. *American Sociological Review* 49: 261–72.

Sherman, L. W. and Cohn, E. G. 1989. The impact of research on legal policy: The Minneapolis violence experiment. *Law and Society Review* 23: 117–44.

Sherman, L. W., Schmidt, J. D., Rogan, D. P., Gartin, P. R., Cohn, E. G., Collins, D., and Bacich, A. 1991. The Milwaukee Spouse Abuse Experiment, Final Report. National Institute of Justice, Grant 86-IJ-CX-K043. Washington, D.C.: U.S. Department of Justice.

Shields, N. and Hanneke, C. R. 1983. Battered wives' reactions to marital rape. In D. Finkelhor, R. J. Gelles, G. T. Hotaling, and M. A. Straus (eds.), *The Dark Side of Families: Current Family Violence Research*. Beverly Hills, Cal.: Sage, 132–47.

Sidel, R. 1986. *Women and Children Last: The Plight of Poor Women in Affluent America*. New York: Viking.

Skogan, W. G. 1989. Social change and the future of violent crime. in T. R. Gurr (ed.), *Violence in America*, volume 1: *The History of Crime*. Newbury Park: Sage, 235–50.

Sonkin, D. J. and Durphy, M. 1985. *Learning to Live Without Violence: A Handbook for Men* (2nd rev. ed.). San Francisco: Volcano Press.

Stark, E., Flitcraft, A., and Frazier, W. 1979. Medicine and patriarchical violence: The social construction of a private event. *International Journal of Health Services* 9: 461–93.

Stets, J. E. and Straus, M. A. 1990. Gender differences in reporting marital violence and its medical and psychological consequences. In M. A. Straus and R. J. Gelles (eds.), *Physical Violence in American Families: Risk Factors and Adaptation to Violence in 8,145 Families*. New Brunswick, N.J.: Transaction Publishers.

Straus, M. A. 1978. Wife beating: how common and why? *Victimology* 2: 576–84.

Straus, M. A. and Gelles, R. J. 1986. Societal change in family violence from 1975 to 1985 as revealed by two national surveys. *Journal of Marriage and the Family* 48: 465–79.

Straus, M. A. and Gelles, R. J., eds. 1990. *Physical violence in American Families: Risk Factors and Adaptations to Violence in 8,145 Families*. New Brunswick, N.J.: Transaction Publishers.

Straus, M. A., Gelles, R. J., and Steinmetz, S. 1980. *Behind Closed Doors: Violence in the American Family*. New York: Anchor Press.

Sykes, G. M. and Matza, D. 1957. Techniques of neutralization: A theory of delinquency. *American Sociological Review* 22: 667–70.

Tauchen, G., Tauchen, H., and Witte, A. D. 1986. *The Dynamics of Domestic Violence: A Reanalysis of the Minneapolis Experiment*. Washington, D.C.: Police Foundation.

U.S. Commission on Civil Rights. 1978. *Battered Women: Issues of Public Policy*. Washington, D.C.: U.S. Government Printing Office.

U.S. Commission on Civil Rights. 1982. *Under the Rule of Thumb: Battered Women and the Administration of Justice*. Washington, D.C.: U.S. Government Printing Office.

U.S. Attorney General. 1984. *Task Force on Family Violence: Final Report*. Washington, D.C.: U.S. Department of Justice.
Walker, L. E. 1979. *The Battered Women*. New York: Harper and Row.
Walker, L. E. 1984. *The Battered Woman Syndrome*. New York: Springer.
Wexler, S. 1982. Battered women and public policy. In E. Boneparth (ed.), *Women, Power and Policy*. New York: Pergamon.
Williams, K. R. and Hawkins, R. 1986. Perceptual research on general deterrence: A critical review. *Law and Society Review* 20: 545–68.
Williams, K. R. and Hawkins, R. 1989a. The meaning of arrest for wife assault. *Criminology* 27: 163–81.
Williams, K. R. and Hawkins, R. 1989b. Controlling male aggression in intimate relationships. *Law and Society Review* 23: 591–612.
Williams, K. R. and Hawkins, R. 1991. Wife assault, costs of arrest, and the deterrence process. *Journal of Research in Crime and Delinquency*, 29 (3), in press.
Wilson, W. J. 1987. *The Truly Disadvantaged*. Chicago: University of Chicago Press.
Wolfgang, M. E. 1958. *Patterns in Criminal Homicide*. New York: John Wiley and Sons.
Wolfgang, M. E. 1967. A sociological analysis of criminal homicide. In M. E. Wolfgang (ed.), *Studies in Homicide*. New York: Harper and Row.
Wolfgang, M. E. and Ferracuti, F. 1967. *The Subculture of Violence: Toward an Integrated Theory of Criminology*. London: Tavistock.
Yllo, K. A. and Straus, M. A. 1984. Patriarchy and violence against wives: The impact of structural and normative factors. *Journal of International and Comparative Social Welfare* 1: 16–29.
Zimring, F. E. and Hawkins, G. J. 1973. *Deterrence*. Chicago: University of Chicago Press.

## Cases Cited:

*Bruno v. Codd*, 396 N.Y.S. 974 1977.
*Scott v. Hart*, No. 6-76-2395 (N.D. Cal: 1976). U.S. District Court for the Northern District of California. Settlement decree between Mary Scott et al., and George Hart et al., Index C76-2395.
*Thurman v. City of Torrington*, 595 F. Supp. 1521 (D. Conn. 1984).

# 9

# Theoretical Formalization, a Necessity: The Example of Hirschi's Bonding Theory

*Marc Le Banc*
*Aaron Caplan*

Two decades ago two events occurred simultaneously. First, Hirschi's volume *Causes of Delinquency* was published, while numerous books were printed on theory construction. Hirschi's theory became the most prominent empirically based criminological theory for the explanation of juvenile delinquency and it has retained that status ever since. Second, modes of theory construction were discussed in various publications (Zetterberg 1965; Willer 1967; Stinchcombe 1968; Dubin 1969; Blalock 1969; and Gibbs 1972) but that subject was rapidly left aside. Why have theory formulation and theory formalization not met to reinforce each other's development? Such a collaboration between a mode of formalization and a discursive theory had proven fruitful in criminology: De Fleur and Quinney (1966) used set theory to formalize Sutherland differential association theory and Empey and Lubeck (1971) relied on formal rules to formulate their axiomatic theory of lower class delinquency.

If this connection between discursive theory and formalization was not pursued, it was not because criminologists did no know about the developments in the modes of theory construction. The differential association and the lower-class delinquency experiences

237

were very useful to reveal the shortcomings of these theories. As well, two of the major writers on theory formalization, Sinchcombe and Gibbs, were also publishing on criminological subjects. If Hirschi's bonding theory was not formalized, it is probably because it was the first criminological theory that was not solely presented in a discursive manner but was also the object of an extensive and elegant empirical verification by the author. Formalization may also not have happened because criminology was entering into a new era of theoretical questions in which theoretical perspectives were more important than theory content. It was the epoch in which conflict and labeling theories were a new fashion and were focusing the debate on a new perspective, social reaction to crime, as Gibbs (1985) analyses the situation. As a consequence of this anarchy of perspectives, two directions were taken by criminologists that were of a positivistic perspective: testing bonding theory and confronting it with existing theories.

In the first direction, the studies were numerous, Kempf (1989) reports over forty studies, and she did not cover studies outside North America (for example: Junger-Tas and Junger 1984, in Holland and Albrecht, 1982, and Dünkel, 1983, in Germany). Rare, however were the studies that used an exact replication of the measure of the dependent and independent variables employed by Hirschi (for an exception see Caplan and Le Blanc 1985). These verifications of control theory could be characterized as an anarchy of operationalizations of bonding theory because, even if the constructs of the theory were referred to, there was no large consensus on the measures to operationalize them (see Kempf 1989, for a review of the measures used). In the second direction, the integration of control theory with other theories, particularily differential association or social learning theory, the attempts were also numerous but mainly at the level of empirical model building and verification (see for example Johnson 1979, or Elliott et al. 1985; and Kempf, 1989, for the list of the variables pertaining to other theories used in conjunction with control variables). However, there is a controversy about the usefulness of such integrations (Messner et al. 1989). Some authors (Hirschi 1989; Thornberry 1989) argue for theoretical elaboration rather than theoretical integration.

Because of these research orientations, bonding theory has not developed very much over the last twenty years. In fact, most of the empirical verifications of this theory have not been real tests because they generally have used different measures of Hirschi's concepts and habitually have relied only on a limited part of his conceptual paradigm. They have not been exact replications—a basic condition of science and a prerequisite for the development of knowledge. Virtually all integrations have been empirical rather than theoretical because they have not tried or could not, reconcile the fundamental premises of various theories such as for example bonding and social learning. Because of this situation, Hirschi's theory has been at a stand still, except for the attempt of its author to argue that it can be seen as a general theory of crime and criminality (Gottfredson and Hirschi 1990; see also Hagan 1985). Over the last twenty years, neither the internal consistency or the structure of bonding theory has been fundamentally challenged or elaborated in a substantive manner. Worse, because of the unbridled empiricism of criminology, bonding theory developed less than strain and cultural deviance theories that were integrated and extended into a mixed model (using Kornhauser 1978, classification) by Cohen (1955) and Cloward and Ohlin (1960) a decade earlier.

In this paper, we formalize Hirschi's theory in order to uncover its shortcomings and propose a revision of its discursive statement. We show that formalization is a necessity in order to replicate and elaborate a theory. What we try to demonstrate is that theoretical progress necessitates formalization. In order to do so, this article will be divided in six parts: (1) a discussion of the advantages and disadvantages of formalization; (2) a presentation of a mode of theory construction; (3) an outline of Hirschi's discursive statement; (4) the formalization of his theory; (5) a presentation of definitional problems and incomplete specifications that are consequences of the formalization; and (6) the proposition of a modified formal and discursive statement of the theory.

## Formalization, Why?

In his book *Causes of Delinquency,* Hirschi presents a theory in the sense suggested by Blalock (1969); he proposes a conceptual scheme, a set of definitions of concepts, and he formulates propositions that interrelate these concepts at least two at a time. Not only does he formulate a theory but he is also concerned with the evaluation of his theoretical system from the standpoint of testing its correspondence with reality; to do this he operationalizes his concepts and tests his propositions with survey data. However, Hirschi's bonding theory is formulated only in a discursive mode since it strictly uses the conventions of a natural language, even if it goes one step further since most of the notions used are operationalized for an empirical test. However, it does not go to the point where it is translated into a formal language through specific rules.

If an axiomatic theory consists of "logically related, logically consistent, and logically complete definitions and propositions" (Winton 1974, 5), two types of rules can be used to transcend a discursive statement: mathematical and formal. The use of everyday language has certain disadvantages. Because of its evocative and abbreviated nature, it tends to produce overgeneralized and insufficiently specified statements (Freese 1980; Hanneman 1988). We will show that this is true of Hirschi's bonding theory. In criminology, theorists rarely move beyond a discursive statement of their theory. The first type of formal rule, mathematical language, is seldom employed. There is an exception with set theory, a formal calculus that has been used once on Sutherland's differential association theory (De Fleur and Quinney 1966). This version of differential association is rarely referred to, probably because most criminologists are not well trained in the uses of mathematical language or because the language used is either too sophisticated for the theory or insufficient to express its complexity. Formal rules have not been much more successful. An exception to this practice occurred with the work of Empey and Lubeck entitled "Explaining Delinquency." In their work they formally stated and tested a body of sociological theory whose most fundamental tenet is that official delinquency is a lower-class phenomenon. From our point of view, Empey and Lubeck contributed to delinquency theory by demonstrating the possibilities of a second and more efficient method of theory presentation, the formally stated theory. Empey and Lubeck (1971) used postulates and theorems to formulate their lower-class theory of delinquency while Bernard (1987) employes definitions and propositions to demonstrate tautologies in Hirschi's definition of commitment. Gibbs (1985) moves further; he uses his sophisticated technique of theory construction to illustrate rapidly its usefulness with differential association, control and anomie theories. No such sophisticated set of formal rules has ever been applied thoroughly on any specific theory in criminology.

We favor formal rules over mathematical rules for three reasons. First, it corresponds more directly to the usual way in which theories are dealt within our discipline. Bonding theory is a good example: concepts are defined, operationalized, and relations between them are stated in hypotheses. Second, as shown by Empey and Lubeck (1971), it is easier to exhaust the major implications of a theory and to test alternatives explanations or theorems. Third, as argued by Hanneman (1988), it has specific advantages: it relies on restrictive but powerful vocabularies and syntax that result in a statement of the theory that cannot be ambiguous and open to interpretation, producing a tightly structured and explicit statement. Before applying the method of formal rules to Hirschi's theory of bonding, we should discuss the advantages and limits of formalizing in this way an existing discursive theory.

*Limits*

We will comment on three principal limits—things that this procedure cannot do—to any attempt at formalizing a theory. Gibbs (1985) claims that formalization does not resolve fundamental questions. It is not aimed at helping criminologists choose between etiology and social reaction, between radical and structural criminology, and so on. It cannot help a researcher in deciding what is the nature of delinquency. Formalization is thus a type of operation that is concerned with the internal content of a theory, its logical coherence, not its relations with the whole field of criminology. In no way can formalization also help clarify obscure questions or decide on the class of events to which a particular theory should apply.

Another limit that Gibbs (1972) and Hanneman (1988) have identified is that the formalization of a theory does not ensure its empirical validity. Even if testable theories are desirable, it is not feasible to propose a theory only composed of empirical assertions because the field vocabulary is not precise enough and it is also impossible to exclude substantive or discursive definitions. Many of the criminological phenomena to be explained are suffering from too few empirical investigations and too primitive theorizations (Freese 1980). Consequently, it is necessary to rely on vague constructs (social disorganization, differential association, attachment, subculture, and so on). It cannot be expected that a theory should be able to avoid them and be exclusively a set of empirical assertions. These unobservable phenomena are limits to the validity of a theory and to its testability that formalization cannot help to resolve.

In fact, theory formalization involves for the theorist many decisions that are technical rather than theoretical. Gibbs (1972, 370) enumerates seven of them: "judge the empirical applicability of sociological terms, assess the research resources of the field, consider alternative space-time relations in formulating empirical assertions, limits assertions to particular types of social units, stipulate formulas for tests of the theory, evaluate the reliability and comparability of various kinds of data, and stipulate procedures for gathering or otherwise obtaining data". These demands impose an important burden on the theorists. Hirschi responds to most of them in his empirical verification but he does not move to formalization per se. This situation creates another type of problem, the personal interpretation of a theory by another scientist.

The first step in moving from discursive to formalized theory is the identification of the theoretical constructs. With regard to Hirschi's theory, this stage of formalization does not appear to create major problems of personal interpretation. Hirschi is very clear in enuciating his theoretical constructs of attachment, commitment, belief, and involvement. But to obtain a complete definition of a theoretical construct, the theorist must present one or more concepts. We wish to emphasize that the identification of the concepts presented in this paper is our personal interpretation of Hirschi's discursive statement. Therefore we may falsely present his concepts, the definition of his theoretical constructs. We believe that if any misrepresentation of definitions does occur, the error would be in the refinement as opposed to general meaning of the definitions. Nevertheless the reader should be aware of this possibility. The definition of an author's theory are rendered empirically applicable by presenting their operationalization. We feel comfortable in our identification of them, since Hirschi's work is one of the few theories in criminology that clearly presents the operational definitions of the theoretical statement. Finally, the theory necessarily specifies relationships between its theoretical constructs. Although each theoretical construct is clearly related to delinquency, the relationship between the constructs in the discursive statement is at times vague or not presented in Hirschi's book. Consequently, the formal statements are the result of our understanding of the relationships between the theoretical statements. Although we would like to think of our efforts at identifying them as accurate, we are not prepared to claim that they are a definitive formalization of the relationship between Hirschi's theoretical constructs. Only the author of the theory could validate our translation of his theory in formal statements.

## Advantages

Perhaps we have labored over our presentation of the major disadvantages of formalizing an existing discursive theory. However at the same time, we do not wish to leave the impression that formalizing a theory is not worth the effort. There are several advantages in formalizing a theory suggested by specialists in their construction (Zetterberg 1965; Willer 1967; Stinchcombe 1968; Dubin 1969; Blalock 1969; and Gibbs 1972, 1985; Winton 1974; Freese 1980; Turner and Beegley 1981; Hanneman 1988).

Formalization obliges the theorist to clearly identify as well as distinguish between the various substantive terms of a theory (construct, concepts, and operational definitions). As a result, the formalized theory provides a systematic procedure for scrutinizing the theory in terms of logical consistency. The requirement for clear definitions and mutual exclusivity of substantive terms can help eliminate, or at least clarify, such conceptual problems. It can help identify tautologies between definitions and redundancies in reasonings. Hirschi, contrary to most theorists, is very helpful when it comes to performing these checks because he generally provides clear operational definitions of his substantive terms. When De Fleur and Quinney (1966) formalized differential association theory they identified such inconsistencies between assertions and they were able to reformulate them in order to avoid confusion and debate.

Formal theory construction is also very useful because it allows the examination of the logical coherence of the theory, its completeness, and the interrelations between its components. That is, it enables the theorist to have a better understanding of the relationship between the substantive terms of the theory and it may help uncover the gaps in the theory. These advantages have been illustrated by Empey and Lubeck (1971) and will also be evident after our formalization of Hirschi's bonding theory. Discursive theory presentation makes it difficult for the reader to appreciate the theory as a logical whole because the emphasis is placed more on each individual hypothesis or proposition. On the other hand, formal theory presentation allows for an understanding of the individual propositions, as well as an overview of the relationship between the theorems. Thus the formalized theory allows the reader to evaluate the weaknesses or missing links in the theory. It was one of the major consequences of the formalization of differential association by De Fleur and Quinney (1966) and they even elaborated the theory by specifying various relationships between assertions that were not originally identified by Sutherland.

Formalized theory also facilitates communication and replication. Since the researcher is obliged to clearly identify as well as distinguish between various substantive terms in addition to demonstrating the derivations of the theorems, the testable assertions, a theory cannot hide behind its discursive rethoric. However to avoid any misinterpretation, the formalized statement should be accompanied by a narrative summary. We believe that the formalized statement can communicate major premises of the theory in a form that eliminates misunderstanding of what the author of the theory is presenting. That is, the formalized theory allows a clear form for discussion in natural language. The clarity of formal statements will allow other criminologist to question our interpretation of Hirschi's theory or, one hopes, contribute to an enlargement of its statement. These precisely defined formal statements will be an excellent starting point for replications that are so rarely performed in criminology and so essential for the formulation of generalizations.

Finally, as argued by Gibbs (1972), the formalization of a theory will also facilitate defensive tests. Because of the rigor it implies for the formulation of substantive and operational definitions and for logical consistency, it should be much more difficult for opponents and supporters to be out of range while testing a theory. A researcher will not be able to claim that a theory has been tested if all its contructs and appropriate measurement or data gathering devises have not been included. The anarchy of operationalization that Kempf (1989) inadvertently demonstrates should not be a natural consequence of the tests of a formalized theory. Formalization sets frontier to human imagination, it is a means of keeping the criminological train on the track, of introducing more rigour in our theoretical discussions. It is too easy to claim that a piece of data is falsifying a theory when there is no perfect continuity between the theorist definition of his constructs and an empiricist operationalization of them.

### Formalization, How?

With these justifications of the usefulness of formalization in mind, we are now in a position to choose a technique of formalization. Having reviewed the basic literature on theory construction, we are in total agreement with Gibbs (1972, 4) when he states that "there is no effective consensus in the field as to the appropriate mode of theory construction and no trend in that direction" but he adds thirteen years later (1985, 24), "*any* formal mode is superior to the discursive mode." Accepting that point of view does not resolve the problem of determining the best technique of theory formalization. After comparing the techniques of Zetterberg (1965), Willer (1967), Stinchcombe (1968), Dubin (1969), and Blalock (1969) with the technique of Gibbs, we conclude that the latter was more elaborate and more complex and that his rules were clearer and much more detailed. These characteristics were in accordance with two principles that we consider prerequisites to theory construction: the technique of formalization must be equally complex as the theory that is formalized and the precision of the rules are highly favorable to replication which is a basic principle of science.

Gibbs (1972) proposes that a method of theory construction should stipulate major divisions of a theory, basic units of a theory, criteria by which basic units are distinguished as to type and identity, rules by which statements are derived from other statements, the procedure for the testing of statements derived from the theory, rules for the interpretation of the tests and criteria for assessing theories. According to Gibbs, a formally constructed theory has an intrinsic and extrinsic part. The extrinsic part defines the terms used in the intrinsic statements that are derived from the discursive theory. The intrinsic part consists of statements in the form of empirical assertions, such as axioms, postulates, propositions, transformational statements, and theorems. This dictionary is composed of the constructs, the concepts, the referentials, and the unit terms to be employed in the formally constructed theory. The proposed method of theory construction states that each intrinsic statement must be distinguished by reference to its position and the nature of the constituent term involve. Since a theory is a combination of various constituent terms (constructs, concepts, and referentials), five types of intrinsic statements are possible (axioms, postulates, propositions, transformational statements, and theorems) and, depending on the complexity of the theory, its structure will be defined in terms of order and division.

In every theory some intrinsic statements are direct assertions (premises) from which other intrinsic statements are derived. As will be seen shortly, direct assertions are not empirically applicable; that is, no tests of these assertions can be conducted. Consequently, the ultimate goal in formal theory construction is the derivation of testable assertions. Each intrinsic statement contains three constituent terms: unit, substantive, and relational. In his definition of a theory, Gibbs mentions that all intrinsic statements refer to properties of a class of events or things. Therefore all intrinsic statements must include a term that specifies the class of events or things as *units*. In Hirschi's theory, the unit term is male adolescents.

*Substantive terms* are used in an intrinsic statement to describe the properties of the unit term. There are three types of substantive terms: constructs, concepts, and referentials. When the definition of a term is neither complete nor empirically applicable, that term is identified as a *construct*. Gibbs (1972) considers a definition of a term complete when it equates a designed property with all other conceivable properties excluded. He stresses that the definition of a construct can be brief and grossly incomplete. For instance, Hirschi's construct of attachment to parents is defined as the adolescent's sensitivity to his parent's opinion, that is, caring about their wishes and expectations. It is obvious that the definition of this construct does not recognize and relate all conceivable dimensions of the property designated by the term.

To obtain a complete definition of a construct, the theorist must present one or more *concepts*. A concept is a definition of a term that is complete but not empirically applicable. A term cannot be empirically applicable without the specification of a formula or measure. Hirschi offers a complete definition of the construct attachment to parents by presenting three concepts: "psychological presence of parents," "impact of parental opinions and expectations" and "mutual participation in the adolescent psychological fields." Consequently Hirschi recognizes and relates all conceivable dimensions of the property designated by the term "attachment to parents". The term "attachment to parents" means nothing more to Hirschi than the three concepts stipulate. To avoid confusion, we will designate constructs in this article with double quotation marks (" ") and concepts with single quotation marks (' ').

For a complete definition to be empirically applicable a *referential* is employed. A referential is an intrinsic term that designates a measure presented in the extrinsic part of a theory. To emphasize that the referential is relative to the theory used, the term appears as a capitalized acronym. For example, MVS, means referential of the psychological presence of parents. Furthermore, any substantive terms (construct, concept, or referential) must state the time period being studied. Since Hirschi's theory is a static explanation of events, all the substantive terms in the analysis will use the temporal quantifier to signify a point in time. In addition, *composite* substantive terms may be formed by combining what would otherwise be two distinct substantive terms.

The third constituent term of an intrinsic statement, the *relational term,* is concerned with the association between substantive terms. Gibbs limits the possible relational terms to "greater, greater" and "greater, less." The reason for this limitation is Gibbs' feeling that the quality of data limits itself to prediction of ordinal differences. For example: Among male adolescents, the greater the 'academic competence at To', the less the 'commission of delinquent acts at To'.

When employing various combinations of the three substantive terms (constructs, concepts, and referentials), five types of intrinsic statements are possible: axioms, postulates, propositions, transformational statements, and theorems. Through the process of derivation, the various types of intrinsic statements allow the theorist to substitute testable relational statements for vague abstract relational statements. The most abstract intrinsic statement is an *axiom*. An axiom is a direct intrinsic statement in which the substantive terms are constructs. For example: Among male adolescents, the greater the "attachment to parents at To", the greater the "conformity to conventional standards of behavior at To". The axiom is abstract since the purpose of the statement is to relate two incomplete terms or constructs.

The theorist is able to complete his definition of the constructs by relating them to concepts. That is a *postulate,* a direct intrinsic statement in which the substantive terms are a construct and a concept. A postulate must stipulate a unit term, a relational term, and a temporal quantifier as follows: Among male adolescents, the greater the "attachment to parents at To", the greater the 'mutual participation in the adolescent psychological fields'. As will be seen later, Hirschi presents four postulates in order to complete his definition of "attachment to parents."

A *proposition* is presented when the formal relationship between two concepts cannot be derived from an axiom or a postulate. A proposition is a direct intrinsic statement in which the substantive terms are concepts. For example: Among male adolescents, the greater the 'academic competence at To', the greater the 'academic performance at To'. The use of propositions is basically limited to two relational situations. First, if several concepts define one construct, the relationship between these concepts must be established by proposition. Hirschi's construct "attachment to parents" is defined by three concepts, thus the relations between the concepts are expressed by propositions, one of which is, Among male adolescents, the greater the 'mutual participation in the adolescent psychological fields', the greater the 'psychological presence of parents at To'. Second, a proposition can also state an intuitive or inductive relationship between concepts. There are a few occasions in Hirschi's book where assertions of this nature are made. For instance, he states that, "it is worth mentioning that the child doing poorly in school is less likely to report close communication with his parents" (109). This statement is translated into the following proposition: Among male adolescents, the greater the 'academic performance at to', the greater the 'mutual participation in the adolescent psychological fields'.

Finally, the relationship between a concept and its empirical application (the referential) is defined by the *transformational statement*. A transformational statement is a direct intrinsic statement in which the substantive terms are a concept and a referential. For example: Among male adolescents, the greater the 'psychological presence of parents at To', the greater the MVS at To. This statement allows the theorist to complete a series of assertions that relate a construct ("attachment to parents at To"), a concept ('psychological presence of parents at To') and a referential (a measure such as MVS). None of the above-mentioned statements can be directly tested. However, as direct intrinsic statements, they enter into the derivation of other statements which in turn enter into tests.

The fundamental purpose in theory construction is the derivation of *theorems,* since they are the only type of intrinsic statement that can be tested empirically. A theorem is a formally derived intrinsic statement in which the constituent substantive terms are referentials. In Gibbs' technique of formalization, the theorems are derived by the "sign rule": the direction of the relation between any two referentials is given by the cumulative product of the intervening relational terms. As mentioned previously, an intrinsic statement contains either one of the two relational terms. The "greater, greater" relational term signifies a direct or positive relation symbolized by a plus sign ( + ), while the "greater, less" relational term specifies a negative or inverse relation expressed by a minus sign $(-)$.

We will complete our presentation of formal theory construction by discussing two notions that identify the structure of a theory: order and division. The *order* of a theory refers to the number of substantive terms in the intrinsic statements. Each intrinsic statement contains two or more substantive terms. The most common form of theory structure is a second order theory in which all intrinsic statements relate two substantive terms in one of the following ways: (1) the greater X, the greater Y, that is, among male adolescents, the greater the "attachment to parents at To", the greater the "conformity to conventional standards of behavior at To"; (2) the greater X, the less Y, that is, among male adolescents, the greater the "conformity to conventional standards of behavior at To", the less the 'commission of delinquent acts at To'. In addition to second order theories, third order or fourth order theories may also be constructed.

The second notion pertaining to the structure of a theory is its *division(s)*. A division of a theory includes three or more interrelated intrinsic statements, so that (1) they have the identical unit term; (2) one of the substantive terms in each of the intrinsic statements is also found in at least one of the other statements; and 3) all of the statements enter into the derivation of at least one specific theorem. However, two sets of intrinsic statements are components of the same division of a theory if one or more substantive terms is used in both sets of intrinsic statements and the unit term is identical for the two sets. Even though two sets of intrinsic statements have the identical unit term, both sets may be considered as separate divisions of a theory if (1) none of the substantive terms in one set are present in the order set; (2) at least one theorem can be derived from each set; and (3) the theorem or theorems of one set specify a type of space-time relation that is different from that specified by the theorem or theorems of the other set.

## Formalization, on What?

Within this section, we will present Hirschi's theory in its discursive form. Hirschi assumes that delinquent acts result when an individual's bond to society is weak or broken. The essence of his theory is a classification and description of the elements of the bond to conventional society. However, before defining the elements of the bond, we should describe what delinquency and the bond are. *Delinquency* is defined by acts, the detection of which is thought to result in punishment of the person committing them by agents of the larger society (Hirschi 1969, 47).

In his discursive statement of the theory, Hirschi does not define an individual's *bond* to society other than to say that it is several institutions constituting the adolescent's source of attention. In essence, the bond is the different spheres of the adolescent's world. In the empirical verification of the theory, three institutions comprising the bond are emphasized: family, school, and peers. The adolescent relates to his world, the above mentioned institutions, via four avenues: attachment, commitment, involvement, and belief. Hirschi attempts to show how each of these elements of the bond is related to delinquent behavior and how they are related to each other.

The most important element of the bond to conventional society is the individual's *attachment*. The importance of this element lies in the number of institutions or segments of society that can define an individual's attachment. Hirschi limits his conceptualization of attachment to the adolescent's parents, friends, and school. Hirschi situates the construct of attachment within the framework of the social norm that states what ought to be. Hirschi assumes that if a person is sensitive to the opinions of others, then he is, to that extent, bound by the norms. Consequently the internalization of norms depends on the individual's attachment to others. Hirschi views attachment to conventional persons as a major deterrent to the commission of delinquent act; the stronger this tie, the more likely it will be considered by the adolescent when and if he considers committing a delinquent act.

In his book, Hirschi looks at the process through which *attachment to parents* presumably works against the commission of delinquent acts. That is, the adolescent's attachment to parents is defined by several concepts. The first concept of parental attachment is the psychological presence of parents. When the adolescent faces the commission of a delinquent act his parents will be psychologically present; the adolescent will give thought to his parents' reaction. Hirschi operationalizes psychological presence indirectly in that he assumes the adolescent who thinks his parents know where he is and what he is doing is the one most likely to consider his parents' reaction. As a result, the adolescent who perceives his parents are unaware of his whereabouts is to that extent free to commit a delinquent act when a situation of potential delinquency arises. Hirschi notes that the psychological presence of the parents is a form of indirect supervision in the sense that parents do not actually restrict the adolescent's activities, nor do the parents necessarily know where the adolescent is; nonetheless, the adolescent is being supervised by virtue of his perception of the parent's concern.

The second concept in the process through which attachment to parents presumably works against the commission of delinquent acts is the mutual participation in the adolescent's social psychological fields. By not discussing his activities with his parents the adolescent is not sharing his inner world with them. Consequently, since the parents are not perceived by the adolescent as a part of his private world, then the reaction to his behavior is of no concern. In a similar vein, the parents who do not communicate their feelings about their child's behavior remove an important source of potential concern for the adolescent; that is, the parents do not try to enter their child's private world. Furthermore, Hirschi defines the relationship between the first two concepts in that he views the psychological presence of the parents depending to a large degree upon the adolescent's interaction with his parents on a personal basis.

In introducing the concept 'psychological presence of parents,' Hirschi assumes that the adolescent considers the expectations and opinions of his parents, that is, he considers the consequences of his act on his parents. As a result, Hirschi is required to add the impact of the parental expectations and opinions on the adolescent as a third concept to the process of attachment. More specifically, does the adolescent care what his or her parents will think? In essence, the process through which attachment to parents presumably works against the commission of delinquent acts can be summarized as the adolescent communicating, caring, and thinking about his parents. That is, for the parents to play an effective role as a controlling agency, the adolescent and parent must first interact with each other on a personal basis. This is what we have called the psychological presence of parents. In the process of interaction, the adolescent becomes aware of his parents' opinions and expectations. The adolescent is cognizant of the consequences of his potential delinquent behavior in terms of his relations with his parents. Secondly, in considering the consequences, the adolescent concludes that he does care what his parents will think. In the process of family interaction, the adolescent has developed an affectional identification with them. The parental opinions and expectations have had an impact. Finally, faced with the actual temptation to commit an act, the adolescent perceives his parents as being psychologically present. The psychological presence of the parents causes the adolescent to give thought to parental opinions and expectations which he considers sufficiently important to deter him from the act. The psychological presence of parents informs the adolescent of the parental opinions and expectations. The impact of the parental expectations and opinions instills within the adolescent their importance. Finally, the psychological presence of the parents recalls the parental expectations and opinions that have been deemed important. In conclusion, the unattached adolescent is more apt to commit delinquent acts because he does not have to consider the impact of his actions on his relations with his parents.

Hirschi also views *attachment to school* as a process that works against the commission of delinquent acts. This process is defined by five concepts. The first concept in this process is academic competence, the adolescent's potential achievement in the school setting. For Hirschi, the higher the boy's academic competence the lower the probability that he will commit delinquent acts. In order to relate academic competence to delinquency, Hirschi is required to introduce two additional concepts: academic performance and sentiments toward the controlling institution. More specifically, the boy who is academically competent has a greater chance of doing well in school. In turn, he is more likely to enjoy school, and consequently, he is less likely to be delinquent. Thus the third concept is the student's self-perceived academic competence. The more competent a boy thinks he is, the less likely he is to commit delinquent acts.

As we mentioned earlier, Hirschi is required to introduce the concept of sentiment toward the controlling institution as the link between ability and performance on the one hand and delinquency on the other. The boy who does poorly in school has less interest in school and consequently is free, to this extent, to commit delinquent acts. Therefore, attitude toward school is the next step in the process. However, Hirschi states that besides the attitude toward school, feelings toward persons in authority is important. According to bonding theory, the boy who is not concerned about what teachers think of him and who perceives himself as being picked on by teachers is most likely to be delinquent. However, the perception of teachers' treatment is not a necessary condition for freeing the child to commit delinquent acts. The boy who values the opinion of his teachers is less likely to become delinquent regardless of how he perceives teachers treating him. Thus, for Hirschi, the bond to school consists of the boy's attitude to school as well as his concern for his teacher's opinions. According to Hirschi, this positive bond to school is the first line of social control within the school setting. A weakening of the bond to school neutralizes its moral force. In control theory, such neutralization is a major link between lack of attachment and delinquency. Consequently the student's feelings about the scope of the school's legitimate authority becomes the final concept in the process. To summarize the process of attachment to school working against the commission of delinquent acts, Hirschi claims that academic competence affects academic performance. In addition, objective ability, academic competence, affects self-perceived ability. Both actual performance and self-perceived ability affect attitudes toward teachers and the school. The bond to school, the attitude toward teachers and the school, affects the student's feelings about the scope of the school's legitimate authority. Finally, rejection of the school's authority is conducive to delinquency.

Hirschi's definition of the process whereby *attachment to peers* affects delinquency can be reduced to a causal ordering of three concepts: stake in conformity, delinquent companions, and delinquent acts. Stake in conformity is an omnibus concept introduced by Hirschi to describe in general terms the constructs of both attachment and commitment. The composite concept of stake in conformity is defined by three concepts: sentiments toward the controlling institution, concern for parental opinion, and the adolescent's achievement orientation. Delinquent companions is the simpler concept within the definition. This element represents the adolescent's exposure to criminal influences, that is, the delinquent friends. A central assumption of control theories, including Hirschi's, is that companionship with delinquents is an incidental byproduct of the real causes of delinquency. Hirschi suggests that the relationship between delinquent companions and delinquency is spurious. However, after testing this hypothesis with his data, Hirschi revises his bonding model to state that delinquent companions have a direct or causal impact on the commission of delinquent acts. Furthermore, in the control model a low stake in conformity leads to the acquisition of delinquent friends as well as having a direct effect on delinquency. Hirschi also suggests that the definition of attachment to peers requires an additional concept: the adolescent's identification with his best friends, that is, the degree to which he respects his friends. However Hirschi is extremely vague in his discursive statement as to the location of this concept within the context of the above mentioned model. Consequently we must assume that identification with best friends is not a primary concept.

The second major element of the bond in Hirschi's theory is *commitment to conformity*. Hirschi views the accumulated time and energy that the adolescent has spent in a conventional activity, such as getting an education, as an investment. Conversely, deviant behavior is considered a cost. Therefore, when an adolescent is faced with the temptation to commit a delinquent act, he must evaluate the costs of his delinquent behavior in relation to the investment he has made in conventional activities. The assumption underlying the idea of commitment to conformity is that the investment of most adolescents would be seriously affected if they were to commit delinquent acts. In Hirschi's theory, commitment to conventional activities is viewed as a constraint on delinquency since the latter would jeopardize the adolescent's possibility of realizing the fruits of his investment. That is, Hirschi suggests that the adolescent is committed to conformity not only by his present investments but also by what he hopes to achieve. As a result, "ambition" and/or "aspiration" play an important role in producing conformity. Hirschi's notion of commitment consists of three constructs or career lines. These career lines are educational, occupational, and the passage to adult status. Only the educational and occupational career lines can be considered as the pursuit of conventional goals. The passage to adult status defines a lack of commitment.

According to bonding theory, those adolescents *committed to educational success* should be least likely to commit delinquent acts. For Hirschi, educational success is defined by two concepts: general achievement orientation and educational expectations. General achievement orientation is designed to tap the students' desire to do well in current activities. This concept is concerned with defining the adolescent's current efforts in creating and/or maintaining his investment. The concept of educational expectations defines the reality component or the adolescent's prospect for the future attainment of his investment, educational success. Hirschi empirically demonstrates that each concept has an independent effect on the commission of delinquent acts. In the early stages of his discursive statement on commitment, Hirschi defines the adolescent's *occupational career* as one component or concept that keeps him continuously bound to conformity by participation in a conventional game. Since Hirschi is formulating a theory of delinquency, his theory pertains to adolescents who, for the most part, do not have a current commitment to an occupational career. At best, this aspect of commitment can be defined in terms of the adolescent's aspirations or expectations, since there is no real basis for evaluating the adolescent's current investment in an occupational career. Consequently, the commitment to a high-status occupation can be defined by either the adolescent's aspirations or expectations. However, later in his discursive statement, Hirschi leaves us with the impression that occupational aspirations, the only form of occupational commitment that he discusses, are not a necessary component of commitment. For this reason, we interpret the occupational component of commitment as being unessential for the formulation of the commitment element of the theory.

Hirschi suggests that an adolescent's early termination of his education is associated with a delayed entrance into a low-status occupation. In order to compensate for this bleak future, adolescents expecting little formal education are likely to engage in adult activities such as smoking, drinking, dating; this situation refers to the *passage to adult status* concept. According to Hirschi, the adolescent claims adult privileges without adult responsibilities. By prematurely claiming adulthood, the adolescent is expressing the right to act contrary to the wishes of adults, which frees himself for the commission of delinquent acts. In summary, the passage to adult status involves two concepts: lack of commitment to the educational system and a premature claim to adulthood. The adolescent not committed to an educational career is likely to prematurely claim adulthood. In order to validate his claim to adulthood, the adolescent engages in adult activities. This claim as well as its validation signifies a contempt for adult expectations. Consequently if the adolescent claims the right to smoke, drink, date, and drive a car, he is more likely to commit delinquent acts. As we have stated before, the passage to adult status defines a lack of commitment on the part of the adolescent.

*Involvement* is the third major element of the bond of the individual to society. The involvement hypothesis states that the greater the involvement of the adolescent in conventional activities, the less time he has to engage in deviant acts. However, Hirschi found that measures of time spent in leisure activities are unrelated to the commission of delinquent acts. In retrospect, Hirschi realized that his definition of delinquency and the involvement hypothesis are incompatible. The involvement hypothesis implies that delinquency is a full-time activity that occupies the better part of the adolescent's day. Consequently when the adolescent is kept busy with conventional things, he cannot find the time to be a delinquent. Viewed in this manner, delinquency is defined as a role, a way of life, a career as proposed by Blumstein et al. (1986). This definition of delinquency is contrary to Hirschi's which is to explain delinquent acts. As defined in his theory, delinquency requires very little time.

Hirschi feels that when defining delinquency by acts, the emphasis should be placed on the nature of the conventional activity as opposed to the quantity of conventional activities. With this position, Hirschi located two types of leisure that are, presumably, to a large degree consequences of commitment to conventional success goals. The two types of activities center around the school and the working-class adult culture. The school dimension is defined as involvement in school-related activities such as time spent on homework. The working-class adult dimension is defined by involvement in working-class adult activities. Hirschi states that these activities are important since school-related activities inhibit delinquent activities, whereas participation in adult activities is positively related to the commission of delinquent acts. Furthermore, each type of involvement is independently related to delinquent activity.

The final component of the bond is the adolescent's *belief*, that is, the extent to which he believes he should obey the rules of society. The adolescent's belief acts as a moral obstacle to the commission of delinquent acts. The less an adolescent believes he should obey the rules of society, the greater the probability that he will commit delinquent acts. However, unlike other control theorists, Hirschi assumes that there is variation in the adolescent's attitude of respect toward the rules of society; many people feel no moral obligation to conform. Hirschi perceives a very subtle relation between beliefs and delinquency; he sees the absence of effective beliefs as the result of weak attachment to conventional others. In other words, attachment to the conventional system and belief in the moral validity of its rules are not entirely independent. The chain of causation is from attachment to parents, through concern for the approval of persons in positions of authority, to belief that the rules of society are binding on one's conduct.

As Hirschi has stated, if the adolescent does not see his parents as part of his private world, he does not have to concern himself with their imagined reaction to his behavior. The adolescent who does not care about the reaction of his parents will tend not to be concerned with the approval of persons in positions of impersonal authority. As a result, the adolescent will be free to reject their normative pattern. When the adolescent is not attached to his parents or persons in positions of impersonal authority, he believes that the only reason to obey rules is to avoid punishment. Hirschi found that there is variation in the extent to which boys believe they should obey the law, and the less they believe they should obey it, the less likely they are to do so. However, Hirschi noted empirically that respect for the law is strongly associated with delinquency when respect for persons in position of impersonal authority and attachment to parents are controlled. That is, although beliefs may demonstrate a weak stake in conformity, beliefs are independently related to delinquency.

Besides defining the four major elements of the bond, Hirschi describes *the relations among these elements*. The components of the bond are not unrelated; consequently, Hirschi establishes discursively the relative importance of three sets of relations: attachment and commitment, commitment and involvement, and attachment and belief. Hirschi assumes that attachment to conventional others and commitment to achievement tend to vary together. The adolescent who is attached to conventional persons is more likely to be committed to conformity. Hirschi does not go beyond this general statement in describing the relationship between these two elements, neither does he state the manner in which the components of these two elements interact.

Hirschi established the relation between commitment and involvement to clarify the meaning of the statement "a boy is free of bonds to conventional society." He stresses that this statement does not imply that a boy will necessarily commit delinquent acts. The only certain interpretation that can be given is that he is more likely to commit delinquent acts than the boy strongly tied to conventional society. The fact that bonding theory relies on conditions that make delinquency possible rather than necessary suggests there is a certain amount of indeterminacy within the theory. Hirschi argues that rather than assume opportunities to commit delinquent acts are randomly distributed through the adolescent population, an assumption which stresses indeterminacy, an attempt can be made to demonstrate how commitment limits one's opportunities by examining the relationship between educational and occupational aspirations (commitment) and involvement in conventional activities. That is, the more one is committed to conformity, the more one will be involved in conventional activities, which in turn will limit one's opportunities to commit delinquent acts. Hirschi accepts Piaget's definition of the relationship between attachment to others and belief in the moral validity of society's rules. Our discussion of the belief element of the bond relies heavily on this relationship between belief and attachment to others. During the discussion, we noted the independent effect of belief in the moral validity of the rules on the commission of delinquent acts. Furthermore, Hirschi states that attachment may produce conformity even in the face of beliefs favorable to nonconformity. However, the adolescent's attachment to others normally will lead to acceptance of the moral validity of society's rules.

## Formalization

Now that a technique of formalization has been chosen and Hirschi's discursive statement of his theory has been described, we are in a position to formalize his bonding theory. Hirschi's theory can be represented by ten axioms, nineteen postulates, eleven propositions, twenty-one transformational statements and thirty-one theorems. The extrinsic part of the theory is presented in appendix 9.1 while the intrinsic part is developed in appendix 9.2 The derivation tables, using axioms, postulates, propositions and transformational statements to derive each theorem, can be obtained from the first author. Gibbs' procedure also reveals that Hirschi's theory is a traditional second order theory in which all the intrinsic statements relate two substantive terms, bond and delinquency. The theory consists of one division since all the theorems specify one type of space-time relation. The thirty-one theorems state explicitly the facts that empirically support the theory and the page numbers at the end of each theorem identify where they are verified in Hirschi's book. But the theory, as stated in the preceding section, can be seen as broader; in its empirical verification, however, the author limits its initial scope. In fact, appendix 9.2 presents the empirically based bonding theory before Hirschi modified it through its empirical verification.

## Formalization, Consequences

Now that we have formally stated Hirschi's theory of bonding, we are in a position to examine its internal consistency and to suggest certain modifications to the theory. These modifications are the result of both inconsistencies in the definition of the theoretical constructs as well as certain incomplete theoretical explanations of the relations between construct or concepts. They will be proposed on the grounds of three types of reasons: the logical flaws revealed by the formalization, the empirical results obtained during the exact replication of Hirschi's study by Caplan (1978) and the empirical and substantive literatures on social control since the publication of Hirschi's book twenty years ago.

Our modified version of Hirschi's bonding theory is presented in appendix 9.3, extrinsic part, and 9.4, intrinsic part. Axioms, postulates, propositions, transformational statements and theorems of the modified theory have been numbered with roman numerals, while the numbers of the initial formalization are given in parentheses. The symbols used in the formalization will be the same as before except for two changes. Because the constructs are very broad, we will introduce subconstructs (denoted by a new type of quotation mark, " '......' ") and in the transformational statements and the theorems some acronym will be referred to by names in italics to indicate that they are unmeasured or latent variables. These measures are equivalent to Hirschi's composite measures. The formal statement of the theory will be presented in four blocks according to the levels of generality of the propositions. The first level will limit itself to the major construct, bond, criminal influence, and conformity; the second block will cover constructs like attachment to persons, commitment to institutions, and so on; the third level will involve constructs, subconstructs, concepts and referentials to give a comprehensive view of the theory; and, the fourth block concerns the middle range theories pertaining to family and school social controls.

The inconsistencies in definition that we will discuss concern the four elements of the bond, as well as the bond itself. Some constructs and concepts are not mutually exclusive as expected in a formal theory, while some referentials introduce the problem of autocorrelations. Particularly, the definition of commitment used in Hirschi's text appears to conflict with the definition of involvement as well as attachment; in turn, the concept stake in conformity and its referential are a good examples of a measure that is constructed with questions also used to operationalize other concepts related to different constructs. The formal statement of the theory also reveals that the proposed set of relationships between the components of the theory is insufficient at all levels. Hirschi did not discuss all the possible relationships between constructs or between concepts, as a consequence there are many gaps in the theoretical statement. For example, the theoretical explanation of attachment to parents as well as attachment to peers appears to be particularily incomplete. Our attempt to elaborate Hirschi's theory will not go beyond the constructs and concepts that are implied by the discursive statement in his 1969 book. We could introduce a whole range of constructs, from social constraint, individual differences, routine activities, and others, that are relevant for an elaboration of the theory without betraying its fundamental postulates; this will be done in a subsequent paper.

For the tautologies and gaps that we will identify, we will propose relevant adjustments to axioms, postulates, propositions, tranformational statements and theorems. New theorems will be derived as well. We will first comment on definitional problems concerning each element of the bond, the processes of attachment, commitment, involvement, and belief. Following this first step, we will be concerned with the relationships between the elements of the bond.

### Definitional Problems

*Commitment*

The definition of commitment used in Hirschi's theoretical formulation and particularily in its empirical test appears to conflict with the definition of attachment as well as involvement. This is also noted by Krohn and Massey (1980) who propose to discard the construct of involvement. It should also be mentioned that Kempf (1989) concludes that there appears to be less consensus regarding the measurement of commitment as compared to the other elements of the bond. It is our opinion that the source of the conflict is not the same for both attachment and involvement; therefore we will analyze the overlapping in definitions separately before we propose a redefinition.

The definition of the construct "commitment" reported previously poses problems with regard to the purity of its meaning. As Hirschi points out, "one is committed to conformity not only by what one has but also by what one hopes to obtain." (Hirschi 1969, 21). That is, the term designates two properties of the adolescent behavior (pursuit) and attitude (desire). This definition conflicts with that of the construct "involvement" which refers to the time devoted to conventional activities. With his definition, Hirschi follows Becker (1960) who states that a person, in order to follow a consistent line of activity, is committed if he "is envisioned as having acted in such a way ("made a commitment") or being in such a state ("being committed")" (35). However, Becker and Hirschi accept that "its seems convenient to retain "commitment" to refer to the specific mechanism of constraint of behavior through previously placed side bets and use such terms as "involvement", "attachment," . . . and so on, to refer to related but distinguishable phenomena" (Becker 1960, 40).

The problem of obscurity of the definition of commitment becomes evident when Hirschi operationalizes his construct. It can be clearly seen in Hirschi's definition of the "passage to adult status," a concept that delimits, in part, the construct of commitment defined as the "development of *attitudes* and *behavior* in ways appropriate only to an adult" (1969, p. 163). Hirschi uses the referential IOIIAA (index of involvement in adult activities) to measure this concept. However, this referential measures only the behavioral aspect of the concept. The attitudinal component of the concept is not measured. Hirschi also uses the same referential IOIIAA to measure the concept 'involvement in working class adult activities,' which defines, in part, the construct involvement. As a result, there is an overlap in the definition when behavior is used to define "commitment" as well as "involvement."

A solution would appear to be the removal of the behavioral element from the definition of the commitment construct. In other words, if the commitment construct were to be defined in an attitudinal perspective while the involvement construct defined in a behavioral perspective, a considerable degree of clarity could be introduced by allowing these two constructs to stand as mutually exclusive. This distinction between behavior and attitude is well grounded in the tradition of sociology and psychology since the seminal paper of Allport (1935). Limiting the construct "commitment" to the attitudinal perspective, what Bernard (1987) calls subjective or psychosocial commitment that is the perceived interests, leaves aside what he refers to as the objective or structural commitment, the accurate calculation of interests, which is a prerequisite to attachment, involvement, and belief. It is beyond the scope of Hirschi's theory and of this paper to integrate that element in our criticism of bonding theory. Recently, in the field of the study of organizations, Mottaz (1989) demonstrated the importance, theoretically and empirically, in distinguishing what he calles attitudinal commitment from behavioral commitment: the first type of commitment refers to an acceptance of the goals and values of an organization, a desire to be a member and a willingness to work for it, while the second type of commitment relates to concrete investments in the organization. The Wiatrowski and Anderson (1987) study of the dimensionality of the bond also makes a clear distinction between school involvement (activities related to school) and attachment (attitude towards school). To follow that tradition and to maintain the mutual exclusivity of the construct and the measures, we will redefine the concepts delimiting "commitment" in an attitudinal perspective while the various concepts delimiting "involvement" will be limited to a behavioral perspective.

Hirschi briefly mentions the acquisition of a reputation as one of the components of his definition of commitment. This desire to maintain a favorable reputation with conventional others defines a commitment to persons. In further elaboration of the definition of commitment, however, stress is placed mainly on educational and occupational careers that represent the commitment to institutions as opposed to persons. As a result, of the definition of commitment being oriented towards both institutions and persons, Hirschi overlaps this definition with the definition of attachment. That is, the very essence of attachment is the desire to maintain a favorable reputation with conventional others. More specifically, attachment means caring about the wishes and expectations of other persons. To distinguish between an adolescents that is attached to his parents and one who is committed to his parents would be tautological. This generic definition is also adopted by Briar and Piliavin (1965) who view "the central processes of social control as commitment to conformity (39). Krohn and Massey (1980), noting this overlap, proposed to limit attachment to persons and commitment to institutions. In that direction, the Wiatrowski and Anderson (1987) study of the dimensionality of the bond also distinguishes clearly between attachment to persons, parents, and teachers, and attachment to school that we would prefer to call commitment. If attachment and commitment are to be included in the same formal theory, we must distinguish between the source of attachment and commitment. Conceptual clarity is introduced if we speak of an adolescent being attached to persons and committed to institutions. The problem created by the failure to distinguish between attachment and commitment is particularily demonstrated in Hirschi's concept of 'stake in conformity'.

In the formal statement of the theory, the "commitment" is defined, in part, by the concept 'stake in conformity.' However, several items used in the referential SIC, which measures 'stake in conformity', are used in constructing referentials that measure other concepts that define attachment. That is, the item "do you like school?" is not only used in constructing the referential SIC, but is also used in measuring the concept 'attitude toward school.' Likewise, the items "Do you share your thoughts and feelings with your mother (father)?" and "How often have you talked over your future plans with your mother (father)?", are used in measuring the concept 'mutual participation in the adolescent psychological fields' as well as the concept 'stake in conformity.' The concept 'attitude toward school' defines, in part, the construct "attachment to school," while the concept 'mutual participation in the adolescent psychological fields,' is used in defining the construct "attachment to parents." As a result, referentials that are used in the measurement of concepts that define different constructs, "attachment to parents" and "attachment to school," are used in the measurement of a concept that defines the construct of "commitment." Since the definition of attachment and comitment are not entirely mutually exclusive, the measurement of these definitions is, in part, overlapping. This practice does not only involve a conceptual tautology but also creates a problem of autocorrelations when these measures are correlated. In order to clearly distinguish between commitment and attachment and avoid statistical problems, we suggest that the concept of 'stake in conformity' be removed from the definition of commitment. The concept must be eliminated due to its broad definition. 'Stake in conformity' measures globally the strength of the bond to conventional society but does not define any one specific element of the bond. Hirschi acknowledges the scope of his concept when he states "throughout the text, I occasionally use stake in conformity in speaking in general of the strength of the bond to conventional society" (Hirschi 1969, 19–20).

In sum, we propose that commitment be limited to institutions, that attachment be restricted to persons and that involvement be confined to activities. The necessity of these distinctions is not only logical from substantive and formal point of views, it is also an empirical requirement. As noted above, the study of the dimensionality of the bond by Wiatrowski and Anderson (1987) clearly shows that the latent variables measuring these constructs are constituted of scales that correspond to the distinctions we are proposing. Kempf's (1989) review also shows that most of the researchers have avoided that problem of overlap since only fourteen studies consider simultaneously these three elements of the bond and only thirteen studies measure commitment and attachment. When they introduce more than one element of the bond, their operationalization of the elements suffers from the same inconsistencies that we have outlined.

The proposed redefinition of the construct of commitment implies the reorganization of certain concepts. For example, the concept 'sentiments toward the controlling institution' can no longer define the construct "attachment to school." Instead this concept more appropriately taps the adolescent's attitude toward school, which indirectly defines this desire to achieve the conventional goal of education ("commitment"). Hirschi includes the concept 'academic performance' under the construct "commitment." However, since we have previously defined the construct "commitment to institutions" in an attitudinal perspective, we prefer not to include the concept 'academic performance' in the subconstruct " 'commitment to education' ". This definitional choice does not imply that the adolescent academic performance does not have a role in the process of commitment to education. We will discuss this role

below. Another reason to leave the concept 'academic performance' out of the subconstruct " 'commitment to education' " is
that Caplan (1978) was unable to construct an internally consistent
measure of attitudinal commitment if it was included.

Above, we demonstrated that the composite concept 'stakes in
conformity' reflects the overlap in Hirschi's definitions of "attachment" and "commitment." We suggested that the concept of
'stakes in conformity' should be eliminated from the theory due to
its broad definition, the overall strength of the bond to conventional
society, which defines both the constructs of attachment and commitment instead of one specific construct. 'Stakes in conformity' is
defined by three concepts: 'mutual participation in the adolescent
psychological fields,' 'achievement orientation,' and 'sentiments
toward the controling institution'. We consider the concept 'mutual
participation in the adolescent psychological fields' to be a concept
that exclusively defines, in part, the adolescent's attachment to his
parents. In his theory, Hirschi uses the concept 'achievement
orientation' as part of the definition of the construct of commitment
to education. As we mentioned above, an adolescent's sentiments
toward the controlling institution now defines, in part, his commitment to education and it is a measure of attitude.

Now that we have eliminated the composite concept 'stakes in
conformity' and reclassified its constituent concepts, we are able to
introduce in the subconstruct "commitment to education" with the
concepts that defined previously the construct "commitment to
school." We are also implying that there are other sorts of institutions towards which commitment can develop: religion, work, or
career, and so on. Since "commitment to school" was defined by
the adolescent's 'educational expectation' and his 'achievement
orientation', these concepts have been employed in the initial
statement of theory: theorem 27 states a direct relationship between
'achievement orientation' and 'commission of delinquent acts' and
theorem 25 proposes an indirect relationship between 'educational
expectation' and 'commission of delinquent acts' through 'involvement in adult activities'. Since this last theorem is neither valid in
Hirschi's data nor in Caplan's data (1978), it has to be eliminated
from the formal statement. It is replaced by proposition xi which
relates the three concepts/'educational expectation', 'academic per-

formance' and 'self-perceived academic competence'. Proposition XI states: Among male adolescents, the greater the 'educational expectation at To' *and* the less the 'academic performance at To', the less the 'self-perceived academic competence at To'. What we are proposing here is an elaboration of the process of commitment integrating educational expectation in that process and thus indicating another source of the self-perceived academic competence. Theorem XXXIX is derived from proposition XI.

'Attitude toward the school setting' is another composite concept that overlaps the definitions of attachment and commitment. This composite concept is defined by the concepts 'sentiments toward the controlling institution' and 'attachment to teacher'. We have reclassified the concept 'sentiments toward the controlling institution' as defining the subconstruct '' 'commitment to education' ''. In addition 'attachment to teacher' defines, in part, the adolescent's attachment. Due to the conceptual overlap, we will eliminate this composite concept from the theoretical statement and theorems 17, 18, and 19 are reformulated to include only the first component of the composite concept; they become theorems XXXIV, XXXVII shown by Caplan (1978), this choice is empirically valid.

Also, as a result of the elimination of this composite concept, we must modify proposition 8 that states that among male adolescents, the greater the 'self-perceived academic competence at To', the greater the 'sentiments toward the controlling institution and attachment to a conventional figure at To'. In his text, Hirschi (1969, 111) states: "The boy who sees himself as capable of doing well in school is likely to find school tolerable and relevant to his future." This suggests that an adolescent's self-perceived academic competence has a greater impact on this attitude toward school than on his attitude toward teachers. This statement is also consistent with proposition VII that hypothesizes a relationship between academic performance and sentiments toward the controlling institution. Therefore, proposition IX incorporates these assumptions by now stating: Among male adolescents, the greater the 'self-perceived academic competence at To', the greater the 'sentiments toward the controlling institution at To'. By modifying proposition 8 in this manner, we are also suggesting that 'self-perceived academic competence' more appropriately defines the construct of ''commitment". Theorem xxxvii is derived from that proposition and it is empirically valid (Caplan 1978).

Since we have redefined an adolescent as being committed as opposed to attached to an institution, such as school, certain concepts that formerly defined the defunct construct "attachment to school" now have been reclassified as concepts defining the adolescent's commitment to education. As the redefinition of the "commitment" construct does not affect the relationship between the concepts academic performance and sentiments toward school, theorem 30 is maintained. That is, proposition v, the basis of theorem xxxv, states: Among male adolescents, the greater the 'academic performance at To', the greater the 'sentiments toward the controlling institution at To'. But the reorganization of the concepts also requires the introduction of a new proposition. That is, we believe that a relationship exists between an adolescent's attitude toward school and his achievement orientation. Before an adolescent can be committed to educational success, which is defined, in part, by the adolescent's achievement orientation, he should logically possess a positive attitude toward school. More specifically, proposition x states: Among male adolescents, the greater the 'sentiments toward the controlling institution at To,' the greater the 'achievement orientation at To'. In introducing this proposition, we are implying that the adolescent's sentiments toward the controlling institution are indirectly related to the commission of delinquent acts via the adolescent's achievement orientation. That is, we are removing theorem 16 that states the direct relationship between the adolescent's sentiments toward the controlling institution and the commission of delinquent acts and introducing theorem xxxviii that states the direct relationship between the adolescent's sentiment toward the controlling institution and his academic orientation (a theorem verified by Caplan 1978).

The elimination of the composite concept 'stakes in conformity' requires us to redefine the relationship between stakes in conformity and delinquent companions as stated in theorem 22. Basically, this theorem states concurrently the relationship between the adolescent's commitment, his attachment, and his delinquent companions. Consequently, we can formulate theorems to state these relationships. That is, we can relate the adolescent's commitment to education to his exposure to criminal influences; this is done by theorem IX. As well, an additional theorem can be introduced to state the relationship between the adolescent's attachment and his delinquent companions. Later in our discussion of the redefinition of the construct attachment, we will present the second theorem that allows us to reformulate theorem 22.

Two of the concepts comprising the former composite concept 'stakes in conformity' are the adolescent's sentiments toward the controlling institution and his achievement orientation. In our redefinition of the construct "commitment" we hypothesized that the process of commitment is such that the adolescent's sentiments toward the controlling institution affects his achievement orientation, which in turn, is related to delinquency. In relating the adolescent's commitment to education with his exposure to criminal influences we hypothesize a similar process. That is, the adolescent's, achievement orientation is directly related to his involvement with delinquent companions. We are able to specify this relationship by axiom XI: Among male adolescents, the greater the " 'commitment to education at To' ", the less the "exposure to criminal influences at To"; theorem XLI, which is derived from this axiom, is empirically valid according to Caplan (1978). The consequence is that the adolescent's sentiments toward the controlling institution are indirectly related to his delinquent companions via the adolescent's achievement orientation.

With these proposed modifications, we are suggesting that the construct "commitment to institutions" could involve several sub-constructs, for example " 'commitment to education' ", " 'commitment to religion' ", " 'commitment to a high status occupation' ", and so on. However, to stay in the limits of the domain marked by Hirschi's discussion and questionnaire, we are confining ourselves to the subconstruct " 'commitment to education' ". It is also the most significant institution for adolescents. This subconstruct is composed for four concepts: 'self-perceived academic competence', 'sentiment toward the controlling institution', 'achievement orientation', and 'educational expectation'. However, two concepts have an important role in the development of the adolescent commitment to education: his 'academic competence' and his 'academic performance'. As Hirschi (1969, 115) points out: "academic competence is linked to delinquency by way of success in and attachment to school."

Several consequences are derived from a clearer distinction between the constructs "attachment to persons", "commitment to institutions", and "involvement in conventional activities" and a reclassification of their original concepts and measures. First, the relationship between the four attitudinal concepts in the process of commitment, is represented by four theorems (XXXVI, XXXVIII, XXXIX, and XLIII). Second, the adolescent's commitment to education represented by the above four attitudes is affected by the academic competence and the academic performance; these relationships are defined by theorems XXXIV, XXXV, XXXVI, and XLII. Third, the adolescent's commitment to education reinforces his conformity to conventional standards of behavior through the direct relation specified by theorem XL and also protects him against the exposure to criminal influence, theorem XLI. Fourth, the adolescent's achievement orientation is a transmitter since all other commitment variables do have an indirect effect on exposure to criminal influences and delinquency through that variable. It is the only attitudinal variable that is directly related to these two variables (theorems XL and XLI). Fifth, the concepts defining the adolescent commitment relate to concepts delimiting, in part, the constructs "attachment to persons" (theorem LIX) and "involvement in conventional activities" (theorems LXII and LXIV).

Finally, because we have proposed to subdivide the formal statement of the theory according to four levels of generality that implied unmeasured variables, new postulates must be introduced to specify the subconstruct " 'commitment to education' "; postulate V creates that subconstruct from the construct and postulate XXII defines the concepts delimiting the subconstruct while the transformational statement V creates the latent variable relative to that subconstruct, ENGSCO. As a consequence of the introduction of this subconstruct two theorems are derived. The origins of theorem VII and IX are respectively axioms V and XI that express a relationship between the adolescent commitment to education and, respectively, his conformity to conventional standards of behavior and his susceptibility to criminal influences that are fundamental in Hirschi's theory.

## Involvement

We have proposed a clear distinction between the constructs of "involvement" and "commitment," restricting the first to behaviors and the second to attitudes. As we have defined "commitment" as the desire to achieve conventional goals, involvement would be defined as the expenditure of energy in the pursuit of conventional activities. Kempf's (1989) review shows that some measures of involvement do not follow this distinction. She also demonstrates that variables that refer to types of activities are more often used and, particularily, the ones that concern the amount of time spent on them account for most of the measures of involvement in conventional activities. However, the nature and variety of conventional activities considered varies greatly from one study to the other. To avoid that kind of disparity, we propose to specify more precisely the concepts that should be included under the construct "involvement in conventional activities".

Since Hirschi has limited his construct of involvement to the concept of 'involvement in school related activities' (theorem XLIV), we see a need for an enlargement of this construct. The concept of 'involvement in adult activities' recuperated from the construct of "commitment" can constitute another component of the construct "involvement". Although this operationalization defines involvement in activities related to two institutions delimiting the bond, school, and, in part, peers, the involvement in conventional activities with parents is excluded. In appendix C of Hirschi's text (1969, 284), four items that measure involvement in conventional activities with parents are presented: How often do you work in the garden with your parents? How often do you make household repairs with your parents? How often do you watch television with your parents? How often do you go to sports events with your parents? These items could be combined to measure 'involvement in conventional activities with parents' and theorem XLVI—Among male adolescents, the greater their 'involvement in conventional activities with their parents at To, the less the 'commission of delinquent acts at To'—can be derived. In a similar vein, Hirschi remains silent on the involvement of adolescents in conventional activities with peers. In appendix C of Hirschi's text, (1969, 284) there is the following item: "Do you belong to any youth clubs?" This item could be used to measure 'involvement in conventional activities with peers' and theorem XLVII could be derived. With these modifications considered, we would be able to verify the degree to which the desire to achieve conventional goals is related to the pursuit of these goals via conventional activities with peers. This theorem states: Among male adolescents, the greater the 'involvement in conventional activities with peers at To, the less the 'commission of delinquent acts at To'.

The concept 'expression of claims to adult status' is now considered as part of the definition of involvement. This concept reflects "the fact that adulthood has been prematurely obtained or claimed by the adolescent" (Hirschi 1969, 165). Hirschi (1969, 163) states that "in the ideal case, the adolescent simultaneously completes his education, begins his occupational career, and acquires adult status." In other words, Hirschi views work in its proper sequence within the life cycle, as an adult activity. However if an adolescent's commitment to education is absent, indicating a premature completion of his educational career, his involvement in work can be seen as a premature claim to the attainment of adulthood. That is, the adolescent not committed to an educational career, works in order to validate his claims to adulthood. This position is supported by the recent work of Greenberger and Steinberg (1986) on the psychological and social costs of adolescent employment while in school. Consequently, we believe the concept 'involvement in adult activities' to be more realistically measured by an adolescent's involvement in work as opposed to his involvement in smoking, drinking, and dating. Furthermore, Caplan (1978) has demonstrated that these supposedly adult activities are not related to the commission of delinquent acts. Theorem 26 has been modified accordingly and is empirically valid according to Caplan's data (1978), it is now theorem XLV which states: Among male adolescent, the greater the adolescent 'involvement in work at To', the greater the 'commission of delinquent acts'.

In sum, the construct "involvement" is composed of four concepts: "involvement in school related activities', 'involvement in work', 'involvement in conventional activities with parents', and 'involvement in conventional activities with peers'. And, the measures of this construct no longer overlap with the variables measuring the construct "commitment to institutions". Another concept could have been retained, namely 'involvement in leisure activities' or 'involvement in sports'. Hirschi, from a note at the bottom of page 190, tells us that there is a weak positive relationship between the time spent in particular activities—watching television, reading, playing games—and delinquency. This type of relationship has been replicated in our data (see Fréchette and Le Blanc 1987), while the involvement in sports has produced contradictory results. Polk and Schaffer (1972) and Landers and Landers (1978) find a negative correlation while Stark et al. (1987) report no correlation between participation in sports and concurrent or later delinquency. The controversial nature of these concepts demands clarification and for this reason we did not include it in our modified formal statement of bonding theory.

*Belief*

Hirschi defines belief as an attitude of respect toward the rules of society as well as their enforcers. The first component of his definition, because it refers to the moral validity of the rules, renders this construct nontautological with the constructs "involvement in conventional activities" and "commitment to institution"; and theorem XII operationalizes the relationship between the moral validity of the rules and the commission of delinquent acts. This theorem is empirically valid according to Hirschi's and Caplan's data (1978) and the review by Elliott et al. (1985) on that question confirms its validity. Most of the seventeen replications of control theory using a belief construct employed this type of measures (Kempf 1989). However the second part of the definition of beliefs, that refers to the attitude of respect toward the enforcers of the rules, can be logically seen as an element of the attachment to persons. We believe that the concept 'concern for the approval of persons in positions of impersonal authority' (the adolescent's attitude of respect toward persons representing authority outside the family unit) should be reclassified under the construct "attachment to persons" and in a later section we will discuss it.

Although Hirschi defines belief as an attitude of respect toward the rules of society; it appears that belief is not an independent element of the bond. "The meaning and efficacy of such beliefs are contingent upon other beliefs and, indeed, on the strength of other ties to the conventional order" (Hirschi 1969, 26). We may interpret this statement as meaning that belief, as an element of the bond, is dependent on "other beliefs" and "the strength of other ties to the conventional order." We can equate "the strength of other ties to the conventional order" as meaning attachment to parents and respect for impersonal authority. However, Hirschi leaves us in the dark as to what might be considered "other beliefs'. This statement leaves us with the impression that he would like to go beyond "belief in the legal institution" in his theory, and include "other beliefs" whatever they may be. He tries to include them, particularily lower-class culture and middle-class values, but empirical data do not support a role for these variables.

We are able to further define the adolescent's attitude of respect toward the rules of society by using two concepts: 'legitimacy of the controlling institution's rules' and 'legitimacy of parental rules'. Hirschi dealt with the first concept in his chapter on attachment to school; on pages 127 and 128, he uses the item "none of school's business if student wants to smoke outside of classroom" to tap that aspect of the adolescent belief in the legitimacy of the school rules. Theorem L specifies the relationship between this concept and delinquency; it is empirically valid in Hirschi's and Caplan's data (1978). The referential for the second concept could be the following question found in appendix B of Hirschi's book: "Do your parents make rules that seem unfair to you?" Accordingly, theorem XLIX can be derived from axiom VII: Among male adolescents, the greater the "belief at To", the greater the "conformity to conventional standards of behavior at To". This theorem was validated empirically by Caplan (1978).

As part of the "belief" construct, Hirschi introduces the concept of techniques of neutralization, borrowed from Sykes and Matza (1957), to "measure the extent to which these techniques are part of the boy's ideological system" (Hirschi 1969, 206). He shows that the techniques of denial of responsibility, of injury and of the victim and condemnation of the condemners are related to the commission of delinquent acts. Replications (Hindelang 1973; Mannle and Lewis 1979; Caplan 1978; Le Blanc et al. 1988b) have used a composite index of neutralization techniques; it is our referential NTEC. Based on axiom VII, theorem LIII states accordingly that the greater the adolescent's adoption of the neutralization techniques the more he will be involved in delinquency. Even if Hirschi did not discuss the source of neutralization techniques, we can easily imagine that the more the exposure to criminal influence the more these techniques will be adopted by the adolescent. Johnson (1979) shows that there is a strong relationship between delinquent associates and delinquent values; from their review, Elliott et al. (1985) conclude that delinquents also perceive some sort of social approval for delinquent acts from their peers. Proposition XIV makes this relationship possible and theorem LI can be derived from it. It states: Among male adolescent, the greater the number of delinquent friends at To, the greater the use of neutralization techniques at To. We can also propose that there should be an inverse relationship between the acceptance of the normative system and the reference to neutralization techniques. Proposition XV states this relationship and theorem LII is consequently derived.

In sum, the construct "belief" is represented by four concepts: 'acceptance of the normative system', 'legitimacy of parental rules,' 'legitimacy of the controlling institution's rules', and 'use of neutralization techniques'. And theorems are relating these variables to the commission of delinquent acts or the exposure to criminal influences.

*Attachment*

In the discursive statement of his theory, in chapter 2 of his book, Hirschi does not introduce the subconstructs " 'attachment to parents' ", " 'attachment to peers' ", and " 'attachment to teachers' ". However, he devotes chapters 6 and 8 respectively to the first two categories of attachment. Kempf's (1989) review shows that thirty-nine out of forty-five studies involved the element of the bond attachment, typically referring to parents (often only to the mother), followed by peers (most often excluding delinquent friends), and then to school (often to teachers). Mathur and Dodder (1985) and Wiatrowski and Anderson (1987) in studies of the dimensionality of the social bond demonstrated the necessity of the distinction between attachment to parents, peers, and teachers. In their study these three dimensions of the adolescent's attachment to persons constitute latent variables and the correlations between themselves are higher than with the other dimensions of the bond. In discussing the construct "attachment to persons" (according to the distinction made with the construct "commitment to institutions"), we will introduce a new construct " 'attachment to persons in positions of impersonal authority' ", revise the construct " 'attachment to parents' ", and reaffirm the importance of the construct " 'attachment to peers' ". Finally, we will review the relationships between the subcomponent of the construct "attachment to persons."

*Attachment to Persons in Positions of Impersonal Authority*

On several occasions in his book Hirschi draws a distinction between attachment to parents and attachment to adult authorities in general. That is, he demonstrates an interest in examining the extend of the carry-over effect from attachment to parents toward teachers (theorem 17) as well as the police (theorem 29). Those two types of authority are treated under the concept 'concern for the approval of persons in positions of impersonal authority' as part of the definition of the construct "belief". We now realize, because we have proposed a clear distinction between the constructs "attachment to persons" and "belief in a normative system", that this concept defines the "attachment to persons variously located in conventional society" (Hirschi 1969, 85). Although both teachers and police represent persons in positions of impersonal authority they are perceived as located in different spheres of conventional society, in different institutions. As a result, it would be appropriate to speak of 'attachment to teachers' and 'respect for police' as two independent concepts defining the sub-construct " 'attachment to persons in positions of impersonal authority' " of the construct "attachment to persons". There could also be other adult figures to represent persons in positions of impersonal authority, such as a coach or a scout leader, but we will limit ourselves to the two figures introduced by Hirschi. Catalano and Hawkins (1986) also propose the introduction of this concept under the name of attachment to conventional others. In the verifications of Hirschi's bonding theory the adolescent's attachment to other adults than parents is very rarely considered (Kempf 1989). The concept of respect for police is used only three times (Hindelang 1973; Caplan 1978; Le Blanc et al. 1988b), while the concept of attachment to the teacher is measured in only five studies (Hindelang 1973; Caplan 1978; Shover et al. 1979; Caplan and Le Blanc 1985; Le Blanc et al. 1988b).

We have drawn a distinction between two forms of attachment to persons in positions of impersonal authority; that is, attachment to teachers and respect for police. As a result, theorem 20 is replaced by three theorems that are derived from axiom IV relating the attachment to persons to delinquency. Theorem XXV states the relationship between the adolescent " 'attachment to persons in positions of impersonal authority' " and the "conformity to conventional standard of behavior": Among male adolescents, the greater the ATTAU at To, the less the IOD at To. Theorem XXIV state a relationships between the concept 'attachment to teacher' and delinquency. In the original statement of the theory an adolescent's stake in conformity was negatively related to the number of his delinquent friends, theorem 22. The removal of the composite concept 'stake in conformity' required us to introduce three theorems in order to express the original relationship stated in theorem 22. Theorem XXI hypothesizes that the more the adolescent is attached to his teacher the lower his probability of having delinquent friends; theorem XXI states that the higher the adolescent's respect for the police the lower the probability of exposure to criminal influences; and, theorem XXIII formulates the same relationship, this time with the unmeasured variable attachment to persons in positions of impersonal authority, ATTAU.

In sum, Hirschi concept 'concern for the approval of persons in positions of impersonal authority' has been transferred from the construct "belief" to the construct "attachment to persons." And, the subconstruct " 'attachment to persons in positions of impersonal authority' '' is now composed of two concepts, 'respect for police' and 'attachment to teacher'. These changes bring more precision in the formal statement of the theory relative to this component but also relative to its relationship to the adolescent beliefs and attachment to parents, which we will discuss below.

### Attachment to Parents

According to Hirschi's presentation, the attachment to parents model is defined by four concepts—'parental expression on child's behavior,' 'concern for parental opinion,' 'impact of parents opinions and expectations,' and 'psychological presence of parents'— and their relationships can be represented by theorems 1 to 5. Our critical analysis of the process of attachment to parents will demonstrate that for conceptual clarity there is a need to group some concepts, to introduce a new concept and a new construct and to revise the relationships between the concepts. It is interesting to note that most of the studies (Kempf 1989) that refer to the attachment to the parents use a summated index to measure that dimension without distinguishing the concepts proposed by Hirschi. Also many of these studies separate attachment to parents according to the target, mother or father, which is futile if we accept Hirschi's demonstration (100–107). Studies that argue for distinguishing between attachment to mother and father, for example Johnson (1987), cannot show results with major differences in the impact of each attachment on delinquency; Johnson reports the following correlations between attachment and delinquency: for boys, mother $-.20$ and father $-.24$, and for girls, mother $-.12$ and father $-.13$.

The concepts 'parental expression on child's behavior' and 'concern for parental opinion' are used by Hirschi in his empirical test, but he often refers to the concept 'mutual participation in the adolescent social and psychological fields' while formulating his theory. During his analysis of the first order theorems Caplan (1978) found that to distinguish between various forms of shared communication did not add any precision to the theoretical model. That is, whether we define mutual participation in the form of parental expression of their child's behavior or the adolescent's concern for parental opinion, our results are equivalent (the two concepts as measured by their referentials IOCPTC and IOCCTP were fairly strongly correlated). For these reasons we have decided to employ one composite referential IOC that combines the two former referentials IOCPTC and IOCCTP to measure the shared communication between the adolescent and his parents. The construction of this composite referential allows us to combine theorem 7 and 8. We can now relate 'share communication' with the 'commission of delinquent acts' without distinguishing whether the flow of communication is between the adolescent and his parents or visa versa. Theorems 7 and 8 are replaced by theorem XIV which is derived from axiom IV: Among male adolescents, the greater the 'attachment to parents at To,' the greater the 'conformity to conventional standards of behavior at To.' For the same reasons theorem 4 and 5 can be combined. In other words, only one theorem, theorem LXVII, is required to express the relationship between the 'share communication' and the 'psychological presence of parents.'

Hirschi assumes that the adolescent considers the expectations and opinions of his parents. This assumption is valid if the focus of the mutual participation or share communication is positive. That is, the adolescent not only considers his parents as part of his private world but also his parents try to enter his private world. However, in order to verify the effect of 'share communication,' the adolescent's perception of parental attitude must be considered. As Nye (1958, p. 73) has stated: "The indifferent or hostile parent is unlikely to give the sympathetic and constructive supervision needed by the adolescent. He will not be concerned about the child getting into trouble until it occurs and embarrasses him. In addition, indifference or hostility is likely in return to breed negative emotions in the adolescent toward the parent."

In other words, the adolescent will feel loved and accepted by his parents only if there is effective share communication with them. Furthermore, the more the adolescent feels loved and accepted by his parents the more he cares about his parents expectations and opinions. More specifically, the concept 'adolescent's perception of parental attitude' intervenes between the concept of 'share communication' and 'impact of the parental expectations and opinions'; this concept is often referred to as the adolescent affectional identification with his parents in Hirschi's discursive statement. In order to represent this theoretical formulation of the process of attachment to parents it is necessary to introduce propositions and , which are as follows: Among male adolescents, the greater the 'share communication at To,' the greater the 'adolescent's perception of parental attitude at To'; and, Among male adolescents, the greater the 'adolescent's perception of parental attitude at To,' the greater the 'affectional identification.' From these propositions theorems and can be derived and they have been empirically validated by Caplan (1978). Also, Hirschi has shown that the adolescent affectional identification is related to his level of delinquency (theorem ).

In our interpretation of the subconstruct " 'attachment to parents' " we believe three concepts are used by Hirschi in his definition of it: 'mutual participation in the adolescents social and psychological fields,' 'impact of the parental expectations and opinions,' and the 'psychological presence of the parents'. In reexamining this latter concept, we realize that 'psychological presence of the parents' does not define the construct "attachment to parents" which has been defined by Hirschi as the adolescent's sensitivity to his parents' opinion. Rather this concept is more closely related to direct control, what Reiss (1951) calls the "ability of social groups or institutions to make norms effective." Hirschi's theory enunciates the elements that are necessary for the adolescent to be bonded to conventional society without clearly explaining how society is able to sanction the adolescent's behavior effectively in the direction of conformity. Hirschi mentions direct control implicitly within his discussion of parental attachment. He notes the importance of discipline with parental attachment and, in a more recent text, he stresses the importance of parental monitoring (Hirschi 1985). In fact, Hirschi's discussion of the role of discipline within the process of parental attachment introduces an autonomous element, direct control, which is treated as a component of attachment to parents. Although we stress the importance of developing the notion of direct control as did many revisions of Hirschi's theory (Conger 1976; Meier and Johnson 1977; Minor 1977; Paternoster et a. 1983; Paternoster 1989), we consider this development as beyond the framework of the present analysis. It is simply necessary at this time to distinguish between the subconstructs " 'attachment to parents' " and the construct "direct control."

The psychological presence of parents, that is, the adolescent giving thought to his parents' reaction when he is faced with a situation to commit a delinquent act, is one way in which parental norms are made effective. In other words, the psychological presence of parents is view as a form of indirect supervision. Consequently, we are required to introduce this new construct that we believe has been omitted from Hirschi's presentation of the theory, that is, the construct "direct control"; the concept of psychological presence of parents can be considered as a partial definition of direct control. The introduction of this new construct does not affect the original theorems 3, 4, 5, and 6 which specify the relationship between the following three constructs: " 'attachment to parents,' " "direct control," and "conformity to conventional standards of behavior"; they are now theorems LIV to LVII.

As we mentioned during our discussion of the redefinition of the construct of commitment, theorem 22, states in part the relationship between the adolescent's attachment and his exposure to criminal influences. The modification of theorem 22 allows us to introduce two additional theorems that state the relationship between the adolescent's attachment to his parents and his delinquent companions in the same way that we have related the attachment to persons of impersonal authority to delinquent companions. The relationship between the adolescent attachment to his parents and his susceptibility to being exposed to criminal influences can be stated by the introduction of axiom x. Among male adolescents, the greater the " 'attachment to parents at To,' " the less the 'exposure to criminal influences at To.' Theorems XVII and XVIII are derived from this axiom and validate by Caplan (1978).

In summary, four modifications are introduced into the formal statement as a result of the redefinition of the subconstruct " 'attachment to parents.' " First, the two referentials measuring the adolescent's shared communication with his parents have been combined to replace theorems 4 and 5 with theorem LVII, as a consequence we can replace theorems 7 and 8 by theorem XIV. Second, the two measures of 'affectional identification with parents' have been reduced to one composite referential. Third, the theorems that relate the 'share communication' and the 'affectional identification' with parents have been replaced by theorems xv and xvi in order to express the intervening role of the 'adolescent's perception of parental attitude' in this relationship. Fourth, theorem xix states that, overall, the process of attachment to parents represented by these relationships has a direct impact on the adolescent conformity. Fifth, a new construct "direct control" has been added to the model, but the theorems involving to the concept 'psychological presence of parents' are not affected by this change (LIV to LVII).

*Attachment to Peers*

Hirschi clearly states that the relationship between peer attachment and delinquent behavior is conditional on the type of peers. "If the peer 'culture' requires delinquent behavior then presumably attachment would foster conformity, that is, delinquency. However, if the peer culture is identical to the conventional culture, then attachment to persons within this culture should foster conformity to conventional standards" (Hirschi 1969, 84). In other words, Hirschi predicts either a negative relationship between delinquency and attachment to conventional peers or a positive relationship between delinquency and attachment to deviant peers. Therefore, peer attachment per se cannot be related to delinquency because the combination of conventional and deviant attachments would cancel out their differential effect. In his analysis, Hirschi dismisses his own explanation concerning the conditional nature of the impact of peer attachment by showing that whatever the number of friends picked up by the police, delinquency increases when attachment to friends weakens (table 50, 151). Caplan (1978) follows up on Hirschi's initial suggestion that the relationship between attachment to peers and delinquency was conditional on the presence of delinquent companions, showing that there no significant association between attachment to peers and delinquency (it is very weak and negative) and that it is not conditional on the existence of delinquent companions. Chapman (1986), however, found a weak negative relationship between attachment to peers and delinquency in two sets of data (Richmond youth survey and Seattle youth study), as in many studies, and shows that it is not conditional on the level of the stake of conformity of the friends.

As a consequence of these results, a theorem has to be introduced (xxvi) to relate the measures of the concepts 'identification with best friends' and 'conformity to conventional standards of behavior.' However, representing the adolescent attachment to friends by only one element, his identification with his best friend, is a rather simplistic view of friendships if we refer to the review by Giordano et al. (1986) on that subject, Kempf's (1989) review of the measures used in the verifications of bonding theory, or Ried's (1989) demonstration that attachment to peers has an indirect effect on drug use through peer expectations and favorable attitude to use. To permit a further elaboration of the theory, which is not the objective of this paper, we include a more general theorem, xxvi, that refers to an unmeasured variable, attachment to peers, and involves a process of attachment to peers that could include elements such as affective identification, communication, contact, influence, and so on.

## Relationships between the Attachment Subconstructs

In summary, we proposed to view the adolescent's attachment as being directed toward his parents, friends, or persons in positions of impersonal authority. However we have revised the former definition of the subconstruct " 'attachment to parents,' " to exclude the concept 'psychological presence of parents' which is now employed as a partial definition of the construct 'direct control.' In addition, we have eliminated the concept 'concern for persons in positions of impersonal authority' which was used in defining the belief construct. Instead we believe the concepts within this composite concept define the construct "attachment to persons in positions of impersonal authority" and we have suggested that two concepts, 'attachment to teachers' and 'respect for the police' should define it. Finally we consider the construct "attachment to peers" to be defined by the concept "identification with best friends." These modifications, resulting from the redefinition of the composite construct "attachment," provide a more precise explanation of the role of attachment within the theoretical statement.

As Hirschi (1969, 131) mentions, "Some control theorists have suggested that lack of respect for and attachment to parents tends to spread to adult authorities and conventional institutions in general." To translate this into the context of the school setting, weak attachment to parents may produce weak attachment to teachers. The relationship between the adolescent's affectional identification and his attitude toward the school setting, stated in theorem 17, indirectly express Hirschi's statement. However, the elimination of the composite concept 'attitude toward the school setting' requires us to redefine this relationship. The derivation of theorem 17 is based on proposition 9 that states: Among male adolescents, the greater the 'affectional identification at To', the greater the 'sentiments toward the controlling institution and attachment to a conventional figure at To'. In keeping with Hirschi's statement, the first modification of proposition 9 involves replacing 'attitude toward the school setting' with " 'attachment to persons in positions of impersonal authority' ". Therefore, proposition 9 is replaced by axiom xv which states: Among male adolescents, the greater the 'attachment to parents at To', the greater the 'attachment to persons in positions of impersonal authority at To'. Theorem xxx, which replaces theorem 17, is derived from that axiom as well as the subsidiary theorems xxviii and xxix that relate the adolescent's attachment to his parents' with his 'attachment to teachers'. In their data set Caplan (1978) and Chapman (1986) show that the adolescent attachment to his parents does, in fact, correlate to his attachment to his teachers. This is the carry-over effect of the attachment to parents to peers postulated by Hirschi (1969, p. 142). Theorem xxxi, derived from axiom xvi, expresses that relationship, as does theorem xxxii that relates the concepts 'affectional identification' and 'identification with best friends'. This type of carry-over is also expected for the adolescent attachment to teachers (theorem xxxiii).

## Incomplete Specification of the Relationships

The previous section discussed definitional problems relative to the mutual exclusivity of constructs, concepts and referentials. In this section, we will comment on three themes: the status of the construct "exposure to criminal influences" within the theory, the interrelations between the elements of the bond and the definition of what is the conventional society. These themes have in common a specific problem, incomplete specification.

*The Theory in its Most General Terms.*

The most synthetic formulation of social control theory states "that delinquent acts result when an individual's bond to society is weak or broken" (1969, 16). This statement tells us that there are two fundamental constructs from which the theory is formulated. In methodological terms these are called an independent variable, bond, and a dependent variable, delinquency. However, in his text (152–58), Hirschi elaborates and verifies a more comprehensive causal model. This causal model employs the construct 'exposure to criminal influences,' which is defined by the concept 'delinquent companions'. The model includes as well the composite construct "bond to conventional society" which is defined by the composite concept 'stakes in conformity'. After the test of different alternatives, the model retained by Hirschi explains delinquency using a triangular set of relationships: the quality of the adolescent's bond to conventional society directly influences his level of delinquency and his level of exposure to criminal influences, while the adolescent situation in regards to criminal influences directly affects his level of delinquency. In this model, bonds have three effects on delinquency: a direct effect, and an indirect effect through the adolescent exposure to criminal influences, and these variables also interact with each other in their effects on delinquency in Hirschi's data.

Most of the replications of social-control theory have addressed this question and the results are consistent. For example, Elliott et al. (1985, 133) conclude using the National Youth Survey data on successive years that "low conventional bonding in conjunction with high bonding to delinquent peers leads to a substantially higher frequency of delinquent behavior." However, even if they had the possibility, they did not check the causal order between these variables with their panel data; if low conventional bonding would precede bonding to delinquent peers and in turn this bonding would imply an increase in delinquency, then the control theory causal model would be more definitely confirmed. The empirical model confirmed by Hirschi, Elliott, et al., and others is perfectly compatible with bonding theory. It could have been declared a comprehensive formulation of control theory based on the data presented by Hirschi. However, the construct "exposure to criminal influences" did not attain a prominent status in his theory even if it was introduced early on in his empirical verification (1969, 98).

We can speculate that Hirschi did not revise his initial formulation of control theory because he refers only to one possible concept to specify the adolescent exposure to criminal influence. This concept is 'delinquent friends', which is rather weakly operationalized by the question "have any of your close friends ever been picked up by the police?" In the verification reviewed by Kempf (1989), or in integrative models such as Johnson (1979), Elliott et al. (1985) or others, researchers have relied on a similar measure. It is understandable in Hirschi's case because his major objective, as shown particularly by chapters 1 and 12 but also throughout his book, was to demonstrate that a bonding explanation of delinquency was more pertinent than a differential association or cultural deviance explanation. It was then logical to carry out his task while using only the concepts 'delinquent companions' when he could have referred to others means by which criminal influence can reach an adolescent. An adolescent can be exposed to criminal influences through his community (Krohn et al. 1984; Simca-Fagan and Schwartz 1986; Chapman 1986;), television and particularly violent television (see Thornton and Voigt 1984, demonstration), parental deviance and criminality (see West and Farrington 1977, results and Hirschi, 1985, discussion), routine activity (Felson 1986; Cohen and Land 1987; Gottfredson and Hirschi 1989;) among other possibilities.

In our modified formal statement of the theory, we propose a prominent status for the construct "exposure to criminal influences." However, we will not go beyond Hirschi's definition of the exposure to criminal influences; we will not elaborate his theory by referring to other means by which it can affect the adolescent. This is outside the scope of this paper. A way to recognize the status of that construct is reflected by the distinction between levels in the formalization of the theory. Each level regroups notions of an equivalent status. At the most general level, three constructs are involved: "bond to conventional society", "exposure to criminal influences", and "conformity to conventional standards of behavior". At the next level, the theory is formalized using the elements of the bond (attachment, commitment, involvement, and belief), at the next level the subconstructs are introduced (attachment to parents, to peers, and to persons in positions of impersonal authority), and at the last level the concepts are considered.

The replacement of the composite concept of 'stake in conformity' by the latent variable *BOND* has not affected the initial formalization of the theory. At the most general level, the theory involves three axioms (I, II and III that were 6, 4, and 3 before), the use of a new postulate and of a new transformational statement for the construct "bond to conventional society" and theorems 22, 23, and 24 become theorems I, II, and III. At the level of the constructs, the removal of the composite concept 'stake in conformity' requires the introduction of new theorems in order to express the original relationship stated in theorems 22 and 23. The new theorems state that an adolescent's attachment to persons (theorem VI and IV) and his commitment to institutions (theorem IX and VIII) affect the likelihood that he will be exposed to criminal influences, and in turn, his level of conformity to conventional standards of behavior. The exposure to criminal influences can also have an impact on the adolescent's beliefs (theorem XIII). These changes, we feel, are not incompatible with the theory even if they have direct consequences at the other levels of the formalization of the theory.

## *The Relationships between the Elements of the Bond*

It is evident that the elements of the bond not only affect the commission of delinquent acts but also that there are several relationships among the elements themselves. We find that the relationship among the elements, cited by Hirschi as important, are either not verified in the empirical presentation or are left unclear. Furthermore, and perhaps more important, Hirschi acknowledges that six possible combinations of elements exist. However he selects only three of these combinations as particularly important without stating why the remaining combinations are excluded from his presentation. The combinations discussed are attachment and commitment, commitment and involvement, and attachment and belief. In this section we would like to introduce new propositions relative to these combinations that will enable us to verify the relationship among the constructs, the subconstructs, and the concepts as redefined in the section of definitional problems of the original theory.

## Attachment and Commitment

If we accept the argument, as described above, that the concept 'stake in conformity' is improperly measured, then there are no referentials that establish the relationship between the adolescent's attachment and his commitment. As a result, Hirschi does not empirically verify his discursive statement that "attachment to conventional others and commitment to achievement tend to vary together" (Hirschi 1969, 28). Since we have redefined the construct of commitment as the adolescent's commitment to institutions, this construct focuses on one major institution within the adolescent's world, education within the school system. In order to define education as an institution we refer to the definitions of education and school found in Webster's dictionary: "the process of being educated" and "something that serves to instruct." These definitions imply that education and school are in themselves inanimate. Therefore, as any other major institution, it is given its meaning by the people that represent them. It is the persons in authority within an institution who allow us to express our sentiments toward such institutions.

Theorem VII is derived from axiom XII that we introduced because Hirschi states that "attachment to conventional others and commitment to achievement tend to vary together" (1969, 28). Axiom XII states: Among male adolescents, the greater the "attachment to persons at To," the greater the "commitment to institutions at To." This axiom opens many avenues for theoretical elaboration because there are many kinds of conventional others. Hirschi (1969, 85) uses one when he states: "Teachers, by inclination and law espouse conventional standards." Therefore, if the adolescent expresses an attachment to his teacher (a conventional figure in a position of impersonal authority) he should, to some degree, internalize the conventional standards espoused by the teacher, the desire to get an education. Theorems LIX and LX express the relationship between the subconstructs " 'attachment to a conventional figure (teacher)' " and " 'commitment to education' " and with the concept 'achievement orientation.' They propose a positive relationship between the constituent variables and they are valid in Caplan's data (1978). Other avenues of elaboration would be to propose relationships between the adolescent's attachment to his parents and his commitment to education, and between his commitment to education and his attachment to peers. There is also the possibility to use other subconstructs of the construct "commitment to institutions" such as commitment to religion, to work, and so on, and to relate them to the subconstructs of the construct "attachment to persons."

*Attachment and Belief*

Hirschi establishes a general relationship between attachment and belief that allows the theory to go beyond a statement concerning the relationship between the adolescent's belief in the moral validity of rules and the conformity to conventional standards of behavior. More specifically, Hirschi (1969, 127) states, "If a person feels no emotional attachment to a person or institution, the rules of that person or institution tend to be denied legitimacy. Just as the child who does not like his parents is likely to consider their rules 'unfair' so the child who does not like school or does not care 'what teachers think' is likely to believe that the school has no right to control him." This general statement allows us to examine beliefs within an additional sphere of the adolescent's world. We are able to establish a relationship between the adolescent's attachment to persons and his belief in the normative system with the introduction of axiom IX: Among male adolescents, the greater the 'attachment to persons at To,' the greater the 'belief at To.' Theorem V is derived from that axiom and some subsidiary theorems can be presented concerning the empirical relationship between the attachment to parents and the acceptance of the normative system (theorems LXVI and LXVII). These subsidiary theorems are empirically valid (Caplan 1978).

With the introduction of this new construct composed of two concepts, we are also required to revise our original theorem relating concern for persons in positions of impersonal authority and acceptance of the normative system (theorem 30). As we mentioned above, the 'concern for persons in positions of impersonal authority' is defined by two concepts, 'attachment to teachers' and 'respect for the police.' Consequently, proposition XXIII allows us to define a more theoretically meaningful relationship between respect for the police and acceptance of the normative system by eliminating the effects of attachment to teachers (theorem LXVIII is derived from that proposition and is empirically valid in Hirschi's and Caplan's data). That is, proposition XXIII states: Among male adolescents, the greater the 'respect for the police at To,' the greater the 'acceptance of the normative system at To.'

*Commitment and Involvement*

Hirschi also suggests that there is a link between educational and occupational aspirations (commitment) and involvement in conventional activities (Hirschi 1969, 29). In the empirical verification of his theory, Hirschi draws a relationship between 'educational expectation' and 'expression of claims to adult status' (theorem 25). Hirschi measures involvement via two leisure activities clustering around involvement in school related activities and working-class adult activities. Hirschi states that boys taking part in the latter type of activity are more likely to commit delinquent acts. This implies that working-class adult activities are not conventional in nature. Since the concepts 'expression of claims to adult status' and 'working-class adult activities' are measured by the same referential IOIIAA (index of involvement in adult activities), we refer to both of these concepts as involvement in adult activities. As stated above, this type of involvement is not conventional in nature. Therefore, theorem 25 does not verify that there is a link between educational and occupational aspirations and involvement.

In redefining the construct of commitment as the desire to

achieve conventional goals we were required to redefine the construct of involvement as the expediture of energy in the pursuit of conventional goals via conventional activities. As a consequence, we propose theorem X, which states the relationship between the constructs "commitment to institutions" and "involvement in conventional activities," that can be formulated on the basis of Hirschi's discussion on pages 28 and 29. With this theorem in mind, we can also verify the relationship between commitment to education and involvement through the relationships between achievement orientation and involvement in adult activities (theorem LXV) and involvement in school related activities (theorem LVIII and LXI) by employing axiom VIII: Among male adolescents, the greater the " 'commitment to education at To' ", the less the 'involvement in conventional activities at To.' These two theorems are valid in Caplan's (1978) replication.

## The Definition of the Conventional Society

In his discursive statement of the theory, Hirschi does not define "conventional society" other than to say that it is eclectic or composed of several institutions. However, in the empirical verifications of the theory three units, or institutions comprising the bond, are emphasized: family, school, and peers. Hirschi does not state whether he considers this empirical definition complete; nor does he rank importance of each institution in the construction of his theory. However, he does discuss the partial relationship between school and family (theorem 11), and family and school (theorem 17). In addition, if we return to our comments on the measurements of the concept 'stake in conformity', we can say that Hirschi inadvertently defines the partial relationship between family, school and peers via theorem 22. Based on the definitional problems outlined earlier, we can conclude that these institutions are socializing the adolescent in the various ways. Discussing bonding in relation to the institutions of conventional society, as did Hirschi, opens the way for the development of middle range social control theories as defined by Merton (1957). Hirschi made some opening statements concerning each institution but much elaboration needs to be done for the family, the school, and the peers.

The family imposes social control through three processes. The process of attachment to parents represented by theorems XIV to XIX, the interaction between the adolescent attachment to his parents and the level of direct control employed by them represented by theorems LIV to LVII, and the interaction between the attachment to parents and the belief in the legitimacy of their rules represented by theorems LXIX. This family model of social control derived from Hirschi's book is rather complex because two elements of the bond, attachment and belief, are mixed with direct control and beliefs within their relationships with exposure to criminal influences and delinquency. However, involvement in the family life is left aside as well as many other important elements such as sanctions, marital relations, parental deviance and criminality, and so on, as implied by Hirschi in a more recent text (1985) or shown by the model tested by Le Blanc (Ouimet 1988a, 1992).

Another institution that defines the conventional society is the peer group. Hirschi discusses only the question of the adolescent attachment to his peers, he never elaborates his theory to include statements concerning the involvement with peers, the commitment to the peer group, or the belief in the value of peer relationships. His theory is very insufficient concerning this institution and it has to be updated to integrate a larger vision of the nature of peer relationships, such as proposed by Giordano et al. (1986).

As established earlier, the process by which an adolescent becomes committed to education involves the development of four favorable attitudes toward school: self-perceived academic competence, achievement orientation, acceptance of school, and educational expectation. The level of commitment depends on the interactions between these attitudes but it is also influenced by two variables: the academic competence, and the actual performance. The school in Hirschi's discursive and empirical statements is a source of social control not only through the development of the commitment, but also because of the interactions between the elements of the bond: attachment to a conventional figure (teacher), commitment to education, belief in the legitimacy of school rules, and involvement in school related activities. He states this process in the following way: "a causal chain runs from academic incompetence to poor school performance to disliking school to rejection of the school's authority to the commission of delinquent acts" (Hirschi 1969, 132). Theorems XXI, XXIV, XXXIV to XLIII and LVIII to LXIV formulate the school control model. Here again, other variables could be active in the mechanism of social control operated by the school, for example, the diverse forms of direct control such as sanctions. Once again the model proposed by Hirschi is insufficiently developed. Even the driving role of academic competence and performance, supported by Caplan's data (1978), is contested by the results of Farnworth et al. (1985). It can be elaborated (see Le Blanc et al. 1992a, b).

## A Modified Discursive Statement of the Theory

Once the rhetoric of discursive theory has been removed not only are the definitional problems clarified, but also the avenues for elaboration are more easily identifiable. The result of that critique of the theory is a modified formal statement proposed in appendixes 9.3 (extrinsic part) and 9.4 (intrinsic part). We are then left with the final task: the formulation of a modified discursive statement of social control theory.

Social control theory assumes that an individual's *conformity* to conventional standards of behavior is obtained when his *bond* to society is solid and when he is not exposed to strong *criminal influences*. Alternatively, delinquency results when social bonds are weak or broken and sufficient criminal influences are present. The theory has two components. The first is a classification and description of the elements of the bond to conventional society. The second proposes relationships between the elements of the bond and between these elements and the other two main constructs: exposure to criminal influences and conformity to conventional standard of behavior. *Delinquency* is defined by acts, the detection of which are thought to result in sanctions by agents of the larger society.

An individual's *bond* to society is manifested towards several institutions constituting the different spheres of the adolescent's world. Three institutions are emphasized for the age group considered family, school, and peers. The adolescent is related to these institutions via four avenues: attachment to persons, commitment to institutions, involvement in conventional activities, and belief in conventional standard of behavior. A central assumption of control theories is that companionship with delinquents is an incidental byproduct of the quality of the bond to society. This assertion suggests that the relationship between delinquent companions and delinquency is spurious. However, after testing this hypothesis with his data, as confirmed by numerous studies, Hirschi revises his bonding model to state that delinquent companions have a direct or causal impact on the commission of delinquent acts. Furthermore, in the new model, a weak or broken bond to society leads to the acquisition of delinquent friends as well as having a direct effect on the level of delinquency. The delinquent friends represents, in part, the adolescent's *exposure to criminal influences*. An adolescent, however, can be exposed to criminal influences through the nature of his community, television, parental deviance and criminality, routine activity, and so on.

## The Elements of the Bond

The most important element of the bond to conventional society is the individual's *attachment to persons*. The importance of this element lies in the number of persons in society that can lead to an individual's attachment. There are three categories of such figures: parents, peers, and persons in positions of impersonal authority. Attachment to persons is situated within the framework of the social norm that states what ought to be. It is assumed that if a person is sensitive to the opinions of others, then he is to that extent bound by the norms. Consequently, the internalization of norms depends on the individual's attachment to persons. Attachment to conventional persons acts as a major deterrent to the commission of delinquent acts in that the stronger this tie, the more likely it will be considered by the adolescent when and if he considers committing a delinquent act. This attachment to persons also counters the impact of criminal influences: a weak or broken attachment to persons increases the susceptibility to criminal influences. The theory defines the process through which attachment to persons works against the commission of delinquent acts and the criminal influences. That is, the adolescent's level of attachment to parents determines his level of attachment to peers and to persons in positions of impersonal authority. The cumulative impact of these attachments protects the adolescent against criminal influences and discourages delinquency. However, these subtypes of attachment are constructed in the following way.

The adolescent's *attachment to parents* is defined by several concepts. The first concept in the process, through which attachment to parents presumably works against the commission of delinquent acts, is the 'share communication.' By not discussing his activities with his parents the adolescent is not sharing his inner world with them. Consequently, since the adolescent does not see his parents as part of his private world, he does not have to concern himself with their reaction to his behavior. In a similar vein, the parents who do not communicate their feelings about their child's behavior remove an important source of potential concern for the adolescent; that is, the parents do not try to enter their child's private world. In sum, the adolescent not only considers his parents as part of his private world but also his parents try to enter his private world. However, in order to verify the effect of 'share communication,' the adolescent's perception of parental attitude must be considered, the second concept involved in the process of attachment to parents. The adolescent will feel loved and accepted by his parents only if there is an effective mutual participation. Furthermore, the more the adolescent feels loved and accepted by his parents, the more he cares about his parents expectations and opinions, the third concept defining the attachment to parents. More specifically, the concept 'adolescent's perception of parental attitude' intervenes between the concept of 'share communication' and 'affectional identification.' The introduction of 'share communication,' assumes that the adolescent considers the expectations and opinions of his parents, that is, he considers the consequences of his act for his parents. More specifically, does the adolescent care what his parents will think?

The adolescent's *attachment to persons in positions of impersonal authority* is described through two concepts. The attachment to a conventional figure, such as the teacher, blocks the criminal influences and fosters conformity to conventional standards of behavior. The respect for persons in positions of formal authority, such as policemen has the same double effect. Finally, the adolescent *attachment to peers,* as expressed by the level of identification with best friend, is also a protection against delinquency.

The second major element of the bond is *commitment to institutions.* The adolescent commitment to institutions could develop towards school, religion, work, or success, and so on, but because of the nature of adolescence it is postulated that the most important institution that is involved in the development of the adolescent's commitment is school. Commitment refers to an attitude of acceptance of an institution, an affective investment in education, religion, and so on. Conversely, deviant behavior is considered a cost. Therefore, when an adolescent is faced with the temptation to commit a delinquent act, he must evaluate the costs of his delinquent behavior in relation to the investment he has made. The assumption underlying the idea of commitment to institutions is that the attitudinal investment of most adolescents would be seriously affected if they were to commit delinquent acts. Commitment is viewed as a constraint on delinquency and a protection against criminal influences since they would jeopardize the adolescent's possibility of realizing the fruits of his investment. That is, it suggests that the adolescent is committed to conformity not only by his present investments but also by what he hopes to achieve.

The adolescent *commitment to education* is viewed as the major process of commitment that works against the commission of delinquent acts and as a protection against criminal influences. This process is described using four endogenous concepts: self-perceived academic competence, attitude towards school, achievement orientation, and educational expectation, and two exogenous concepts: academic competence and academic performance. The starting point in this process is academic competence, that is, the adolescent's potential achievement in the school setting. The higher the boy's academic competence the lower the probability that he will commit delinquent acts. In order to relate academic competence to delinquency, the introduction of two additional concepts are required: academic performance, and self-perceived academic competence. More specifically, the boy who is academically competent has a greater chance of doing well in school. In turn, the more competent a boy thinks he is, the less likely he is to commit delinquent acts. The source of this self-perceived academic competence is not only the adolescent's potential but also the gap between his academic performance and his educational expectation. High expectations and weak performance will result in a poor self-perception of competence; this will lead to an unfavorable attitude toward school. The introduction of this concept, sentiment toward the controlling institution, is also necessary as the link between performance and achievement orientation on the one hand and delinquency and criminal influences on the other. The boy who does poorly in school diminishes his interest in school and, in turn, his achievement orientation; consequently he is free to receive criminal influence and to commit delinquent acts. In sum, the impact of the two exogenous and four endogenous variables is indirect on the susceptibility to criminal influences and delinquency; and it is mediated by the adolescent's level of achievement orientation.

*Involvement in conventional activities* is the third major element of the bond of the individual to society. The involvement hypothesis states that the greater the involvement of the adolescent in conventional activities, the less time he has to engage in deviant acts and the less chance there is that he could be exposed to criminal influences. When defining delinquency by acts, the emphasis should be placed on the nature of the conventional activity as opposed to the quantity of conventional activities. With this position, four types of activities are presumably important. These activities center around the family, the peers, the school, and work. The school dimension is defined as involvement in school-related activities such as time spent on homework. The work dimension is defined by involvement in work while studying. These two types of activities are important since school-related activities inhibit delinquent activities, whereas participation in work is positively related to the commission of delinquent acts. The other two types of involvements, activities with parents and peers, are viewed as a protection against the commission of delinquent acts.

The final component of the bond is the adolescent's *belief in conventional standards of behavior*, that is, the extent to which he believes he should obey the rules of society. The adolescent's belief acts as a moral obstacle to the commission of delinquent acts. The less an adolescent believes he should obey the rules of society, the greater the probability that he will commit delinquent acts. However, there is variation in the adolescent's attitude of respect toward the rules of society; many persons feel no moral obligation to conform. Four types of belief are potentially important: acceptance of the normative system, use of neutralization techniques, legitimacy of rules imposed by parents and of controlling institution.

## The Relations among the Elements of the Bond

Besides defining the four major elements of the bond, the theory describes the relations among these elements. The components of the bond are not unrelated; consequently, the theory establishes the relative importance of three sets of relations: attachment and commitment, commitment and involvement, and attachment and belief. It is assumed that attachment to persons and commitment to institutions tend to vary together. The adolescent who is attached to conventional persons is more likely to be committed to education. As a consequence, not only does attachment to persons directly affect the commission of delinquent acts, but also indirectly through commitment and exposure to criminal influences. These statements mean that the tighter the attachment to persons, the stronger the commitment to education and the lower the susceptibility to criminal influences; but also, the tighter the attachment to persons and the stronger the commitment to education, the less probable is the commission of delinquent acts.

There is also a relation between commitment to institutions and involvement in conventional activities, to clarify the meaning of Hirschi's statement "a boy is free of bonds to conventional society." The fact that control theory relies on conditions that make delinquency possible rather than necessary suggests that there is a certain amount of indeterminacy within the theory. It can be argued that rather than assume that opportunities to commit delinquent acts are randomly distributed through the adolescent population, an assumption that stresses indeterminacy, an attempt can be made to demonstrate how commitment limits one's opportunities by examining the relationship between commitment and involvement. That is, the more one is commited to education, the more one will be involved in conventional activities, which in turn will limit one's opportunities to commit delinquent acts.

There is a very subtle relation between beliefs and delinquency: the absence of effective beliefs is the result of weak attachment to conventional others. In other words, attachment to persons and belief in the moral validity of its rules are not entirely independent. The chain of causation is from attachment to parents, through concern for the approval of persons in positions of authority, to belief that the rules of society are binding on one's conduct. The situation is even more complex if the exposure to criminal influences is considered. Above we have stated that the stronger the attachment to persons, the less the susceptibility to criminal influences. But it can also be expected that an adolescent who is the subject of criminal influences will alter his beliefs in the norms of conventional society. He should be subject to a more frequent use of techniques of neutralization for example. Based on these relationships, another causal chain can be proposed: the weaker the attachment to persons and the greater the exposure to criminal influences, the less the belief in the normative system and, consequently, the greater the commission of delinquent acts.

As Hirschi has stated, if the adolescent does not see his parents as part of his private world, he does not have to concern himself with their imagined reaction to his behavior. The adolescent who does not care about the reaction of his parents will tend not to be concerned with the approval of persons in positions of impersonal authority. As a result, the adolescent will be free to reject their normative pattern. When the adolescent is not attached to his parent or persons in positions of impersonal authority, he believes that the only reason to obey rules is to avoid punishment. Since there is variation in the extent to which boys believe they should obey the law, respect for the law is strongly associated with delinquency when respect for persons in position of impersonal authority and attachment to parents are controlled. That is, although beliefs may demonstrate a weak bond to society, the acceptance of the moral validity of society's rules is independently related to delinquency.

## Middle Range Control Theories

The definition of conventional society identifies three institutions towards which the bond can be constructed by the adolescent: family, peers, and school. As implied by our discussion of Hirschi's theory, his discursive statement can be read in two dimensions. Up until now, we have read the theory from a horizontal point of view giving priority to the relationships between the elements of the bond independently of the three institutions. In the next paragraphs, however, we will read it vertically considering the relationships between the elements of the bond but only relative to a specific institution of conventional society. This point of view is referred to as a middle range theory as compared to the global theory of bonding stated above.

## Family Control Model

The impact of the family control model on delinquency depends on the adolescent's attachment to parents, his involvement in conventional activities with them, his belief in the legitimacy of their rules and on the level of direct control they exercise. Since we have defined previously how each of the four elements is related to delinquency and exposure to criminal influences, we will limit our discuss in this section to the relationships between them.

The new concept introduced by this list of components of the family is the direct control or the psychological presence of parents. It is present in Hirschi's discursive statement, but as part of the process of attachment to parents. We have argued above that it should be considered a construct independent of the four elements of the bond. When the adolescent is faced with a situation to commit a delinquent act his parents will be psychologically present; he will give thought to his parents' reaction. The direct control is indirectly referred to because it is assumed that the adolescent who thinks his parents know where he is and what he is doing is the one most likely to consider his parents' reaction. As a result, the adolescent who perceives his parents as unaware of this whereabouts is, to that extent, free to commit a delinquent act when a situation of potential delinquency arises. The psychological presence of parents is a form of indirect supervision in the sense that parents do not actually restrict the adolescent's activities, nor do the parents necessarily know where the adolescent is; nonetheless, the adolescent is being supervised inasmuch as he perceives that his parents are aware of this location.

In essence, the process through which family control presumably works against the commission of delinquent acts can be summarized as the adolescent communicating, caring, and thinking about his parents. That is, for the parents to play an effective role as a controlling agency, the adolescent and parent must first interact with each other on a personal basis. This is what we have called share communication. In the process of interaction, the adolescent becomes aware of his parents' opinions and expectations concerning his behavior. He is cognizant of the consequences of his potential delinquent behavior for his relations with his parents. Secondly, in considering the consequences, the adolescent concludes that he cares what his parents will think. In the process of interacting with his parents, the adolescent has developed an affectional identification with them; the parental opinions and expectations have had an impact on him. Thirdly, faced with the actual temptation to commit an act, the adolescent perceives his parents to be psychologically present. The psychological presence of parents causes the adolescent to give thought to parental opinions and expectations that he considers sufficiently important to deter him from the act. The share communication informs the adolescent of the parental opinions and expectations. The impact of the parental expectations and opinions instills within the adolescent their importance. Fourthly, if the adolescent communicates, cares and thinks about his parents, the legitimacy of their rules will not be contested. This will reinforce the conformity to conventional standards of behavior. Finally, the psychological presence of parents recall the parental expectations and opinions that have been deemed important. In conclusion, the unattached adolescent is more apt to commit delinquent acts because he does not have to consider the impact of his actions on his relations with his parents and because he does not believe in the legitimacy of their rules.

*School Control Model*

Hirschi states that besides the commitment to education, the feelings toward persons in authority is important. The boy who is not concerned about what teachers think of him should be most likely to be delinquent. The boy who values the opinion of teachers is less likely to become delinquent regardless of how he perceives teachers treating him. The boy who is not commited to education is also less likely to be involved in school-related activities. Thus, the bond to school consists of the boy's commitment to education as well as his attachment to his teacher and his involvement in school-related activities. This positive bond to school is the first line of social control within the school setting. A weakening of the bond to school neutralizes its moral force as it has been stated earlier. In control theory, such neutralization is a major link between lack of attachment and delinquency. Consequently, the student's feelings about the scope of the school's legitimate authority become the final concept in the process.

However, this bond to school is not without support from academic competence and academic performance. Academic incompetence thus keeps a link with delinquency by way of the lack of success in and commitment to education. Academic incompetence thus encourages poor school performance. A dislike of school is then developed, and the rejection of school authority that follows, a situation that favors delinquency. This summarizes the process of how school control works against the commission of delinquent acts. However, rejection of the school's authority as well as the absence of commitment to education are also conductive of a greater exposure to criminal influences which in turn favors the commission of delinquent acts.

## An Agenda for Theoretical Elaboration

In Gibbs' model of theory construction, the purpose of articulating a formal theory is to interpret, test, and assess the statements representing the theory as a means to advance it. We have fulfilled the task of interpreting Hirschi's theory with our modified formal and discursive statement of bonding theory. The modified version of this theory is also empirically valid since all its theorems are supported in Caplan's test (1978) and/or by Hirschi's data or other researchers data (Kempf 1989). The theorems must be replicated with different age groups, for females and minorities, in other cultures and over time. If the tasks of interpretation and testing have begun, there is still a third task, assessment. The appraisal of a theory can only be done in relation to the overall corpus of theoretical knowledge in a discipline. During our discussion of Hirschi's constructs, we have proposed some possibilities in that direction.

The construct 'exposure to criminal influences' has not only been promoted to a more prominent role within the theory, we have also stressed that there are other sources of criminal influences than the delinquent peers. The theory indicates some types of involvements and commitments that are considered important. However, there are numerous other institutions or types of activities that could strengthen the bond to conventional society that are not mentioned by Hirschi. We have also proposed to limit the adolescent's attachment to persons to parents, peers, and persons in positions of impersonal authority. There could also be other adult figures to represent such persons. Finally, although Hirschi defines belief as an attitude of respect toward the rules of society, it appears that belief is not an independent element of the bond. However, other authors have shown that beliefs beyond the respect for the rules of society, referred to as moral values, may play a role in the explanation of delinquency (Szabo et al. 1972).

We have previously affirmed that there are two major gaps in the formulation of bonding theory, constraint and personality (Le Blanc 1983). Earlier, we argued that Hirschi departs from previous social control theorists by explicitly stressing only one element of control: internal control. The control theories of Reiss (1951), Nye (1958) and Reckless (1967), have emphasized both internal and external social control. In other words, for a theory to be classified within the control perspective, it must emphasize the socialization process or the internalization of norms (internal control) as well as the role of sanctions (external control) in developing the adolescent's behavior effectively in the direction of conformity. Our position is that a control theory cannot be considered comprehensive if it does not explicitly integrate these two sorts of controls. Hirschi's explanation of delinquency should be enlarged to include a formal statement about the elements and the operation of direct control. The elements of the bond explain *what* an adolescents accepts or submits to. Social rewards and punishments explain *how* adolescent behavior is controlled or developed in the direction of acceptance or submission. It is this process of control that must be elaborated to complete the theory. We proposed to call constraints the construct that incorporates internal and external controls.

Control theorists are not closed to the question of individual differences and the consideration of this dimension does not contradict bonding theory as affirmed by Kornhauser (1978). Freud is a control theorist according to Empey (1977) and Durkheim (1924) refers to individual differences in his book titled *De l'éducation morale*. Reckless (1967) was the first to introduce the psychological construct, 'self-concept'. After the publication of Hirschi's book, some integrative models used some psychological variables (Aultman 1979; Le Blanc 1983; Kaplan et al. 1984; Le Blanc et al. 1988). And, in a recent publication, Gottfredson and Hirschi (1990) introduce low self-control. They refer to traits such as aggressiveness, impulsivity, self-centeredness, and intelligence, that are rooted in the individual activity level. Fréchette and Le Blanc (1987) propose to call the construct referring to individual differences 'egocentrism.' This construct is built on six dimensions and thirteen psychological traits that are relevant to crime, traits that are strongly correlated with each other and that distinguish conventional adolescents from delinquents. The developmental task of the individual being to move out of egocentrism to allocentrism, it is expected that the psychological development of the delinquent along that continuum will lag. As shown by the verification of our elaborated model (Le Blanc et al. 1988), the individual level of allocentrism reinforces the bond to conventional society and the receptivity to social constraints.

A formal theory has a unit term. In the case of Hirschi's theory, it is defined as male adolescents. His bonding theory is then only appliable to that group. Before it can be adapted for females, minority groups, and so on, questions have to be resolved. Are there constructs or concepts that have to be included or put aside in new social groups or contexts? Are there referentials to be modified when the unit term is changed?

In this paper, we have tried to demonstrate that formalization is the most rigorous instrument for the analysis and the criticism of a theory. We have completed that laborious task in order to demonstrate that discursive statements are useful but that they do not encourage exact replications which is a fundamental condition of science. Conversely, formal statements not only guarantee the internal coherence and a common understanding of the content of the theory, but also renders exact replications much simpler. In that context, the researcher who wants to start an empirical test of a theory has to choose between two alternatives. Be creative and modify constructs, concepts, and referentials or be rigourous and formalize the theory before beginning its test.

With the first choice, the researcher will introduce more confusion as shown. With the second choice, there is more chance that the researcher will build knowledge progressively on common ground.

We believe that neither choice alone is fruitful for the development of a discipline. Rigor and imagination are necessary for theoretical progression. We think that there are times to be inventive and times to be systematic. Bonding theory was the product of an original blending of theoretical imagination and empirical facts. The numerous empirical verifications and the various integrative models that followed the statement of the theory by Hirschi have proven that the theory is very well grounded in the reality of delinquency. We believe that it is now time for rigor. It is time for an optimal development of control theory, it is time for formalization, elaboration and exact replications in diverse social settings and for different classes of peoples.

### Appendix 9.1 - Initial Formal Version of Hirschi's Theory, Extrinsic Part.

**Unit term:** Male adolescents attending junior and senior public high schools.

**Substantive terms:** (*composite construct, concept, or referential)

**constructs:** Eight of the terms in the intrinsic statements are constructs, each of which is defined below. (1) Attachment to parents: The adolescent's sensitivity to his parent's opinion, that is, caring about their wishes and expectations. (2) Attachment to school: The adolescent's concern about the wishes and expectations of the school setting and its agents. (3) Exposure to criminal influences: The adolescent's association with criminals. (4) Commitment to education: The adolescent's pursuit and desire to further his education. (5) Bond to conventional society*: The adolescent's sensitivity to the opinion of others as well as his pursuit and desire to achieve conventional goals. (6) Involvement: The adolescent's expenditure of time in conventional activities. (7) Belief: The adolescent's attitude of respect toward the rules of society as well as their enforcers, a moral obligation to conform. (8) Conformity to conventional standards of behavior: Adolescent behavior which is acceptable to the agents of the larger society.

It should be noted that all the temporal quantifiers To, are designating one point in time. The same temporal quantifiers apply to all substantive terms (constructs or otherwise).

**concepts:** Nineteen concepts enter into the intrinsic statements

*Attachment to parents* (1) Psychological presence of parents: The adolescent's perception that his parents are aware of his activities at any given moment. (2) Share communication: The adolescent's willingness to share his mental life with his parents, seeking or getting their opinion about his activities, as well as the parent's willingness to explain situation and personal feelings to their child, telling him how they feel about his behavior. (3) Affectional identification: Consideration of parents in a situation of temptation, caring what parents will think, the adolescent's attitude toward his parents.

*Attachment to school* (1) Academic performance: The adolescent's success in school course work. (2) Self-perceived academic competence: The degree to which the adolescent believes he possesses the necessary skills to make school a place of potential achievement and satisfaction. (3) Sentiments toward the controlling institution: The adolescent's attitude toward school. (4) Attachment to a conventional figure: The adolescent's concern for the opinion of persons in authority within the school setting. (5) Legitimacy of the controlling institution's rules: The adolescent's willingness to accept the school's role in establishing rules to control the student body.

*Exposure to criminal influences.* Delinquent companions: The adolescent's association with peers who have had contact with the agents of the larger society.

*Commitment to education.* (1) Educational expectations: The level the adolescent expects to achieve. (2) Achievement orientation: The adolescent's concern about grades, about effort expended in school, as well as in general undertaking.

*Bond to conventional society.* Stake in conformity*: The adolescent's attachment to school and family as well as his general desire to achieve conventional goals.

*Involvement.* Involvement in adult activities: The adolescent's adoption of adult attitudes and behaviors. (2) Involvement in school-related activities: The adolescent's expenditure of time in activities emanating from the school setting.

*Belief.* (1) Concern for the approval of persons in positions of impersonal authority: The adolescent's attitude of respect toward persons representing authority outside the family unit. (2) Acceptance of the normative system: The adolescent's perception of the rules of society, the adolescent's attitude toward the law.

*Conformity to conventional standards of behavior.* Commission of delinquent acts: The adolescent performing certain acts, the detection of which is thought to result in his punishment by agents of the larger society.

*Construct undefined.* Academic competence: The adolescent's possession of the necessary skills to make school a place of potential achievement and satisfaction.

**referentials**: The vast majority of the twenty-one referentials are derived from the items of a self-report questionnaire. Two of the referentials are based on school records.

*Psychological presence of parents*: *MVS*: (1) "Does your mother (father) know where you are when you are when you are away from home?" and (2) "Does your mother (father) know whom you are with when you are away from home? "The response categories are: "Usually," "Sometimes," and "never." The two items are combined, equally weighted, so that the parents of boys obtaining a score of 4 "usually know where they are and whom they are with."

*Share communication*: (1) *IOCPTC*: "When you don't know why your mother (father) makes a rule, will she (he) explain the reason?" "When you come across things you don't understand, does your mother (father) help you with them?" and, "Does you mother (father) ever explain why she (he) feels the way she (he) does?"

(2) *IOCCTP*: "When you don't know why your parents make a rule, do they explain the reason?" and "How often have you talked over your future plans with your mother (father)?" The items are combined equally weighted, such that boys with the highest scores often share their thoughts and talk over their plan with their parents, while the boys with the lowest scores never have such communication.

*Affectional identification AIWP*: "Would you like to be the kind of person your mother (father) is?"

*Share communication and impact of parental expectations and opinions IOCAI*\* is created by combining IOCCTP and AIWP.

*Academic competence*: *DAT*: The verbal score of the differential aptitude test.

*Academic performance*: *GPA*: is the English and mathematics grades as recorded on the school file.

*Self-perceived academic competence*: *SPAC*: "How do you rate yourself in school ability compared with other students in your school?"

*Sentiments toward the controlling institution*: *ATS*: "In general, do you like or dislike school?"

*Attachment to a conventional figure*: *FOT*: "Do you care that teachers think of you?"

*Sentiments toward the controlling institution and attachment to a conventional figure*: *ATSS*\*: "Do you like school?" and "Do you care what teachers think of you?"

*Legitimacy of the controlling institution's rules*: *NOSB*: "It is none of the school's business if a student wants to smoke outside of the classroom?"

*Delinquent companions*: *NDF*: "Have any of your close friends ever been picked up by the police?"

*Educational expectations*: *EE*: "How much schooling do you actually expect to get?"

*Achievement orientation*: *IOAO*: (1) "I try hard in school." (2) "How important is getting good grades to you personally?" and (3) "Whatever I do, I try hard."

*Stake in conformity*: *SIC\** is constructed by dichotomizing three items: "Do you like school?" (ATS), index of achievement orientation (IOAO) and intimacy of communication with parent (IOCCTP). The items are weighted in the order listed.

*Involvement in adult activities IOIIAA*: "Do you smoke cigarettes? "Do you drink beer, wine or liquor away from home?" and "Do you date?" If the student smokes or drinks, he is given a score of 2 on the index. If he dates, he is given a score of 1. The scores on the index may thus be interpreted as follows: 0 = Does not smoke, drink, or date; 1 = Dates but does not smoke or drink; 2 = Smokes or drinks, but does not date; 3 = Smokes or drinks, and dates; 4 = Smokes and drinks, but does not date; 5 = Smokes, drinks, and dates.

*Involvement in school related activities TDTH*: "On the average, how much time do you spend doing homework outside school?"

*Concern for the approval of persons in positions of impersonal authority*: *COTRP\**: (1) "Do you care what teachers think of you?" and (2) "I have a lot of respect for the police."

*Acceptance of the normative system*: *RFTL*: "It is alright to get around the law if you can get away with it."

*Commission of delinquent acts IOD*: 1. Have you ever taken little things (worth less than $2.00) that did not belong to you? 2. Have you ever taken things of some value (between $2.00 and $50.00) that did not belong to you? 3. Have you ever taken things of large value (worth over $50.00) that did not belong to you? 4. Have you ever taken a car for a ride without the owner's permission? 5. Have you ever banged up something that did not belong to you on purpose? 6. Not counting fights you may have had with a brother or sister, have you ever beaten up anyone or hurt anyone on purpose? The index (a recency index) is based on the number of acts committed during the year prior to the administraiton of the questionnaire.

## Appendix 9.2—Initial formalization of Hirschi's theory, intrinsic part

Ama: must be read among male adolescents.

Because of space limitation, the term *at To* is not attached to each construct, concept and referential.

**Axiom 1:** Ama, the greater the "attachment to parents", the greater the "conformity to conventional standards of behavior".

**A 2:** Ama, the greater the "attachment to school", the greater the "conformity to conventional standards of behavior".

**A 3:** Ama, the greater the "exposure to criminal influence", the less "conformity to conventional standards of behavior".

**A 4:** Ama, the greater the "bond to conventional society", the less the "exposure to criminal influences".

**A 5:** Ama, the greater the "commitment to education", the greater the "conformity to conventional standards of behavior".

**A 6:** Ama, the greater the "bond to conventional society", the greater the "conformity to conventional standards of behavior."

**A 7:** Ama, the greater the "commitment to education", the greater the "involvement".

**A 8:** Ama, the greater the "involvement", the greater the "conformity to conventional standards of behavior".

**A 9:** Ama, the greater the "attachment to parents", the greater the "belief".

**A 10:** Ama, the greater "the belief", the greater the "conformity to conventional standards of behavior".

**Postulate 1:** Ama, the greater the "attachment to parents", the greater the 'psychological presence of the parents'.

**P 2:** Ama, the greater the "attachment to parents", the greater the 'mutual participation in the adolescent's social and psychological fields'.

**P 3:** Ama, the greater the "attachment to parents", the greater the 'affectional identification'.

**P 4:** Ama, the greater the "attachment to parents", the greater the 'share communication and 'affectional identification'.

**P 5:** Ama, the greater the "attachment to school", the greater the 'academic performance'.

**P 6:** Ama, the greater the ''attachment to school'', the greater the 'self-perceived academic competence'.

**P 7:** Ama, the greater the ''attachment to school'', the greater the 'sentiments toward the controlling institution'.

**P 8:** Ama, the greater the ''attachment to school'', the greater the 'attachment to a conventional figure'.

**P 9:** Ama, the greater the ''attachment to school'', the greater the 'sentiments toward controlling institution and attachment to a conventional figure'.

**P 10:** Ama, the greater the ''attachment to school'', the greater the 'legitimacy of the controlling institution's rules'.

**P 11:** Ama, the greater the ''exposure to criminal influences'', the greater the 'delinquent companions'.

**P 12:** Ama, the greater the ''commitment to educationat to'', the greater the 'educational expectations'.

**P 13:** Ama, the greater the ''commitment to education'', the greater the 'achievement orientation'.

**P 14:** Ama, the greater the ''bond to conventional society'', the greater the 'stake in conformity'.

**P 15:** Ama, the greater the ''involvement'', the less the 'involvement in adult activities'.

**P 16:** Ama, the greater the ''involvement'', the greater the 'involvement in school related activities'.

**P 17:** Ama, the greater the ''belief'', the greater the 'concern for the approval of persons in positions of impersonal authority'.

**P 18:** Ama, the greater the ''belief'', the greater the 'acceptance of the normative system'.

**P 19:** Ama, the greater the ''conformity to conventional standards of behavior'', the less the 'commission of delinquent acts'.

**Proposition 1:** Ama, the greater the 'share communication', the greater the 'affectional identification'.

**Pr 2:** Ama, the greater the 'impact of parental expectations and opinions', the greater the 'psychological presence of parents'.

**Pr 3:** Ama, the greater the 'share communication', the greater the 'psychological presence of parents'.

**Pr 4:** Ama, the greater the 'academic competence', the greater the 'academic performance'.

**Pr 5:** Ama, the greater the 'academic performance', the greater the 'share communication'.

**Pr 6:** Ama, the greater the 'academic performance', the greater the 'sentiments toward the controlling institution'.

**Pr 7:** Ama, the greater the 'academic competence', the greater the 'self-perceived academic competence'.

**Pr 8:** Ama, the greater the 'self-perceived academic competence', the greater the 'sentiments toward the controlling institution and attachment to a conventional figure'.

**Pr 9:** Ama, the greater the 'affectional identification', the greater the 'sentiments toward the controlling institution and attachment to a conventional figure'.

**Pr 10:** Ama, the greater the 'sentiments toward the controlling institution and attachment to a conventional figure', the greater the 'legitimacy of the controlling institution's rules'.

**Pr 11:** Ama, the greater the 'concern for the approval of persons in positions of impersonal authority', the greater the 'acceptance of the normative system'.

**Transformational statements 1:** Ama, the greater the 'psychological presence of parents', the greater the MVS.

**T 2:** Ama, the greater the 'share communication', the greater the IOCTPC.

**T 3:** Ama, the greater the 'concern for parental opinion', the greater the IOCCTP.

**T 4:** Ama, the greater the 'affectional identification', the greater the AIWP.

**T 5:** Ama, the greater the 'share communication and affectional identification', the greater the IOCAI.

**T 6:** Ama, the greater the 'academic competenece', the greater the DAT.

**T 7:** Ama, the greater the 'academic performance', the greater the GPA.

**T 8:** Ama, the greater the 'self-perceived academic competence', the greater the SPAC.

**T 9:** Ama, the greater the 'sentiments toward the controlling institution', the greater the ATS.

**T 10:** Ama, the greater the 'sentiments toward the controlling institution and attachment to a conventional figure', the greater the ATSS.

**T 11:** Ama, the greater the 'attachment to a conventional figure', the greater the FOT.

**T 12:** Ama, the greater the 'legitimacy of the controlling institution's rules', the less the NOSB.

**T 13:** Ama, the greater the 'delinquent companions', the greater the NDF.

**T 14:** Ama, the greater 'the educational expectations', the greater the EE.

**T 15:** Ama, the greater the 'achievement orientation', the greater the IOAO.

**T 16:** Ama, the greater the 'stake in conformity', the greater the SIC.

**T 17:** Ama, the greater the 'involvement in adult activities', the greater the IOIIAA.

**T 18:** Ama, the greater the 'involvement in school related activities', the greater the TDTH.

**T 19:** Ama, the greater the 'concern for approval of persons in positions of impersonal authority', the greater the COTPR.

**T 20:** Ama, the greater the 'acceptance of the normative system', the greater the RFTL.

**T 21:** Ama, the greater the 'commission of delinquent acts', the greater the IOD.

**Theorems:** To facilitate their understanding, it is indicated in parenthesis beside the theorem number which axioms, postulates, propositions, and transformational statements are used to derive each theorem.

**Th 1:** (From T3, Pr1, T4): Ama, the greater the IOCCTP, the greater the AIWP (p. 93).

**Th 2:** (From T2, Pr1, T4): Ama, the greater the IOCPTC, the greater the AIWP (p. 108).

**Th 3:** (From T4, Pr2, T1): Ama, the greater the AIWP', the greater the MVS (pp. 91–92).

**Th 4:** (From T3, Pr3, T1): Ama, the greater the IOCPTP, the greater the MVS (p. 90).

**Th 5:** (From T3, Pr3, T1): Ama, the greater the IOCCTP, the greater the MVS (p. 90).

**Th 6:** (From T1, P1, A1, P19, T21): Ama, the greater the MVS, the less the IOD (p. 88).
**Th 7:** (From T2, P2, A21, P19, T21): Ama, the greater the IOCPTC, the less the IIOD (p. 108).
**Th 8:** (From T3, P2, A1, P19, T21): Ama, the greater the IOCCTP, the less the IOD (p. 91).
**Th 9:** (From T4, P3, A1, P19, T21): Ama, the greater the AIWP, the less the IOD (p. 92).
**Th 10:** (From T6, Pr4, T7): Ama, the greater the DAT, the greater the GPA (p. 115).
**Th 11:** (From T7, Pr5, T3): Ama, the greater the GPA, the greater the IOCTP, (p. 109).
**Th 12:** (From T7, Pr6, T9): Ama, the greater the GPA, the greater the ATS (p. 120).
**Th 13:** (From T6, Pr7, T8): Ama, the greater the DAT, the greater the SPAC (p. 177).
**Th 14:** (From T8, Pr8, T10): Ama, the greater the SPAC, the greater the ATS (p. 129).
**Th 15:** (From T8, P6, A2, P19, T21): Ama, the greater the SPAC, the less the IOD (p. 117).
**Th 16:** (From T9, P7, A2, P19, T21): Ama, the greater the ATS, the less the IOD (p. 115).
**Th 17:** (From T4, Pr9, T10): Ama, the greater the AIWP, the greater the ATSS (p. 131).
**Th 18:** (From T10, P9, A2, P19, T21): Ama, the greater the ATSS, the less the IOD (p. 127).
**Th 19:** (From T10, Pr10, T12): Ama, the greater the ATSS, the less the NOSB (p. 127).
**Th 20:** (From T11, P8, A2, P19, T21): Ama, the greater the FOT, the less the IOD (p. 125).
**Th 21:** (From T12, P10, A2, P19, T21): Ama, the greater the NOSB, the greater the IOD (p. 128).
**Th 22:** (From T16, P14, A4, P11, T13): Ama, the greater the SIC, the less the NDF (p. 159).
**Th 23:** (From T16, P14, A6, P19, T21): Ama, the greater the SIC, the less the IOD (p. 155).
**Th 24:** (From T13, P11, A3, P19, T21): Ama, the greater the NDF, the greater the IOD (p. 156).

**Th 25:** (From T14, P12, A7, P15, T17): Ama, the greater the EE, the less the IOIIAA (p. 156).

**Th 26:** (From T14, P15, A8, P19, T21): Ama, the greater the IOIAA, the greater the IOD (pp. 168–169).

**Th 27:** (From T15, P15, A5, P19, T21): Ama, the greater the IOAO, the less the IOD (p. 178).

**Th 28:** (From T18, P16, A8, P19, T21): Ama, the greater the TDTH, the less the IOD (p. 194).

**Th 29:** (From T5, P4, A9, P17, T19): Ama, the greater the IOCAI, the greater the COTPR (p. 200).

**Th 30:** (From T19, Pr11, T20): Ama, the greater the COTPR, the greater the RFTL (p. 200).

**Th 31:** (From T20, P18, A10, P19, T21): Ama, the greater the RFTL, the less the IOD. (p. 204).

### Appendix 9.3—The modified formal version of Hirschi's theory, extrinsic part

When a term is not defined, refer to appendix 9.1 for the definition.
**Unit term:** Male adolescents attending junior and senior high schools.

It should be noted that all the temporal quantifiers at To, are designating one point in time. The same temporal quantifiers apply to all substantive terms (constructs or otherwise).

**Substantive terms:** (a * refers to an unmeasured construct or subconstruct)

**Constructs:** Three of the terms in the intrinsic statement are major or generic constructs:

(1) Bond to conventional society*: (2) Exposure to criminal influences: The degree to which an adolescent is exposed to criminal or different nature. (3) Conformity to conventional standards of behavior: Adolescent behavior which is acceptable to the agents of the larger society.

Five of the terms in the intrinsic statement are constructs: (1) attachment to persons*: the adolescent's sensitivity to other persons whatever their age, that is, caring about their wishes and expectations. (2) commitment to institutions*: the adolescent's pursuit and desire to be part of such institutions such as school, education, and so on. (3) Involvement in conventional activities*: (4) Belief in society's normative system*:

(5) Direct control: the means used by society to sanction the adolescent's behavior effectively in the direction of conformity.

Four of the terms in the intrinsic statement are subconstructs: (1) Attachment to parents: (2) Attachment to peers: (3) Attachment to persons in positions of impersonal authority: The adolescent's concern about the wishes and expectations of the school setting and its agents. (4) Commitment to education: The adolescent's pursuit and desire to further his education.

**Concepts:** Twenty three concepts enter into the intrinsic statements.

*Attachment to parents.* * (1) Share communication: (2) Perception of parental attitude: The adolescent sentiment that he is loved and accepted by his parents (3) Affectional identification:

*Attachment to persons in positions of impersonal authority**

(1) Respect for police: The adolescent's attitude of respect toward persons representing authority outside the family unit. (2) Attachment to a conventional figure: The adolescent's concern for the opinion of persons in authority within the school setting, the teacher.

*Attachment to peers.* Identification with best friends: The adolescent's affectional closeness to friends.

*Commitment to education.** (1) Self-perceived academic competence: (2) Sentiments toward the controlling institution: (3) Educational expectations: (4) Achievement orientation:

*Exposure to criminal influences.* Delinquent companions:

*Involvement in conventional activities.** (1) Involvement in work: The adolescent's quantity of time devoted to work while studying. (2) Involvement in school related activities: The adolescent's expenditure of time in activities emanating from the school setting. (3) Involvement in conventional activities with parents: The adolescent's expenditure of time in conventional activities with parents. (4) Involvement in conventional activities with peers: The adolescent's expediture of time in conventional activities with peers.

*Belief in society's normative system.** (1) Acceptance of the normative system: (2) Legitimacy of the controlling institution's rules: (3) Legitimacy of parental rules: The adolescent's willingness to accept parental rules. (4) Use of neutralization techniques: The extent to which the adolescent adopts definitions favorable to violations of law.

*Direct control:* Psychological presence of parents:

*Conformity to conventional standards of behavior.* Commission of delinquent acts:

*Construct undefined.* (1) Academic competence: (2) Academic performance:

**Referentials**: The vast majority of the twenty-three measured referentials are derived from the items of a self-report questionnaire. Two of the referentials are based on school records. The items constituting the referentials are combined equally weighted. There are also seven unmeasured variables that are defined as the sum of the constituting measured referentials; however, latent variables could also be constructed, they are in italics.

*Psychological presence of parents:* MVS:

*Share communications:* IOC is constructed from the following items: "When you don't know why your mother (father) makes a rule, will she (he) explain the reason?" "When you come across things you don't understand, does your mother (father) help you with them?" and "Does your mother (father) ever explain why she (he) feels the way she (he) does? "When you don't know why your mother (father)?" and "How often have you talked over your future plans with your mother (father)?"

*Perception of parental attitude:* EATP: "Do you feel rejected, unloved by one of your parents?" "Would your parents stick by you if you got into trouble with the police?" "Do your parents seem to understand you?"

*Affectional identification* AIWP:

*Identification with best friend* IWBF: "Would you like to be the kind of person your best friend is?"

*Academic competence:* DAT:

*Academic performance:* GPA:

*Self-perceived academic competence:* SPAC:

*Sentiments toward the controlling instituion:* ATS:

*Attachment to a conventional figure:* FOT:

*Legitimacy of the controlling institution's rules:* NOSB:

*Delinquent companions:* NDF:

*Educational expectations:* EE:

*Achievement orientation:* IOAO:

*Involvement in work* IOIIAA: "On the average, how many hours a week do you work for pay now, while you are attending school?"

*Involvement in school related activities* TDTH:

*Involvement in conventional activities with peers:* IOICPE: "Do you belong to any youth clubs?"

*Involvement in conventional activities with parents:* IOICPA: How often do you work in the garden with your parents?

How often do you make household repairs with your parents? How often do you watch television with your parents? How often do you go to sports events with your parents?

*Concern for the approval of persons in positions of impersonal authority*: RFTP: "I have a lot of respect for the police".

*Acceptance of the normative system:* RFTL:

*Legitimacy of parental rules*: LORP: "Do your parents make rules that seem unfair to you?"

*Neutralization techniques*: NTEC: "Most criminals shouldn't really be blamed for the things they have done." I can't seem to stay out of trouble no matter how hard I try." "Most things that people call 'delinquency' don't really hurt anyone." "The man who leaves the keys in his car is as much to blame for its theft as the man who steals it." "Policemen try to give all kids an even break."

*Commission of delinquent acts* IOD:

*Belief in society's normative system* BEL: NTEC and NOBS and LOPR and FRLT

*Involvement in conventional activities* INCA: IOIIAA and TDTH and IOICPA and IOICPE

*Commitment to education* ENGSCO: DAT and GPA and SPAC and ATS and EE and IOAO

*Attachment to parents* ATTPAR: IOC and EATP and AIWP

*Attachment to persons in positions of impersonal authority:* ATTAU: FOT and RFTP

*Attachment to persons:* AP: ATTPA and ATTAU and ATTPE

*Bond to conventional society* BOND: AP and ENGSCO and BEL and INCA

## Appendix 9.4—Modified formal version of Hirschi's theory, intrisic part

Axioms, postulates, propositions, transformational statements, and theorems are classified in five groups according to the level of generality of the substantive terms: major constructs, constructs, subconstructs and concepts. They are also ordered from the most general to the most specific (roman numbers), but the numbers used in referring to the original formalization (appendix 9.2) are kept in parenthesis. Terms in italic are referring to unmeasured or latent variables.

Ama reads among male adolescents

Because of space limitation, the term *at to* is not attached to each construct, concept and referential.

**The theory at the level of the major constructs**

**Axiom-I** (A6): Ama, the greater the "bond to conventional society", the greater the "conformity to conventional standards of behavior".

A-II (A4): Ama, the greater the "bond to conventional society", the less the "exposure to criminal influences".

A-III (A3): Ama, the less the "exposure to criminal influence", the greater the "conformity to conventional standards of behavior".

**Postulate I**: Ama, the greater the "bond to conventional society", the greater the "attachment to persons" *and* the "commitment to institutions" *and* the "involvement in conventional activities" *and* the "belief in society's normative system".

P-II (P11): Ama, the greater the "exposure to criminal influences", the greater the 'delinquent companions'.

P-III (P19): Ama, the greater the "conformity to conventional standards of behavior", the less the 'commission of delinquent acts'.

**Transformational statement I** (T13): Ama, the greater the 'delinquent companions', the greater the NDF.

**T-II** (T21): Ama, the greater the 'commission of delinquent acts', the greater the IOD.

**T-III**: Ama, the greater the "attachment to persons" *and* the "commitment to institutions" *and* the "involvement in conventional activities" *and* the "belief in society's normative system", the greater the *BOND*.

**Theorem I** (Th22): (From: TIII, PI, AII, PII, TI): Ama, the greater the *BOND*, the less the NDF.

**Th-II** (Th23): (From: TIII, PI, AI, PIII, TII): Ama the greater the *BOND*, the less the IOD.

**Th-III**(Th24): (From: TI, PII, AIII, PI, TIII): Ama the greater the NDF, the greater the IOD.

**The theory at the level of the constructs**

**Axiom IV** (A1): Ama, the greater the "attachment to persons", the greater the "conformity to conventional standards of behavior".

**A-V** (A5): Ama, the greater the "commitment to institutions", the greater the "conformity to conventional standards of behavior".

**A-VI** (A8): Ama, the greater the "involvement in conventional activities", the greater the "conformity to conventional standards of behavior".

**A-VII** (A10): Ama, the greater "the belief in society's normative system", the greater the "conformity to conventional standards of behavior".

**A-VIII** (A7): Ama, the greater the "commitment to institutions", the greater the "involvement in conventional activities".

**A-IX** (A9): Ama, the greater the "attachment to persons", the greater the "belief in society's normative system".

**A-X**: Ama, the greater the "attachment to persons", the less the "exposure to criminal influences".

**A-XI**: Ama, the greater the "commitment to institutions", the less the "exposure to criminal influences".

**A-XII**: Ama, the greater the "attachment to persons", the greater the "commitment to institutions".

**A-XIII**: Ama, the greater the "exposure to criminal influences", the less the "belief in society's normative system".

**Postulate IV**: Ama, the greater the "attachment to persons", the greater the " 'attachment to parents' " *and* the " 'attachment to conventional peers' " *and* the " 'attachment to persons in position of impersonal authority' ".

**P-V**: Ama, the greater the "commitment to institutions", the greater the " 'commitment to education' ".

**P-VI**: Ama, the greater the "involvement in conventional activities'', the less the 'involvement in work' *and* the greater the 'involvement in school related activities' *and* the 'involvement in conventional activities with parents' *and* the 'involvement in conventional activities with peers''.

**P-VII**: Ama, the greater the ''belief in the conventional normative system'', the greater the 'acceptance of the normative system' *and* the greater the 'legitimacy of parental rules *and* the 'legitimacy of the controlling institutions' rules *and* the less the 'use of neutralization techniques'.

**Transformational statement IV**: Ama, the greater the '' 'attachment to parents' '' *and* the '' 'attachment to conventional peers' '' *and* the '' 'attachment to persons in position of impersonal authority' '', the greater the *AP*.

**T-V**: Ama, the greater the '' 'commitment to education' '', the greater the *ENGSCO*.

**T-VI**: Ama, the less the 'involvement in work' *and* the greater the 'involvement in school related activities' *and* the 'involvement in conventional activities with parents' *and* the involvement in conventional activities with peers', the greater the *INCA*.

**T-VII**: Ama, the greater the 'acceptance of the normative system' *and* the 'legitimacy of parental rules' *and* the 'legitimacy of the controlling institutions' rules' *and* the less the use of 'neutralization techniques', the greater the *BEL*.

**Theorem IV**: (From: TIV, PIV, AIV, PIII, TII): Ama, the greater the *AP*, the less the IOD.

**Th-V**: (From: TIV, PIV, AIX, PVII, TVII): Ama, the greater the *AP*, the greater the *BEL*.

**Th-VI**: (From: TIV, PIV, AX, PII, TI): Ama, the greater the *AP*, the less the NDF.

**Th-VII**: (From: TIV, PIV, AXII, PV, TV): Ama, the greater the *AP*, the greater the *ENGSCO*.

**Th-VIII**: (From: TV, PV, AV, PIII, TII): Ama, the greater the *ENGSCO*, the less the IOD.

**Th-IX**: (From: TV, PV, AXI, PII, TI): Ama, the greater the *ENGSCO*, the less the NDF.

**Th-X**: (From: TV, PV, AVIII, PVI, TVI): Ama, the greater the *ENGSCO,* the greater the *INCA*.

**Th-XI**: (From: TVI, PVI, AVI, PIII, TII): Ama, the greater the *INCA*, the less the IOD.

**Th-XII**: (From: TVII, PVII, AVII, PIII, TII): Ama, the greater the *BEL*, the less the IOD.

**Th-XIII**: (From: TI, PII, AXIII, PVII, TVII): Ama, the greater the NDF, the less the *BEL*.

**The theory at the level of the sub-constructs and concepts**
**Attachment to persons—Attachment to parents**

**Postulate VIII**: Ama, the greater the " 'attachment to parents' ", the greater the 'adolescent's perception of parental attitude'.

**P-IX** (P2): Ama, the greater the " 'attachment to parents' ", the greater the 'share communication'.

**P-X** (P3): Ama, the greater the " 'attachment to parents' ", the greater the 'affectional identification'.

**P-XI**: Ama, the greater the " 'attachment to parents' ", the greater the 'share communication' *and* 'the adolescent's perception of parental attitude' *and* 'the affectional identification'.

**Proposition I**: Ama, the greater the 'share communication', the greater the 'adolescents's perception of the parental attitude'.

**Pr-II**: Ama, the greater the 'adolescent's perception of parental attitude', the greater the 'affectional identification'.

**Transformational statement VIII** (T2 & T3): Ama, the greater the 'share communication', the greater the IOC.

**T-IX**: Ama, the greater the 'adolescent's perception of parental attitude', the greater the EATP.

**T-X** (T4): Ama, the greater the 'affectional identification', the greater the AIWP.

**T-XI**: Ama, the greater the 'share communication', *and* the 'adolescent's perception of parental attitude' *and* the 'affectional identification', the greater the *ATTPAR*.

**Theorem XIV** (Th7 & Th8): (From: TVIII, PIX, AIV, PIII, TIII): Ama, the greater the IOC, the less IOD.

**Th-XV**: (From TVIII, PIX, PrI, PVIII, TIX): Ama, the greater the IOC, the greater the EATP.

**Th-XVI**: (From TIX, PVIII, PrII, PX, TX): Ama, the greater the EATP, the greater the AIWP.

**Th-XVII**: (From: TX, PX, AX, PII, TI): Ama, the greater the AIWP, the less the NDF.

**Th-XVIII**: (From: TXI, PXI, AX, PII, TI): Ama, the greater the *ATTPAR*, the less the NDF.

**Th-XIX**: (From: TXI, PXI, AIV, PIII, TII): Ama, the greater the *ATTPAR*, the less the IOD.

**Th-XX** (Th9): (From: TX, PX, AX, PIII, TII): Ama, the greater the AIWP, the less the IOD.

**Attachment to persons in position of impersonal authority**

**Postulate XII**: Ama, the greater the " 'attachment to persons in position of impersonal authority' ", the greater the 'attachment to a conventional figure'.

**P-XIII**: Ama, the greater the " 'attachment to persons in position of impersonal authority' ", the greater the 'respect for the police'.

**P-XIV**: Ama, the greater the " 'attachment to persons in position of impersonal authority' ", the greater the 'respect for the police" *and* the 'attachment to a conventional figure'.

**Transformational statement XII** (T11): Ama, the greater the 'attachment to a conventional figure', the greater the FOT.

**T-XIII**: Ama, the greater the 'respect for the police', the greater the RFTP.

**T-XIV** (T10): Ama, the greater the 'concern for approval of persons in positions of impersonal authority', the greater the *ATTAU*.

**Theorem XIII**: (From:TXII, PXII, AX, PII, TI): Ama, the greater the FOT, the less the NDF.

**Th-XXII**: (From TXIII, PXIII, AX, PII, TI): Ama, the greater the RFTP, the less the NDF.

**Th-XXIII**: (From: TXIV, PXIV, AX, PII, TI): Ama, the greater the *ATTAU*, the less the NDF.

**Th-XXIV** (Th20): (From: TXII, PXII, AIV, PIII, TII): Ama, the greater the FOT, the less the IOD.

**Th-XXV** (Th20): (From: TXIV, PXIV, AIV, PIII, TII): Ama, the greater the *ATTAU*, the greater the IOD.

**Attachment to peers**

**Postulate XV:** Ama, the greater the " 'attachment to peers' ", the greater the 'identification with best friend'.

**Transformational statement XV:** Ama, the greater the " 'attachment to peers' ", the greater the *ATTPER*.

**T-XVI:** Ama, the 'identification with best friend', the greater the *IWBF*.

**Theorem XXVI**: (From: TXV, PXV, AIV, PIII, TII): Ama, the greater the *ATTPER*, the less the IOD.

**Th-XXVII**: (From: TXV, PXV, AIV, PIII, TII): Ama, the greater the IWBF, the less the IOD.

**Relations among the attachment sub-constructs and concepts of attachment to persons**

**Axiom XV**: Ama, the greater the " 'attachment to parents' ", the greater the " 'attachment to persons in position of impersonal authority' ".

**A-XVI**: Ama, the greater the " 'attachment to parents' ", the greater the " 'attachment to peers' ".

**Proposition III**: Ama, the greater the 'mutual participation in the adolescent's social and psychological fields, the greater the 'respect for police'.

**Pr-IV**: Ama, the greater the 'affectional identification', the greater the 'attachment to a conventional figure'.

**Pr-V**: Ama, the greater the 'affectional identification', the greater the 'identification with best friends'.

**Theorem XXVIII**: (From: TVIII, PIX, PrIII, PXIII, TXIII); Ama, the greater the IOC, the greater the RFTP.

**TH-XXIX**: (From: TX, PX, PrIV, PXII, TXII): Ama, the greater the AIWP, the greater the FOT.

**Th-XXX**: (From: TXI, PXI, AXV, PXIV, TXIV): Ama, the greater the *ATTPAR*, the greater the *ATTAU*.

**Th-XXXI**: (From: TXI, PXI, AXVI, PXV, TXV): Ama, the greater the *ATTPAR*, the greater the *ATTPER*.

**Th-XXXII**: (From: TX, PX, PrV, PXV, TXV): Ama, the greater the AIWP, the greater the IWBF.

**Th-XXXIII**: (From: TXi, PXI, AXV, PXII, TXII): Ama, the greater the ATTPAR, the greater the FOT.

**Commitment to education**

**Postulate XVIII** (P6): Ama, the greater the " 'commitment to education' ", the greater the 'self-perceived academic competence'.

**P-XVIX** (P7): Ama, the greater the " 'commitment to education' ", the greater the 'sentiments toward the controlling institution'.

**P-XX** (P12): Ama, the greater the " 'commitment to education' ", the greater the 'educational expectations'.

**P-XXI** (P13): Ama, the greater the " 'commitment to education' ",
the greater the 'achievement orientation'.

**P-XXII**: Ama, the greater the " 'commitment to education' ", the
greater the 'self-perceived academic competence' *and* the 'sentiments toward the controlling institution' *and* the 'educational expectations' *and* the 'achievement orientation'.

**Proposition VI** (Pr4): Ama, the greater the 'academic competence',
the greater the 'academic performance'.

**Pr-VII** (Pr6): Ama, the greater the 'academic performance', the
greater the 'sentiments toward the controlling institution'.

**Pr-VIII** (Pr7): Ama, the greater the 'academic competence', the
greater the 'self-perceived academic competence'.

**Pr-IX** (Pr8): Ama, the greater the 'self-perceived academic competence', the greater the 'sentiments toward the controlling institution'.

**Pr-X**: Ama, the greater the 'sentiments toward the controlling
institution', the greater the 'achievement orientation'.

**Pr-XI**: Ama, the greater the 'educational expectation' *and* the less
the 'academic performance', the less the 'self-perceived academic
competence'.

**Pr-XII**: Ama, the greater the 'academic performance', the greater
the 'achievement orientation'.

**Pr-XIII**: Ama, the greater the 'self-perceived academic competence', the greater the 'achievement orientation'.

**Transformational statement XVII** (T6): Ama, the greater the 'academic competence', the greater the DAT.

**T-XVIII** (T7): Ama, the greater the 'academic performance', the
greater the GPA.

**T-XIX** (T8): Ama, the greater the 'self-perceived academic competence', the greater the SPAC.

**T-XX** (T9): Ama, the greater the 'sentiments toward the controlling
institution', the greater the ATS.

**T-XXI** (T14): Ama, the greater the 'educational expectations', the
greater the EE.

**T-XXII** (T15): Ama, the greater the 'achievement orientation', the
greater the IOAO.

**Theorem XXXIV:** (Th10): (From TXVII, PrVI, PXVII, TXVIII):
Ama, the greater the DAT, the greater the GPA.

**Th-XXXV:** (Th12): (From TXVIII, PXVII, PrVII, PXIX, TXX): Ama, the greater the GPA, the greater the ATS.

**Th-XXXVI:** (Th13): (From TXVII, PrVIII, PXVIII, TXIX): Ama, the greater the DAT, the greater the SPAC.

**Th-XXXVII:** (Th14): (From TXIX, PXVIII, PrIX, PXIX, TXX): Ama, the greater the SPAC, the greater the ATS.

**Th-XXXVIII:** (From TXX, PXIX, PrX, PXXI, TXXII): Ama, the greater the ATS, the greater the IOAO.

**Th-XXXIX:** (From: TXXI & TXVIII, PXX & PXVII, PrXI, PXVIII, TXIX): Ama, the greater the EE *and* the less the GAP, the less the SPAC.

**Th-XL** (Th27): (From: TXXII, PXXI, AV, PIII, TII): Ama, the greater the IOAO, the less the IOD.

**Th-XLI:** (From: TXXII, PXXI, AXI, PII, TI): Ama, the greater the IOAO, the less the NDF.

**Th-XLII:** (From: TXVIII, PXVII, PrXII, PXXI, TXXII): Ama, the greater the GAP, the greater the IOAO.

**Th-XLIII:** (From: TXIX, PXVII, PrXIII, PXXI, TXXII): Ama, the greater the SPAC, the greater the IOAO.

**Involvement in conventional activities**

**Postulate XXIII** (P15): Ama, the greater the "involvement in conventional activities", the less the 'involvement in work'.

**P-XXIV** (P16): Ama, the greater the "involvement in conventional activities", the greater the "involvement in school related activities'.

**P-XXV:** Ama, the greater the "involvement in conventional activities", the greater the 'involvement in conventional activities with parents'.

**P-XXVI:** Ama, the greater the "involvement in conventional activities", the greater the 'involvement in conventional activities with peers'.

**Transformational statement XXIII** (T17): Ama, the greater the 'involvement in work', the greater the IOIIAA.

**T-XXIV** (T18): Ama, the greater the 'involvement in school related activities', the greater the TDTH.

**T-XXV:** Ama, the greater the "involvement in conventional activities with parents', the greater the IOICPA.

**T-XXVI**: Ama, the greater the "involvement in conventional activities with peers', the greater the IOICPE.

**Theorem XLIV**: (Th28): (From TXXIV, PXXIV, AVI, PIII, TII): Ama, the greater the TDTH, the less the IOD.

**Th-XLV**: (Th26): (From TXXIII, PXXIII, AVI, PIII, TII): Ama, the greater the IOIIAA, the greater the IOD.

**Th-XLVI**: (From TXXV, PXXV, AVI, PIII, TII): Ama, the greater the IOICPA, the less the IOD.

**Th-XLVII**: (From TXXVI, PXXVI, AVI, PIII, TII): Ama, the greater the IOICPE, the less the IOD.

**Belief**

**Postulate XXVII** (P18): Ama, the greater the "belief in society's normative system'', the greater the 'acceptance of the normative system'.

**P-XXVIII**: Ama, the greater the "belief in society's normative system'', the greater the 'legitimacy of parental rules'.

**P-XXIX**: Ama, the greater the "belief in society's normative system'', the greater the 'legitimacy of the controlling institution's rules'.

**P-XXX**: Ama, the greater the "belief in society's normative system'', the less the "use of neutralization techniques'.

**Proposition XIV** Ama, the greater the "acceptance of the normative system', the less the 'use of neutralization techniques'.

**Pr-XV**: Ama, the greater the 'exposure to criminal influences', the greater the 'use of neutralization techniques'.

**Transformational statement XVI** (T20): Ama, the greater the 'acceptance of the normative system', the greater the RFTL.

**T-XXVII**: Ama, the greater the 'legitimacy of parental rules', the greater the LOPR.

**T-XXVIII** (T12): Ama, the greater the 'legitimacy of the controlling institution's rules', the greater the NOBS.

**T-XXIX**: Ama, the greater the 'use of neutralization techniques', the greater the NTEC.

**Theorem-XLVIII**: (Th31): (From TXXVII, PXXVII, AVII, PIII, TII): Ama, the greater the RFTL, the less the IOD.

**Th-XLIX**: (From: TXXVIII, PXXVIII, AVII, PIII, TII): Ama, the greater the LORP, the less the IOD.

**Th-L** (Th21): (From: TXXVIII, PXXIX, AVII, PIII, TII): Ama, the greater the NOSB, the less the IOD.

**Th-LI**: (From: TI, PII, PrXIV, PXXX, TXXIX): Ama, the greater the NDF, the greater the NTEC.

**Th-LII**: (From: TXXVII, PXXVII, PrXV, PXXX, TXXIX): Ama, the greater the RFTL, the less the NTEC.

**Th-LIII**: (From: TXXIX, PXXX, AVII, PIII, TII): Ama, the greater the NTEC, the greater the IOD.

**The theory at the level of the institutions**

**Family**

**Axiom XVII**: Ama, the greater the "attachment to parents", the greater the "direct control".

**A-XVIII**: Ama, the greater the "direct control", the greater the "conformity to conventional standards of behavior".

**Postulate XXXI** (P1): Ama, the greater the "direct control", the greater the 'psychological presence of parents'.

**Proposition XVI** (Pr3): Ama, the greater the 'mutual participation in the adolescent's social and psychological fields', the greater the 'psychological presence of parents'.

**Pr-XVII** (Pr2): Ama, the greater the 'affectional identification', the greater the 'psychological presence of parents'.

**Transformational statement XXX** (T1): Ama, the greater the 'psychological presence of parents', the greater the MVS.

**Theorems** (See also theorems relative to attachment to parents)

**Th-LIV**: (From: TXI, PXI, AXII, PXXXI, TXXX): Ama, the greater the *ATTPAR*, the greater the MVS.

**Th-LV:** (Th3): (From TX, PX, PrXVII, PXXXI, TXXX): Ama, the greater the AIWP', the greater the MVS.

**Th-LVI** (Th6): (From TXXX, PXXXI, AXVIII, PIII, TII): Ama, the greater the MVS, the less the IOD.

**Th-LVII** (Th4 & Th5): (From TVIII, PIX, PrXVI, PXXXI, TXXX): Ama, the greater the IOC, the greater the MVS.

**School**

**Proposition XVIII** Ama, the greater the 'achievement orientation', the greater the 'involvement in school related activities'.

**Pr-XVIX**: Ama, the greater the 'attachment to a conventional figure', the greater the 'achievement orientation'.

**Pr-XX** (Pr10): Ama, the greater the 'attachment to a conventional figure', the greater the 'legitimacy of the controlling institution's rules'.

**Pr-XXI**: Ama, the greater the 'sentiments toward the controlling institution', the greater the 'legitimacy of the controlling institution's rules'.

**Theorems** (See also theorems relative to commitment to education and involvement in school related activities)

**Th-LVIII:** (From: TV, PV, AVIII, PXXIV, TXXIV): Ama, the greater the *ENGSCO*, the greater the TDTH.

**Th-LIX:** (From: TXII, PXII, AXII, PV, TV): Ama, the greater the FOT, the greater the ENGSCO.

**Th-LX:** (From: TXII, PXII, PrXIX, PXXI, TXXII): Ama, the greater the FOT, the greater the IOAO.

**Th-LXI:** (From; TXXII, PXXI, PrXVIII, PXXIV, TXXIV): Ama, the greater the IOAO, the greater the TDTH.

**Th-LXII:** (From: TXII, PXII, PrXIX, PXXIX, TXXVIII): Ama, the greater the FOT, the greater the NOBS.

**Th-LXIII** (Th 19): (From: TXIX, PXX, PrIX, PXXIX, TXXVIII): Ama, the greater the ATS, the greater the NOBS.

**The theory at the level of the relationships between constructs**
**Commitment and involvement**

**Proposition XXII**: Ama, the greater the 'achievement orientation', the less the 'involvement in work'.

**Theorems** (see also **Th-LVIII** and **LXI**)

**Th-LXIV:** (From: TV, PV, AVIII, PXXII, TXXII): Ama, the greater the ENGSCO, the less the IOIIAA.

**Th-LXV:** (From TXXII, PXXI, PrXXII, PXXIII, TXXIII): Ama, the greater the IOAO, the less the IOIIAA.

**Attachment and belief**

**Proposition XXIII:** Ama, the greater the 'respect for the police', the greater the 'acceptance of the normative system'.

**Pr-XXIV:** Ama, the greater the 'affectional identification', the greater the 'legitimacy of parental rules'.

**Theorems** (see also **th-LXII**)

**Th-LXVI:** (From TXI, PXI, A1X, PXXVIII, TXXVIII): Ama, the greater the *ATTPAR*, the greater the LOPR.

**Th-LXVII:** (From TX, PX, PrXXIV, PXXVIII, TXXVIII): Ama, the greater the AIWP, the greater the LOPR.

**Th-LXVIII**: (From TXIII, PXIII, PrXXIII, PXXVII, TXXVII): Ama, the greater the RFTP, the greater the RFTL.

## References

Albrecht, H.-J. 1982. Criminal law and general prevention. In G. Kaiser (ed.), *Research in Criminal Justice: Stock-Taking of Criminological Reserch at the Max-Planck-Institute for Foreign and International Penal Law after a Decade* (286–307). Freiburg: Criminological research unit, Max Planck Institute.

Allport, G. W. 1935. Attitudes. In C. Murchison (ed.), *A Handbook in Social Psychology* Worcester: Clark University Press.

Aultman, M. G. 1979. Delinquency causation: A typological comparison of path models. *Journal of Criminal Law and Criminology* 70 (2), 152–63.

Bernard, T. J. 1987. Structure and control: Reconsidering Hirschi's concept of commitment. *Justice Quarterly* 4 (3), 409–24.

Blalock, H. M. 1969. *Theory Construction: From Verbal to Mathematical Formulations*. Englewood Cliffs, N.J.: Prentice Hall.

Blumstein, A., Cohen, J., Roth, J. A., and Visher, C. A. 1986. *Criminal Career and "Career Criminals"*. Washington, D.C.: National Academy Press.

Caplan, A. 1978. *A formal statement and extension of Hirschi's theory of social control.* Unpublished doctoral thesis, School of Criminology, Université de Montréal.

Caplan, A. and Le Blanc, M. 1985. A cross-cultural verification of a social control theory. *International Journal of Comparative and Applied Criminal Justice* 9 (2), 123–38.

Catalano, R. F. and Hawkins, J . D. 1986. *The Social Development Model: A Theory of Antisocial Behavior* Center for Social Welfare Research, School of Social Work, University of Washington.

Chapman, W. R. 1986. *Delinquency Theory and Attachment to Peers.* PhD, The University of New York at Albany.

Cloward, R. A. and Ohlin, L. E. 1960 *Delinquency and Opportunity: A Theory of Delinquent Gangs*. New York: Free Press.

Cohen, A. K. 1955. *Delinquent Boys: The Culture of the Gang*. New York: Free Press.

Cohen, L. E. and Land, K. C. 1987. Sociological positivism and the explanation of criminality. In M. R. Gottfredson and T. Hirschi (eds.). *Positive Criminology* (43–55). Beverley Hills, Cal.: Sage Publications.

Conger, R. 1976. Social control and social learning models of delinquency: a synthesis. *Criminology* 14 (1), 17–40.

DeFleur, M. L. and Quinney, R. 1966. A reformulation of Sutherland's differential association theory and a strategy for an empirical verification. *Journal of Research in Crime and Delinquency* 3 (1), 1–22.

Dubin, R. 1969. *Theory Building*. New York: Free Press.

Durkheim, E. 1924. *De l'éducation morale*. Paris: Presses universitaires de France.

Elliott, D. S., Huizinga, D., and Ageton, S. S. 1985. *Explaining Delinquency and Drug Use*. Beverly Hills, Cal.: Sage Publications.

Empey, L. T. 1977. *American Delinquency: Its Meaning and Construction*. Homewood, Ill.: Dorsey Press.

Empey, L. T. & Lubeck, S. G. 1971. *Explaining Delinquency: Construction, Test and Reformulation of a Sociological Theory*. Lexington, Mass.: Heath Lexington Books.

Farnworth, M., Schweinhart, L. J., and Berruta-Clement, J. R. 1985. Preschool intervention, school success and delinquency in a high-risk sample of youths. *American Educational Research Journal* 22 (3), 445–64.

Felson, M. 1986. Linking criminal choice, routine activities, informal control and criminal outcomes. In D. B. Cornisk and R. V. Clarke (Eds.), *The Reasoning Criminal: Rational Choice Perspectives on Offending* (119–28). New York: Springer-Verlag.

Fréchette, M. and Le Blanc, M. 1987. *Délinquances et délinquants*. Chicoutimi: Gaétan Morin Éditeur.

Freese, L. and Sell, J. 1980. Constructing axiomatic theories in sociology. In L. Freese (ed.), *Theoretical Methods in Sociology: Seven Essays* (263–368). Pittsburgh: University of Pittsburgh Press.

Gibbs, J. 1972. *Sociological Theory Construction*. Hinsdale, Ill.: The Dryden Press.

Gibbs, J. 1985. The methodology of theory construction in criminology. In R. F. Meier (ed.), *Theoretical Methods in Criminology* 23–50). Beverly Hills, Cal.: Sage Publications.

Giordano, P. C., Cernkovich, S. A., and Pugh, M. D. 1986. Friendships and delinquency. *American Journal of Sociology* 91 (5), 1170–1202.

Gottfredson, M. R. and Hirschi, T. 1989. A propensity-event theory of crime. In W. S. Laufer and F. Adler (eds.), *Advances in Criminological Theory* (57–68). New Brunswick, N.J.: Transaction Publishers.

Gottfredson, M. R. and Hirschi, T. 1990. *A General Theory of Crime*. Stanford, Cal.: Stanford University Press.

Greenberger, H. and Steinberg, L. 1986. *When Teenagers Work: The Psychological and Social Costs of Adolescent Employment*. New York: Basic Books Inc.

Hagan, J. 1985. *Modern Criminology: Crime, Criminal Behavior and its Control*. New York: McGraw-Hill.

Hanneman, R. A. 1988. *Computer Assisted Theory Building. Modeling Dynamic Social Systems*. Beverley Hills, Cal.: Sage Publications.

Hindelang, M. 1973. Causes of delinquency: A partial replication and extension. *Social Problems* 20 (4), 471–82.

Hirschi, T. 1969. *Causes of Delinquency*. Berkeley: University of California Press.

Hirschi, T. 1979. Separate an unequal is better. *Journal of Research in Crime and Delinquency* 16 (1), 34–38.

Hirschi, T. 1985. Crime and family policy. In R. A. Weisheit and R. C. Culberston (eds.), *Juvenile Delinquency: A Justice Perspective* (53–67). Prospect Height, Ill.: Waveland Press.

Hirschi, T. (1989). *Exploring Alternatives to Integrated Theory*. In Messner, S. F., Krohn, M. D., Liska, A. E. (eds.). *Theoretical Integration in the Study of Deviance and Crime: Problems and Prospects*. Albany: State University of New York Press.

Hirschi, T. and Gottfredson, M. R. 1986. The distinction between crime and criminality. In T. Hartnagel and R. Silverman (eds.), *Critique and Explanation* (55–69). New Brunswick, N.J.: Transaction Publishers.

Hirschi, T. and Gottfredson, M. R. 1988. Toward a general theory of crime. In W. Buickhuisen and S. Mednick (eds.), *Understanding Crime: Interdisciplinary Perspectives* Leiden: Brill.

Johnson, R. E. 1979. *Juvenile Delinquency and Its Origins: An Integrated Approach*. Cambridge: Cambridge University Press.

Johnson, R. E. 1987. Mother's versus father's role in causing delinquency. *Adolescence* 22 (86), 305–15.

Junger-Tas, J. and Junger, M. 1984. *Juvenile Delinquency: Backgrounds of Delinquent Behavior*. Ministery of Justice, Nederlands.

Kaplan, H. B., Martin, S. S. and Robbins, C. 1984. Pathways to adolescent drug use: Self-derogation, peer influence, weakening of social controls and early substance use. *Journal of Health and Social Behavior* 25 (2), 270–89.

Kempf, K. 1989. *Hirschi's Theory of Social Control: Is it Fertile but not yet Fecund?* University of Missouri, St. Louis.

Kornhauser, R. R. (1978). *Social Sources of Delinquency: An Appraisal of Analytic Models*. Chicago: University of Chicago Press.

Krohn, M. D., Lanza-Kaduce, L., and Akers, R. L. (1984). Community context and theories of deviant behavior. An examination of social learning and social bonding theories. *Sociological Quarterly* 25 (3), 353–71.

Krohn, M. D. and Massey, J. L. 1980. Social control and delinquent behavior: An examination of the elements of the social bond. *Sociological Quarterly* 21: 529–43.

LaGrange, R. I. and Raskin White, H. 1985. Age differences in delinquency: a test of theory. *Criminology* 23 (1), 19–45.

Landers, D. M. and Landers, D. M. 1978. Socialization via interscholastic athletics. Its effects on delinquency. *Sociology of Education* 51 (4), 299–303.

Le Blanc, M. 1983. Delinquency as an epiphenomenon of adolescence. In R. R. Corrado, M. LeBlanc, and J. Trépanier (eds.), *Current Issues in Juvenile Justice* (31–48). Tornoto: Butterworths.

Le Blanc, M. and Ouimet, G. 1988a. Système familial et conduite délinquante au cours de l'adolescence à Montréal en 1985. *Santé mentale au Québec* 13 (2), 119–34.

Le Blanc, M., Ouimet, M., and Tremblay, R. E. 1988b. An integrative control theory of delinquent behavior: a validation 1976–1985. *Psychiatry* 51: 164–76.

Le Blanc, M., Vallière, E., and McDuff, P. 1992a. Adolescents' school experience and self-reported offending, a longitudinal test of a social control theory. *International Journal of Youth and Adolescence* 5, 1: 42–63.

Le Blanc, M., Vallière, E., and McDuff, P. 1992b. School Experience,

Self-Reported Delinquency, and Adult Criminality: The Predictive Power of a Social Control Theory for Male Adolescent. *Canadian Journal of Criminology* 34, 3: 181–203.

Le Blanc, M. 1992. Family dynamics, Adolescent Delinquency and Adult Criminality. *Psychiatry* 55, 1: 24–42.

Mannle, H. W. and Lewis, P. W. 1979. Control theory reexamined: Race and the use of neutralizations among institutionalized delinquents. *Criminology* 17 (1), 58–74.

Mathur, M . and Dodder, R. A. 1985. Delinquency and the attachment bond in Hirschi's control theory. *Free inquiry in creative sociology* 13 (1), 99–103.

Meier, R. F. and Johnson, W. T. (1977). Deterrence as social control: The legal and extralegal production of conformity. *American Sociological Review* 42: 292–304.

Merton R. K. 1957. *Social Theory and Social Structure*. New York: Free Press.

Minor, W. W. 1977. A deterrence control theory of crime. In R. F. Meier (ed.), *Theory in Criminology, Contemporary Views* (117–38). Beverly Hills, Cal.: Sage.

Messer, S. F., Krohn, M. D., and Liska, A. E. 1989. *Theoretical Integration in the study of Deviance and Crime: Problems and Prospects*. Albany: State University of New York Press.

Mottaz, C. J . 1989. An analysis of the relationship between attitudinal commitment and behavioral commitment. *Sociological Quarterly* 30 (1), 143–48.

Nye, F. I. (1958). *Family Relationships and Delinquent Behavior*. New York: Wiley.

Paternoster, R., Saltzman, L. E., Waldo, G. P., and Chiricos, T. G. 1983. Perceived risk and social control: do sanctions really deter? *Law and Society* 17 (3), 425–26.

Polk, K. and Schaffer, N. E. 1972. *School and Delinquency*. Englewood Cliffs, N.J.: Prentice-Hall.

Reckless, W. C. 1967. *The Crime Problem*. New York: Appleton Century Crofts.

Reiss, A. J. 1951. Delinquency as the failure of personal and social controls. *American Sociological Review* 16 (2), 196–207.

Shover, N., Norland, S., James, J. and Thorton, W. E. 1979. Gender roles and delinquency. *Social Forces* 58 (2), 162–75.

Simca-Fagan, O. and Schwartz, J. E. 1986. Neighborhood and delinquency: An assessment of contextual effects: *Criminology* 24 (4), 667–703.

Stark, R., Kent, L., and Finke, R. 1987. Sports and delinquency. In M. R. Gottfredson and T. Hirschi (eds.), *Positive Criminology* (115–124). Beverly Hills, Cal.: Sage.

Stinchombe, A. L. 1968. *Constructing Social Theories*. Chicago: The University of Chicago Press.

Sykes, G. M. and Matza, D. 1957. Techniques of neutralization: A Theory of delinquency. *American Sociological Review* 22 (4), 664–70.

Szabo, D., Gagné, D., and Parizeau, A. 1972. *L'adolescent et la société.* Bruxelles: Dessart.

Thornberry, T. P. 1989. *Reflections on the advantages and disadvantages of theoretical integration.* In Messner, S. F. Krohn, M. D., and Liska, A. E. 1989. *Theoretical Integration in the study of Deviance and Crime: Problems and prospects.* Albany: State University of New York Press.

Thornberry, T. P. 1987. Toward an interactional theory of delinquency. *Criminology* 25 (4), 963–92.

Thornton, W. and Voigt, L. 1984. Television and delinquency: A neglected dimension of social control. *Youth and Society* 15 (4), 445–68.

Turner, J. H. and Beeghley, L. 1981. *The Emergence of Sociology.* Homewood, Ill.: Dorsey.

West, D. J. and Farrington, D. P. 1977. *The Delinquent Way of Life.* London: Heineman.

Wiatrowski, M. and Anderson, K. L. 1987. The dimensionality of the social bond. *Journal of Quantitative Criminology* 3 (1), 65–81.

Willer, D. 1967. *Scientific Sociology: Theory and Method.* Englewood Cliffs, N.J.: Prentice Hall.

Winton, C. 1971. *Theory and Measurement in Sociology.* New York: John Wiley.

Zettenberg, H. L. (1965). *On Theory and Verification in Sociology.* Totowa, N.J.: Bedminster Press.

# 10

# Control Theory and Punishment: An Analysis of Control Theory as a Penal Philosophy

*Michael J. Lynch*
*Graeme R. Newman*
*W. Byron Groves*

Hirschi's (1969) reformulation of Durkheim's (1925) doctrine on social bonding resulted in one of the most influential contemporary theories of criminal etiology: "control theory." While Durkheim employed his control model to explain punishment[1], Hirschi's reformulation recast the control model primarily as a theory of crime causation. In so doing, Hirschi established a tradition that has separated itself from control theory's origins as a theory of punishment.

It is surprising that previous research has neglected the punitive basis of control theory, especially in light of Durkheim's (1925, 1966, 1968) work which dealt extensively with the problem of punishment as control. To do so, Durkheim adopted a mixed platform consisting of utilitarian and retributive perspectives. Durkheim's model, in short, is a hybrid theory of punishment. Most discussions of punishment, however, are monolithic, advancing *one* preferred theory of punishment (e.g., see Hirschi and Gottfredson's, 1989, 1987a, 1987b, recent work which employs a classical utilitarian understanding of crime and punishment).

In this paper we investigate the punitive nature of control theory further. Since control theory is explicitly derived from the work of Durkheim (Hirschi 1969) we devote the first part of this paper to assessing Durkheim's control theory, paying special attention to his view of punishment. In the second part, we review the punitive basis of modern control theories ala Hirschi. The third part discusses the connection between a control theory of punishment and the causes of delinquency. In the fourth section we examine the connection between control theory and general deterrence. In the final section we examine Durkheim's structural-level views of the punishment process.

## Durkheim on Punishment

### The Impetus Behind Durkheim's Control Theory

Many versions of control theory exist (e.g., Hirschi 1969; Durkheim 1925; Reiss 1951). However, the basic values underlying the theory are found in Durkheim's *Moral Education*. In *Moral Education* Durkheim strove to produce a scientific theory of society that established a secular rather than a religious foundation for social order. His purpose was to discover "the sources of social solidarity which were . . . the fundamental conditions of collective life and social cohesion" (Garland 1990, 23). The problem Durkheim faced was how to understand "moral order" without introducing any religious trappings. Even with this goal in mind, Durkheim advocated that the secular production of "moral individuals" was similar to the techniques that served as the foundation of religious moral order he described in *Elementary Forms of Religious Life* (1915): both types of moral order relied on the imposition of an external authority, often seemingly arbitrary, and always all powerful. The problem Durkheim faced in *Moral Education* was how to explain the historical shift in the foundation of society's moral order from the religious to the secular.

Durkheim argued that in primitive societies, "important duties are not the duties of man towards other men but of man toward his gods" (1925, 6). In contemporary society, however, the moral individual's duty to God was supplanted by a duty to society.

Society, by which Durkheim meant the shared rules that existed over and above the individual, became the external source of authority. Hence, society acquired a "Godlike" yet secular nature, captured in Durkheim's claim that society "is like a jealous and formidable God, the stern lawmaker allowing no transgression of his orders" (Durkheim 1925, 92–93)[2]. This argument suggests that the contracts, exchanges, and so on that society promotes and that in turn promote bonding appear on the surface to be evidence for a utilitarian, rational, self-interest model (Garland 1990, 28). However, hidden beneath this surface were, in Durkheim's view, "submerged moralities" that gave punishment its "moral significance and moralizing social functions" (Garland 1990, 29).

For the purposes of a control theory of punishment the issue of a secular foundation for order is important for two reasons. First, it shows a connection between Durkheim's approach and the utilitarian tradition in penology (e.g., with Bentham and Hobbes). This tradition stands for a conception of an ordered society that would avoid inevitable chaos or a "war of all against all." In this view, an egoistic, unordered society could only be avoided if society successfully imposed its will over the will of the individual—if the individual was completely controlled. If society accomplished this goal there would be a natural balance or harmony between the individual and society. We must be aware, however, that this "harmony" is achieved at the cost of controlling or subjugating individual wills to the social will. The question of *how* individual wills are to be controlled is a crucial problem for Durkheim's theory, as it is for all theories derived from Utilitarian roots. As we shall see, Durkheim goes beyond many of the principles adhered to by Utilitarians to escape some of these potential problems.

Second, the translation of the details of this theory into actual practical or policy guidelines is of great interest. Durkheim considered policy or the practical application of theory to be the ultimate justification for research (Wilson 1974, x)[3]. In contrast, modern control theorists, preoccupied with causation, have virtually ignored the question of policy, *especially* as it relates to the question of *punishment*.

## The Basis of Secular Order and Morality

As noted above, Durkheim's mission was to outline the development of a secular morality and explain how forces external to the individual legitimized a secular morality. Drawing upon the Utilitarian tradition, Durkheim located the secular source of morality in the heavy hand of order itself: authority. It is understandable that Durkheim should "discover" this source of morality since he was writing *Moral Education* for a secular school system, and it is in schools that the strongest tendencies towards totalitarianism is located.[4]

In order to bolster his position, Durkheim pursued a detailed discussion of discipline as it existed above and beyond individuals and as it related to authority. For Durkheim, discipline and authority became the two forces that joined to form the basis of secular morality. How exactly did these forces work?

Durkheim argued that discipline was an observable "social fact," or concrete rules that guided behavior. But, why should the individual obey such rules? What caused the individual to conform? The essential, mysterious and quasireligious concept Durkheim used to describe this process was the idea of *attachment*, a concept later sanctified (quantified) by its translation into the idea of the social bond by a number of theorists (e.g., Hirschi 1969).

The central feature of Durkheim's control theory is his discussion of the processes that established and maintained attachment. Bonding is a social process; an essential element of this process is the assertion of authority. In turn, authority hinges on the concepts of order (as expressed in the social fact of regularity) and obedience. The primacy Durkheim grants obedience and order in his control theory is easy to demonstrate from his writings:

> The content of moral precepts . . . promote regularity . . . this is why transients and people who cannot hold to specific jobs are always suspect . . . their moral temperament is fundamentally defective. . . . Such people are subject to momentary impulses. (Durkheim 1925, 27)

> Morality is not . . . a system of customary conduct. It is a system of commandments. (Durkheim 1925, 31)

Durkheim asserts that order and obedience result from discipline, or that regularity and authority are combined in the concept of discipline. In making this argument Durkheim stated that "it is good that man is disciplined, independent of the acts to which he finds himself constrained" (1925, 32). On this point, Durkheim's position differs from his Utilitarian forebears such as Bentham, and suggests that constraints on the individual's desires are *good* because they are "demanded by nature herself" or by the nature of human social life.[5] The contrasting view (from Bentham to Freud) is the individual pitted in an heroic fight against him/herself, fighting against society's impositions and repressions. When all is said and done, however, it is difficult to see any substantial difference between Durkheim's view of society and that of Hobbes or Freud. Durkheim, for instance, insists that man's basic nature consists of "inclinations, instincts, and desires" that, if left unopposed, will bring "our behavior willy-nilly to the level of its natural inclinations" (1925, 46). Considerable constraints are therefore necessary to place limits on human behavior (i.e., to eliminate egoism and anomie, and establish a balanced society). For all intents and purposes Durkheim has reproduced the Utilitarian conception of both human nature and social order. We will return to further consideration of this connection throughout this paper.

## *The Punitive Basis of Durkheim's Control Theory*

It is at this point in Durkheim's argument— at the point where he has established the basis of secular order and morality, and discussed the roles of authority, attachment, bonding, obedience, and discipline in maintaining secular order and morality—that the concept of punishment becomes important. The argument here can be reduced to the simple assertion that discipline cannot be established without punishment.[6] Thus, attachment, though related to authority, discipline, order, and bonding, is at its heart the result of *punishment*. In adopting this model, Durkheim's argument closely parallels the social process that he previously argued undergirds all religious controls in *Elementary Forms of Religious Life*. As Garland (1990, 23) has noted, in Durkheim's view "punishment was an institution which was connected to the very heart of society."

## Durkheim's Predilection for Order

Durkheim tried to play down the harshness of his predilection for order and discipline with two simple assertions: first, discipline and order are "good" for us, and second, we value such constraints because they attach us to society and give our lives meaning. A formidable question facing Durkheim can be drawn from Freud's perspective: "Why should we value social attachments when we are, at the same time, tempted by our individual desires?" Durkheim is unable to explain such questions except with the mystical concept of "the will." One can only interpret this concept as similar to, though not as well developed as the rational calculus model used by Utilitarians.

For Durkheim, a disciplined, *rational* person would choose order over chaos, and would choose society over her/himself because society offered the most returns for the individual's sacrifice. This position, while based on a Utilitarian model of rational decision making, is more deterministic than the model offered by Utilitarians. The Utilitarian model holds out the possibility that rational individuals choose crime when the rewards of crime outweigh its costs. Durkheim's position does not allow for such a possibility: since *order*, regularity and society are the *highest good*, *rational* individuals would *always choose conformity* and regularity over crime. Thus, we can assume that those who do not choose the highest good—order, regularity, or society—are irrational social actors. However, such an assumption does not fit with widely held interpretations of Durkheim's position on crime (i.e., that crime is normal, not pathological).

Durkheim's position on liberty and regulation also developed from the general claims made by Utilitarians. For example, while both Durkheim and Freud (following the Hobbesian Utilitarian tradition) claimed that liberty is made possible by regulation, they also insisted that total liberty was the way to wanton destruction (or loss of security). These theorisits differed considerably, however, with reference to the price paid for liberty. Freud argued that individuals paid a very high price for liberty—repression, guilt, and neurosis. Durkheim, however, insists that there is no price for obedience and yielding to authority—no price for being controlled:

the social actor, imbued with society in his/her very being, will want to yield to society, will place society before his/her individual wants and will feel happy in doing so.

In a sense, while Durkheim drew some of his inspiration from the Utilitarian tradition, he *has* gone further than Bentham or Hobbes. To the Utilitarians, individuals grudgingly gave up a little of their liberty in order to satisfy their individual desires. Thus, the individual and society exist as separate yet dependent entities. Durkheim argued that the process of discipline produced truly social beings or individuals who cannot define themselves apart from society. This social individual is deeply attached to others, not in any direct sense of "being friends" but rather through the abstract idea of society which collects us together:

> there is in us a host of states which something other than ourselves—that is to say, society—expresses in, or through, us. Such states constitute society itself, living and acting in us. . . We are fused with it . . . [it is] the thing to which we are bound. (Durkheim 1925, 71)

While Durkheim eclipsed the Utilitarian tradition, his position continued to reflect many Utilitarian beliefs. For example, toward the end of section 1 of *Moral Education,* he sums up morality as "A system of rules, external to the individual, which impose themselves on him from outside; not . . . by any physical force, but by virtue of the ascendancy that they enjoy" (1925, 107).

## Discipline without Punishment?

It is interesting to note that in *Moral Education* Durkheim, who offered such strong arguments in favor of authority and obedience maintained by discipline, does not once elaborate on punishment, generally considered to be the negative aspect of discipline. Rather, he shrewdly refers to discipline as a kind of "self discipline;" provided us with a long essay on "autonomy" which suggested that the "will" was the source of discipline; argued that this will was formed out of the deep attachment one developed with society; and that attachment and the development of the will is bound up in the process of becoming a social being. The argument, however, is tautological. How can external impositions be impositions if they are engaged in willingly? One must ask the prior question: how does it come about that the individual willingly obeys?

Durkheim confronted this question in section two of *Moral Education,* "The Establishment of Morality in Children." Here we see the tension in his argument clearly. While he at once insisted that punishment should be used as little as possible in the school in order to maintain discipline, he admitted that "it is certainly true that there must be some fairly close connection between the idea of rule and the idea of punishment curbing infraction of the rule" (Durkheim 1925, 160)—apparently the principle of deterrence.

Once again, Durkheim indulged in circularity. He claimed that the majority of school children are well disciplined and obedient and, therefore, that punishment is hardly necessary. He also argued that the use of punishment for "deterrent purposes" (that is, to intimidate children into not committing delinquent acts) is *indefensible* because it leads to excess and unjustly disproportionate punishments (here we see Durkheim's rejection of Utilitarian principles and an attempt to supplant that tradition with some other form of explanation). Our interest again returns to the unanswered question: "why are children obedient in the first place?"

In short, throughout his discussion of discipline, in claiming that authority rather than punishment should be used as the main source of discipline, Durkheim begs the question concerning the origins of authority. This criticism is also true of modern theories of punishment that employ the idea of social bonding (see, especially, Braithwaite 1989). Yet in so doing Durkheim admitted that punishment actually *is* necesary to establish social bonds. His reasons for this assertion are most revealing.

### Pain: The Necessary Evil

Durkheim criticized the deterrent use of punishment (both as a specific and general deterrent through threats) according to now familiar arguments. His primary objection stems from the assertion that crime is normal and a natural part of social life (Durkheim 1966, 67, 70). Consequently, punishment cannot serve as a deterrent since all known societies and all healthy societies have crime, and in order to remain healthy society cannot repress crime into nonexistence: "Crime . . . must no longer be conceived as an evil that cannot be too much suppressed" (Durkheim 1966, 72).

However, Durkheim also criticized the "retributive" model, noting that "pain *is* evil, and it is clearly absurd to think that one evil can compensate for another or nullify it" (Durkheim 1925, 165). Furthermore, he argued that punishments do not penetrate into the will because they are external to the individual, and thus treat matters of obedience only superficially. But one may ask, if pain is so evil and so harsh a sensation, what more effective way to penetrate into the innermost soul of the individual? What better method is there to internalize rules?

Durkheim dismissed this idea: he is not concerned with whether or not punishment is internalized—rather his concern was that *authority* should be internalized. Once more, we see Durkheim move beyond the simple cost-benefit approach adopted by the Utilitarians: punishment does not deter because it is a cost, its purpose is to bond people to moral authority. In order to penetrate the will and reinforce authority, punishment must stand for the idea of rules in society. Thus punishment, to Durkheim, was the empirical manifestation of an abstract process and served to express "the external index of feeling that must assert itself in the face of violation" (Durkheim 1925, 167). That is, authority must assert itself at any cost. The content of the violation and the content of the punishment are secondary if not irrelevant. Of prime importance is the emotional disapproval expressed through punishment (for similar thoughts see Braithwaite's (1989) theory of reintegrative shaming). And here we have the very soul, the basis of Durkheim's argument: punishment, even as the manifestation of sociologically abstract processes, lies at the very base of discipline and authority and serves as the empirical manifestation of abstract social processes such as authority and moral order.

Despite this line of reasoning, Durkheim continued to see value in punishment (this may be why he failed to deal with the negative consequences of punishment, since he continually attempted to examine the functions of punishment). In the same passage in which he explained his position on punishment, Durkheim criticized the theory of punishment expounded by Rousseau (1906) and others.

This theory claimed that adults should not impose punishments on children but should instead allow nature to provide the punishment or consequences. Rousseau believed that all acts had their natural consequences; if a child does something wrong, one leaves it to nature to provide the punishment (e.g., "If he is not ready in time, you leave without him"). This was well argued by Rousseau in his famous essay, *Emile* (1906). It is strange that Durkheim could not embrace this philosophy since it seems consistent with his lectures on the sources of duty and the social being (i.e., that it is from nature that order comes, and that by giving oneself up to this natural order, there are no self-imposed constraints).

Yet, even given these similarities, Durkheim harshly criticizes Rousseau's position, and argued that natural consequences sometimes took too long to emerge and resulted in the individuals' inability to link their actions to the punishment.[7] Punishment must include some type of intervention that helps connect actions and consequences. This principle—the principle of celerity—is one of the earmarks of the Utilitarian tradition. Once more, we witness Durkheim shifting between retributive and utilitarian principles, never espousing either view as complete in itself.

And what kind of intervention is appropriate? Durkheim is quite clear that the intervention should be *punitive*:

> It is not a matter of making him suffer, as if suffering involved some sort of mystical virtue, or as if the essential thing were to intimidate or terrorize. Rather, it is a matter of reaffirming the obligation at the moment it is violated, in order to strengthen the sense of duty, both for the guilty party and for those witnessing the offense—those whom the offense tends to demoralize. Every element of the penalty that does not promote this end, and all severity that does not contribute to this end, is bad and should be prohibited. (1925, 182)

This statement is neither wholly utilitarian nor retributive, and again demonstrates Durkheim's debt to both perspectives. We see here that duties should be reinforced (retribution); that punishment has a concrete nature (retribution); that just measures of punishment should be created (retribution); that punishing strengthens the sense of moral duty (utilitarian); and that deterring the offender and the social audience is part of punishment (utilitarianism).

But how far could one go in punishing? How much pain could be applied to rule breakers? Although Durkheim believed corporal punishment should not be employed in school (though its use in the family was another matter!), the logic of his argument suggests that almost *any* amount and type of punishment could be used if it helped establish and reinforce authority. We can think of certain closed institutions and other types of strict organizations that justify extremely severe punishments that instill a sense of duty and respect for authority (e.g., the military, cf., Foucault 1979).

One of Durkheim's main objections to corporal punishment was that it could have an unintended effect: that is, it could result in fear and intimidation rather than reverence for order and authority. Since Durkheim clearly recognized that the consequences of severe punishment often *are* fear and intimidation, he indulged in wishful thinking when he suggested that its use is justified so long as it does not threaten and intimidate. If he embraced punishment, he must also embrace its less desirable consequences, whether wanted or not.

We have thus far argued that Durkheim's theory of control rests upon an undeniably punitive base that consists of an elaborately concealed theory of deterrence as well as portions of the retributive model. We now ask whether this punitive dimension of the theory plays a role in modern control theory.

### The Punitive Basis of Modern Control Theory

If we examine the dominant version of control theory as spelled out in Hirschi's *The Causes of Delinquency* (1969), we find a clear debt to Durkheim. The only major difference bewteen Hirschi and Durkheim is that Hirschi incorporates pieces of Durkheim's *The Division of Labor* (1933) and reverts to an earlier version of Utilitarianism that Durkheim rejected.

Hirschi claimed that there are four elements of the bond: attachment, commitment, belief, and involvement. In actual fact, Hirschi's four elements may be reduced to one: the concept of attachment, which Durkheim painstakingly demonstrated included the remaining "bonds," commitment and belief (see Durkheim 1925).

Hirschi's revision of Durkheim included an avoidance of the issue of "internalization"—that is, the process whereby attachment to society is established, so carefully laid out by Durkheim. Hirschi argued that because this "internal" conscience is not observable (i.e., not measurable) it is invalid theoretically. Yet Hirschi is heavily disposed to accept Durkheim's overall view by quoting him approvingly: "We are moral beings to the extent that we are social beings" (Hirschi 1969, 18).

Hirschi qualifies Durkheim by downplaying the implied internal aspects of Durkheim's view of the "social being," but nevertheless concludes that "To violate a norm is . . . to act contrary to the wishes and expectations of other people" (1969, 18). At all times Hirschi tries to reduce the abstractions of Durkheim's theory to what are, in his opinion, measurable concepts. Thus, he translates "society," a complex concept in Durkheim's work, into "other people." He discards completely Durkheim's fuzzy concept of "will" as a process of internalization that cannot be measured. This constitutes a dramatic departure from Durkheim, who described the process of internalization as manifested in the application of discipline and authority to the child, a process best captured in Hirschi's use of the term "commitment": "Few would deny that men on occasion obey rules simply from fear of the consequences. This rational component of conformity we call commitment" (Hirschi 1969, 20). What closer statement to the idea of deterrence could one get? While Durkheim rejected the notion of using punishment to instill obedience through fear—through deterrence—Hirschi embraces it. In fact, having more or less minimized the role of "internalization" as a control on delinquent deviant behavior, Hirschi is left with little else in terms of the implied psychological state of the actor. In short, Hirschi reduces the individual's psychological processes to the rational calculations involved in commitment. Indeed, the final comment in his chapter on control theory is most telling: "The question is, 'Why don't we do it?' There is much evidence that we would if we dared" (1969, 34). Utilitarians from Hobbes to Bentham, and all modern deterrence advocates, would heartily agree.

Hirschi's version of control theory employs a much stronger utilitarian strategy than Durkheim's. Where Durkheim rejected deterrence as the main objective of punishment (though we saw above that his rejection was more apparent than substantive),

Hirschi holds it out as the appropriate objective, and his recent writings make this even clearer (Hirschi and Gottfredson 1987a, 1987b, 1989; Gottfredson and Hirschi 1987).

Hirschi's treatment of "belief" is not much different. After a lengthy discussion on why people behave in a manner contrary to their beliefs, Hirschi offers this conclusion: "the less a person believes he should obey the rules, the more likely he is to violate them" (1969, 26).

Obedience is the central element of control theory—Durkheim or Hirschi. It matters not what the content of the rules are (according to Durkheim) so long as they are obeyed. According to Hirschi, since the rules are agreed upon by everybody (a kind of primitive consensus theory), all that needs to be done is to demonstrate that some individuals believed in them less, and a sufficient cause to explain rule-breaking behavior is supported.

Thus far Hirschi's control theory suggests (somewhat tautologically) that deviants come from the ranks of the disobedient, and that disobedience is caused by inadequate discipline. There is one final element of control theory introduced by Hirschi to which we now wish to turn our attention: "involvement."

For Durkheim, involvement in social groups was all important in a person becoming a social being, and was so important as to count as the main source of "discipline." In fact, the role of group involvement was to minimize the need for punishment. Hirschi employs the concept of "involvement" in two different ways: involvement through the work *ethic* and involvement through the peer group. First, Hirschi argues that the more time individuals spend in nondelinquent activities—i.e., the more involved the individual—the less likely is delinquency. In this simplified conceptual form, individuals will not have time to get into trouble if they are involved in numerous activities. Involvement, however, has less to do with the idea of establishing the individual as a social being and more to do with another value also strongly countenanced by Durkheim: *work*. Durkheim argued that work—regular work—provided the consistency and security of everyday life. Furthermore, by providing an ordered life, one that was well regulated, the idea of limits was clearly established in the minds of men, and anomie therefore kept at bay. Hirschi does not mention work directly.

Rather, for Hirschi involvement is defined by what it is not—and it is not leisure. In fact, he quotes approvingly the old adage, "idle hands are the devil's workshop," and concludes, "in the end then, the leisure of the adolescent produces a set of values, which, in turn, leads to delinquency." The problem with this position is that it views work simply as a constraint on time while neglecting its other important contributions, especially those related to discipline (cf., Foucault 1979).

Hirschi also argued that involvement with any group, delinquent or not, will militate against delinquency. In order to understand this point we must return to Durkheim. Durkheim was severely taken to task by Piaget (1965) for his failure to consider the importance of peers in establishing respect for rules. This is one area in which Hirschi's conceptualization of the control model exceeds the parameters established by Durkheim.

We demonstrated above that Durkheim believed that the sole source of respect for authority and obedience came from authority itself, especially as applied by teachers against their charges. Piaget took a middle ground on this issue and demonstrated from his intensive interviews with children that respect for authority and rules could be learned within groups of peers, especially peer groups that incorporated different age levels. Hirschi favorably notes this finding, and thus finds support for his idea that so long as one is attached to something social, even if it is a delinquent gang, then one is much less likely to become delinquent.

We may simply pause to ask here: what kind of discipline would emerge from a gang structure? Since gangs have been described as organized on many different lines ranging from highly structured and totalitarian (the Chicano gangs described by Horowitz and Schwartz 1974, for example) to those that are loosely structured (such as Yablonsky's "near group"), this is difficult to determine. However, we may say that gangs that are not leaderless are often structured in a way which ensures that individuals obey the rules of the group or suffer severe consequences from ostracism to physical injury. Indeed, the entire process of gang violence and feuding is based on the use of threats and fear to enforce group loyalty (Thrasher 1927; Suttles 1971) out of a "need" to enforce social rules. Either way, this aspect of control theory supports our general thesis that the theory is based on utilitarian as well as retributive principles.

## The Control Theory of Punishment and the Causes of Delinquency

The most difficult problem for control theory is to establish the extent to which those who are less obedient are less so because of poor discipline, or because they were unable to understand the significance of their punishments. To address this issue we review the connection between poor school performance and delinquency.

One would expect, given control theory's emphasis on discipline (Hirschi 1983) that we would find the most glaring delinquents or sources of delinquency in the school setting. To many, this assumption may seem contrary to the logic of control theory. However, we believe that such a view is completely consistent with control theory for the following reasons.

First, it is in schools that we find a close to totalitarian organization that is designed to utterly control the individual and make him/her submit to social rules or the social will. Second, it is in schools where we also see how totalitarian rules are applied to otherwise "free" individuals. Third, it is also here that regular training, specific punishment for rule breaking and all the other trappings of discipline so well outlined by Durkheim can be found. And fourth, we should expect that those who become delinquent while still in school are those for whom the process of establishing the bond of obedience did not work. While there may be many reasons for the failure of discipline to work with all students, we propose by way of example a theory based on the work of Jules Henry (1963, 1965).

From Henry we extract the idea that in addition to the well-entrenched role of authority in the classroom and the school, there is another source of authority (and hence punishment)—competition. The preoccupation with grading, honors systems, and so on ensures that a large portion of students must see themselves as failures; they have failed to succeed in a competitive struggle with other students in a system that imposes externally validated rules in an apparently impartial atmosphere. Furthermore, since grades are given out at the discretion of teachers, their source of authority is greatly enhanced. Thus, while it is true that corporal punishment has decreased in high schools over the past twenty years, it may nevertheless be argued that the amount and severity of discipline, as evident in the assignment of grades, tracking, and the assignment of individuals to honors and remedial programs, has increased discipline dramatically. Unfortunately, this discipline has the unintended side effect of diminishing the self-worth of students. Since it is in relation to authority that respect develops and from which the idea of an individual as a truly "social being" derives, it follows that the more these individuals are disciplined, the less attached they will become to society (since their social being is degraded). As Hirschi or Matza might say, they become free to deviate.

Control theorists have not attended to this possible interpretation of their theory—that nonpunitive disciplinary methods *sever* rather than form bonds. Rather, they have most often slipped back into a kind of primitive psychological explanation (which Hirschi severely criticized on page 31 of *Causes of Delinquency*), arguing that certain psychological attributes (e.g., low intelligence) explain the failure of individuals to respond appropriately to discipline (Hirschi and Hindelang 1977). In short, control theory specifies that the appropriate response to discipline (to punishment) is *obedience*.

This is an especially strange position for control theorists to adopt given, as we saw above, that they abide by the old utilitarian idea that individuals give up a little of their liberty in order to gain a certain amount of pleasure. But this liberty is given up grudgingly, according to the classic utilitarians. Why should we not conclude that those who commit delinquent acts do so out of belligerence against a society that demands too much obedience, while simultaneously failing to reward its members with adequate doses of "selfhood?" Why, in other words, should we not conclude that this individual is acting rationally, making calculations and coming to the rational conclusion that conforming—that yielding to discipline and authority—is less pleasurable than the freedom of deviation? In Durkheim's view, truly social individuals, of course, could not reach such a conclusion since they valued society above all else. Anything that violated social rules was not rational because it challenged the authority of society and could lead to its downfall. However, Durkheim's insights from *Division of Labor* may come into play here, and we will review these insights shortly. For now, it is important to note that Durkheim's structural model of punishment (*Division*), suggests that deviation is normal and necessary. Therefore, one could also assume that individuals who deviated did so for rational reasons: so that society could have individuals to make example of and thus define the limits of the collective conscience. It may, however, be stretching the point to claim that those who deviate realize that society needs deviants, and that deviants are sacrificing themselves to perform a necessary social function.

The question of whether rational individuals are deterred by punishment, or whether their rationality impels them to violate rules for the long-range benefit of social order leads us to some of the more interesting contradictions within deterrence theory (see below) and control theory. As far as control theory is concerned, it is higly likely—if our above summary is correct—that many socialization processes are responsible for driving individuals into deviance. Thus, the problem may not be whether or not individuals are bonded, but may lie in the very socialization processes used to train individuals and inculcate social values. Such a view of control theory requires that it be recast as a structural model (e.g., see Groves and Sampson 1987; Lynch and Groves 1989, 77–81). Given this interpretation, below we turn to an examination of Durkheim's structural view of punishment for further insights.

### A Control Theory and General Deterrence

So far we have confined our analysis to the problem of control and punishment at the individual level as discussed in *Moral Education*. We began there because it was from that work that modern control theory was primarily derived. As we have seen, in *Moral Education* Durkheim discussed the ability of punishment to generate commitment of the individual to authority which bonded her/him to society. Yet in *The Division of Labor in Society* (1933) *Suicide* (1951) and *The Rules of Sociological Methods* (1966) Durkheim argued that one cannot reduce social to individual facts, or vice versa. Today this is indeed a widely held tenet by sociologists (Maghen 1980). Yet, this is exactly the mistake Durkheim appears to have made in *Moral Education*: to generalize from the individual to the social level.

In *Division*, Durkheim makes an argument that is more consistent with the structural approach he argued for in *Rules*. Here, he argued that punishing criminals reaffirmed or reinforced the moral boundaries and authority of society.[8] In this case, punishment is thought to ensure conformity and increase commitment among noncriminals by strengthening the noncriminals' bonds to society. This appears to be a thinly veiled theory of general deterrence, and recent work has interpreted the theory in this way (see Gottfredson and Hirschi 1990, Hirschi and Gottfredson 1987a, 1987b, 1989). Yet, Durkheim's analysis of the history of punishment (1968, 85–96) demonstrated time and again that punishment is at its core, *retributive*:

> It is error to believe that vengence is but useless cruelty. . . . [V]engence is far from having had the negative and sterile role in the history of mankind which is attributed to it. It is a defensible weapon which has its worth . . . The whole difference [between the punishments of today and yesterday] derives from the fact that it now produces its effects with a much greater understanding of what it does. . . . [P]unishment has remained . . . a work of vengeance. (Durkheim 1968, 87–88)

> [T]he nature of punishment has not been changed in essential. All we can say is that the need of vengeance is better directed today than heretofore. . . . [*Vengeance*] *remains the soul of punishment*.[9] (90, emphasis added)

Notwithstanding this argument, Durkheim still implied that masses of people are made to conform (were deterred) by the spectacle of punishment (for an alternative interpretation of the spectacle of punishment see Foucault 1979; Newman 1985; Rusche and Kirchheimer 1968). Yet, the appearance of utilitarian goals in modern society does not erase the retributive basis of punishment: "Modern penal systems may try to achieve utilitarian objectives, and to conduct themselves rationally and unemotively, but at an underlying level there is still a vengeful, motivating passion which guides punishment and supplies its force" (Garland 1990, 31). As Garland later notes with regard to Durkheim's work, "To think of punishment as a calculated instrument for rational control of conduct is to *miss its essential character*, to mistake *superficial form* for *true content*" (1990, 32, emphasis added).

Examining *all* of Durkheim's work, it becomes clear from that he believed in a hybrid explanation for punishment; one that exposed the retributive underpinnings of punishment, particularly at the structural level, and one that was mixed at the individual level, comprised of retributive and utilitarian underpinnings. The reason Durkheim relied upon such a mixed penal model are revealing. It would appear that Durkheim believed punishment had different effects at different levels of social structure. At the broadest structural level, as in *Division*, we see a retributive model in Durkheim's work, dominated by the idea that vengeance is the soul of punishment (1968, 90), with utilitarian undertones (punishment acts as a general deterrent). At lower levels of social interaction (i.e., the individual level), we see a mixed model, dominated by utilitarian concerns with retributive undertones.

### The Necessity of Penalty: Durkheim's Structural View

At a broad structural level of analysis pursued in *Division*, we again witness Durkheim's distaste for punishment, even though he has acknowledged its usefulness and the strong connection between punishment and retribution. This view is part and parcel of Durkheim's functionalism.

Durkheim believed that punishment, like crime, was not only necessary but functional (1968, 96, 107–9)—a positive social force that contributed to social solidarity and social integration. Such a view, however, overlooks the negative aspects of punishment (what functionalist call its dysfunctional consequences). For example, in order to be effective (i.e., provide control and discipline), modern punishments like imprisonment must divide and label or rely upon panoptic methods of control (Foucault 1979), as well as scientific divisions and classifications (Foucault 1975; Smart 1983). Such a procedure alienates those who come into contact with the system from society, and ensures that bonds will *not* be formed between the criminal and society. Thus, punishing criminals may promote the formation of subcultural (deviant) bonding that drives the criminal further from society. This point of view has long been argued in the punishment literature (Skinner 1953; Bettleheim 1987, 98–110), and informs Foucault's (1979) analysis of the change from corporal punishment to imprisonment, and his argument that corporal punishment has lost its authority—become something "ugly" and repulsive—turning the criminal into "an object of pity and admiration" (1979, 9). Again, it is this "ugly," negative aspect of punishment that control theory fails to come to grips with, especially the idea that punishment might *tear apart* rather than *weave together* the social fabric. For example, if punishment creates boundaries between criminals and noncriminals, this is hardly a process promoting solidarity; It is rather a process of societal division. By calling punishment "normal" Durkheim has watered down its negative connotations and made it look like a positive force, just as in *Moral Education*, where he attempted to make authority look like a positive force by divorcing it from punishment.

The very process of punishment ensures general deterrence of its enduring popularity, for without infractions and the criminals who commit them there would be no one to punish. And with no one to punish, individuals could not serve as examples to others, and thus no general deterrent effect would result. Such a view of punishment as the remedy for crime is ironic in light of Durkheim's view of crime that implies that no society devoid of crimes and punishments can exist:

> Imagine a society of saints, a perfect cloister of exemplary individuals. Crimes, properly so called, will then be unknown; but faults which appear venal to the layman will create the same scandal that the ordinary offense does in ordinary consciousness. (Durkheim 1985, 68–69)

Here Durkheim indulges in the most widely used excuse for visiting punishment on individuals when he claimed that punishing to establish order is somehow more morally acceptable than is vengeance itself. But there is no historical evidence to support the claim that vengeance is any more "primitive" than deterrence (e.g., see Marongiu and Newman 1987) and, as we have noted above, even Durkheim acknowledged the retributive heart of penalty and punishment.

In the end Durkheim ends up with a retributive/deterrent hybrids as an excuse to punish, just as his forebears did in the seventeenth and eighteenth centuries (Newman 1985, 79–124). He advocates the use of punishment because (1) the offenders "deserve it"[10]; (2) the masses have vengeful desires that should be expressed; (3) it promotes bonding; (4) it deters the offender; (5) it deters the social audience; (6) it links actions and their consequences; (7) it reinforces the moral boundary; (8) it reinforces authority and the moral social order.

The harshness of Durkheim's theory of punishment has been hidden by his assertion that punishment will reinforce solidarity and moral boundaries (will bond individuals to the social order). We raise the possibility that punishment may work in the opposite direction, by reinforcing and forming social divisions that are unlikely to be overcome.

That is, of course, if today's punishments have any effect at all and there is some reason to think that they may not. For example, as Foucault (1979) and Newman (1983, 1985) have demonstrated, the "progress" from community level corporal (and very public) punishments to centralized systems of incarceration controlled by the state has removed the individual being punished and the community from the punishment process. Once removed from direct community control, punishment becomes an abstract social process that loses its meaning for the offender and the community. In fact, in its modern form punishment may lose its ability to reinforce the social bond. The current popularity of "community corrections" is a desperate attempt to reproduce the idealistic traditional society of "mechanical solidarity" in an already fragmented society. Unfortunately, punishment seems to have little credibility unless it is concrete; modern punishments are abstract (Newman 1983, 1985).

## Conclusions

In this this paper we have argued that the preoccupation of control theory with crime causation has led to the neglect of an important aspect of this theory: its punitive base and by implication its significance, if any, for penal policy.

We have demonstrated that policies derived from control theory—policies that supposedly would strengthen an individual's bonds to society—are deeply embedded in the idea of punishment as an authoritative instrument. The theory clearly assumes that without punishment an individual—*any* individual—cannot be bonded to society. The policy seems to apply at both the individual and social level, but in different ways.

At the individual level, control theory is primarily a utilitarian, proactive model of punishment: discipline and obedience to authority must be instilled in the individual for the social good, to prevent deviation and to bond to society the individual being punished in order to prevent deviance. Thus, punishment is justifiable *before* deviation, at least at the individual level in Durkheim's analysis.

At the social or macrolevel, control theory presents a punishment model based in retribution that manifests itself as utilitarian concerns. Here individuals are punished to set and maintain social boundaries of acceptable behavior; to exact retribution on individuals; to bond others (those who observe punishment or know of its consequences) more strongly to the social order. Punishments must be both proactive and reactive; proactive to satisfy the utilitarian portions of Durkheim's perspective, and reactive to meet his concerns with the retributive nature of punishment.

The obvious contradictions and complexities of the implications of control theory on punishment suggest that further, more specific, analysis should be done to assess each element of theory, especially its retributive and deterrent aspects. Control theory has dominated criminology for many years as a theory of crime causation, and more recently, as a theory of utilitarian origins (Gottfredson and Hirschi 1990; Hirschi and Gottfredson 1987a, b, c; 1989). It is time to give serious attention to its implications as a theory promoting retribution.

## Notes

1. Although much has been written about Durkheim in general, little specifically analyzes his theory of punishment. See Nisbet (1974, 221–27) and Garland (1990, 23–82) for overviews.
2. Durkheim's concern with this issue is apparent early on in his writings: "The types of conduct or thought are not only external to the individual but are, moreover, endowed with coercive power, by virtue of which they impose themselves upon him, independent of his individual will" (Durkheim 1895:2).
3. We are unaware of any published research bearing directly on the practical application of control theory. While there are surely some studies, there is nothing that compares to projects such as "Mobilization for Youth" derived from strain and opportunity theory.

4. For example, see Illich (1971). The work of anthropologist Jules Henry (1965) lays bare the totalitarian structure of schools and families. See also, Henry (1963); and Bowles and Gintis (1976).
5. "When I fulfill my obligations as brother, husband, or citizen, when I execute my contracts, I perform duties which are defined externally to myself and to my acts . . . in law and custom. *Even if* they conform to my own sentiments and I feel their reality subjectively, such reality is still *objective*, for I did not create them" (Durkheim 1895, 1).
6. It is interesting that Durkheim makes this argument because he displayed a great displeasure with retributive punishments even though he endorsed various aspects of retribution throughout his writings (e.g., Durkheim, 1966, 66, 70, 71).
7. Durkheim believed that one could not take such risks: "The educator must intervene and link to the rules of discipline sanctions that anticipate those in later life" (1925, 173).
8. "Penal law . . . does not say . . . as civil law does: Here is the duty; but rather, Here is the punishment" (Durkheim 1968, 75).
9. Durkheim asserted that "[Punishment consists of a passionate reaction . . . especially in less cultivated societies . . . [where] primitive people punish for the sake of punishing . . . and making [the criminal] suffer . . . without seeking any advantage for themselves" (1968, 85–86). This assertion again demonstrates Durkheim's commitment to a retributive understanding of penalty.
10. Durkheim continually employs an orthodox retributive position arguing that punishment "makes its presence felt by the tendency to surpass in severity the action against which it is reacting" (1968, 86; for further discussion see Newman 1985, 189–221).

## References

Becker, Ernest. 1973. *Denial of Death*. New York: The Free Press.
Bettleheim, Bruno. 1987. *A Good Enough Parent: A Book on Child Rearing*. New York: Vintage Books.
Blumstein, A., J. Cohen, and D. Nagin, eds. 1978. *Deterrence and Incapacitation: Estimating the Effects of Criminal Sanctions on Crime Rates*. Washington, D.C.: National Academy of Sciences.
Braithwaite, John. 1989. *Crime, Shame and Reintegration*. Cambridge: Cambridge University Press.
Bowles, S. and Gintis, H. 1976. *Schooling in Capitalist America: Educational Reform and the Contradictions of Economic Life*. New York: Basic Books.
Colvin, M. and J. Pauly. 1983. "A Critique of Criminology: Toward an Integrated Structural-Marxist Theory of Delinquency Production." *American Journal of Sociology* 90, 3: 513–51.
Durkheim, E. 1951 [1897]. *Suicide*. New York: The Free Press.
Durkheim, E. 1961 [1925]. *Moral Education*. New York: The Free Press. (First published as L'Education Morale, Librarie Felix Alcan, 1925.)
Durkheim, E. 1966 [1895]. *The Rules of Sociological Method*. New York: The Free Press.

Durkheim, E. 1968 [1893]. *Division of Labor in Society*. New York: Free Press.

Foucault, Michel. 1979. *Discipline and Punish*. New York: Vintage.

Foucault, Michel. 1975. *The Birth of the Clinic: An Archeology of Medical Perception*. New York: Vintage Books.

Freud, S. 1961. *Civilization and Its Discontents,* trans. J. Strachey. New York: W. W. Norton.

Garland, David. 1990. *Punishment and Modern Society*. Chicago: University of Chicago Press.

Gottfredson, M . and T. Hirschi, eds. 1987. *Positive Criminology*. Beverly Hills, Cal.: Sage.

Groves, W. Byron and Robert J. Sampson. 1987. "Traditional Contributions to Radical Criminology." *Journal of Research in Crime and Delinquency* 24, 3: 181–214.

Henry, Jules. 1963. *Culture Against Man*. New York: Vintage.

Henry, Jules. 1965. *Pathways to Madness*. New York: Vintage.

Hirschi, T. 1969. *The Causes of Delinquency*. Berkeley: University of California Press.

Hirschi, T. 1983. "Crime and the Family," In James Q. Wilson (ed.), *Crime and Public Policy*. San Francisco: ICS Press.

Hirschi, Travis and Michael Gottfredson. 1989. "The Significance of White-Collar Crime for a General Theory of Crime." *Criminology* 27, 2: 359–71.

Hirschi, Travis and Michael Gottfredson. 1987a. "Causes of White-Collar Crime." *Criminology* 25, 4: 949–74.

Hirschi, Travis and Michael Gottfredson. 1987b. "A General Theory of Crime for Cross-National Criminology." Paper presented at the Fifth Asian-Pacific Conference on Juvenile Delinquency, Taipei, Taiwan.

Hirschi, T. and M. Hindelang. 1977. "Intelligence and Delinquency: A Revisionist Review." *American Sociological Review* 42: 592–87.

Horowitz, I. C. and Schwartz, G. 1974. "Honor, Normative Ambiguity and Gang Violence." *American Sociological Review* 39: 238–51.

Illich, Ivan. 1971. *Deschooling Society*. New York: Harper and Row.

Kornhauser, R. 1978. *Social Sources of Delinquency*. Chicago: University of Chicago Press.

Lynch, Michael J. and W. Byron Groves. 1989. *A Primer in Radical Criminology*. New York: Harrow and Heston.

Mayhen, B. 1980. "Structuralism versus Individualism: Part I, Shadow Boxing in the Dark." *Social Forces* 59: 335–75.

Marongiu, P. and Graeme Newman. 1987. *Vengenace: The Fight Against Injustice*. Totowa, N.J.: Littlefield Adams.

Marx, K. 1977. *Capital,* vol. 1. New York: Inkunanne Publishers.

Melossi, D. 1982. "Punishment and Social Structure." In A. Platt and P. Takagi (eds.), *Punishment and Penal Discipline*. San Francisco: Crime and Social Justice Associates.

Melossi, D. and M. Pavarini. 1980. *The Prison and the Factory*. London: Macmillan.

Newman, Graeme. 1983. *Just and Painful*. New York: Macmillan.

Newman, Graeme. 1985. *The Punishment Response*. New York: Harrow and Heston.

Nisbet, R. 1974. *The Sociology of Emile Durkheim*. New York: Oxford.

Piaget, J. 1965. *Moral Judgement of the Child,* trans. Marjorie Gabain. New York: The Free Press.

Reiss, Albert J. 1956. "Delinquency as the Failure of Personal Social Controls." *American Sociological Review* 16: 196–207.

Rieff, P. 1961. *Freud the Mind of the Moralist*. New York: Doubleday.

Rousseau, J. J. 1963 [1906]. *Emile*. London: Dent.

Rusche, G. and O. Kirchheimer. 1968 [1939]. *Punishment and Social Structure*. New York: Russell and Russell.

Skinner, B. F. 1953. *Science and Human Behavior*. New York: Macmillan.

Smart, Barry. 1983. "On Discipline and Social Regulation: A Review of Foucault's Genealogical Analysis." In D. Garland and P. Young (eds.), *The Power to Punish*. London: Heinemann.

Suttles, G. 1971. *The Social Order of the Slum*. Chicago: University of Chicago Press.

Thrasher, F. M. 1927. *The Gang*. Chicago: University of Chicago Press.

Toby, Jackson, 1957. "Social Disorganization and Stake in Conformity: Complementary Factors in the Predatory Behavior of Hoodlums." *Journal of Criminal Law, Criminology and Police Science*. 48: 12–17.

Wilson, Everett. 1974. "Introduction" to Durkheim, E., *Moral Education*. New York: The Free Press.

# 11

# Power-Control vs Social-Control Theories of Common Delinquency: A Comparative Analysis

*Gary F. Jensen*

One of the most popular works on crime and delinquency in the 1970s and 1980s was Travis Hirschi's *Causes of Delinquency* (1969). Hirschi elaborated a "social control" theory of delinquency that could be contrasted with competing dominant perspectives at that time (cultural deviance and strain theories) and conducted what he considered to be crucial tests of the theory. The central assumption in social control theory is that the weaker the bonds to conventional people, goals, beliefs, or activities the greater the probability of breaking laws. Youths are relatively "free" to commit delinquent acts when the social and moral costs are minimal. Hirschi draws most heavily on a Durkheimian tradition wherein rates of deviance are attributed to variations in the intensity of social and moral bonds.

Earlier control theories with a similar emphasis on barriers rather than motivation were proposed by Reiss (1951), Toby (1957), Nye (1958), and Briar and Piliavin (1965). Youths who were free from personal and social controls (Reiss), external or internal controls (Nye) or who had few "stakes in" (Toby) or "commitments to" (Briar and Piliavin) conformity were candidates for involvement in delinquency. The range of specific barriers to delinquency varied but all of these theories included both external constraints and internal constraints, including emotional bonds to other people and conventional institutions and acceptance of conventional moral standards or "norms."

In more recent years a different type of control theory has been proposed, drawing on Marxist and neo-Marxist traditions and terminology. John Hagan, A. R. Gillis, and John Simpson propose a theory of common delinquency that uses the concept of "power" to make predictions about class, gender and their interaction in the explanation of what they call "common delinquency." This "power-control" theory has been elaborated in subsequent works (Hagan, Gillis, and Simpson 1987) and in the award-winning monograph *Structural Criminology* (1989). As they state it, "the core assumption of our theory is that the presence of power and the absence of control create conditions of freedom that permit common forms of delinquency (Hagan, Gillis, and Simpson 1985, 1174)."[1] They test their theory using data from Toronto and have responded to criticisms, ultimately concluding that "the essence of the theory endures (Hagan, Gillis, and Simpson 1990)."

However, such confidence is considerably premature for several reasons. First, if the essence of a theory were the ability of its "core assumption" to explain prior findings and generate verifiable predictions about the relevance of racial, occupational, and gender-based stratification to delinquency, then (as will be elaborated below) the theory has major problems. It yields predictions about structural and individual correlates that are contradicted by research.

Second, since prior "social control" theories explain delinquency in terms of the absence of control, the unique property of their theory is the *addition* of "power" to control theory. This addition requires demonstration that the presence of power has an impact on delinquency independent of the "absence of control" since the latter is already central to social control theory. The theory has to be judged in terms of the addition of power rather than in terms of variables introduced by control theorists decades ago.

Third, the theory has to be judged in terms of the variables omitted in comparison to other theories as well. Power-control

theory, like other structural theories emphasizing external constraints and opportunity (i.e., rational choice and routine activities
theories), does not include moral or normative variables. This
property of the theory not only sets it apart from social control
theories but differentiates it from social learning theory (Akers
1977; Akers et al. 1978), cultural deviance theory (Sutherland and
Cressey 1974; Miller 1958) and all subcultural or contractultural
theories (e.g. Cohen 1955; Cloward and Ohlin 1960). Neither does
power-control theory include the wide range of social bonds and
institutions characteristic of other versions of "social" control
theory. The emphasis is on parental power and family relationships.
Thus, the explanatory merits of power-control theory compared to
prior theory will require a demonstration that power has to be
added and that other variables can be omitted with little or no loss
in explanatory power.

## Power-Control Theory as a General Theory

When first proposed, power-control theory was presented as a
derivative of a classical criminological theory developed by William
Bonger (1916). The first article in the series was presented as the
first application of Marxian ideas to delinquency to be empirically
tested and the first to address the relationship between gender and
delinquency (1985, 1173). That first analysis dealt with class defined
in terms of power relationships, gender and class-gender interactions. Subsequent analyses (1987, 1990) have concentrated on gender, patriarchy as inferred from household class categories and
patriarchy based on power relationships between mothers and
fathers in high status neighborhoods.

There are two important points to note with regard to the theory
as originally presented. For one, while criminologists were criticized for neglecting classical criminological theory, power-control
theory is inconsistent with the same classical criminological theory.
The core assumption of power-control theory leads them to propose
a positive relationship between class and delinquency whereas
William Bonger and other applications of Marxist ideas posit a
negative relationship (Greenberg 1979; Colvin and Pauly 1983). In
fact, one of the applications cited, Colvin and Pauley (1983), uses

similar neo-Marxist notions involving power-relationships in occupations to explain why the obey classes have *higher* delinquency
rates than children in the command classes.

Hagan, Gillis, and Simpson deal with this inconsistency in a
footnote where it is suggested that class might be negatively related
to crimes more serious than those measured in their study. Of
course, their measure of common delinquency included activities
that would be recorded as grand theft, assault, and motor vehicle
theft as well as less serious offenses and their own data show no
meaningful variation by seriousness of offense. Neither their hypothesis about class nor their limitation of the hypothesis to common delinquency can be derived from the traditions cited.

The second important point with regard to the theory as originally presented is that its core assumption was used to generate
integrated propositions about class itself as well as about gender
and class-gender interactions. Class was predicted to be positively
related to delinquency because children of the command classes
were hypothesized to have the power to deviate with impunity,
were freer from both formal and informal controls and were bigger
risk-takers than children in the obey classes as a product of socialization. In subsequent work this image was presented as particularly applicable to boys since households where fathers were in the
command class and mothers were in obey classes were patriarchal,
controlling girls but socializing boys to be risk-takers and setting
them free to deviate.

In a recent critique of power-control theory, Jensen and Thompson (1990) ask, "What's class got to do with it?" They argue that
power-control theorists have not shown class to be an important
predictor of delinquency among either girls or boys whether measured in terms of power or in more traditional ways. Hagan, Gillis,
and Simpson respond by criticizing the class measures used by
Jensen and Thompson but gloss over the central criticism that class
has trivial effects in the power-control theorist's own data. Moreover, Singer and Levine (1987) have measured class in the exact
same fashion as Hagan, Gillis, and Simpson and their data fail to
show a significant positive relationship between class and delinquency and yield the opposite class-gender interactions. Finally,

Hagan, Gillis, and Simpson limit their most recent analysis (1990) to high status neighborhoods and class is not treated as a variable. In sum, their theory predicts a relationship between class and delinquency contrary to that predicted by Bonger and other applications of Marxist ideas. It predicts relationships that have not been replicated in subsequent tests no matter how class is measured. With regard to predictions about class and delinquency the essence of the theory is empirically unsubstantiated.

When applied to dimensions of stratification other than gender, the core assumption generates predictions contrary to research as well. If children of advantaged command classes are freer to deviate than children in the obey classes, then whites should be freer to deviate than blacks. Research using nearly the same indices of delinquency as Hagan, Gillis, and Simpson have shown either no relationship or higher delinquency rates for blacks. In fact, the very research cited by power-control theorists as support for using regression techniques and interval level measures of delinquency (Elliott and Ageton 1980) reports race differences contrary to power-control theory. The only offenses where whites exceed blacks are status offenses and the least risky forms of theft. *Contrary to power-control theory* blacks are greater risk-takers than whites. Race is ignored in the power-control theorist's own tests despite the obvious implication of the theory that whites should have higher rates than blacks.

In sum, power-control theory generates hypotheses about race and class that are negated by most theory and research. The gender-class interaction they propose has not been found in other tests (Singer and Levine 1987) and the pattern revealed in their own data is not uniformly supportive of their theory (Jensen and Thompson 1990). Hence, the gender difference in delinquency is the only pattern predicted on the basis of their core assumption and that difference has been predicted and/or explained by a variety of alternative sociological perspectives. In fact, the relationship between gender and delinquency has been shown to be very weak when measures of activities, commitments, and social bonds are controlled without introducing specifications by class (See Jensen and Eve 1976).

## Distinguishing Power From the Absence of Control

The absence of control has been central to social control theories of delinquency for close to four decades (Reiss 1951; Nye 1958; Toby 1957; Briar and Piliavin 1965; Hirschi 1969). Moreover, researchers have added variables such as perceived risk of punishment (Minor 1977; Johnson 1979) and have shown variations in external and internal control to be relevant to gender differences in delinquency (Jensen and Eve 1976). Thus, to qualify as a distinctive theory, power-control theory has to conceptualize and operationalize "power" as distinct from the absence of control. If power *is* inferred from the absence of control alone, then the theory is not unique and the concept of power is redundant.

Consistent with accepted definitions of power (See Gibbs 1989) Hagan, Gillis, and Simpson measure parents' occupational power in terms of freedom from control by others as well as the ability to command others. Children in such command class households are allegedly subject to fewer external constraints and are socialized into entrepreneurial risk-taking. Their privileged status is also supposed to lower the risk of apprehension and punishment. Yet, the emphasis when extending the theory to youth is on freedom from control rather than the reproduction of power relationships. If parents' command status at work is reproduced in control relationships between parents, then why is it not reproduced in parent-child relationships as well? If father or mother has power (i.e., control others) at work, why is it not reproduced in greater control of children (i.e., power rather than control)? If youth are being prepared for command-class futures, then command-class parents could prepare them for such futures by allowing them to have influence within the family rather than controlling them. Similarly, command-class parents may reproduce their power by encouraging their childrens' exercise of power in other contexts such as school.

Both the core assumption that power is positively related to crime and the assumption that parental power relationships are reproduced in their children's characteristics imply that juveniles who have command status over others should have higher rates of common delinquency than juveniles who lack such command status. If control of others is central to parental command status, then it should be "reproduced" in some form among their children other than through mere freedom. In fact, command class of parents is depicted as important to juveniles (especially boys) because they are prepared by parents for future command class careers. Boys are depicted as reproducing father's command status and increases in mother's power is supposed to increase girl's delinquency through similar processes.

However, power-control theory is as subject to question when considering power and delinquency among juveniles as it is when considering race and class in relation to delinquency. If we consider characteristics of youth from which legitimate power might be inferred (i.e., characteristics of youth that parallel adult command status), then most prior research is contrary to the theory. For example, high school dropouts are not likely to be destined for command status careers, nor to come from command-status families. Yet, dropouts have significantly higher rates of subsequent criminal conduct than juveniles who stay in school (Thornberry, Moore, and Christenson 1985). If command-class families are raising their children to take risks and setting them free to do so, then youths who aspire towards command-status futures should have higher rates of delinquency than those who do not. If research on delinquency and college and occupational aspirations are considered, then the theory will have to explain why youths who exhibit the prerequisite aspirations for such futures have lower rather than higher rates of delinquency (See Hirschi 1969 and Hindelang 1973). Moreover, if grades are correlated with parental status, then it appears that youths with the highest potential for such futures are least likely to engage in delinquency (Hirschi 1969; Hindelang 1973; Johnson 1979; Paterson and Dishion 1985). Since school sports can also serve as a source of status and power we would expect that high school athletes would have higher rates of delinquency than nonathletes but what little research there is suggests either no difference or an inhibiting effect among obey-class youth (Shaefer 1969). There may be sources of popularity and power in adolescent society such as money and cars (Hirschi 1969; Cullen et al. 1985) that facilitate some forms of delinquency but they would have to be shown to affect delinquency through their association with power over others rather than through freedom from parental or adult control.

Research on family power and delinquency is inconsistent with power-control theory as well. Such research does enable a separation between "freedom" from parental control and power. Consistent with social-control theory, youths in families where they are totally free from adult control have very high rates of delinquency. In fact, it was freedom from parental control that led Bonger to predict a higher rate of crime for children in disadvantaged classes. However, as noted above, freedom from control does not necessarily imply any level of control over others. Children in families where they have input into family decisions, where power is "shared" to some degree, have lower rates of delinquency than children in families where they feel they make no difference (Nye 1958). Youth who are free from such controls do not have power in the sense implied by parallel notions of occupational command status.

Many of the characteristics of youth and their families that inhibit delinquency can be argued to be more common among youth whose parents are in command status occupations than among youth whose parents are in the obey classes. Power-control theory ignores the deviance-inhibiting side of command class membership stressed in other applications of Marxist ideas. Based on the same neo-Marxist framework, Colvin and Pauley argue that children of the obey classes have higher rates of delinquency than children from command classes because their parents are likely to use direct and punitive forms of control that are less effective than the types of indirect and normative control emphasized in command-class families. Command-class youth are depicted as subject to greater normative constraints than obey-class youth. As they state it "The more coercive this structure of control, the more negative the bonds produced in the child (537)" and "the coerciveness of family control structures, conditioned by parents' work experiences, contributes at least indirectly to the production of delinquency" (1983, 537).

Moreover, contrary to power-control theory, close parental supervision—taken as an indicator of lack of power—can be interpreted as a correlate of preparation for command-class futures. To quote Marwell (1966, 46) "Close supervision is usually part of a pattern of training and grooming children for power in other contexts. It is supervised instruction and practice in skills and habits that will pay off in school and other settings—the price the child pays early for added dividends in power later on." In short, the types of control and socialization styles likely to predominate in command-class families should decrease delinquency relative to obey-class families. Thus, even if there is greater training for "risk taking" in a capitalist-entrepreneurial sense as argued by power-control theorists, there may also be greater training relevant to other prerequisites for command-class futures such as academic achievement, commitment to distant goals and avoiding trouble—prerequisites that inhibit delinquency.

To summarize, power-control theorists have not shown the presence of power to add to the explanation of delinquency independent of the absence of control. Indeed, what evidence there is cannot be predicted from their core assumption. Moreover, the exact opposite predictions are derived from other applications of the same ideas—applications that take into account different forms of socialization and control in different classes. It is not surprising that class should make so little difference in the results of delinquency research when totally contrary predictions can be derived by focusing on different aspects of class. If the causal forces generating such diverse possibilities were all at work, we might anticipate that the most common finding would be little or no relationship between class and delinquency.

## Variables Omitted

A third contrast between social control and power control theory is the focus of power control theory on supervision and risk as compared to the wider range of controlling forces characterizing social control theory. For example, Hagan, Gillis, and Simpson have no normative or belief variables in power control theory. The theory posits that youths enjoy risk taking to variable degrees and vary in their perceptions of risks of punishment. Variations in normative socialization or acceptance of the law as morally binding are not included. Yet, such normative variables are not logically excluded from the theory. "Ideology" is a controlling and constraining force in other Marxist criminologies (See Young 1975) and the notion of "false consciousness" can encompass acceptance of values, norms, and beliefs that serve the interests of dominant groups. The view that people can be controlled to some degree by what they are taught to believe is perfectly consistent with a Marxist approach. Hagan, Gillis, and Simpson provide no justification for ignoring belief variables.[3]

Aspirations and commitments are ignored as well. Again, such variables are not inconsistent with a Marxist perspective. From a Marxist perspective youth are part of a surplus labor force that is controlled to some degree by the promise of better things to come (See Schwendinger and Schwendinger 1976 and Greenberg 1979). Those who learn to wait patiently while pursuing good grades, degrees, and training will be most likely to succeed. Girls who defer marriage and children until they meet the most promising candidates for economic success will have a better life than those who prematurely make such choices. Those who pursue the status indicators used to propel people upward in the system will be rewarded for such attainment. Commitments to such conventional goals are generally presumed to inhibit crime and delinquency, at least to some degree. Of course, all such arguments implicitly assume a negative relationship between class and delinquency that may be one of the reasons they are not included in power-control theory. Variables that traditionally have been presumed to be positively related to class and negatively related to delinquency are not readily encompassed by a theory proposing a positive association between class and delinquency.

Finally, the focus in power-control theory as formulated is on parental supervision and control as compared to the broader focus of social-control theory on conventional people and institutions. Social-control theory does stress parental supervision and attachment to parents as important to the explanation of delinquency but includes attachments and commitments involving teachers and school as well. Since power-control theory is concerned with linking class dominance to household dominance, the focus is on parents and the impact of household patriarchy on gender differences. The reproduction of class dominance and patriarchy in other institutions could be incorporated into the theory but, in its present form, the emphasis is on the household.

The omission of such variables is not a serious problem unless they have been shown to be relevant to explaining delinquency and for explaining the relevance of other correlates. In the case of moral or normative variables not only are they important for explaining delinquency but an important unresolved controversy is whether structural or interactional variables have an impact on delinquency that *is not* mediated by normative variables. In 1982 Ross Matsueda mounted a challenge to social-control theory by showing that when latent structure analysis is used the all other variables studied were indirectly related to delinquency through their impact on the types of subcultural "definitions" stressed in cultural-deviance differential-association theory. Parental supervision was found to make a difference for delinquency because youth who were supervised were more likely to define law breaking in unfavorable moral terms. More recent analyses (Matsueda and Heimer 1987) report similar findings with regard to normative variables. Variation in acceptance of conventional and unconventional moral standards is crucial to the explanation of delinquency and the impact of other variables on delinquency. If such findings are problematic for social-control theory (because it posits that nonnormative bonds have independent relevance to explaining delinquency), then they constitute an even more serious threat to power-control theory where only external constraints and risk-related utilities are included.

While family relationships are correlated with experiences and bonds in other contexts measures of performance and attachment at school have been found to be independently related to common delinquency (e.g., Hirschi 1969; Johnson 1979; Wiatrowski et al. 1981). Indeed, some of the research suggests that school variables and moral beliefs mediate the effect of family and structural variables on delinquency. If school variables have an effect on delinquency independent of the family and class background, then theories positing such effects fare better in that regard than theories limiting control to the family. Moreover, as noted above, most measures of a youth's command-class standing in school (i.e., occupation of legitimate positions involving power over others) would likely yield results contrary to power-control theory.

## Explaining Gender Differences

In response to Jensen and Thompson's question "What's class got to do with it?", Hagan, Gillis and Simpson chide their critics for failing to ask "What's sex got to do with it?" Of course, the relevance of class to delinquency is a major controversy in criminology while very few criminologists have challenged the relevance of gender. Gender is a significant correlate of common delinquency and an even stronger correlate of serious delinquency (see Jensen and Rojek 1980). Not only is gender an accepted correlate of delinquency but it has been explained by every major theory as well. Moreover, it has already been shown (Jensen and Eve 1976) that much of the relation between gender and self-reported delinquency can be explained by variations in social control.

Class differences and gender-class interactions, not gender differences per se, are the source of controversy and it is claims about those specific issues that have not been replicated. If gender differences were the focus, then power control theory has to be assessed in comparison to other explanations. For example, competing sociological theories include "normative" or "moral" variables in the form of "beliefs," (Hirschi), definitions (Sutherland and Creesey, Matsueda), normative learning (Akers), subcultural or contracultural values and norms (Miller, Cohen). In earlier research, Jensen and Eve (1976) reduced the variance in self-reported delinquency attributable to gender to one or two percent by introducing measures of attachment, commitment, activities, and beliefs. Power control theory explains some portion of the gender difference with parental supervision, perceptions of risk and taste for risk taking. However, it has not been shown that such variables explain the gender difference better than variables derived from other theories. At present, there is no reason to accept power-control theory as a superior explanation of gender differences when compared to social control, social learning, or a variety of other prior theories.

## Summary

By identifying the unique characteristics of power-control theory in comparison to other theories, especially social-control theory, we have attempted a preliminary assessment of the theory based on prior research and research on common delinquency conducted by power-control theorists.

The most crucial difference is reflected in the name assigned the theory. Power-control theory proposes to add power to the explanation of delinquency and to link delinquency to parental occupational power. However, unless power is clearly and operationally differentiated from weak social control, power-control theory cannot be distinguished from social control theory. Since such differentiation is lacking in power-control research and prior research implies alternative possibilities, we can conclude that power has not been demonstrated to explain delinquency in the manner proposed.

Second, if the variables stressed in social-control theory but omitted from power-control theory have significant and independent effects on delinquency and contribute to the explanation of differences among demographic categories, then social-control theory would be preferable in terms of explanatory power. Since the literature suggests that such variables are important and do contribute to the explanation of delinquency and sociodemographic variations in delinquency, social-control theories and other theories including such variables are empirically superior.

Third, if the limited type of controls stressed by power-control theorists are the only controls necessary for an adequate explanation of delinquency and other control theory inhibitors can be omitted without a loss in explanatory power, then power-control theorists would have made a contribution by specifying prior control theory. They would still have to differentiate power from freedom to become more than a specification of prior theory.

In sum, when attempts to test the theory are considered together with existing research we have to conclude that, contrary to their claims, the "essence" of power-control threory does not "endure." The essence of the theory should be those characteristics that differentiate if from prior theory. It predicts that sociodemographic categories with power will have the highest rates of delinquency. There is little support for this proposition and racial differences are contrary to it. No evidence is provided to support the argument that the presence of power facilitates delinquency independent of freedom from control. Finally, there is no evidence that the gender differences in delinquency has been explained any better than it was explained years ago using variables derived from prior theories.

Since the variables distinguishing social control theories (as well as many other types of theories such as social learning theory) and power-control theory have not been included simultaneously in comparative tests we cannot say which applies best to the gender difference. Progress in explaining delinquency and the gender difference requires a return to the agenda of comparative and crucial tests started by Hirschi in the late 1960s. Without such comparative analysis we can extend the question asked in other critical work and challenge power-control theorists to provide a better answer to the question "What's power got to do with it?" We already knew that freedom from control had a great deal to do with common delinquency.

## Concluding Observations on Class and Delinquency

The most iconoclastic claim characterizing power-control theory is that command-class membership is positively related to common delinquency. The criminological debate over social class and criminality has most often hinged on whether there is an inverse relationship or none. Attempts to defend the importance of class against claims that the relationship is a myth have defended a negative relationship. In contrast, power-control theory posits a positive relationship based on arguments about power, control, and risk taking.

We have seen that other theories with a similar heritage posit negative relationships based on other correlates of command-class membership. Prerequisites likely to be stressed for command-class occupations in socialization of children (e.g., achievement, preparing for college, homework, leadership) inhibit delinquency. If we consider measures of adolescent power defined in terms similar to those embodied in command-class occupations, the theory is even more problematic since measures of legitimate power over others are likely to be negatively related to common delinquency.

If contrary preditions can be derived from different ideas within the same theoretical framework, then it is plausible to propose that class will enter into weak positive, negative, or null relationships with measures of common (and uncommon) delinquency, depending on the balance of countervailing influences. Command-class membership can set people free to break the law through some mechanisms and constrain people from breaking laws through other mechanisms. Preparation of youth for command-class futures may encourage delinquency through socialization into command-class norms of entreepreneurial risk taking but discourage delinquency through other socialization processes affecting aspirations, academic, and social performance and a variety of other types of control.

There has been no systematic development of a neo-Marxist theory in which a variety of "potentially" countervailing mechanisms are identified. We have suggested ways in which variables central to social-control theory fit within such a framework. While other critics (See Gibbs 1989) have noted that Marxists and neo-Marxits theories of crime are typically control theories of crime no one has delineated the full implications of diverse arguments about class defined in terms of power relationships.

There has been no research simultaneously varying measures of class and delinquency as well as measuring the full range of intervening mechanisms that have been introduced individually to advance contrary predictions about class and delinquency. It is completely possible that contrary theories survive and are repeatedly resurrected because the proposed mechanisms are real but countered by contrary processes that are equally real. Thus, while identification of crucial differences and comparative tests are vital for adjudicating among competing ideas in terms of their general explanatory power, identification of countervailing mechanisms could unravel the criminological mystery surrounding social class and delinquency.

This manuscript is a revised version of a paper presented at the Annual Convention of the American Society of Criminology, Baltimore, Maryland, 1990.

## Notes

1. The concept of power has been introduced into earlier explanations of delinquency. For example, in addressing presumed higher rates of delinquency

New Directions in Criminological Theory

among lower-class youths, Gerald Marwell 1966, 44) argued nearly twenty-five years ago that "middle-class adolescents simply have more rewards at their command than lower-class children, particularly in the form of money, and thus are not as powerless." The economic and political "marginality" *or lack of power* of adolescents in Western capitalist systems is introduced as the major source of *high* rates of delinquency among adolescents in other Marxist theories (Schwendinger and Schwendinger 1976; Greenberg 1979). Thus, whether at the individual or aggregate level high probabilities of delinquency have been attributed by others to a lack of power.

2. Another contrast between social control and power control theory is the introduction of "tastes for risk" in power control theory. Social control theory was proposed as an *amotivational* theory and did not require that some specific motivation be introduced into the explanation of delinquency. While enjoyment of risk taking might be one of the many diverse and common sources of the motivation to deviate, such variables are not accorded explanatory significance as compared to the strength of barriers. The inclusion of such a variable in power control theory reflects the attempt of the theory to link control to class and household dominance in a capitalist society. Children of dominant classes and boys in particular are most likely to be encouraged to take risks and are, allegedly, more likely to believe they can do so with impunity. Since power entails the ability to control others and freedom from control by others, the powerful are freer to take risks with impunity. However, this variable has also been included in theories of delinquency that do not require a relation between class and tastes for risk or class and delinquency—social-learning theory (Akers 1977; Akers et al. 1979) and utility theory as delineated by Tittle (1977).

3. In a recent longitudinal, latent-structure analysis of the relation between belief and minor forms of deviance Matsueda (1989) finds little relation between the two. However, while he views such findings as contrary to Hirschi's argument that the correlates of minor and serious deviance are the same he does not view the findings as a demonstration of the irrelevance of moral beliefs to more serious crimes. Moreover, since power-control theorists have tested their theory using cross-sectional data, findings based on cross-sectional research are a legitimate basis for comparison with social control theory. Longitudinal results are potentially as problematic for power-control theory as social control theory.

# References

Akers, R. L. 1977. *Deviant Behavior: A Social Learning Approach*, Belmont, Cal.: Wadsworth.

———, M.D. Krohn, L. Lanza-Kaduce, and M. Radosevich. 1978. "Social Learning and Deviant Behavior." *American Sociological Review* 44 (August): 636–55.

Bonger, W. 1916. *Criminality and Economic Conditions*. Boston: Little, Brown and Company.

Briar, S., and I. Piliavin. 1965. "Delinquency, Situational Inducements, and Commitments to Conformity." *Social Problems* 13 (1): 35–45.

Cernkovich, S. A. 1978. "Evaluating Two Models of Delinquency Causation." *Criminology* 16: 335–52.

Cloward, R. A. and L. E. Ohlin. 1960. *Delinquency and Opportunity*. New York: Free Press.

Cohen, A. K. 1956. *Delinquent Boys*. New York: Free Press.

Colvin, M. and J. Pauley. 1983. "A Critique of Criminology: Toward an Integrated Structural Marxist Theory of Delinquency Production." *American Journal of Sociology* 89: 513–55.

Cullen, F. T., M. T. Larson, and R. A. Mathers. 1985. "Having Money and Delinquency Involvement." *Criminal Justice and Behavior* 12 (June): 171–92.

Elliott, D. S. and S. S. Ageton. 1980. "Reconciling Race and Class Differences in Self-Reported and Official Estimates of Delinquency." *American Sociological Review* 45: 95–110.

Gibbs, J. P. 1989. *Control: Sociology's Central Notion*. Urbana: University of Illinois Press.

Giordano, P., S. Cernkovich, and M. Pugh. 1986. "Friendships and Delinquency." *American Journal of Sociology* 91: 1170–1202.

Greenberg, D. 1979. "Delinquency and the Age Structure of Society." Pp. 586–620 in *Criminology Review Yearbook*, S. Messinger and E. Bittner (eds.). Beverly Hills, Cal.: Sage Publications.

Hagan, J. 1989. *Structural Criminology*. New Brunswick, N.J.: Rutgers University Press.

———, A. R. Gillis, and J. Simpson. 1985. "The Class Structure of Gender and Delinquency: Toward a Power-Control Theory of Common Delinquent Behavior." *American Journal of Sociology* 90: 1151–78.

———. 1987. "Class in the Household A Power-Control Theory of Gender and Delinquency." *American Journal of Sociology* 92: 788–816.

———. 1990. "Clarifying and Extending Power-Control Theory." *American Journal of Sociology* 95: 1024–37.

Hindelang, M. J. 1973. "Causes of Delinquency: A Partial Replication and Extension." *Social Problems* 21 (Spring): 471–87.

Hirschi, T. 1969. *Causes of Delinquency*. Berkeley: University of California Press.

Jensen, G. F. and R. Eve. 1976. "Sex Differences in Delinquency." *Criminology* 13 (February): 427–48.

——— and D. G. Rojek. 1980. *Delinquency: A Sociological View*. Lexington, Mass.: D. C. Heath and Company.

——— and K. Thompson. 1990. "What's Class Got to Do With It? A Further Examination of Power-Control Theory." *American Journal of Sociology*. 95: 1009–23.

Johnson, R. E. 1979. *Juvenile Delinquency and Its Origins: An Integrated Theoretical Approach*. Cambridge: Cambridge University Press.

Krohn, M. and J. Massey. 1980. "Social Control and Delinquent Behavior: An Examination of the Elements of the Social Bond." *Sociological Quarterly* 21: 529–43.

Marwell, G. M. 1966. "Adolescent Powerlessness and Delinquency." *Social Problems* 14: 35–47.

Matsueda, R. L. 1982. "Testing Control Theory and Differential Association." *American Sociological Review* 47: 489–504.

———. 1989. "Moral Beliefs and Deviance." *Social Forces* 2: 428–57.

———— and K. Heimer. 1987. "Race, Family Structure, and Delinquency: A Test of Differential Association and Social Control Theories." *American Sociological Review* 52: 826–40.

Merton, R. K. 1957. *Social Theory and Social Structure*. New York: Free Press.

Miller, W. 1958. "Lower Class Culture as a Generating Milieu of Gang Delinquency." *Journal of Social Issues* 14: 5–19.

Minor, W. 1977. "A Deterrence-Control Theory of Crime." Pp. 117–137 in R. F. Meier (ed.), *Theory in Criminology: Contemporary Issues*. Beverly Hlls, Cal.: Sage Publications.

Nye, F. I. 1958. *Family Relationships and Delinquent Behavior*. New York: John Wiley.

Paterson, G. R. and T. J. Dishion. 1985. "Contributions of Family and Peers to Delinquency." *Criminology* 23: 63–79.

Reiss, A. J., Jr. 1951. "Delinquency as the Failure of Personal and Social Controls." *American Sociological Review* 16: 196–207.

Schaefer, W. E. 1969. "Participation in Interscholastic Athletics and Delinquency: A Preliminary Study." *Social Problems* 17 (Summer): 40–47.

Schwendinger, H. and J. S. Schwendinger. 1976. "Marginal Youth and Social Policy." *Social Problems* (December): 84–91.

————. 1985. *Adolescent Subcultures and Delinquency*. New York: Praeger.

Singer, S. I. and M. Levine. 1988. "Power-Control Theory, Gender and Delinquency: A Partial Replication with Additional Evidence on the Effect of Peers." *Criminology* 26: 627–47.

Shaw, C., and H. McKay. 1942. *Juvenile Delinquency and Urban Areas*. Chicago: University of Chicago Press.

Sutherland, E. H. 1939. *Principles of Criminology*. Philadelphia: J. B. Lippincott.

———— and D. R. Cressey. 1974. *Criminology*, 9th ed. Philadelphia: J. B. Lippincott.

Taylor, I., P. Walton, and J. Young. 1973. *The New Criminology*. New York: Harper and Row.

Thornberry, T. P., M. Moore, and R. L. Christenson. 1985. "The Effect of Dropping Out of High School on Subsequent Criminal Behavior." *Criminology* 23: 3–18.

Tittle, C. R. 1977. "Sanction Fear and the Maintenance of Social Order." *Social Forces* 55: 579–96.

Toby, J. 1957. "Social Disorganization and Stake in Conformity: Complementary Factors in the Predatory Behavior of Hoodlums." *Journal of Criminal Law, Criminology and Police Science* 48: 12–17.

Wiatrowski, M. D., D. Griswold, and M. K. Roberts. 1981. "Social Control Theory and Delinquency." *American Sociological Review* 46: 525–41.

Young, J. 1975. "Working-Class Criminology." In I. Taylor, P. Walton and J. Young (eds.), *Critical Criminology*. London: Rutledge and Kegan Paul.

# Comments

## The Power of Control in Sociological Theories of Delinquency

*John Hagan*
*A. R. Gillis*
*John Simpson*

Gary Jensen has completed a trilogy of critiques of power-control theory (Jensen and Thompson 1990; Jensen 1990; Jensen 1991) that leads to the following conclusion:

> In earlier research, Jensen and Eve (1976) reduced the variance in self-reported delinquency attributable to gender to one or two percent by introducing measures of attachment, commitment, activities and beliefs. Power control theory explains some portion of the gender difference with parental supervision, perceptions of risk and taste for risk-taking. However, it has not been shown that such variables explain the gender difference better than variables derived from other theories.

Jensen is sufficiently impressed with the success of his 1976 analysis and especially its use of control theory variables that he ignores the importance of any scope conditions affecting the results of his study. Since so much of the covariance between gender and delinquency was explained away by his analysis, Jensen assumes a decade and a half later that nothing further is required. However, variation in the context of the relationships between variables can

381

be as important as the structure of propositions themselves. (An extreme version of this view is the historicist's argument that context is indeed everything. For a recent discussion, see Kiser and Hechter 1991).

## A Gender-Based Theory of Self-Control

By arguing that the 1976 analysis fully accounts for the gender-delinquency relationship, and then providing no scope conditions or specifications for this argument, Jensen assumes that this analytic framework can anywhere and everywhere account for the gender-delinquency relationship, which he assumes further to be always and in all places the same. This argues that the effect of gender on delinquency is invariant across social conditions, and that this relationship is therefore independent of historical, cultural or structural context.

This demands dubious assumptions (cf., Rosebaum and Lasley 1990). It requires the assumption that social conditions including social controls either do not vary across time and place, or if they do vary that they are not related to gender and delinquency in ways that influence this relationship and its explanation. Both assumptions are unlikely, and we offer evidence of this below. Note first, however, that both assumptions further imply a constancy to the gender-delinquency relationship that can only be explained by features inherent to the genders themselves. What else could produce this relationship and presumably keep it so constant? Within the tradition of control theory, this constitutes a gender-based theory of self-control.

Gottfredson and Hirschi (1991) have articulated a theory of self-control and Jensen has adopted an extreme form of its assumptions for the study of gender and delinquency (although it is unlikely that Jensen has done this consciously by asserting an unconditional gender-delinquency relationship). Tittle (1991) notes that taken to an extreme, this kind of theory of self-control constitutes an outright rejection of the place of sociology in the explanation of delinquency. Such a rejection involves reconceptualizing the social bond, which is given primacy in Hirschi's social-control theory, as the *product* rather than the cause of self-control. Here the social bond is seen as the result of a process of self-selection in which individuals with a propensity for self-control form ties to parents, peers, and other partners in a social web of conformity that is the *consequence* of inherent predisposition. Jensen's assumption of an unconditional constancy or invariance in the gender-delinquency relationship across time and place associates gender with such differences in propensities for self-control.

Said differently, Jensen offers a theory of "kinds of people" and their resulting social characteristics. As applied to gender and delinquency, this theory asserts, for example, that girls have a greater propensity for self-control than boys, which makes them more likely to build nurturing and supportive relationships with their parents, peers, and other partners in the life course. Since the source of differences in self-control resides internally in the propensities of the kind of people here distinguished by gender, this theory is assumed to apply in the same way in Jensen's 1976 analysis as in any more recent or past, foreign or domestic setting we might choose.

## Enter Power-Control Theory

In contrast, power-control theory articulates a more sociological version of control theory. It does so by not only highlighting social origins of control, but by also calling attention to the characteristically hierarchical forms of this control and to variation in the strength of this control across social and historical settings. Power and control both involve hierarchical influences in social relationships that impose (conformity with) the wants and wishes of others. These wants and wishes may be most influential when they are felt to come from within the individual; but they are also prominently located, in an exogenous causal sense, in the interests and desires of others. This is the power of external control in sociological theories of delinquency that Jensen regards as needless and so easily assumes away. Jensen's critiques of power-control theory are noteworthy illustrations of how these powerful sources of control can be obscured and ignored, with a corresponding loss of understanding.

It is interesting to note that Jensen's implicit assumption of inherent gender differences has some parallels within feminist scholarship. For example, Carol Gilligan (1982) argues in *A Different Voice* that the genders are distinct in inherent ways. She notes that while males rely predominantly on a kind of detached and impersonal logic in their moral decision making, females more often take into account relationships involving caring, affection, and identification. Naffine (1987) adopts this kind of perspective and applies it to the explanation of gender differences in delinquency when she argues that daughters are less delinquent than sons because they are tied more strongly, in relational terms, to their mothers. Note that this could as easily be called a theory of social support as a theory of social control.

However, the point of power-control theory is not to deny these differences. Indeed, this theory makes these differences explicit by distinguishing between instrumental controls, involving supervision and surveillance, and relational controls, involving caring and identification. Furthermore, power-control theory emphasizes that these instrumental and relational controls bind mothers and daughters together with ties that are characteristically stronger than those involving fathers and sons, and that these constraints set in motion processes that reduce risk preferences and ultimately delinquency among daughters compared to sons. The distinction is that power-control theory does not assume that these differences come from within the genders, that is, that these differences are inherent. Rather, power-control theory focuses on variations in family structures and on the social and economic conditions that produce these variations. More specifically, power-control theory proposes that variation in the gender-delinquency relationship (that Jensen assumes is constant) is conditioned by the influence of a patriarchal family structure and the social circumstances that produce this family form.

Of course, this approach to accounting for the origins of gender differences is prominent in feminist scholarship as well. For example, while Catherine MacKinnon (see *Buffalo Law Review* 1985) notes that the relational qualities Gilligan associates with women are important and distinctive, she also warns against the tendency to assume that this difference is inborn. In fact, she argues that this relational emphasis is at least partly an adaptation to oppressive circumstances. MacKinnon (27) writes that

> the voice that we have been said to speak in is in fact in large part the 'feminine' voice, the voice of the victim speaking without consciousness. But when we understand that women are forced into this situation of inequality, it makes a lot of sense that we should want to negotiate, since we lose conflicts. It makes a lot of sense that we should want to urge values of care, because it is what we have been valued for. . . . It makes a lot of sense that women should claim our identity in relationships because we have not been allowed to have a social identity on our own terms.

So this different voice is at least partly a product of circumstances, patriarchal circumstances that we discuss further below, that vary outside the self rather than from within.

### Historical Research on Gender and Crime

The *constancy* and therefore the inherency of the gender-delinquency relationship assumed by Jensen can be tested, using historical data and research, against the assumption of power-control theory that this relationship *varies* with social conditions that produce external differences in social control by gender. Historical studies indicate that the variance predicted by power-control theory does indeed occur, and that therefore the constancy assumed in Jensen's perspective is misleading.

For example, Feeley and Little (1991) have undertaken an exhaustive analysis of criminal cases in London's Old Bailey Court from 1687 to 1912. This analysis reveals that women made up to three to four times the proportion of felony defendants during the first half of the eighteenth century (peaking at more than 40 percent of all defendants) than they have in the twentieth century (when they have accounted for less than 10 percent). The implication of such a finding is that the strength of the gender-delinquency relationship that Jensen treats as a constant is actually variable and historically specific. Although Feeley and Little's research provides the most systematic analysis to date, there are other studies that anticipate and reinforce their conclusions. Phillips (1977) in a study of Victorian England, Sharpe (1984) in an analysis of early modern

England, Langbein (1983) in an examination of eighteenth-century criminal trials, and Hull (1987) in a consideration of colonial Massachusetts, all report a substantially greater involvement of women in crime prior to the twentieth century. Similarly, a near-century long-time series from Toronto (Boritch and Hagan, 1990) between 1859 and 1955 shows a steady and significant decline in arrests of women. It may not commonly be realized that *overall* crime rates declined in most Western industrialized nations during the latter part of the last century and the first part of this century (see Gillis 1989), but what is more impressive is that during this period *female* criminal involvements declined more dramatically than did male involvements, leading to an intensification of the gender-criminality relationship.

These findings (see also Beattie 1975; McCarthy and Hagan 1987) establish an historical context that is anticipated by power-control theory for Jensen and others' contemporary findings about gender and delinquency. Significantly, this is part of power-control theory that Jensen ignores. This part of the theory (see Hagan 1989a, 154–58) draws on Weber (1947) to talk about the separation of the workplace from the home during industrialization, and the creation during this period of what Weber called the production and consumption spheres. A result of this transition was that a social reproduction of gender roles has become a prominent part of both spheres, with men largely assigned reproductive functions through the state (involving the police, courts, and correctional agencies) in the production sphere, and women largely assigned such functions through the family in the consumption sphere.

Both the state and family are prominently involved in creating, maintaining, and reproducing gender roles, but it is particularly the patriarchal structure of the family that establishes a "cult of domesticity" around women (Welter 1966), reducing substantially female involvement in activities like crime and delinquency. Power-control theory gives particular attention to a gender division of roles that reproduces this outcome in more patriarchal families, through an instrument-object relationship in which fathers and especially mothers (i.e., as instruments of social control) are expected to control their daughters more than their sons (i.e., as objects of social control). Braithwaite (1990, 93, see also Sacco 1990) incorporates this framework into his broader theory in *Crime, Shame and Reintegration* when he writes that, "Elaborating the seminal work of Hagan et al. (1979), we predict that females will be more often the objects and the instruments of reintegrative shaming, while males will be more often the objects and instruments of stigmatization."

Feeley and Little (1991, 39) echo this kind of explanation for the historical decline of women in crime from the eighteenth to nineteenth century. They write that, "in the broadest terms, there was a redefinition of the female, and a shift and perhaps an intensification of private patriarchal control of women within the household." They then bring this line of argument to the following conclusion:

> By the end of the nineteenth century, there was a clear separation of home and work, a firmer sexual division of labor, the exclusion of women from the public sphere and from productive work, and the confinement of women to reproductive and domestic work in the home. Our data indicate that there was also a decline in female criminal court involvement during this period.

Feeley and Little are clear in noting that this was a period in which women lost power in the economic sphere of production, and at the same time became more involved and subject to domestic social control within the family. They conclude that "the trends thus point to possible explanations for our vanishing female defendant."

We now move from the broad macrolevel sweep of historical studies of social change to the microlevel detail of cross-sectional survey data. These different kinds of data can address shared theoretical concerns in complementary ways, and this is especially the case with regard to power-control theory. For example, while historical time series analyses can provide insights into changing social relationships as they occur in real time, they seldom can provide the direct measures we need to explore intervening causal processes of interest. This is why cross-sectional survey data often are used in a contextual fashion to simulate "slices of history" and the causal processes assumed to operate within particular periods of interest (see Ross et al., 1983, 809).

In testing power-control theory, we have used cross-sectional survey methodology to contextualize the operation of a core model of interest. This model, displayed in figure C.1, links together

FIGURE C.1.
Power-Control Model

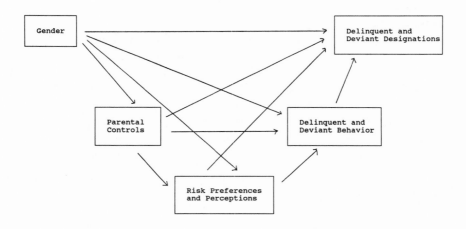

gender, parental controls, risk preferences and perceptions, delinquent and other forms of deviance, and responses to these behaviors in the form of deviant designations. Although this core model
has been used to study police responses to delinquency (Hagan et
al., 1979), and the relationship between gender and depressive
symptoms and thoughts (Hagan 1989b), the greatest attention has
focused on the casual relationship between gender and delinquent
behavior (e.g., Hagan et al. 1985, 1987, 1990). The challenge in
these studies has been to establish the conditional contexts in which
the core model does and does not apply. A central tenant of power-
control theory is that this model will work best in accounting for a
robust relationship between gender and delinquency in more patriarchal families, the kind of family that is a prominent part of the
historical development of Western industrial societies. This is the
kind of conditional analysis that Jensen resists and that an unconditional theory of self-control presumably does not require.

## A Power-Control Model of Teenage Smoking

Patriarchy is a concept that resists specific operational definition (Curtis 1986), however, it seems safe to say that patriarchal families are characteristically ones in which males are dominant and females are subordinate. Identifying families in which this kind of power imbalance operates is a challenging task. We began our work by operationalizing patriarchy in terms of class measures of the work positions of family heads and spouses, and more recently we have used more direct measures of marital power. These measures have been used primarily to establish the family contexts and conditions in which our core model applies. Jensen has systematically ignored this point and stressed instead the main effect of class on delinquency, which has never been a paramount part of power-control theroy (see Hagan et al. 1985, 1155; 1990, 1026). To clarify how power-control theory can be explored usefully with the contextual approach we propose, we turn next to an analysis of teenage smoking. This analysis is based on original data gathered in Toronto and used previously to analyze gender differences in minor theft (see Hagan et al. 1990).

One of the most perplexing problems of recent decades has involved the increasing rates of smoking among adolescent girls and lung cancer among women. Krohn et al. (1986, 147) report that "Not only does it appear that more females are smoking on a regular basis . . . but some studies have found an increase in the proportion of heavy smokers among females." Studies fluctuate in their findings, and there may be signs that this pattern is levelling out, however, a concern persists about the health implications of increases in smoking among adolescent girls.

Concern about the active and passive effects of smoking is so great that strict new laws are being passed to control smoking behavior. We may even come to see smoking again criminalized, as it was for some age groups, times, and places in the past. In any case, it is commonly argued that smoking is analogous to forms of crime and delinquency (Hirschi 1969; Akers 1984; Gottfredson and Hirschi 1990). In a social sense of the term, it can be argued that smoking is one of the most common forms of delinquency, a kind of "common delinquency" that power-control theory was originally intended to explain (Hagan et al. 1985).

About as many women as men may today smoke. This possibility is reflected in the survey we undertook in 1989 of adolescents in a wealthy section of Toronto called Forest Hill (see Hagan et al. 1990). Slightly more than 20 percent of males and females in this setting smoked. Power-control theory suggests that this parity is linked to the increased freedom and power experienced by mothers and daughters in some contemporary families. Coser (1985) suggests that this increased freedom and power coincides with the enlarged participation of women in the labor force and a declining division between the consumption and production spheres. She suggests that the results of these changes are most apparent in affluent communities like Forest Hill. If this is the case, it may be possible to treat differences in power relationships within the families of this community as analogues to more general changes in family power relationships over time.

We used a measure of marital power in this survey that asked who decides where to live, where to go on vacation, whether both spouses should work, and whether to move if the husband gets a job in another city. The item with greatest variance in responses in the scale indicated that while a majority (58 percent) of the wives decided on their own whether to work, a large remaining proportion decided this issue along with their husbands. The sample was split roughly in half on the basis of their scale scores, into more and less patriarchal families. Recall that in the overall sample, about equal proportions of sons and daughters smoked. However, when the sample is split in terms of the scale scores sons are more likely than daughters to smoke in more patriarchal families (24.6 percent vs. 16 percent), while daughters are more likely sons to smoke in less patriarchal families (29.9 percent vs. 22.5 percent). Note that the increase in female smoking in less patriarchal families is pronounced, nearly doubling from 16 to almost 30 percent. So the effect of gender on smoking is strongly conditioned by family structure.

However, not only the relationship between gender and smoking, may be effected by the conditioning influence of family structure, but the intervening relationships in the power-control model as well. To explore this possibility we estimated a LISREL model (Jorskog and Sorbom 1981) in which each concept, with the exception of gender, is measured with two indicators. This model uses concepts and indicators that we have introduced before (see Hagan et al. 1990), with the exception that self-reported smoking behavior is measured with items that indicate regularity of heavy smoking (i.e., more than seven cigarettes a day) and the average number of cigarettes smoked per day. A model was estimated with the sample divided into the less and more patriarchal groupings. Results are summarized in the accompanying figure C.2, with path coefficients for students from less patriarchal families placed first on the diagram, followed by those for students from more patriarchal families. As well, a summary of total, direct and indirect effects is presented in the accompanying lower right hand box in the figure.

The total effects indicate (as in the percentaged results reported above) that sons smoke more than daughters in more patriarchal families, while daughters smoke more than sons in less patriarchal families. Much of the total effect that results in boys smoking more than girls in more patriarchal families is a direct effect of gender. However, a substantial part of the total effect is also a result of sons in these families being more inclined to take risks than daughters [(.115) (.251)], as well as these sons being less controlled than daughters by their mothers [(-.137) (-.587) (.251) + (-.137) (-.221)].

In less patriarchal families, some of the tendency of daughters to smoke more than sons is suppressed by the tendency of daughters to still be less inclined to take risks [(.216) (.404)]. When this counteracting tendency is taken into account, the direct effect of gender on smoking is larger than previously apparent: -.215. Meanwhile, there is little opportunity for maternal relational or instrumental controls to reduce the smoking of daughters, since in these less patriarchal families the links between gender and these controls are miniscule, indicating that daughters are treated much like sons in these families, at least in terms of maternal control.

So the relationship between gender and smoking is not constant in the way that a theory of self-control predicts, but instead is conditioned by family experiences. In this instance, power-control theory accurately anticipates substantial gender differences in

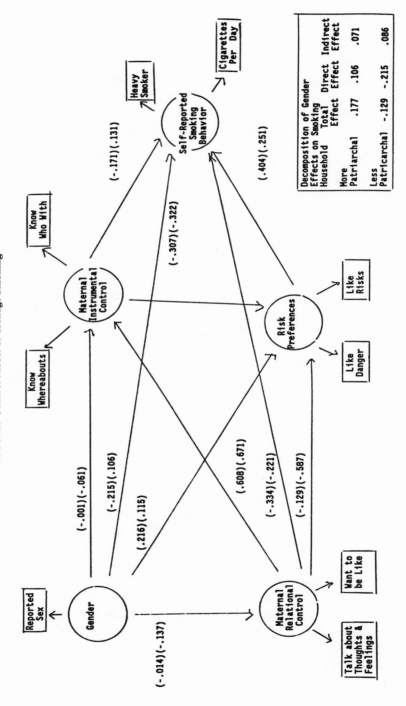

FIGURE C.2.
A Power-Control Model of Teenage Smoking

smoking behavior that are conditioned by the experiences of sons and daughters in more and less patriarchal families of an affluent community. As well, the emphasis of this theory on links between gender and maternal controls and attitudes toward risk-taking explains some of the tendency of sons to smoke more than girls in the more patriarchal families. Furthermore, the specification of the theory in terms of family structure directs us to a different pattern of linkages in less patriarchal families, indicting that daughters like sons can gain freedom to become involved in smoking in these families. However, a continuing difference between sons and daughters in terms of attitudes toward risk taking reduces what might otherwise be an even greater tendency of daughters in these families to smoke. This suggests that our application of power-control theory would probably be of further benefit if it included measures of perceptions of risks of smoking per se. Unfortunately, these measures are not available in the data set and must await further research.

## Some Conclusions

There is growing evidence that power and control are essential concepts for the theoretical understanding of delinquency. Each of these concepts makes its own contribution, as in the literature that continues to elaborate and confirm the influence of social control on delinquency (e.g., Wiatrowski et al. 1981; Liska and Reed 1985), and the research that is developing new measures of power and its impact on delinquency (e.g., Cullen et al. 1985; Agnew 1990; Hagan and Kay 1990). Abelson (1989, 171) even brings these concepts together in her fascinating study of middle-class women shoplifters in the Victorian department store, noting that, "As women began to move from the limited framework of domesticity and into a different self-definition . . . they were exercising both power and control." However, the distinct contribution of power-control theory emphasizes the role of power in conditioning and conceptualizing the influence of control in the causation of common delinquency (Empey 1991, 432–34). Power-control theory does this by emphasizing that males are freest to deviate in settings where they have greater power, as for example in the patriarchal family, and by emphasizing the hierarchal dimension of relationships of control between members of the family, especially in the patriarchal family. Of course, the family is not the only hierarchically organized institution notable for its gender-related effects on adolescents, so that Rosenbaum and Lasley (1990, 511) also indicate that, ''our findings suggest that power-control theory is the most appropriate conceptual framework for explaining the class-related effects of schooling on delinquency.''

Sociological criminology is a fertile source of theories about crime and delinquency, and power-control theory is part of a growing set of theories that gives particular attention to gender as an important new starting point for our more general understanding of crime. Sacco (1990, 502) observes that ''In one sense, the potential contribution of the power-control theory may be seen as building up rather than offering an alternative to existing criminological accounts.'' Several contemporary theories have in common a focus on changing gender roles that gives them a dynamic quality and that counteracts a tradition of regarding the relationship between gender and criminality as inherent and invariant. In different ways, Adler (1975), Simon (1975), Cohen and Felson (1979), and O'Brien (1991) have all speculated about the ways changing gender roles have influenced the variable female experience of crime.

In one way or another all of these theories have encountered the objection that they associate a positive development, the advancement of women, with a negative outcome, increased criminal involvement and victimization. Yet this is a short-sighted view of the contributions of these theories, and we believe it is particularly misguided in relation to power-control theory. Consider the following.

Power-control theory is a theory of common delinquency, not serious delinquency or adult crime. It was intentionally introduced as such (Hagan et al. 1985) because its central concerns with power, risk preferences, and perceptions build into the theory a brake on assumptions that the advancements of women will increase their exposure to serious criminal involvements. The fact that as power-control theory anticipates, during industrialization female involvement in crime decreased as women lost power and were increasingly subjected to informal and domestic social control, does not mean that these involvements will rise with new access to the occupational sphere. Rather, as women advance in occupational and other power spheres of society, they in classic control theory terms build investments in and commitments to conformity, so that they should reduce their preferences for risk taking through crime, while increasing their perceptions of the risks that criminal involvements pose to their advancements. This is acknowledged in a central way by power-control theory.

It may still be, as other gender theories have proposed, that the serious delinquent and adult criminal involvements of females will increase, as for example when economic advancements are blocked or even decline for whose who are disadvantaged in gender related ways. However, this has not been the central concern of power-control theory, which has focused on relatively minor but very frequent forms of delinquency, especially petty theft and smoking. These adolescent indiscretions have little impact on adult lives, other than often to anticipate and symbolize claims to autonomy from adult domination and control. We should not be surprised, and perhaps we should be encouraged, to discover that in a world of more balanced gender relations, daughters as well as sons experience the freedom to engage in some common indiscretions that are characteristic of adolescence.

## References

Abelson, Elaine. 1989. *When Ladies Go A-Thieving: Middle-Class Shoplifters in the Victorian Department Store*. New York: Oxford University Press.

Adler, Freda. 1975. *Sisters in Crime*. New York: McGraw-Hill.

Agnew, Robert. 1990. "Adolescent Resources and Delinquency." *Criminology* 28: 535–66.

Akers, Ronald. 1984. "Delinquent Behavior, Drugs and Alcohol: What is the Relationship." *Today's Delinquent* 3: 19–47.

Beattie, John M. 1975. "The Criminality of Women in Eighteenth Century England." In D. Kelly Weisberg (ed.) 1982. *Women and the Law: A Social Historical Perspective* 1. Cambridge, Mass.: Schenkman Publishing Co., Inc.

Boritch, Helen and John Hagan. 1990. "A Century of Crime in Tornoto: Gender, Class and Patterns of Social Control, 1859–1955." *Criminology* 28: 567–95.

Braithwaite, John. 1990. *Crime, Shame and Reintegration*. Cambridge: Cambridge University Press.

*Buffalo Law Review.* 1985. "Feminist Discourse, Moral Values, and the Law—A Conversation." 34:11–87.

Cohen, Lawrence and Marcus Felson. 1979. "Social Change and Crime Rate Trends: A Routine Activity Approach." *American Sociological Review* 44: 588–608.

Coser, Ruth. 1985. "Power Lost and Status Gained." Paper presented at the meeting of the American Sociological Association, Washington, D.C.

Cullen, F., M. Larson and B. Mathers. 1985. "Having Money and Delinquency Involvement: The Neglect of Power in Delinquency Theory." *Criminal Justice and Behavior* 12: 171–92.

Curtis, Richard. 1986. "Household and Family in Theory on Equality." *American Sociological Review* 51: 168–83.

Empey, Lemar and Mark C. Stafford. 1991. *American Delinquency: Its Meaning and Construction.* 3rd ed. Belmont, Cal.: Wadsworth.

Feeley, Malcolm and Deborah Little. 1991. "The Vanishing Female: The Decline of Women in the Criminal Process, 1687–1912." Paper presented at the Law & Society Association Meetings, Amsterdam, June.

Gilligan, Carol. 1982. *In A Different Voice: Psychological Theory and Women's Development.* Cambridge, Mass.: Harvard University Press.

Gillis, A. R. 1989. "Crime and State Surveillance in Nineteenth Century France." *American Journal of Sociology* 95: 307:41.

Gottfredson, Michael and Travis Hirschi. 1991. *A General Theory of Crime.* Stanford, Cal.: Stanford University Press.

Hagan, John. 1989a. *Structural Criminology.* New Brunswick, N.J.: Rutgers University Press.

Hagan, John. 1989b. "The Structuration of Gender and Deviance: Gender, Vulnerability to Crime, and the Search for Deviant Role Exists." *Canadian Review of Sociology and Anthropology* 27: 137–56.

Hagan, John and Fiona Kay. 1990. "Gender and Delinquency in White-Collar Families: A Power-Control Perspective." *Crime and Delinquency* 36: 391–407.

Hagan, John, John Simpson, and A. R. Gillis. 1979. "The Sexual Stratification of Social Control." *British Journal of Sociology* 30: 25–38.

Hagan, John, A. R. Gillis and John Simpson. 1985. "The Class Structure of Gender and Delinquency." *American Journal of Sociology* 90: 1151–78.

———. 1987. "Class in the Household: A Power-Control Theory of Gender and Delinquency." *American Journal of Sociology* 92: 788–816.

———. 1990. "Clarifying and Extending Power-Control Theory." *American Journal of Sociology* 95: 1024–37.

Hirschi, Travis. 1969. *Causes of Delinquency.* Berkeley: University of California Press.

Hull, N. E. H. 1987. *Female Felons: Women and Serious Crime in Colonial Massachusetts.* Urbana: University of Illinois Press.

Jensen, Gary and Kevin Thompson. 1990. "What's Class Got to Do with

It? A Further Examination of Power-Control Theory." *American Journal of Sociology* 95: 1009–23.

Jensen, Gary and Raymond Eve. 1976. "Sex Differences in Delinquency: A Test of Popular Sociological Explanations." *Criminology* 3: 427–48.

Jensen, Gary. 1990. "The Lingering Promise of a Structural Criminology." *Contemporary Sociology* 19: 12–14.

———. 1991. "Power-Control vs. Social Control Theories of Common Delinquency: A Comparative Analysis." *Theoretical Advances in Criminology* (this volume).

Joreskog, Karl and Dag Sorbom. 1981. *LISREL V User's Guide*. Chicago: National Educational Resources.

Kiser, E. and M. Hechter. 1991. "The Role of General Theory in Comparative-Historical Sociology." *American Journal of Sociology* 97 (1): 1–30.

Krohn, Marvin, William Skinner, James Massey, and Michelle Naughton. 1986. "Adolescent Cigarette Use." *Advances in Adolescent Mental Health* 1: 147–94.

Langbein, John H. 1983. "Shaping the Eighteenth-Century Criminal Trial: A View from the Ryder Sources." 50 *University of Chicago Law Review* 1.

Liska, Allen and Mark Reed. 1985. "Ties to Conventional Institutions and Delinquency: Estimating Reciprocal Effects." *American Sociological Review* 50: 547–60.

McCarthy, William and John Hagan. 1987. "Gender, Delinquency and the Great Depression: A Test of Power-Control Theory." *Canadian Review of Sociology and Anthropology* 24: 153–77.

Naffine, Nagire. 1987. *Female Crime: The Construction of Women in Criminology*. Sydney: Allen & Unwin.

O'Brien, Robert. 1991. "Sex Ratios and Rape Rates: A Power-Control Theory." *Criminology* 29: 99–114.

Phillips, David. 1977. *Crime and Authority in Victorian England*. London: Croom Helm.

Rosebaum, Jill and James Lasley. 1990. "School, Community Context, and Delinquency: Rethinking and Gender Gap." *Justice Quarterly* 7: 494–513.

Ross, Catherine, John Mirowsky, and Joan Huber. 1983. "Dividing Work, Sharing Work and In-Between: Marriage Patterns and Depression." *American Sociological Review* 48: 809–23.

Sacco, Vince. 1990. "Gender, Fear and Victimization: A Preliminary Application of Power-Control Theory." *Sociological Spectrum* 10: 485–506.

Sharpe, J. A 1984. *Crime in Early Modern England 1550–1750*. London: Longman Group Limited.

Simon, Rita. 1975. *Women and Crime*. Lexington, Mass.: Lexington Books.

Tittle, Charles and Rober Meier. 1990. "Specifying the SES/Delinquency Relationship." *Criminology* 28: 271–99.

Tittle, Charles. 1991. Review of *A General Theory of Crime*. *American Journal of Sociology* 96: 1609–11.

Weber, Max. 1947. *The Theory of Social and Economic Organization*. Glencoe, Ill.: Free Press.

Wiatrowski, Michael, David Griswold and Mary Roberts. 1981. "Social Control Theory and Delinquency." *American Sociological Review* 46: 525–41.

# Contributors

MICHAEL BUERGER, assistant professor at the University of Wisconsin, Oshkosh.

AARON CAPLAN, director of statistics, Department of Justice, Ottawa, Canada.

JEFFERY FAGAN, associate professor, School of Criminal Justice and director of the Center for Research on Urban Violence at Rutgers University.

A. R. GILLIS, professor and faculty of sociology at the University of Toronto.

W. BYRON GROVES (deceased), was associate professor of humanistic studies at the University of Wisconsin, Green Bay.

JOHN HAGAN, professor and faculty of Sociology and law at the University of Toronto.

GARY F. JENSEN, professor, Department of Sociology, Vanderbilt University.

KIMBERLY L. KEMPF, assistant professor of criminology and criminal justice at the University of Missouri.

MARC LE BANC, professor and chair of the School of Psychoeducation at the Universite de Montreal.

MICHAEL J. LYNCH, associate professor, Program in Criminal Justice, Florida State University.

LISA MAHER, Ph.D. candidate, School of Criminal Justice at Rutgers University.

GRAEME R. NEWMAN, professor of criminal justice at the State University of New York at Albany.

ROBERT NASH PARKER, senior research scientist, Prevention Research Center, Berkeley California.

ANTHONY PETROSINO, Ph.D. candidate, School of Criminal Justice at Rutgers University.

EDWARD W. SIEH, associate professor of criminal justice at Niagara University, New York.

LAWRENCE SHERMAN, professor of the Institute of Criminal Justice and Criminology and president of the Crime Control Institute at the University of Maryland.

JOHN SIMPSON, professor and faculty of sociology at the University of Toronto.

SALLY SIMPSON, assistant professor of the Institute of Criminal Justice and Criminology at the University of Maryland.

RUTH A. TRIPLETT, assistant professor of the Criminal Justice Center at Sam Houston State University.

AUSTIN T. TURK, professor and chair of the Department of Sociology at the University of California, Riverside, California.

DAVID WEISBURG, associate professor, and director of the Center for Crime Prevention Studies, School of Criminal Justice at Rutgers University.

CHARLES F. WELLFORD, director and professor of the Institute of Criminal Justice and Criminology at the University of Maryland.

# Index